AF479060

Medieval manuscripts from the collection of
T. R. Buchanan in the Bodleian Library, Oxford

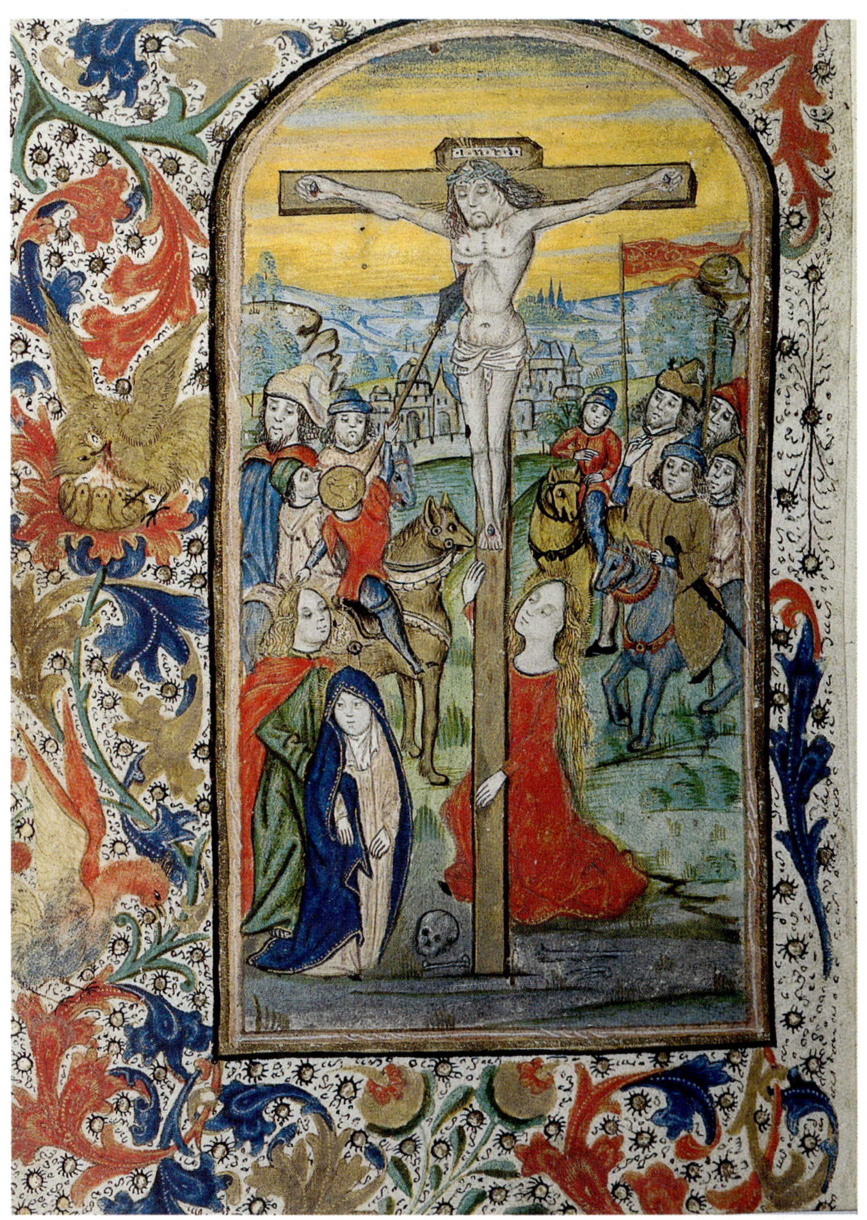

MS. Buchanan f. 1, fol. 57v.

Medieval manuscripts from the collection of T. R. Buchanan in the Bodleian Library, Oxford

Peter Kidd

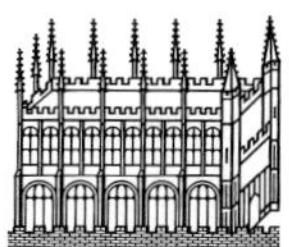

Bodleian Library
University of Oxford
2001

Design Sue Clarke

Typesetting Graham Wilkins

Printed in Great Britain at the Alden Press, Oxford

ISBN: 1-85124-059-4

Preface

The 24 medieval manuscripts in the Buchanan collection were presented to the Bodleian in two instalments, in 1939 and 1941, by Mrs. Emily Octavia Buchanan, in accordance with the wishes of her late husband, Thomas Ryburn Buchanan. The Keeper of Western Manuscripts' letter of thanks referred to 'this munificent benefaction ... the most remarkable and valuable accession to our illuminated manuscripts of the Middle Ages ... for many years'. The collection, with its preponderance of late medieval devotional books from France, the Netherlands and renaissance Italy, is typical of the small private libraries of later 19th-century English amateur collectors. What makes it remarkable is the inclusion of manuscripts notable for their early and fine bindings, their humanistic texts and their provenance. Mrs. Buchanan's gift also included later manuscripts, for the most part notable for their bindings.

A generous grant from the Higher Education Funding Council for England, under the Specialised Research Collections in the Humanities initiative, funded the appointment of Peter Kidd on a four-year project to catalogue the Latin and vernacular medieval and renaissance manuscripts acquired by the Bodleian since 1915 (i.e. those not included in Clapinson & Rogers, *Summary Catalogue of post-medieval manuscripts* ... (1991), where the later Buchanan manuscripts are described at SC 37931-37948). The Library records its grateful thanks to the Funding Council for making possible the resumption of cataloguing of its medieval collections. The grant has facilitated both active experimentation with automation and publication in traditional printed format. Descriptions of all the manuscripts within the scope of the project will be made available, with selected images, on the network. It is anticipated that full descriptions of further groups of medieval manuscripts will be published in a series of catalogues of which the Buchanan collection is the first. The dual nature of the project reflects the transitional stage both of manuscript cataloguing and of publishing as we reach the end of the twentieth century. Whatever the medium, the Bodleian remains committed to the dissemination of knowledge of its manuscripts collections world-wide.

Mary Clapinson

November 1999

Contents

Overview of the manuscripts

MS. Buchanan c. 1
Leonardus Aretinus (Leonardo Bruni), *Historiarum Florentini populi libri XII*,
and *Rerum suo tempore gestarum commentarius*, in Latin.
Italy, Florence; 15th century, 1440 or later (*c.*1440-50).
Illumination attributed to Bartolomeo d'Antonio Varnucci; original binding;
from the libraries of the Earls of Hopetoun and William Morris.

MS. Buchanan d. 4
Poggio Bracciolini, *De varietate fortunae*, in Latin.
Italy, Florence; dated by the scribe 1455.
From the libraries of S. Marco, Florence, and William Morris.

MS. Buchanan e. 2
Book of Hours, Use of Paris, in Latin and French.
France, Paris; 14th century, last quarter.
fine semi-grisaille miniatures.

MS. Buchanan e. 3
Book of Hours, Use of Rouen, in Latin and French.
France, Rouen; late 15th or early 16th century.

MS. Buchanan e. 4
Book of Hours, Use of Rome, in Latin and French.
France; late 15th or early 16th century.

MS. Buchanan e. 5
Book of Hours, Use of Rome, in Latin.
Flanders/Hainault; 15th century, third quarter.

MS. Buchanan e. 7
Book of Hours, Use of Rome, in Latin.
Italy, Florence; late 15th century.
Illumination attributed to Mariano del Buono di Jacopo;
with the arms of the ?Bellacci family, Florence.

MS. Buchanan e. 8
Book of Hours, Use of Paris, in Latin and French.
France, Paris; late 15th or early 16th century.

MS. Buchanan e. 9
    Book of Hours, Use unidentified, in Latin and French.
    North(?) France; 15th century, second quarter.
    Illumination attributed to the Rohan Master.

MS. Buchanan e. 10
    Book of Hours, Use of Paris, in Latin and French.
    France, Paris; late 15th or early 16th century.
    Parisian fanfare binding.

MS. Buchanan e. 11
    Book of Hours, Use unidentified, in Latin and French.
    French Flanders; early 15th century.

MS. Buchanan e. 12
    Book of Hours, Use of Bayeux, in Latin and French.
    France, Normandy; late 15th or early 16th century.
    From the library of John Payne Collier.

MS. Buchanan e. 13
    Book of Hours, Use of Rouen, in Latin and French.
    France, Rouen; 15th century, last quarter.

MS. Buchanan e. 14
    Book of Hours, Use of Evreux, in Latin and French.
    France, Normandy; late 15th or early 16th century.

MS. Buchanan e. 15
    Ps.-Fenestella, *De Romanorum magistratibus*, in Latin.
    Italy, Venice; 15th century, third quarter.
    Signed by the scribe '.P.E.F.A.'; illumination attributed to the Master of the Putti;
    with the arms of the Erizzo family, Venice; original binding; from the library of
    William Morris.

MS. Buchanan e. 18
    Book of Hours, Use of Rome, in Latin and Netherlandish.
    Flanders, Bruges; 15th century, third quarter, after 1461.
    Illumination in the style of Willem Vrelant.

MS. Buchanan f. 1
    Book of Hours, in Dutch, mainly in the translation of Geert Grote.
    Northern Netherlands, Enkhuizen(?); 15th century, last quarter, after 1471.
    Illumination attributed to the Bezborodko Master(s).

MS. Buchanan f. 2
> Bridgettine Breviary, in Latin.
> Netherlands, Diocese of Liège, Mariënwater; 15th century, last quarter.
> Panel-stamped binding.

MS. Buchanan f. 3
> Book of Hours, in Dutch, mainly in the translation of Geert Grote.
> The Netherlands, diocese of Utrecht(?), for use in the diocese of Cologne(?);
> 15th century, second quarter.
> Panel-stamped binding.

MS. Buchanan f. 4
> Rubricated Breviary, Use of Rome, in Latin.
> Italy, Milan, S. Giovanni in Conca; dated 1464 and 1465.
> Signed and dated by the priest Dionisius de Castello.

MS. Buchanan g. 1
> Book of Hours, Use of Rome, in Latin.
> Italy, Florence; late 15th century.
> Illumination related to the style of Giovanni di Giuliano Boccardi and Mariano
> del Buono di Jacopo.

MS. Buchanan g. 2
> Psalter, in Latin.
> Flanders, Ghent(?); late 13th or early 14th century.
> Remains of original binding.

MS. Buchanan g. 3
> Ferial Psalter, in Latin.
> Italy, North-East, Venice(?); 15th century, third quarter.
> Written for a Benedictine house of the Congregation of Sta. Giustina.

MS. Buchanan g. 4
> Private prayers and devotions (perhaps an imperfect Book of Hours), in Latin
> and Italian.
> Italy; 15th century, second half.

List of illustrations

Introduction

The Buchanan collection at the Bodleian Library consists of twenty-four medieval illuminated manuscripts dating from before the mid-16th century, described in this catalogue;[1] a further seventeen later manuscripts, previously catalogued in Clapinson & Rogers, *Post-medieval*; and over five hundred volumes of printed books.[2] The books were all in the collection of Thomas Ryburn Buchanan (d. 1911), and were given to the Library in two consignments by his widow, Mrs Emily Octavia Buchanan, in 1939 and 1941, as will be described below.

   The collection may owe its nucleus to the art collections of Buchanan's uncle, also called Thomas, who seems to have owned at least two of the fifteen Books of Hours given in 1939;[3] and it is probable that Buchanan's father bought the other thirteen. These fifteen form a coherent group in so far as they are all later medieval illuminated Books of Hours, of which more than half are French and date from the 15th or early 16th century.

   If these volumes did indeed belong originally to Buchanan's uncle and father, as I shall suggest below, it is interesting to see what the remaining books tell us about Buchanan's own taste: they considerably widen the scope of the collection. As well as another two Books of Hours, one of them in Dutch, and what is probably a fragment of a Book of Hours, he added three Italian humanistic texts, a Bridgettine Breviary, a Milanese Breviary, a ferial Psalter, and a Psalter of *c.*1300. Significantly, some of these do not contain very extensive decoration, but five are in their original bindings, and the binding of another is very unusual[4]—the printed books in the collection clearly demonstrate the extent to which bindings were one of Buchanan's main interests. Another contrast that may be drawn between the manuscripts he probably inherited, and those he bought himself, is in the prices paid: we know that Buchanan's uncle paid the equivalent of £52 for three volumes *c.*1857, and either his uncle or father paid £105 for four more in 1862, yet it seems that Buchanan himself rarely paid more than £15 for any book, frequently much less, even thirty years later.[5]

---

1. Concise typescript descriptions of the medieval manuscripts have been available at the Bodleian for many years, but remain unprinted; very brief mentions were published in 'Fifteen illuminated *Horae*', *BLR* 1 no. 7 (1939), 115-6; 'Western manuscripts: donations of MSS.', *Oxford University Gazette* (1 Dec. 1939), 185-6; and S. Gibson, 'Bookbindings in the Buchanan Collection', *BLR* 2 no. 16 (1941), 6-12. Brief but useful notes, with some plates, are in the first two volumes of Pächt & Alexander.
2. Included in *The Bodleian Library: pre-1920 catalogue of printed books* (CD-ROM, Oxford [1993]).
3. MS. Buchanan e. 5, and [pr. bk.] Buchanan e.136; and perhaps also MS. Buchanan e. 7.
4. MS. Buchanan g. 4.
5. The increase in the understanding of the artistic merits of illuminated manuscripts in the immediately preceding generations is described by A. N. L. Munby, *Connoisseurs and medieval miniatures 1750-1850* (Oxford, 1972).

Thomas Ryburn Buchanan (1846-1911)

T. R. Buchanan was born in 1846, third son of John Buchanan, of Patrick Hill, Glasgow, of a family who claimed descent from George Buchanan (1506-82), the Scottish historian and scholar.[6] He was first educated locally, then at Sherborne School, whence he came up to Balliol College, Oxford, in 1865. Here he had a distinguished academic career: in 1868 he won the Stanhope Prize Essay,[7] and gained a First Class in classical and mathematical moderations; the following year he gained a First Class in 'Greats'; and in 1871 he was elected to a Fellowship at All Souls College, where he was Librarian of the Codrington Library, just a few paces from the Bodleian, from 1878 until 1882. During his Librarianship, he was responsible for the publication of *Bookbinding in the Library of All Souls College: twelve plates drawn by John James Wild, Ph.D.* (1880),[8] 'the first book to call attention to the wealth of fine bindings in Oxford libraries'.[9] (It has been stated that his interest in illuminated manuscripts, early printed books, and fine bindings dates from this period, but this interest seems to have been fostered considerably earlier by his uncle and his father.) In 1881 he entered parliament as MP for Edinburgh, and remained an MP for most of the rest of his life; he became Financial Secretary to the War Office in 1906, and Under Secretary of State for India and Privy Councillor in 1908.[10] He retired in 1909 due to ill health, and died in 1911, aged 65. The twin interests of his adult life, politics and books, are compared in an obituary which states that 'He was indeed a genuine lover of books, and his knowledge in this department was highly appreciated by Mr. Coxe, the Librarian of Bodley. In fact, at one time he had thoughts of becoming a candidate for a vacant Sub-Librarianship; but politics had always possessed for him a strong attraction.'[11]

6. This biographical sketch owes much to Gibson, as in n. 1 above, at 6-8, to which the reader is directed for further details.
7. Published as *The effects of the Renaissance upon England* (London, Oxford, and Cambridge, 1868).
8. Buchanan's own copy is now Buchanan b.16.
9. Gibson, as in n. 1 above, at 6.
10. See *Who was who, vol. I, 1897-1915: a companion to Who's who containing the biographies of those who died during the period 1897-1915* (5th edn., London, 1966); further information is supplied by the obituary in *The Times*, 8 April 1911, p. 11.
11. H. W. G[arrod], 'Obituary: Thomas Ryburn Buchanan', *The Oxford Magazine* 29 no. 18 (11 May 1911), 299-300; Gibson, as n. 1 above, 6 n. 1 and 12, attributes the obituary and this remark to Sir William Anson.

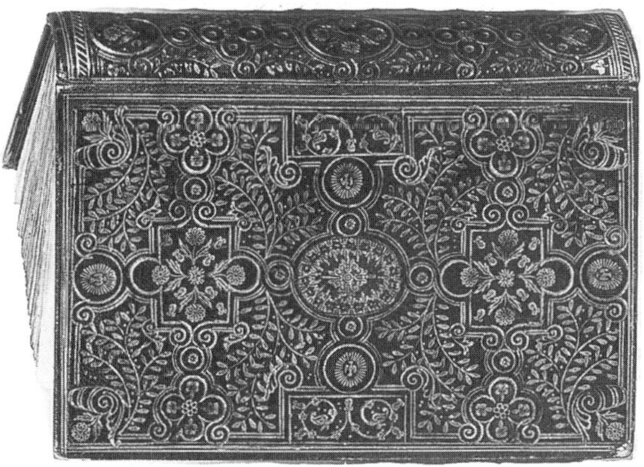
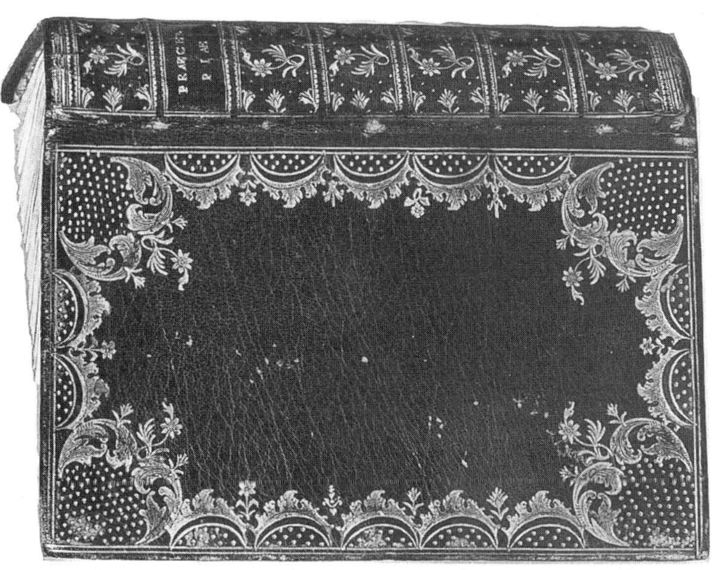

1. *Lower covers of (from left to right:) MS. Buchanan e. 5, MS. Buchanan e. 10, and MS. Buchanan e. 15*

The two donations, in 1939 and 1941

A few words need to be said about the way in which the Bodleian received Buchanan's manuscripts, in order to clarify some of what follows, and to explain the change in the shelfmarks of some of them.

The correspondence concerning the Buchanan Collection begins on 9 July 1939, with war imminent, when Mrs Buchanan wrote a letter from her house in central London to Edmund Craster, Bodley's Librarian, which starts:

> 'I have a small collection of valuable manuscripts which by my husband's desire I have bequeathed by will to the Bodleian. I think that with the possibilities of bombs, it would be wiser to give them away now.'[12]

A few days later she wrote again:

> 'The M.S.S. are mostly Books of Hours, only 12 [*sic*]. I dare say you have more than you want? I do not know why my late husband suggested the Bodleian rather than All Souls Library. I think, perhaps, it may have been his friendship with the Librarian of his time ...'.[13]

Arrangements were made for Noël Denholm-Young, the recently appointed Keeper of Western Manuscripts, to visit Mrs Buchanan two weeks later, and by the end of the month he was writing to thank Mrs Buchanan for 'this most munificent benefaction' of '15 Liturgical manuscripts', which had by then arrived safely at the Library. In the same letter he thanks her for 'the brief descriptive notes and the letter which you kindly lent me', and fortunately, the transcriptions he made of these notes and the last page of this letter survive, and are kept in Library Records.

Though we lack its first page(s), the letter is plainly from Buchanan to his father John, being signed from 'your affectionate son | T. R. Buchanan'. It is dated April 1874, and describes an afternoon spent showing some manuscripts to H. O. Coxe, Bodley's Librarian.[14] The copy of the letter makes reference to 'the printed prayer-book you have got, that by Hardonyn [*sic*]', and mentions that 'The Bodleian is very rich in English work of which I don't think there are any specimens in your possession'; it ends, 'Any further information I get I will let you know.' These and other passages suggest not only that Buchanan's father had a collection of early books; but indeed that it was his father's books, not his own, that he was showing to Coxe.

The fifteen Books of Hours given in 1939 consist of the printed Book of Hours just mentioned, and fourteen manuscripts, all illuminated. These were accessioned with the general Bodleian series of such material, and shelfmarked as MSS. Lat. liturg. e. 22-35 and MS. Dutch f. 1 (see Concordance of Shelfmarks, pp. xxx–xxxi); the shelfmark and accession date were pencilled usually at the bottom centre of the first folio of each manuscript, apparently by Denholm-Young.[15]

12. Library Records d. 1025, fol. 5.
13. *ibid.*, fol. 6.
14. *ibid.*, fol. 9.
15. The pencil notes accompanying the shelfmark, usually in the middle at the bottom edge of the first leaf of the manuscript (e.g. MS. Buchanan ... D. vi. 41) represent the means and date of acquisition (D=Donated, P=Purchased, Dep=Deposited).

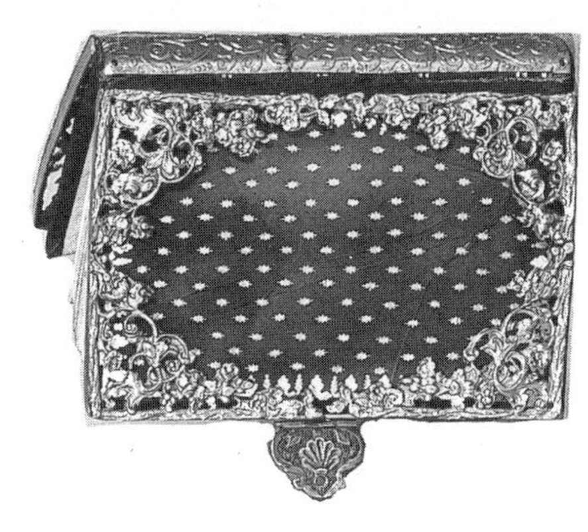

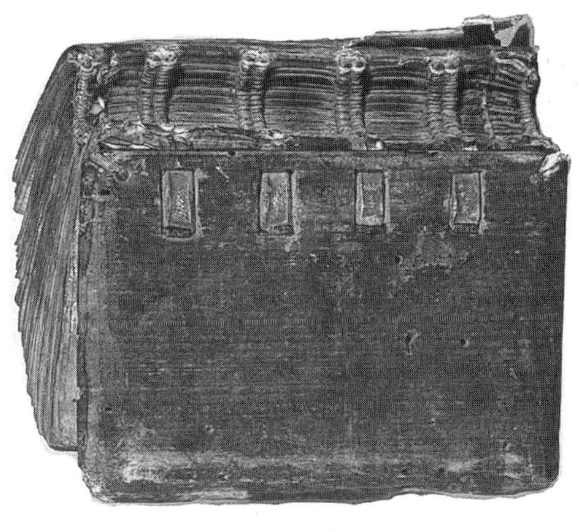

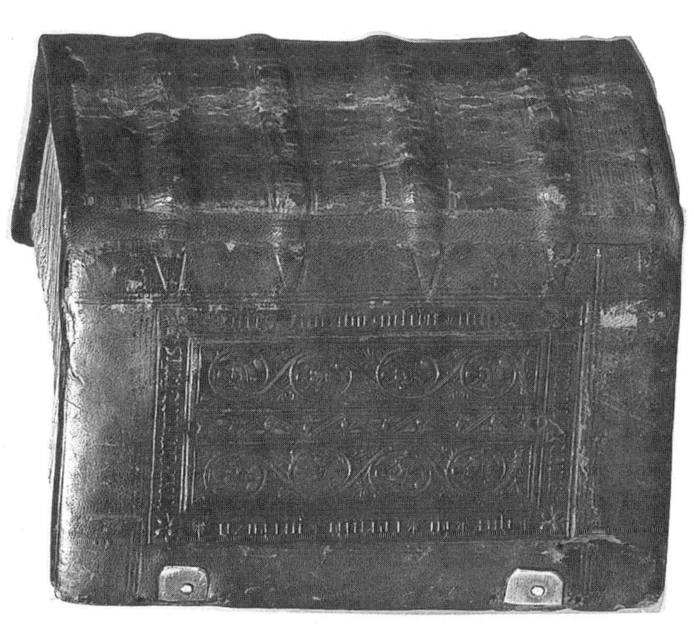

2. *Lower covers of (from left to right:) MS. Buchanan f. 2, MS. Buchanan g. 2, and MS. Buchanan g. 4*

In September 1940, Mrs Buchanan wrote to the Bodleian again:

> 'My valuable books which by my husband's desire I was to leave by will to the Bodleian & All Souls Libraries are in their book cases at 52 Mount St [and] of course they are in imminent danger of destruction.'

Soon after, about 650 books were sent from London to Oxford for appraisal and safe-keeping, but others remained in London, and by May 1941 Mrs Buchanan was writing yet again:

> 'The matter presses as the house ... has already been bombed three times and may be set on fire at any minute.'

A four-way correspondence continued until the end of the year, between the elderly Mrs Buchanan at her house in Cornwall, her secretary at the house in London, the Bodleian, and Sir Charles Oman of All Souls College; an added complication being that a number of Buchanan's books were being stored at a relative's house in Wokingham. Eventually the matter was sorted out to everyone's satisfaction: the Bodleian selected all the manuscripts, and over five hundred printed books, including many notable for their fine bindings, and many editions of the works of George Buchanan;[16] All Souls selected thirty-two books of those that remained, wanting only those relating to law or history; the remainder were sent to Mrs Buchanan's nephew in Edinburgh;[17] and Mrs Buchanan was delighted with Strickland Gibson's account of her husband and of the donation, which he published in *The Bodleian Library Record*.[18]

With the accession of this sizable and important second donation, the new shelfmark 'Buchanan' was created, and the fifteen Books of Hours previously received in 1939 were re-referenced accordingly, with shelfmarks starting 'MS. Buchanan ...'.[19]

16. See 'Printed books, etc.: chief donations of printed books: Buchanan collection', in *Annual report of the curators of the Bodleian Library for 1940-1* (Oxford, 1941), 15; Gibson, as n. 1 above; and Edmund Craster, *History of the Bodleian Library 1845-1945* (Oxford, 1952, repr. 1981), 286-7.
17. Those that no one wanted were sold at Sotheby's, 11 November 1941, lots 242-258.
18. As n. 1 above.
19. Later still, the illuminated printed book was removed from the 'MS. Buchanan' to the 'Buchanan' series, hence the gap in the sequence between MSS. Buchanan e. 5 and e. 7.

Notes on the sources of Buchanan's manuscripts

One of the manuscripts and the illuminated printed Book of Hours bear the inscription 'Tho Buchanan', and the manuscript is also dated 'Oct 1857',[20] all apparently in an adult hand. At this date T. R. Buchanan would have been only 11 years old, and we must therefore assume that these books belonged to T. R. Buchanan's uncle, also called Thomas, who is known to have collected art, and lived at Cadder, not far from the younger Buchanan's family home in Glasgow. It is reported that it was at his uncle's house that the young Buchanan 'first acquired his taste for things of beauty.';[21] when his uncle died in 1864 the whole family moved into the house at Cadder, and these two books presumably passed to Buchanan's father by bequest. It is possible that Buchanan's uncle owned more than just these two books, but they are the only two he signed.

The notes referred to above, transcribed by Denholm-Young 'From a small MS. notebook (6.4" x 3.9") lent to me by Mrs Buchanan',[22] consist of a numbered list of fifteen manuscripts, headed 'Missals'; the numbers on the list correspond to numbers inscribed in pencil at the front of the books themselves. Each book on this list has between two and twenty lines of description, some including notes on where, and for how much, they were bought. The list starts: 'The four following missals were bought at Boone's New Bond Street on April 16th 1862.', and their prices are given as £30, £30, £25, and £20 respectively.[23] No. 5 on the list has the note 'This MS. & Nos. [followed by a blank space, perhaps '6 & 7' was intended] were bought in Paris in October 1857 & cost 52£ (800 fr.)'; No. 12 on the list provides the price, 38 shillings, but not the source.[24]

This is a second piece of evidence which suggests that some, at least, of the manuscripts belonged first to Buchanan's father before passing to Buchanan himself: it seems very unlikely that as a 16-year-old youth, apparently with very little knowledge of manuscripts, Buchanan would have spent £105 on a single day for the first four manuscripts on the list. This is further evidence then, that in 1874 Buchanan was showing books to Coxe on behalf of his father, and was given or bequeathed them at a later date.

It follows from this that the list with numbered descriptive notes on the fifteen Books of Hours was probably compiled by Buchanan's father, and that all fifteen once belonged to him: Buchanan himself did not number his other manuscripts or printed books, and there is no evidence that he compiled a descriptive list of them. And if the several books seen by Coxe did indeed belong to Buchanan's father, we may perhaps assume that *all* the manuscripts in the numbered list were his, and were possibly all bought before 1874. Of the other eleven illuminated manuscripts now in the collection but not on the numbered list,[25] we have firm evidence for the date of acquisition of six of them, and all of these were acquired in 1875 or later.[26]

20. MS. Buchanan e. 5, and Buchanan e.136.
21. Library Records c. 1026, fol. 44r, repeated by Gibson, as n. 1 above.
22. Library Records, d. 1025, fols. 10-12.
23. They are MSS. Buchanan g. 1, e. 2, e. 3, and e. 4, respectively.
24. It is MS. Buchanan e. 12.
25. MSS. Buchanan c 1, d. 4, e. 15, e. 18, f. 2, f. 3, f. 4, g. 2, g. 3, and g. 4.
26. MSS. Buchanan c. 1, d. 4, e. 15, e. 18, f. 4, and g. 3.

It is probable that Buchanan shelved the books given to him by his father physically separate from those that he bought himself, since Mrs Buchanan seems only to have been aware of this group of fifteen when she presented them in 1939.

It may well have been as a result of the meeting with Coxe in 1874 that Buchanan began to collect manuscripts himself, and it may have been Coxe who impressed on him the value of recording the source of such acquisitions, for we find a number of purchases from 1875 onwards (especially 1875 and 1876) which bear either a cutting from the auctioneer's or bookseller's catalogue, or else a handwritten note of the purchase. But these are the exception; Buchanan did not usually write in his books the place, date, or cost of their acquisition. It is, however, possible to piece together a general picture of his buying habits, which is presented below for what it reveals about the formation of the collection, and in the hope that it may aid future investigations into the provenance of these and other manuscripts. This is also done partly in order to prevent the Provenance section of each catalogue entry from becoming disproportionately lengthy, and partly to minimise repetition where more than one manuscript comes from a single bookseller.

There are very few published sources relating to Buchanan's book-collecting, and the information they provide is scanty.[27] In the absence of further secondary sources of information,[28] almost all the material for the investigation of their provenance lies within the books themselves. By examination of the books, both manuscript and printed, it has been possible to make a number of links between the small percentage which bear an explicit indication of their source, and the remainder, which do not. Thus, where a book bears a distinctive form of bookseller's price-code, and evidence revealing the identity of the bookseller from which it was purchased, the probability has been examined that other manuscripts bearing the same price-code came from the same dealer. Sometimes a bookseller who left a distinctive mark in the books he sold cannot be identified; but one can nonetheless be confident that, on the evidence of such marks, all the books bearing a particular mark came from the same source, or at least passed through the hands of the same dealer. From the books bearing indications of the source and/or date and/or place of acquisition, it has been possible to sketch out an impression of where and when Buchanan was buying most actively, which dealers he favoured, as well as his forays into the sale-room to bid in person—the latter relatively unusual for a gentleman collector at that date.

27. The only 19th-century account of any of Buchanan's manuscripts (apart from booksellers' and auctioneers' catalogue descriptions) appears to be E. Gordon Duff and S. T. Prideaux, *Burlington Fine Arts Club: exhibition of bookbindings* (London, 1891), which includes MS. Buchanan f. 2 and twenty-seven of his printed books.
28. Thirty trunks full of 'largely unsorted' personal papers are in private ownership (see Chris Cook *et al.*, *Sources in British political history 1900-1951, volume 3: a guide to the private papers of Members of Parliament, A-K* (London and Basingstoke, 1977), 66-7; and the Royal Commission on Historical Manuscripts's *Papers of British politicians 1782-1900* (Guides to sources for British history based on the National Register of Archives, 7: London, 1989), 15 no. 89); there is no reason to suppose that they contain substantial information regarding Buchanan's manuscripts, and they have not been consulted in the preparation of this catalogue.

Messrs. Boone

As we have seen, four manuscripts were bought by Buchanan's father (or perhaps uncle?) from Messrs. Boone in April 1863.[29] MS. Buchanan e. 3 is inscribed in pencil 'Boone' on fol. i verso, and bears a distinctive form of price-code in the top right corner of the front pastedown, with a variant form in the top left corner of the back pastedown; the same price-code occurs in equivalent positions in MSS. Buchanan e. 2 and g. 1, and other books which passed through Boone's hands, and must, therefore, be their price-code.[30]

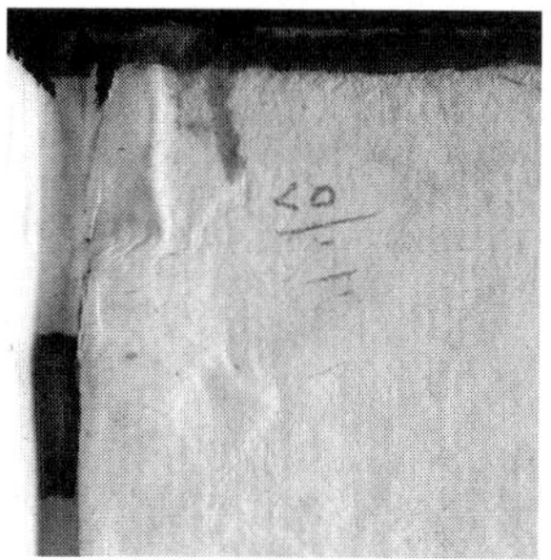

3. *MS. Buchanan e. 3,*
top left corner of lower
pastedown, detail

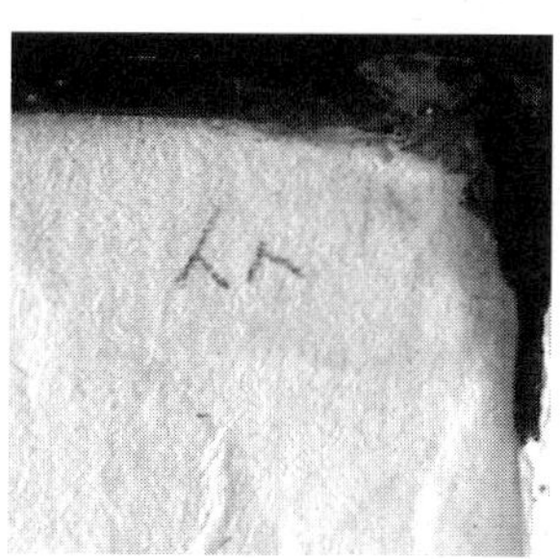

4. *MS. Buchanan e. 3,*
top right corner of upper
pastedown, detail

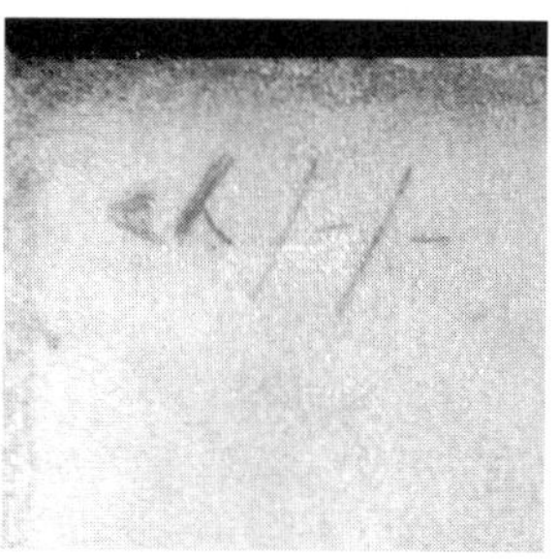

5. *MS. Buchanan e. 2,*
top left corner of lower
pastedown, detail

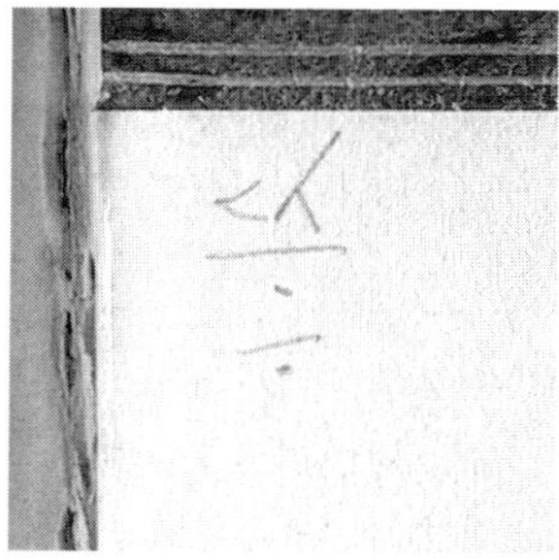

6. *MS. Buchanan g. 1,*
top left corner of lower
pastedown, detail

29. On this business see A. N. L. Munby, *The formation of the Phillipps library from 1841 to 1872* (Phillipps Studies, no. 4: Cambridge, 1956), 3-4; David Pearson, *Provenance research in book history: a handbook* (The British Library Studies in the History of the Book: London, 1994), 159; and George Smith and Frank Benger, *The oldest London bookshop: a history of two hundred years* (London, 1928). It is unlikely that the four Buchanan manuscripts ever appeared in a Boone catalogue: they have not been found in that of 1862 or those of 1863 available at the Bodleian. Like other dealers, Boone did not generally list many illuminated manuscripts in their catalogues, stating instead, under the heading 'Illuminated Horæ, Missals, &c.', that 'The Advertisers have in stock the largest and choicest Collection of these Superb Reliques of the Middle Ages for sale in Europe ... Feeling that no mere description can possibly convey an accurate idea of a Work of Art the Advertisers content themselves with this simple announcement ...'.

30. The same price-code occurs in a number of manuscripts from the library of Carlo Archinto, now in the British Library (Add. MSS. 25449, 25450, 25454), and Los Angeles, J. Paul Getty Museum, MS. 26, all of which passed through Boone's hands; Bodleian Library MS. Add. A. 188, MS. Auct. T. inf. 2. 9, and MS. Auct. T. 5. 34 all bear the price-code, and were acquired from Boone, but are *not* from the Archinto library.

Thomas Arthur & William Ridler

There is one form of price-code in Buchanan's manuscripts and printed books which occurs far more frequently than any other.

*7. MS. Buchanan c. 4,
front flyleaf, detail*

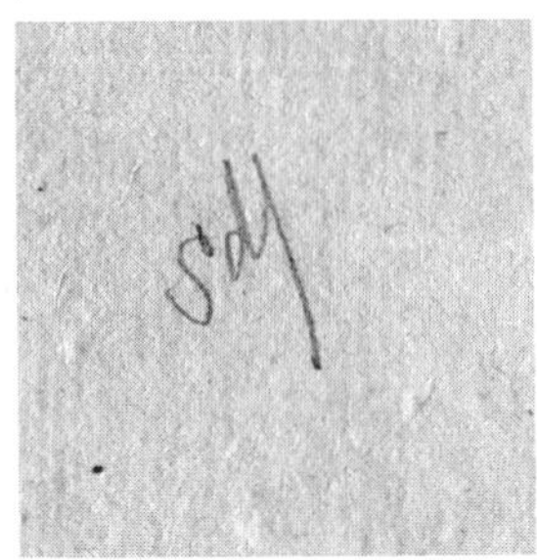

*8. MS. Buchanan d. 1,
upper pastedown, detail*

Their presence at first threatened to undermine the method of attributing particular books to particular dealers based on such price-codes, since this single type of price-code can be found in books which contained other explicit evidence to indicate that they came not from a single dealer, but from two different booksellers: Thomas Arthur, and William Ridler. In due course the solution to the apparent problem was revealed: a single business was owned successively first by Arthur, and then by Ridler. Ridler presumably adopted Arthur's price code, since much of the shop's stock would already have borne it, and to have two price-codes in use concurrently would have been to invite problems. The bookshop was at 45 Holywell St. (better known as Booksellers' Row), Strand, London W.C. This street no longer exists, but can be found on Victorian maps, running approximately west-east parallel to the Strand from the northern side of the church of St. Mary-le-Strand to the northern side of the church of St. Clement Danes on the site now occupied by Bush House. That the price-code is indeed distinctive enough to make such attributions can perhaps be demonstrated by the fact that an example was immediately recognisable in MS. Lat. liturg. e. 39 (part of the Chertsey Breviary), and subsequent enquiry confirmed that this had indeed been bought at auction by Ridler in 1889.

There seems to be very little written about Arthur and Ridler; the most informative source is a single paragraph in William Roberts, *The book-hunter in London* (London, 1895), p. 230:

> 'Two of the earliest and best-known of the more important Holywell Street booksellers passed away some years ago. 'Tommy' Arthur, who made a respectable fortune out of the trade, and whose shop and connections are now in the possession of W. Ridler, who is a successful trader, and a man of considerable independence as regards the conventionalities of appearances.[31] (Our artist's

---

31. Buchanan apparently thought of the business as continuous from one proprietor to the other: Buchanan e.24 has an inscription by him dated September 1892, in which the source was first given as 'Arthur', and then this was crossed through and corrected to 'Ridler'.

portrait of this celebrity in his brougham, indulging in the extravagance of a clay pipe, had not arrived at the time of going to press, so it must be held over until the next edition of this book.)'.[32]

With so little to go on, we must look elsewhere to flesh out the picture. Arthur and Ridler catalogues do not seem to survive in many libraries, though a reasonably complete set could be formed by combining those held at the Bodleian and at the Grolier Club, New York.[33] From these we can see that Arthur issued catalogues at approximately monthly intervals, as was common, and can get an idea of how long he was in business. The earliest catalogue I have found is at the Bodleian, dated March 1856, and numbered 'Part IV'; the latest is at the Grolier Club, and is the last of two series (each described as a 'new series'), and is numbered 88, dated December 1876. We thus know that Arthur was in business at Holywell St. for at least these two decades, 1856-1876.

The date at which Ridler took over from Arthur, referred to in vague terms by Roberts, can be deduced from other sources. In the second edition (1876) of *Kelly's Directory of stationers, printers, booksellers, publishers, and paper makers*, Arthur is listed at 45 Holywell St., but by the time of the third edition (1880), he is absent, and that address is occupied by Ridler. The date of the change is even more closely deduceable from one of Buchanan's printed books: Buchanan d.22 has an inscription stating that it was bought from Ridler in October 1877. Furthermore, since the Grolier Club collection includes an apparently unbroken run of about 150 Arthur catalogues, of which the last is that for December 1876, it is likely that the hand-over of the business occurred at the start of 1877. Ridler presumably started a new series, numbered from 1 onwards, and had reached 'Part 71' by April 1882, suggesting that he too issued catalogues at approximately monthly intervals. The last Ridler catalogue at the Bodleian is Part 113, for December 1884, but it is apparent that he continued in business well into the 20th century, since the Bodleian purchased a manuscript from him as late as 23 December 1903.[34] He is also present in the eighth to eleventh editions (1904-12) of Kelly's directory (having moved between 1900 and 1904 from Bookseller's Row to Bloomsbury), but absent from the 12th edition (1916): he presumably retired or died within a couple of years of 1914.

It may well be that Buchanan's first purchase from Ridler included the printed book just referred to: it is one of a set of six volumes of which the first, Buchanan d.22, has the inscription 'Bought from Ridler Oct 77 | £3.3/. | TRB', written near the bookseller's purchase price in his characteristic code, and the retail price:

---

32. It is regrettable that a second edition was never published, both because it would have been interesting to have had Ridler's portrait, and because it might have offered an expanded version of the paragraph on Buchanan himself (pp. 319-20).

33. A few are held by the Bibliothèque royale, Brussels, (see Jeanne Blogie, *Répertoire des catalogues de ventes de livres imprimés appartenant à la Bibliothèque royale Albert Ier, III: catalogues Britanniques* (Collection du Centre national de l'archéologie et de l'histoire du livre: Brussels, 1988), including one where it has been possible to a match the complete copy with a clipping pasted into a manuscript (MS. Buchanan e. 18).

34. MS. Lat. class. b. 1.

'£4-4-0'. Ridler was offering Buchanan a generous discount on the marked price—perhaps as a sign of goodwill to one of Arthur's regular customers—but he seems not to have made a loss on the transaction, since the price-code 'x/-/-' indicates that the set of books had cost him only £3![35]

On at least one occasion, Buchanan seems to have commissioned Ridler to execute bids on his behalf, at the Baron Seillière sale, in February 1887: numerous Buchanan books were knocked down to Ridler,[36] but none of these have the usual price-code, which suggests that they did not enter Ridler's stock, and instead went directly to Buchanan.

Raguin, Paris

Buchanan recorded a number of purchases from Raguin of Paris, usually hand-written in ink on slips of thin paper inserted along the gutter margin at the front of the volume. Several bear the date November 1875,[37] others are dated April 1876,[38] and all have a form of price-code inscribed in pencil in the top left corner of the back pastedown (or the last flyleaf), which closely resembles those in MSS. Buchanan f. 2 and g. 3. It therefore seems reasonable to propose that these two medieval manuscripts came from this source.

Adolphe Labitte, 4, rue de Lille, 4e Arr., Paris

Three medieval manuscripts (MSS. Buchanan e. 5, e. 7, and e. 14) appear to have come from a single dealer, since they all share a common form of price-code, inscribed in brown ink on the final flyleaf or lower pastedown; the illuminated printed Book of Hours (Buchanan e.136) bought by Buchanan's uncle in Paris, has a similar inscription at the front, with a note in French recording the number of large and small miniatures.

9. MS. Buchanan e. 7,
top right corner of lower
pastedown, detail

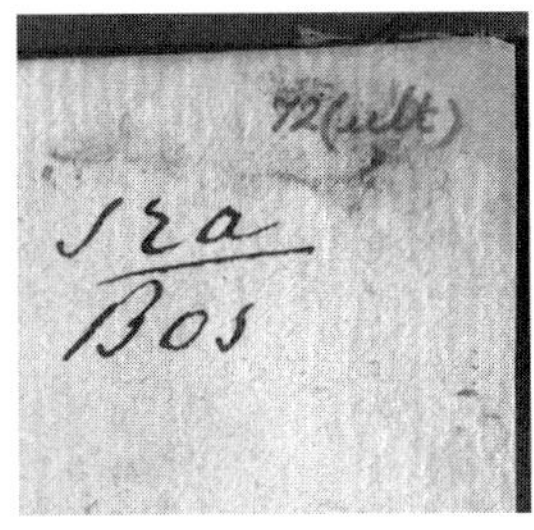

10. MS. Buchanan e. 14,
top right corner of lower
pastedown, detail

35. The price-code seems to have been based on a word like 'taxidermys' (where t=1, a=2, etc.), but I have not found enough books whose auction-price is known, to be certain. See pl. 36 for a price-code, where the auction-price is known.

36. Including, among others, lots 8 (Buchanan d.45), 11 (d.42), 27 (f.56), 83 (c.11), 117 (e.59), 167 (d.36), 725 (c.20-21), etc.

37. MSS. Buchanan d. 2, and g. 15-16, as do the printed books Buchanan d.2, f.36, f.44-45, f.70, f.156, g.15, and g.34.

38. Buchanan e.3, e.65, e.67, f.123, f.132, f.136.

Several other printed books bear codes that appear to relate closely to these; of these, Buchanan c.3, which was acquired before 1891, has a pasted-in cutting from a bookseller's catalogue, cut from the top of the page, thus preserving the running titles in capital letters: 'LIBRAIRE DE ADOLPHE LABITTE' and '4, RUE DE LILLE, 4.'. Buchanan d.53, e.74, f.54, f.131 also have cuttings from Labitte catalogues,[39] and notes by Buchanan stating that they were bought in April 1876 (i.e. the same month he was buying from Raguin, see above).

Other Paris booksellers

Buchanan e.15 has a note stating that it was bought from Jouin, Paris, in April 1876; Buchanan e.51, f.142, and f.179 were bought in the same month from Hérault;[40] and Buchanan g.48 was bought from the libraire A. Rouquette (69-73 passage Choiseul) in 1881. Buchanan f.37 was bought in Paris in 1874, Buchanan f.169 in May of the same year, and Buchanan d.65 in Nov. 1875, but the vendors are not recorded. Buchanan g.41 was also bought in Paris, but neither the date nor the vendor are known. It has not been possible, however, to link any of these booksellers with any of the medieval manuscripts.

Sotheby's

Many manuscripts and printed books in the Buchanan collection bear one of two sorts of annotation which can be attributed to Sotheby's. There is commonly an encircled number inscribed in pencil towards the upper left corner of the upper pastedown (see e.g. pl. 11); much less commonly the number is enclosed within a triangle (e.g. in MS. Buchanan f. 4). That these marks must have been added by Sotheby's is shown by the fact that they occur in books bound for Baron Seillière (thus they cannot pre-date his ownership), which passed from his collection directly through Sotheby's to Buchanan, bidding in person at the auction (thus they cannot have been added by an intermediary bookseller). They presumably relate instead to a preliminary inventorying of books before removal from the owner's to Sotheby's premises,[41] or at least prior to the preparation of a catalogue, since the numbers do not correspond to lot numbers.

39. Which state, from 1873/4 onwards, that he was 'Libraire de la Bibliothèque nationale'.
40. This is perhaps Henry Auguste Hérault, who co-wrote, with Théodore Berrier, the *Histoire et description de la Bibliothèque Mazarine* (Paris [1884]).
41. During Buchanan's life Sotheby's was at Wellington St., opposite the western wing of Somerset House, just north of Waterloo Bridge, just a few minutes walk from Booksellers' Row.

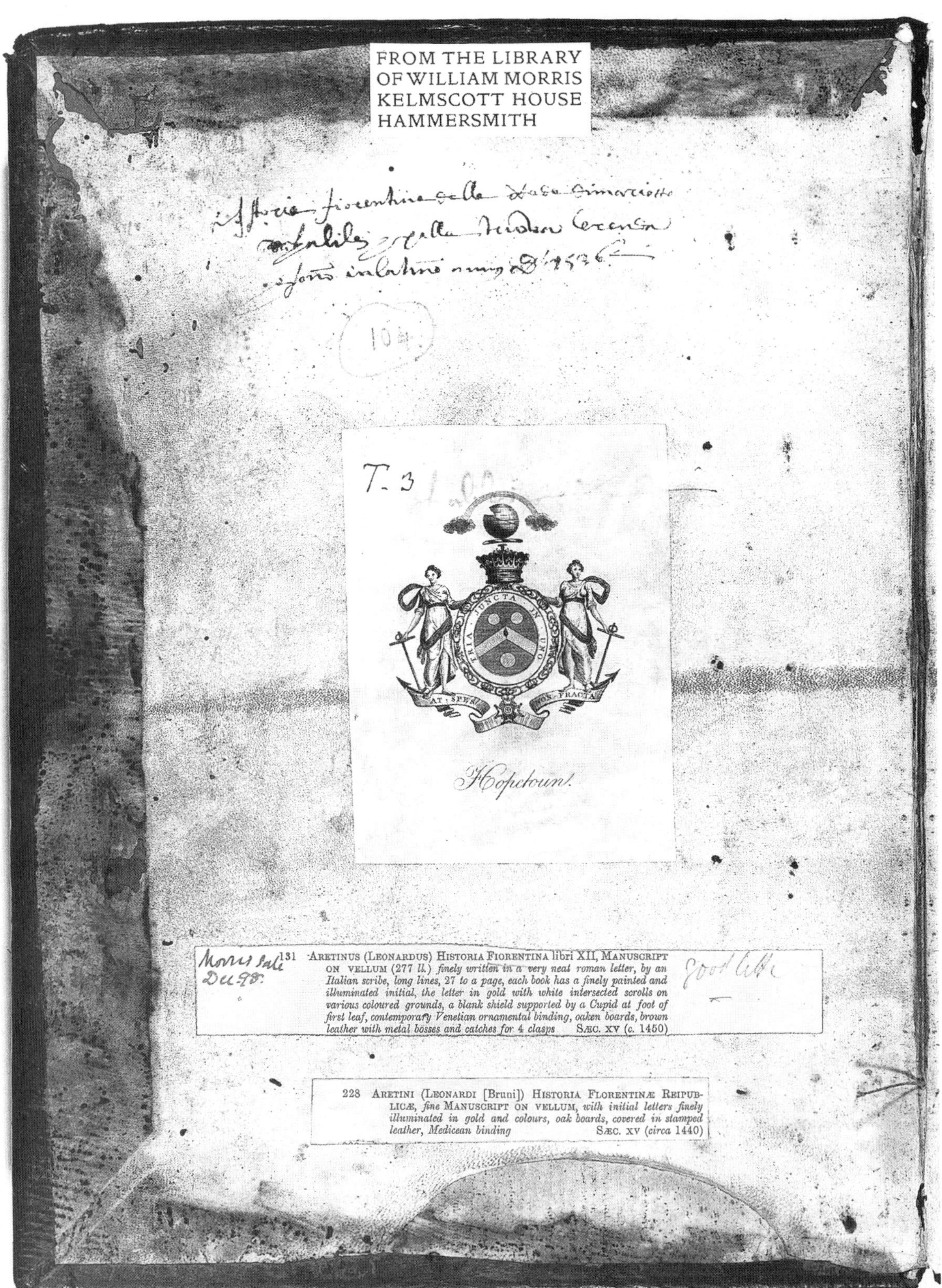

11. *MS. Buchanan c. 1, upper pastedown [Considerably reduced]*

The 'Morris' sale

Shortly after William Morris's death in 1896, the bookseller F. S. Ellis, co-executor with Sydney Cockerell of Morris's will, drew up a '... valuation of the principal books in the library ... [in which] prices fixed were as near as possible those paid by Morris ...'. In this inventory the manuscripts are listed separately before the printed books, mostly in alphabetical order;[42] and the three Buchanan manuscripts appear as nos. 6, 42, and 70.[43] The numbers assigned to the manuscripts in this inventory are usually found inscribed in pencil in the top left corner of the upper pastedown or first flyleaf (e.g. MS. Buchanan d. 4; see pl. 12).

In April 1897 Richard Bennett, of Riversdale, Manchester, an eccentric collector of manuscripts and early printed books,[44] bought Morris's library through Pickering and Chatto (for £18,000, according to Cockerell), and then re-sold the great majority, including all but thirty-one of the manuscripts—and most of those which are more than 13 inches tall, such as MS. Buchanan c. 1—in the 'Morris' sale at Sotheby's on 5 December 1898 and five following days; earlier the same year he had commissioned a posthumous booklabel in Kelmscott 'Golden' type:[45] 'FROM THE LIBRARY | OF WILLIAM MORRIS | KELMSCOTT HOUSE | HAMMERSMITH', which is usually found stuck at the top of the upper pastedown (see pl. 11).[46] Buchanan seems to have viewed the sale personally (making notes in his copy of the catalogue) and then bid in person, coming away with three manuscripts.[47]

Morris had certainly bought a number of his manuscripts from Messrs. J. & J. Leighton,[48] binders of the Kelmscott books, and they are probably responsible for the re-backing of the two Morris-Buchanan manuscripts in wood boards.

42. Inaccurately pr. in *The collected letters of William Morris*, IV, ed. Norman Kelvin (Princeton, 1996), as Appendix B: 'William Startridge Ellis, *Valuation of the library of William Morris 1896*', 401-33. I am very grateful to the present owner of the inventory, Mr. Sanford L. Berger, for supplying me with photocopies of the pages listing the medieval manuscripts.

43. As follows: 6. Aretini (Leon.) Historia Florentini. circa 1450 [£]19 10
    42. Fenestella. De Romanorum magistratibus. Italian. c.1470 sm. 4to [£]15
    70. Poggius (Joh.) De var. Fortunae libri \IV/ Ital. 8° [£] 5
    A fourth Morris MS. is at the Bodleian, MS. Lat. th. b. 4 (Gregory's Decretals, dated 1241 by the scribe), and is recorded in the Ellis inventory as no. 107.

44. On whom see Seymour de Ricci, *English collectors of books & manuscripts (1530-1930) and their marks of ownership* (Cambridge, 1930, repr. 1969), 171-3.

45. See Brian North Lee, *British bookplates* (Newton Abbot, etc., 1979), 154 no. 252.

46. Occasionally the label is inside the lower board when there is insufficient free space available inside the upper; sometimes the label seems to have been removed (e.g. MS. Lat. th. b. 4), possibly for unscrupulous re-use in another volume.

47. On Morris's medieval manuscripts, see Barbara Rosenbaum and Richard Pearson, eds., *Index of English literary manuscripts, volume IV: 1800-1900, part 3: Landor - Patmore* (London and New York, 1993), the introduction to William Morris, especially the sections on 'The dispersal of manuscripts and Morris collections', 475-7, and 'Morris's library and lists of manuscripts', 503-7. I am very grateful to Mark Samuels Lasner for bringing these sources to my attention.
    A complete list of Morris's medieval manuscripts is in preparation by William Stoneman, which will include their Ellis inventory number, 'Morris' sale lot number, provenance, and present whereabouts, where known. I am very grateful to him for making copies of his working lists available to me.

48. On whom see the discursive article by Hugh William Davis, 'Some famous English bookshops, I. Notes on the firm of J. & J. Leighton and the Old House at Brewer Street', *The Library World* 34 nos. 395-6 (1932), 149-55 and 177-83; and David Pearson, *Provenance research in book history: a handbook* (The British Library Studies in the History of the Book: London, 1994), 161.

Codex æc: XV

Codex iste nitidissimus idem
est, quem Auctor Nicolao V.
obtulit, habemus editum
inter Opera Poggij

This note is quite correct, with the
exception that this is not the copy
presented to Nicolas V, and that
it is not printed in the works of
Poggio

Other auctions

A large number of printed Buchanan books were bought at various auctions, and in at least one instance their appeal seems to have been partly due to their Scottish/Edinburgh connections. These include books from the Auchinleck, Gibson-Craig, Laing, Makellan, and Mackenzie of Seaforth sales; a particularly large group were bought at the sale of the library of Sir William Fettes Douglas, President of the Royal Scottish Academy, at Dowell's, Edinburgh, 7 Dec. 1891 and four following days.

Concordance of shelfmarks

Post-*c.*1500 manuscripts have been catalogued in Clapinson & Rogers, *Post-medieval*; their *Summary Catalogue* (*SC*) numbers are given here. 'P&A' refers to the volumes by Pächt & Alexander (see the list of Abbreviations, p. xliii).

Present shelfmark	Former shelfmark	P&A vol. & no.	SC no.
[There are no 'a' size Buchanan manuscripts]			
b. 1		P&A, 1, no. 262	*SC* 37933
c. 1		P&A, 2, no. 230	
c. 2		P&A, 1, no. 897	*SC* 37939
c. 3		P&A, 1, no. 874	*SC* 37945
c. 4		P&A, 1, no. 906	*SC* 37941
d. 1			*SC* 37938
d. 2		P&A, 1, no. 903	*SC* 37940
d. 3		P&A, 2, no. 1030	*SC* 37936
d. 4		P&A, 2, no. 265	
d. 5		P&A, 2, no. 1022	*SC* 37935
d. 6			*SC* 37937
e. 1	no manuscript was assigned to this shelfmark		
e. 2	*olim* MS. Lat. liturg. e. 23	P&A, 1, no. 609	
e. 3	*olim* MS. Lat. liturg. e. 24	P&A, 1, no. 807	
e. 4	*olim* MS. Lat. liturg. e. 25	P&A, 1, no. 777	
e. 5	*olim* MS. Lat. liturg. e. 26	P&A, 1, no. 329	

Present shelfmark	Former shelfmark	P&A vol. & no.	SC no.
[pr. bk.] e.136	*olim* e. 6 *olim* MS. Lat. liturg. e. 27		
e. 7	*olim* MS. Lat. liturg. e. 28	P&A, 2, no. 325	
e. 8	*olim* MS. Lat. liturg. e. 29	P&A, 1, no. 797	
e. 9	*olim* MS. Lat. liturg. e. 30	P&A, 1, no. 678	
e. 10	*olim* MS. Lat. liturg. e. 31	P&A, 1, no. 798	
e. 11	*olim* MS. Lat. liturg. e. 32	P&A, 1, no. 303	
e. 12	*olim* MS. Lat. liturg. e. 33	P&A, 1, no. 803	
e. 13	*olim* MS. Lat. liturg. e. 34	P&A, 1, no. 752	
e. 14	*olim* MS. Lat. liturg. e. 35	P&A, 1, no. 804	
e. 15		P&A, 2, no. 558	
e. 16			*SC* 37946
e. 17			*SC* 37947
e. 18		P&A, 1, no. 327	
e. 19			*SC* 37932
e. 20		P&A, 1, no. 835	*SC* 37934
f. 1	*olim* MS. Dutch f. 1	P&A, 1, no. 245	
f. 2		P&A, 1, no. 247	
f. 3		P&A, 1, no. 207	
f. 4		P&A, 2, no. 731	
f. 5			*SC* 37942
f. 6			*SC* 37931
f. 7			*SC* 37948
g. 1	*olim* MS. Lat. liturg. e. 22	P&A, 1, no. 324	
g. 2			
g. 3			
g. 4			
g. 5			*SC* 37944
g. 6		P&A, 1, 866	*SC* 37943

The form of entries

The manuscripts are listed alphabetically by shelfmark. A concordance of current and former shelfmarks is on the two preceeding pages.

Each catalogue entry is presented according to the following system. The main heading consists of the shelfmark, given in the single correct form in which it should always be cited, followed by two lines giving author and/or title, and language; and the place and date of production. In the absence of explicit evidence, the latter are based on the style of writing and decoration. Serving as an overview of the manuscripts in the catalogue, slightly expanded versions of these headings (including, for example, notes on binding, ownership, and style of illumination) may be found on pp. vii–ix. The body of the catalogue entry itself is divided into six main sections: Text, Decoration, Physical description, Binding, Provenance, and Bibliography, each of which deserves a few words of explanation.

Text

The textual contents of each volume are presented as a numbered list for ease of reference, and the division into separate items usually reflects divisions in the manuscript, marked by a hierarchy of painted initials or other means. Because information concerning the Bodleian's medieval collections is sought by a large number of non-specialists (such as non-academic publishers and picture-researchers), texts are identified in English, even where the quoted rubric and/or incipit makes the nature of the text apparent. Incipits are usually not given for very common texts, or where the manuscript corresponds to the published edition cited.

Where textual and/or scribal divisions correspond to the physical divisions between quires, this is noted in square brackets on a separate line. Quotations from manuscripts are given within single quote marks; italics are used to indicate rubrics, or headings otherwise distinguished, for example by underlining; unambiguous abbreviations are usually expanded silently, but are occasionally expanded within round brackets where a more diplomatic transcription may be desirable (for example, in ownership inscriptions); orthography and capitalization follow the manuscript, except that a majuscule letter after a large initial is rendered as a minuscule; partially illegible readings, and other editorial comments are given within square brackets '[ ]'; a slash '/' indicates a break between notional lines of verse; a vertical bar ' | ', indicates a break between lines of text as laid out on the page (or binding), while a double vertical bar ' | | ' indicates a more major break, including the abrupt beginning or ending of an imperfect text. Wherever possible, reference has been made to a printed version of each text, with the exception of common yet variable texts such as the Hours of the Virgin. Some common texts, such as the Verses of St. Bernard, are given such a reference only at their first occurrence in the catalogue, with subsequent examples cross-referenced to such a manuscript. Hours of the Cross and of the Holy Spirit are of the 'short' variety unless otherwise stated.

Within catalogue entries, bibliographical references are given in full as they occur, unless the printed source refers to the manuscript being described (in which case it will be given in full in the Bibliography section at the end of the entry) or unless it is included in the list of abbreviations on pp. xxxix-xliii.

Decoration

Decoration is usually listed hierarchically from the most to the least elaborate; but the description may be divided into sections, where applicable, for decoration of different periods or in different styles. The subject-matter of a scene is not described in detail if it is unexceptional in its context, but individual features are sometimes noted to help distinguish between different forms of common compositions.

Physical description

The physical description is arranged under sub-headings in the following order:

(i) Material: parchment is of unexceptional quality and weight unless otherwise specified. There are no paper manuscripts described in the present catalogue; paper flyleaves may be described under Binding.

(ii) Dimensions of leaves are given in millimetres, height before width, usually in the form of a range (e.g. '173-6 x 97-100 mm.') to give an impression of the usual degree of variation.

(iii) The (total) number of leaves is given, with flyleaves in lower-case roman numerals followed by an indication of their material and date in brackets; it should be stressed that these totals do not necessarily correspond to the foliation.

(iv) Foliation: the *actual* numbering of the leaves is given here, with an indication of medium and date ('modern' can here usually be taken to mean 'probably after acquisition by the Bodleian'). All the manuscripts in the present catalogue are foliated, not paginated. It is Bodleian practice that any incorrect folio number be cancelled by encircling it (*not* by crossing through it; that leaves which were omitted in a previous foliation are numbered and distinguished alphabetically; and that the last leaf of any sequence of foliation be marked '(ult.)', though the '(ult.)' should not be included when citing the folio number of such a leaf. Thus, for example, the sequence:

... 112, 113, [then four unfoliated leaves], 114, 115, ...

would be re-foliated as:

... 112, 113a, 113b, 113c, 113d, 113e (ult.), 114, 115, ...

(v) Collation is expressed first as a general prose summary, then as a formula in which the quires are numbered in upper-case roman numerals, with superscript arabic numerals to represent gatherings of the notionally intact bifolia, followed where applicable by further superscript numbers to indicate the total number(s) of any leaves added or removed, and further explanation in brackets; each run of regular quires, and each irregular quire, is followed by an indication of its present folio references; where a division between quires corresponds to a scribal/textual division, this is indicated by a vertical bar: '|'; where catchwords and/or quire signatures and/or leaf signatures are present, they are described here (unless otherwise stated, *leaf* signatures may be assumed to occur on the rectos of the leaves in the first half of the quire, taking the form of a quire-letter-plus-leaf-number, similar to the signatures in printed books; and *quire* signatures are numbers on the last versos of quires, which served a function equivalent to catchwords).

(vi) Ruling: the ruling medium, number of ruled lines per page, ruling pattern, and dimensions of the ruled space are described; where prickings are present, they are also described under this sub-heading.

(vii) Script is characterized briefly; then the number of written lines per page, and the dimensions of the written space are given. The style of the script can be assumed to be appropriate to its context, unless stated to the contrary; thus the 'gothic' of an Italian 15th-cent. Book of Hours, and the 'gothic' of a Flemish 13th-cent. Psalter, will each be typical of such books. Unless stated to the contrary, each manuscript appears to have been written by a single scribe, though there may be variation in the handwriting within the book.

(viii) The term 'rubrication' is used here to cover headings in red and other colours, and articulation of the text at a level below that which is described under Decoration, i.e. simple paraphs, one-line initials, touches of colour on capital letters, etc.

(ix) 'Sec. fol.' is used as the abbreviation for *secundo folio*; more than one *sec. fol.* is given wherever there is scope for ambiguity. The *secundo folio* is recorded for every manuscript, not only those which might have been in an institutional library during the Middle Ages, because *secundo folio* references have been recorded in inventories and catalogues up to the present day, and may therefore be useful in determining post-medieval provenance.

Binding

The sewing, material of the boards, their covering material, decoration, and any other markings, are described usually in that order. Flyleaves can be assumed to be paper, without visible watermarks, and of the same date as the binding, unless specified to the contrary.

Provenance

The history of ownership and use of each manuscript is listed chronologically, as far as it has been possible to determine the significance and relative chronology of various types of evidence. Further notes on provenance of are to be found in the Introduction, pp. xiii-xxix.

Bibliography

The bibliography lists in chronological order all the published references (and some unpublished sources) of which we are aware; readers of this catalogue are encouraged to bring others to our attention. Selected images from a large number of Bodleian manuscripts are represented in 35mm. colour filmstrips published by the Library (see *Colour transparencies (35 mm) available from the Bodleian Library, Oxford. Part 1: filmstrips* (Oxford, 1983, repr. 1996), but these are only recorded here where the majority of images on a filmstrip is taken from a single manuscript (in the present catalogue, this only applies in two cases: MSS. Buchanan e. 3 and e. 18).

On-line descriptions of Bodleian manuscripts

It is a condition of the funding from HEFCE (the Higher Education Funding Council for England) which enabled the preparation of these and other descriptions of manuscripts, that the descriptions be made available electronically. This has affected a number of decisions in the style of cataloguing: for example, one is the general avoidance of cross-references such as 'see above' and 'see below', since the end user may be able to reformat the order in which data is presented in the electronic version; another is the decision to use roman numerals in the collational formula, since this will help to distinguish the quire numbers from the numbers of leaves on monitors which do not display superscript characters clearly. More significantly, the intention to create cumulative indexes from this and other catalogues of medieval and post-medieval materials has had an impact on the indexing style used.

Acknowledgments

A number of specialists have given me the benefit of their expertise, for which I am very grateful: A. C. de la Mare confirmed her attribution of the decoration of MS. Buchanan c. 1 to Bartolomeo d'Antonio Varnucci; Gregory Clark sent me extensive notes on the artist of MS. Buchanan e. 5; David Rundle supplied invaluable comments on the authorship and text of MS. Buchanan e. 15; Margriet Hülsmann answered questions about MS. Buchanan f. 1 and Books of Hours from Enkhuisen, and provided photocopies of published and unpublished materials not otherwise available to me; Ulla Sander Olsen answered questions about MS. Buchanan f. 2 and the provenance of manuscripts from Mariënwater; and Jonathan Alexander re-examined the Italian manuscripts with me and confirmed, or suggested revisions to, his and Otto Pächt's attributions of almost 30 years ago.

Special thanks are owed to Bruce Barker-Benfield and Martin Kauffmann, who provided advice and expertise at every stage of the preparation of the catalogue, and each meticulously checked an early draft of the descriptions against the manuscripts themselves; they also read the indexes and other parts with equal care; they are in no way responsible for any errors which have subsequently been introduced.

List of abbreviations

Alexander and de la Mare, *Abbey cat.*
    J. J. G. Alexander and A. C. de la Mare, *The Italian manuscripts in the library of Major J. R. Abbey* (London, 1969).

Alexander and Temple, *Oxford college libraries*
    J. J. G. Alexander and Elżbieta Temple, *Illuminated manuscripts in Oxford college libraries, the University Archives, and the Taylor Institution* (Oxford, 1985).

Analecta hymnica
    Guido Maria Dreves and Clemens Blume, eds., *Analecta hymnica medii aevi* (55 vols., Leipzig, 1886 - 1922).

Bertalot, *Initia humanistica*
    Ludwig Bertalot, ed., *Initia humanistica latina: Initienverzeichnis lateinischer Prosa und Poesie aus der Zeit des 14. bis 16. Jahrhunderts, Band I: Poesie* (Tübingen, 1985), *Band II/I: Prosa A - M* (Tübingen, 1990).

BL
    British Library.

BLR
    Bodleian Library Record 1 - (1939 -).

BnF
    Bibliothèque nationale de France.

Bruylants, *Oraisons*
    P. Bruylants, *Les oraisons du missel romain: texte et histoire* (Études Liturgiques, 1: 2 vols., Louvain, 1952).

Clapinson & Rogers, *Post-medieval*
    Mary Clapinson and T. D. Rogers, *Summary catalogue of post-medieval western manuscripts in the Bodleian Library, Oxford, acquisitions 1916-1975 (SC 37300-55936)* (3 vols., Oxford, 1991).

Corpus orationum
    Jean-Marie Clément, Eugène Moeller, and Bertrand Coppieters 't Wallant, eds., *Corpus orationum* (Corpus Christianorum, Series Latina, 160, 160A- : Turnhout, 1992-).

Colker, *Trinity College Dublin cat.*
    Marvin L. Colker, *Trinity College, Dublin: descriptive catalogue of the medieval and renaissance Latin manuscripts* (2 vols., Aldershot, 1991).

Cottineau, *Répertoire topo-bibliographique*
L. H. Cottineau, *Répertoire topo-bibliographique des abbayes et prieurés* (2 vols., Mâcon, 1935-7); supplementary vol. III prepared by Grégoire Poras (Mâcon, 1970).

Crollalanza, *Dizionario storico-blasonico*
G. B. di Crollalanza, *Dizionario storico-blasonico delle famiglie nobili e notabili italiane estinte e fiorenti* (3 vols., Pisa, 1886-90).

de la Mare, *Lyell cat.*
Albinia de la Mare, *Catalogue of the collection of medieval manuscripts bequeathed to the Bodleian Library, Oxford, by James P. R. Lyell* (Oxford, 1971).

de Ricci, *Census*
Seymour de Ricci and W. J. Wilson, *Census of medieval and renaissance manuscripts in the United States and Canada* (3 vols., New York): *I [Alabama - Massachusetts]* (1935, repr. 1961), *II [Michigan - Canada]* (1937, repr. 1961), *III: Indices* (1940).

DNB
Dictionary of national biography (21 vols. and supplements: London, 1885-), and CD-ROM, including supplements published up to 1993 (Oxford, 1995).

Dutschke, *Huntington cat.*
C. W. Dutschke, *Guide to the medieval and renaissance manuscripts in the Huntington Library* (2 vols., San Marino, CA, 1989).

G.E.C.
Vicary Gibbs. *et al.*, eds., *The complete peerage of England, Scotland, Ireland, Great Britain, and the United Kingdom; extant, extinct, or dormant; by G. E. C.; new edition, revised and much enlarged* (14 vols., London, 1910-98).

Gesamtkatalog der Wiegendrucke
Gesamtkatalog der Wiegendrucke, vols. I-VII (Leipzig, 1925-38), vols. VIII- (Stuttgart, etc., 1978-).

Grotefend, *Zeitrechnung des deutschen Mittelalters*
H. Grotefend, *Zeitrechnung des deutschen Mittelalters und der Neuzeit* (3 vols. in 2, Hanover): I: *Glossar und Tafeln* (1891); II, pt. 1: *Kalendar der Diöcesen Deutschlands, der Schweiz und Skandinaviens* (1892); II, pt. 2: *Ordenskalender, Heiligenverzeichniss, Nachträge zum Glossar* (1898).

Hobson, *Les reliures à la fanfare*
Geoffrey D. Hobson, *Les reliures à la fanfare: le problème de l'S fermé ($); une étude historique et critique de l'art de la reliure en France au XVIe siècle fixée sur le style à la fanfare et l'usage de l'S fermé,* (2nd ed., with a supplement of revisions and corrections by Anthony R. A. Hobson, Amsterdam, 1970).

Hoskins, *Sarum and York Primers*
Edgar Hoskins, *Horæ Beatæ Mariæ Virginis, or, Sarum and York Primers with kindred books and Primers of the reformed Roman Use* (London, etc., 1901).

Gambier Howe, *Franks bequest*
E. R. J. Gambier Howe, *Franks bequest: catalogue of British and American book plates bequeathed to the Trustees of the British Museum by Sir Augustus Wollaston Franks, K.C.B., F.R.S., P.S.A., Litt.D.* (3 vols., London, 1903-4).

James, *Fitzwilliam McClean cat.*
Montague Rhodes James, *A descriptive catalogue of the McClean collection of manuscripts in the Fitzwilliam Museum* (Cambridge, 1912).

Ker, *MMBL*
N. R. Ker, *Medieval manuscripts in British libraries* (4 vols., Oxford); *I: London* (1969); *II: Abbotsford - Keele* (1977); *III: Lampeter - Oxford* (1983); with A. J. Piper, *IV: Paisley - York* (1992); index vol. in preparation.

Kristeller, *Iter italicum*
Paul Oskar Kristeller, *Iter italicum: a finding list of uncatalogued or incompletely catalogued humanistic manuscripts of the Renaissance in Italian and other libraries* (7 vols., Leiden and London, 1963-97; vols. I-VI on CD-ROM, Leiden, etc., 1995).

Leroquais, *Bréviaires*
V. Leroquais, *Les bréviaires manuscrits des bibliothèques publiques de France* (6 vols., Paris, 1934).

Leroquais, *Livres d'heures*
V. Leroquais, *Les livres d'heures manuscrits de la Bibliothèque nationale* (3 vols., Paris, 1927).

Leroquais, *Sacramentaires*
V. Leroquais, *Les sacramentaires et les missels manuscrits des bibliothèques publiques de France* (4 vols., Paris, 1924).

Levi d'Ancona, *Miniatura e miniatori a Firenze*
Mirella Levi d'Ancona, *Miniatura e miniatori a Firenze dal XIV al XVI secolo: documenti per la storia della miniatura* ([Storia della miniatura, studi e documenti, 1:] Florence, 1962).

Ottosen, *Office of the Dead*
Knud Ottosen, *The responsories and versicles of the Latin Office of the Dead* (Aarhus, 1993).

Pächt & Alexander
Otto Pächt and J. J. G. Alexander, *Illuminated manuscripts in the Bodleian Library, Oxford* (3 vols., Oxford): *1: German, Dutch, Flemish, French and Spanish schools* (1966, repr. with corrections, 1969); *2: Italian school* (1970); *3: British, Irish, and Icelandic schools* (1973).

Perdrizet, *Calendrier Parisien*
Paul Perdrizet, *Le calendrier Parisien à la fin du moyen âge d'après le bréviaire et les livres d'heures* (Publications de la Faculté des lettres de l'Université de Strasbourg, fasc. 63: Paris, 1933).

Randall, *Walters Art Gallery cat.*
Lilian M. C. Randall, *Medieval and renaissance manuscripts in the Walters Art Gallery* (Baltimore and London): *I: France, 875-1420* (1989); *II: France, 1420-1540* (2 vols., 1992); *III: Belgium, 1250-1530* (2 vols., 1997).

Repertorium hymnologicum
Ulysse Chevalier, *Repertorium hymnologicum: catalogue des chants, hymnes, proses, séquences, tropes en usage dans l'église latine depuis les origines jusqu'à nos jours* (6 vols., Louvain, etc.): *I: A-K (Nos. 1-9935)* (1892); *II: L-Z (Nos. 9936-22256)* (1897); *III: A-Z (Nos. 22257-34827)* (1904); *IV: A-Z (Nos. 34828-42060)* (1912); *V: Addenda et corrigenda* (Brussels, 1921); *VI: Préface - tables* (Paris, 1919).

Rézeau, *Répertoire*
Pierre Rézeau, *Répertoire d'incipit des prières françaises à la fin du moyen âge: addenda et corrigenta aux répertoires de Sonet et Sinclair, nouveau incipit* (Publications romanes et françaises, 174: Geneva, 1986).

Rietstap, *Armorial général* and *Planches*
J. B. Rietstap, *Armorial général: précédé d'un dictionnaire des termes du blason* (2nd edn.; 2 vols., Gouda, 1884-7); the plates in six vols., the first titled: *Armoires des familles contenues dans l'Armorial général de J. B. Rieststap* [sic] *publiées par l'Institut Héraldique Universel* (Paris, 1903); the remainder: *Planches de l'Armorial général de J-.B. Rietstap*; vols. II-IV, by V. Rolland, cover C-O (Paris, [n.d.]-1912); vols. V-VI, by H. [and] V. Rolland, cover P-Z (The Hague, 1921-6).

Saenger, *Newberry cat.*
Paul Saenger, *A catalogue of the pre-1500 western manuscript books at the Newberry Library* (Chicago and London, 1989).

SC
Falconer Madan, *et al.*, *A summary catalogue of western manuscripts in the Bodleian Library at Oxford* (7 vols in 8, Oxford, 1895-1953); *I: Historical introduction and conspectus of shelf-marks* (1953); *II, part I: (collections received before 1660 and miscellaneous MSS. acquired during the first half of the 17th century), nos. 1-3490* (1922); *II, part II: (collections and miscellaneous MSS. acquired during the second half of the 17th century) [nos. 3491-8716]* (1937); *III: (collections received during the 18th century) [nos. 8717-16669]* (1895); *IV: (collections received during the first half of the 19th century) nos. 16670-24330* (1897); *V: (collections received during the second half of the 19th century and miscellaneous MSS. acquired between 1695 and 1890) nos. 24331-31000* (1905); *VI: (accessions, 1890-1915) nos. 31001-37299* (Oxford, 1924); *VII: index* (1953).

Schutzner, *Library of Congress cat.*
Svato Schutzner, *Medieval and renaissance manuscript books in the Library of Congress: a descriptive catalog, I (Bibles, liturgy, Books of Hours)* (Washington, DC, 1989).

Sinclair, *French devotional texts, first supplement*
Keith V. Sinclair, *French devotional texts of the Middle Ages: a bibliographic manuscript guide. First Supplement* (Westport, CT, 1982).

Sonet, *Répertoire*
Jean Sonet, *Répertoire d'incipit de prières en ancien français* (Société de publications romanes et françaises, 54: Geneva, 1956).

van der Horst, *Utrecht University Library cat.*
Koert van der Horst, *Illuminated and decorated medieval manuscripts in the University Library, Utrecht: an illustrated catalogue* (Maarssen, etc., 1989).

van Dijk, *Handlist of Latin liturgical MSS.*
S. J. P. van Dijk, *Handlist of the Latin liturgical manuscripts in the Bodleian Library* (unpublished typescript; 6 vols. in 7, Oxford): *I: Mass books* (1957); *II(i): Office books* (1957); *II(ii): Office lectionaries* (1957); *III: Rituals & directories* (1958); *IV: Books of Hours* (1959); *V: Fragments - Mass books* (1959); *VI: Fragments - Office books, rituals, directories* (1960); *VII: Indexes* (1960).

VCH
The Victoria history of the counties of England (London, etc., 1900-).

Warner and Gilson, *Royal and King's cat.*
George F. Warner and Julius P. Gilson, *Catalogue of western manuscripts in the old Royal and King's collections* (4 vols., London, 1921).

Watson, *Dated and datable, British Library*
Andrew G. Watson, *Catalogue of dated and datable manuscripts c. 700-1600 in the Department of Manuscripts, The British Library* (2 vols., London, 1979).

Watson, *Dated and datable, Oxford*
Andrew G. Watson, *Catalogue of dated and datable manuscripts c.435-1600 in Oxford libraries* (2 vols., Oxford, 1984).

Weale, *Bookbindings in the National Art Library*
W. H. James Weale, *Bookbindings and rubbings of bindings in the National Art Library, South Kensington* (2 vols., London; repr. in one vol., 1962): *I: Introduction* (1898); *II: Catalogue* (1894).

Wilmart, *Auteurs spirituels*
André Wilmart, *Auteurs spirituels et textes dévots du moyen âge latin: études d'histoire littéraire* (Paris, 1932).

Wordsworth, *Horae Eboracenses*
Christopher Wordsworth, *Horae Eboracenses: the Prymer or Hours of the Blessed Virgin Mary, according to the Use of the illustrious Church of York with other devotions as they were used by the lay-folk in the Northern Province in the XVth and XVIth centuries* (Surtees Society, 132: Durham and London, 1920).

The Catalogue

MS. Buchanan c. 1

Leonardus Aretinus (Leonardo Bruni), *Historiarum Florentini populi libri XII*, and *Rerum suo tempore gestarum commentarius*, in Latin
Italy, Florence; 15th century, 1440 or later (*c*.1440-50)

Text
[Books I-VII of item 1 occupy quires I-VII, Books VIII-XII occupy quires VIII-XXIV]

1. (fols. 1r-238v) Leonardus Aretinus (Leonardo Bruni), *Historiarum Florentini populi libri XII* (ed. Emilio Santini, Rerum Italicarum Scriptores, 19, pt. 3: Città di Castello, 1914) with one or more lines left blank for a rubric before the preface and before each book, except for Book I (fol. 1v) which runs straight on from the preface (marked later with '1/' in the margin), and Books XI (fol. 212v) and XII (fol. 229r), which run on from Book X without break; incipits and explicits of each book are the same as in the pr. ed., except that the manuscript has an extra passage at the end of Book XI (fol. 228v, third line from the bottom, to fol. 229r line 1): 'Hec omnia sic ab eo fiebant ... populorum motus'; and the manuscript omits the first sentence of Book XII of the pr. ed.

[Item 2 occupies quires XXV-XXVI]

2. (fols. 239r-257r) Leonardus Aretinus (Leonardo Bruni), *Rerum suo tempore gestarum commentarius* (ed. Carmine di Pierro, Rerum Italicarum Scriptores, 19, pt. 3: Bologna, 1926) with a line left blank for a rubric; the order of the fourth and fifth words of the incipit reversed: 'Qui per italiam excelluerint homines ...', the correct order indicated with a superscript 'b' and 'a' by the scribe; similar corrections made elsewhere (e.g. fol. 257r, third line from the bottom); fols. 257v-258v ruled, otherwise blank; fols. 259r-260v, original flyleaves, blank.

Decoration
One inhabited five-line initial D[iuturna] of burnished gold enmeshed in white vine-scroll decoration, containing a yellowish lion (fol. 1r); the lower margin with a roundel formed of penwork, gold dots, and painted foliage and flowers, enclosing a winged putto holding a blank shield (pl. 13).

Ten similar but less elaborate initials, each 4-5 lines high at the start of most of the books of the *Historia*: Book II (fol. 19v); Book III (fol. 43r); Book IV (fol. 61r); Book V (fol. 88r); Book VI (fol. 116r); Book VII (fol. 139r); Book VIII (fol. 159r); Book IX (fol. 182v); Book X (fol. 201r); and the start of the *Commentarius* (fol. 239r).

A. C. de la Mare has attributed the illumination to Bartolomeo d'Antonio Varnucci (1412-5? - 1479) (on whom see Levi d'Ancona, *Miniatura e miniatori a Firenze*, 29-37; Annarosa Garzelli, 'Le immagini, gli autori, i destinatari', in *La miniatura fiorentina del Rinascimento, 1440-1525: un primo censimento* ed.

Annarosa Garzelli (Inventari e cataloghi toscani, 18-19: 2 vols., Florence, 1985),
I, 5-391, at 29-31; II, ills. 53, 73-81; and Anna De Floriani, 'Per Bartolomeo
Varnucci: un *Messale* e alcune precisazioni', *Miniatura* 5/6 (1996), 49-60): in
Alexander and de la Mare she compared the present manuscript to the former
Abbey MS. J. A. 3227 (subsequently in the Ludwig Collection, Aachen, and the
J. Paul Getty Museum, MS. Ludwig XI. 2; de-accessioned in 1997); in 'Vespasiano
da Bisticci as producer of classical manuscripts in fifteenth-century Florence', in
*Medieval manuscripts of the Latin classics: production and use. Proceedings of The
Seminar in the History of the Book to 1500, Leiden, 1993* ed. Claudine Chavannes-
Mazel and Margaret M. Smith (Los Altos Hills, CA, and London, 1996), 166-207,
at 169 n. 10, she attributes the former Ludwig manuscript to Bartolomeo
Varnucci, along with those she compared with it in the Abbey catalogue, and she
gives bibliography and attributes the decoration of further manuscripts to him.
Not mentioned is Lincoln College, MS. Lat. 20, containing further Leonardo
Bruni texts (see Alexander and Temple, *Oxford college libraries*, no. 919).

Physical Description

MATERIAL: parchment, often with a marked difference between hair and flesh
sides and often with irregular edges, though generally of fine quality.

DIMENSIONS: the leaves 351-3 x 256-7 mm.; approximately every fifth quire
(quires III, VIII, XIII, XIX, XXIII) projects somewhat further at the fore-edge than its
neighbours, but the projecting quires were not affected by the binding straps, so
this is probably the result of gradual creepage.

NUMBER OF LEAVES: i (original parchment) + 258 + ii (original parchment).

FOLIATION: i, 1-260: fols. 1-34 have near-contemporary(?) foliation in ink in
arabic numerals, probably by the hand that added marginal dates (see under
Provenance); the remaining leaves are foliated in modern pencil.

COLLATION: mostly in quires of 10 leaves (but see the Note below): an original
flyleaf, conjoint with the pastedown, then: I-XIII^{10} (fols. 1-130), XIV^8 (fols. 131-
138) | XV-XXIV^{10} (fols. 139-238) | XXV-XXVI^{10} (fols. 239-258); followed by two
original flyleaves, conjoint with two pastedowns; quires arranged with hair-sides
outermost (on the arrangement of the quires, see the Notes below); CATCHWORDS
are present at the end of all quires except XIV, XVI, XXIV, and XXVI (see the Note
below), written horizontally near the centre of the lower margin, in the same
hand as the main text, usually between two dots; contemporary quire signatures
'.5.', '10' and '14' in ink remain at the lower outer edge of the final versos of
quires VI, XI, and XV (sic) (fols. 60v, 110v, and 148v), respectively; leaf signatures
partially cropped, consisting of a letter and a number, are present only in quires
which contain an illuminated initial (see the Note below).

RULING: 28 lines ruled in pale brown ink, with single vertical bounding lines,
extending the full height of the page, ruled on the flesh side of the leaves with an
instrument which produced a scored line, but also often left a brown 'crayon'
trace; the ruled space 230-2 x 146-9 mm.; prickings are often visible in the
upper and lower margins, and in the outer margin *c.*7 mm. below the bottom
ruled line.

[D]iuturna michi cogitatio fuit et sepe in alterutra parte sententia
pronior faciundu ne foret ut res gestas florentini populi
forisq et domi contentiones habitas et uel pace uel bello inclita
facta mandare litteris aggrederer. Excitabat quippe me ipsa
magnitudo rey quibus hic populus primo inter se ciuili uariosq discidio deinde
aduersus finitimos egregie gestis tandem nostra etate potentia inmodice adauctus
et cu mediolanensium potentissimo duce et cu ladislao bellicosissimo rege ita cotedit
ut ab alpibus in apuliam quanta italie longitudo protenditur cuncta armoy strepitu
quateret ac transalpinos insuper reges magnosq exercitus ex gallia et germania co-
moueret. Accedunt ad hec ipse capte quam ego urbem uel diuersitate animoy uel
emulatione potentie uel exitu belli recte alterum carthagine ut michi uideor appella-
rum. Cuius extrema debellatio atq obsidio pari obstinatione apud uictos uictoresq
agitate ita multa memoratu digna continent ut antiquis illis maximis rebus quas
legentes admirari solemus nulla ex parte inferiores appareant. Hec in perdigna
litteris et memoria uidebantur ac eaydem cognitione rey utilissimam priuatim
et publice arbitrabar. Nam cu prouecti etate homines eo sapientiores habeantur
quo plura uiderunt in uita quanto magis historia nobis si accurate legerimus hac
prestare poterit sapientia in qua multay etatum facta consiliaq cernuntur ut
et quid sequare et quid uites faciliter sumas excellentiumq uiroy gloria ad uirtue
excitere. Ex aduerso labor ingens ac partim obscura partim interrupta quoydam
tepor notitia nominu demoq asperitas uix cuiusq elegantie patiens multe preterea
difficultates uehementer auertebant. Tandem uero his inter se multu diuq pesatis
in hac potissimu sententia constiti ut censerem quacuq scribendi ratione torpenti
silentio esse preferendam. Itaq ea scribere aggressus sum non ignarus quidem
ipse mei nec quantu onus suscipiam nescius. Sed cepti spero fautor deus aderit

13. MS. Buchanan c. 1, fol. 1r. [Considerably reduced]

SCRIPT: written in a fine humanistic script, probably by a single scribe, with 27 lines of text per page; the written space 224-5 x 146-52 mm.; enlarged capital letters are written to the left of the ruling when a sentence starts on a new line (e.g. fols. 13v-14v); various corrections (including an omitted line and a half, supplied in the lower margin of fol. 178r) are by the original scribe.
RUBRICATION: spaces were left for rubrics but these were never executed.
SEC. FOL.: 'notitia aperiendum'.

Note

Most of the quires which contain an illuminated initial—and *only* these quires —have the cropped remains of a series of leaf signatures consisting of a letter and number (notionally from a1-a6 in quire I, to h1-h6 in quire XVII): quire II has 'b5' extant (fol. 15r), quire V has 'c1', 'c2', and part of 'c3' (fols. 41r-43r), quire IX has 'e2'-'e6' extant (fols. 82r-86r), quire XII has parts of 'f2'-'f6' (fols. 112r-116r), quire XV has 'g1'-'g5' (fols. 139r-143r), and quire XVII has parts of 'h1'-'h5' (fols. 159r-163r). These leaf signatures were presumably provided to facilitate the re-assembly of the bifolia of each of these quires in the correct order after they had been disassembled, so that the illuminator could work on them. Each quire has a catchword *except* when the following quire contains an illuminated initial: presumably the binder assembled the quires according to catchwords, and on encountering a quire without a catchword, he followed it by a quire with leaf signatures, in alphabetical order. The purpose of the quire numbers at the end of quires VI, XI, and XV is unclear; and the reason why they are each one ahead of the true quire number is obscure unless a prefatory quire is now lost; the numbers may possibly have been part of a tally of the amount of parchment used.

The collation shows that the makers of the book wanted to keep open the possibility that the *Historia* would be bound in two volumes, perhaps without the *Commentarius*, since the *Commentarius* starts on a new quire, and in the *Historia* the end of Book VII falls at the end of a short quire. Several copies of the *Historia* are divided into two volumes at this point; see Emilio Santini, 'Leonardo Bruni aretino e i suoi *Historiarum florentini populi libri XII*', *Annali della R. Scuola Normale Superiore di Pisa 22*, Filosofia e Filologia (1910), (separately paginated:) 1-173, 125-9, nos. II, III, VIII, XI, XVIII, XIX.

Binding

Contemporay blind-tooled binding. Sewn on five wide split/double straps, the seven sewing-stations (for kettle-stitching and five straps) marked out by prickings near the gutter-edge of the leaves (clearly visible, e.g. fol. 1; cf. MS. Buchanan d. 4); each strap pegged into its channel using (wood?) pegs and pairs of ferrous nails; with (faded) green and yellow five-core end-bands; bound in polished brown leather over wood boards, each decorated in blind with the same design; working inwards from the edges are: a plain band flanked by fillets, a band of interlace with four-pointed starlets in the interstices, and another plain

band flanked by fillets, all enclosing a rectangle of ropework containing a central
square panel, in which is an eight-pointed star design filled with further
ropework; all these areas, except the interlace, have punched circlets, often with
traces of copper-coloured gilding or paste; the upper board with a rounded brass
boss at each corner (one at the centre missing), and the remains of four textile
strap fastenings (two at the fore-edge, and one each at top and bottom; the straps
themselves all missing), each held with three nails (one missing) in a triangular
pattern, the nail-heads with a punched star pattern; the lower board with four
bosses at the corners (one missing), and one in the centre, and four brass
rounded fleur-de-lis-shaped clasp fittings, corresponding to those on the upper
board, each secured with three round-headed nails (the whole board ill. in Hobson,
Humanists and bookbinders, fig. 11); the flat spine with five slightly raised double
bands, each compartment tooled in blind with a simple lattice; the second and
fourth compartments lettered in gilt, probably for William Morris, perhaps by
Messrs. Leighton (see under Provenance; cf. MS. Buchanan e. 15): 'L. ARETINI
| HISTORIA | FLORENTINÆ | REIPUBLICÆ' and 'MS. | IN | MEMBRANIS'.
Boxed, 1987.

Provenance
1. The text of the *Commentarius* goes as far as the year 1440, providing the
terminus post quem; the empty shield on fol. 1r suggests that the book was copied
and decorated without a particular recipient in mind (de la Mare, 'New research');
it is possible that the book was produced on spec in the workshop of Vespasiano
da Bisticci, for whom the illuminator of the present manuscript, Bartolomeo di
Antonio Varnucci, is known to have worked.

2. Unidentified 15th- and/or 16th-cent. Italian owners: the foliation of fols. 1-34;
marginal corrections (e.g. fols. 24v, 27r); and dates (e.g. fols. 72r, 72v); a 'Nota'
mark (fol. 101r); other inscriptions in humanistic script (e.g. fols. 143v, 144v);
and the illegibly scrawled inscription: 'I.storii.flori.mini'(??) on the lower
pastedown, were presumably added by early owners.

3. Unidentified Italian owner, 1536: inscribed semi-legibly: 'Istorie fiorentine
della[?] []ade[?] di marciotto[?] | ..[?] haliles[??] etc.[?] alla nuova[??] lerenda[??]
| e son(n)o in latin(n)o anno D' 1536 —', on the upper pastedown; another
inscription, partially visible under the bookplate (see below), seems also to read
'haliles'(?) (see pl. 11).

4. Unidentified 17th-cent. Italian collection; inscribed with a title and
shelfmark(?) (fol. i recto): 'Historia Florentine Reipublice | Authore Leonardo
Aretino | H. 769'.

5. John Adrian Louis Hope (1860-1908), 7th Earl of Hopetoun and 1st Marquis
of Linlithgow (on whom see *DNB*, Second Supplement, II (1912), 299-301;
G.E.C., VI, 575-6; and 'Sir James Hope of Hopetoun' cd. Quaritch): with the
(later?) larger Hopetoun bookplate (see Gambier Howe, *Franks bequest*, II, no.
15273) pasted to the upper pastedown, inscribed with a shelfmark(?) 'T-3',

in brown ink in a shaky hand (see pl. 11); above the title and shelfmark(?) on
fol. i recto (see above) is, written by another hand, 'O.3.20' (the '20' corrected
from '19'), between two roughly horizontal lines. Very similar inscriptions
(usually without horizontal lines or correction) occur on the bookplates and
flyleaves of other manuscripts from the Hopetoun collection (e.g. Bodleian, MS.
Lat. misc. c. 5, which has 'F-9' and 'O.3.9'); according to Quaritch, *op. cit.*, the
7th Earl was not a bibliophile, so it is probable that the manuscript had already
been in the family for at least one generation; it was in the 7th Earl's sale at
Sotheby's, 25 Feb. 1889, lot 228, bought by Leighton for £12 10s., with the
description cut from the sale catalogue glued to the upper pastedown (see pl. 11).

6. Messrs. J. & J. Leighton (see Introduction, p. xxvii): erased pencil notations,
perhaps include a price starting '£15[...]'?, below and to the right of the centre
of fol. i recto, and a price-code(?) in the bottom gutter corner of the pastedown
(cf. MS. Buchanan e. 15).

7. William Morris (1834-96) (see Introduction, p. xxvii); apparently acquired
after 1890, since it does not appear in the Morris catalogue compiled during
1890-1 (see Paul Needham, 'William Morris: book collector', in *William Morris
and the Art of the Book* (London, 1976), 21-47, at 32-3); no. 6 in the inventory
drawn up by F. S. Ellis after his death (*ibid*, pl. 9).

8. Richard Bennett (see Introduction, p. xxvii), with his posthumous Morris
book-label on the upper pastedown; sold at the 'Morris' sale, Sotheby's, 5 Dec.
1898, lot 131, bought by Buchanan for £25; inscribed probably by Sotheby's in
pencil: '104', encircled, on the upper pastedown (see Introduction, p. xxv, and
pl. 11).

9. Rt. Hon. T. R. Buchanan (1846-1911), 1898; bought at the 'Morris' sale
(cf. MSS. Buchanan d. 4 and e. 15); with the description from the sale catalogue
(erroneously describing the volume as having 277 leaves) glued to the upper
pastedown, and inscribed by Buchanan in pencil: 'Good title', presumably before
the sale; and in ink: 'Morris Sale | Dec. 98.', after it (see pl. 11); given to the
Bodleian by his widow, Mrs E. O. Buchanan, in 1941.

Bibliography

Sotheby, Wilkinson & Hodge, *The Hopetoun Library: catalogue of the library of the
Right Honourable the Earl of Hopetoun, which will be sold by auction ... 25th of
February, 1889, and three following days* (London), p. iii and lot 228.

'Sir James Hope of Hopetoun (died 1661) and his descendants Earls of
Hopetoun', in *Contributions towards a dictionary of English book-collectors as also
of some foreign collectors whose libraries were incorporated in English collections or
whose books are chiefly met with in England* ed. Bernard Quaritch (issued in 14
parts: London, 1892-1921), pt. V (1894), (separately paginated:) 1-3, at 2.

Sotheby, Wilkinson & Hodge, *Catalogue of a portion of the valuable library of manuscripts, early printed books, &c. of the late William Morris, of Kelmscott House, Hammersmith, which will be sold by auction … 5th of December, 1898 and five following days* (London), lot 131.

S. Gibson, 'Bookbindings in the Buchanan Collection', *BLR* 2 no. 16 (1941), 6-12, at 8.

Alexander and de la Mare, *Abbey cat.*, 31.

Pächt & Alexander, 2, no. 230, pl. XX (fol. 1r, details).

Alexander and Temple, *Oxford college libraries*, under no. 919.

Albinia de la Mare, 'New research on humanistic scribes in Florence', in *La miniatura fiorentina del Rinascimento, 1440-1525: un primo censimento* ed. Annarosa Garzelli (Inventari e cataloghi toscani, 18-19: Florence, 1985), 395-574, at 398 n. 21.

Anthony Hobson, *Humanists and bookbinders: the origins and diffusion of the humanistic bookbinding 1459-1559 with a census of historiated plaquette and medallion bindings of the Renaissance* (Cambridge, etc., 1989), 19 fig. 11 (back board of binding).

Kristeller, *Iter Italicum* IV (1989), 245.

James Hankins, *Repertorium brunianum: a critical guide to the writings of Leonardo Bruni, I: handlist of manuscripts* (Fonti per la storia dell'Italia medievale. Subsidia, 5: Rome, 1997), 129 no. 1771.

cura & negotio uacua. scribendi exercitio
uacent egere. Sed pessimum malo♃ om
nium rectissime a sapientibus uiris in
gratitudo appellatur; que maxime in
habitaculis principum uersari solet. ho
mines certe ex arce rationis deiciat; nul
loq; boni uiri officio uti sinit. Id uitium
cum semp horrueris ueluti pnitiosam pe
stem. certus sum de nequaq̃ alio♃ cul
pam esse imitaturum.

EXPLICIT PROEMIVM.

POGGII FLORENTINI DE VARIE
TATE FORTVNE LIBER PRIMVS
INCIPIT. AD NICOLAVM PAPA V.

VPER CVM PONTIFEX
martinus paulo anteq̃ diem
situm obiret. ab urbe in agrũ
tusculanum secessisset uale
tudinis gratia. nos autem es
semus negotiis curisq; publicis uacui;
uisebamus sepius deserta urbis antonius
luscus uir clarissimus ego q; admirates

MS. Buchanan d. 4

Poggio Bracciolini, *De varietate fortunae*, in Latin
Italy, Florence; dated 1455

Text
(fols. 2r-122r) Poggio Bracciolini, *De varietate fortunae* (ed. Outi Merisalo, stating,
p. 33, that this is the earliest dated manuscript of his Phase III (cf. p. 15)) with
the rubric (fol. 2r): 'AD NICOLAVM PAPAM .V. POGGII FLORENTINI DE
VARIETATE FORTUNE INCIPIT PROEMIUM' ('INCIPIT PRO' over an erasure;
see Watson, *Dated and datable, Oxford*, II, pl. 524), and a similar rubric at the start
of Book I (see pl. 14); fol. 1r-v ruled in ink, otherwise originally blank; fols. 122v-
123v ruled in drypoint, otherwise blank.

Decoration
The preface with a four-line white vine-stem initial M[ulta] with foliate ornament
extending up and down the inner margin (fol. 2r; *ibid.*); Books I-IV (fols. 4v, 32v,
66v, 96r) each with a three- to five-line initial in gold on a green and/or red
ground framed in blue (see pl. 14).

Physical Description
MATERIAL: parchment.
DIMENSIONS: the leaves 234-6 x 147-9 mm.
NUMBER OF LEAVES: i (paper) + 123 + i (paper).
FOLIATION: modern, in pencil: i, 1-124.
COLLATION: mostly in quires of 10 leaves: I¹⁰⁺¹ (1st leaf added, fol. 1, glued to fol. 2)
(fols. 1-11), II-XII¹⁰ (fols. 12-121), XIII² (fols. 122-123); quires arranged flesh side
outermost; horizontal CATCHWORDS present throughout, in the script of the
main text, in the lower right margin, the start of the catchword usually aligned
with the leftmost of the vertical bounding lines.
RULING: 25 lines ruled in drypoint on the hair side, with double vertical bounding
lines extending the full height of the leaf, the first and last horizontal extending
the full width of the page, the ruled space 149-50 x 82-3 mm. (95-6 mm. including
the bounding lines); fol. 1 without visible prickings, ruled with 30 lines in pale
brown ink, between double vertical bounding lines ruled the full height of the
page (the outermost vertical significantly fainter); the ruled space 168 x 89 (97)
mm.; PRICKINGS usually visible in the fore-edge margin of quires I-II, pricked
from the front of the quire to the back, and in the upper and lower margins
throughout, pricked from the hair to the flesh side; the upper and lower margins
occasionally re-pricked from the opposite side; quire II is pricked for 25 lines
throughout; the second and centre bifolia of quire I (fols. 3 & 10, 6 & 7), however,
have 31 prickings in the outer margin, of which the lowest 25 are pricked from
the back of the quire to the front: thus it seems that after pricking for 25 lines,
these two bifolia were inverted, the wide bottom margin now being at the top,

necessitating the extra prickings in the upper margin; other bifolia also have
double sets of pricking (e.g. lower margin of fols. 103 & 110, 107 & 108).
SCRIPT: written in humanistic script, attributed to ser Giovanni di Piero da Stia
(see under Provenance), with 25 lines of text per page, written above top line;
the written space 151-2 x 83-91 (97) mm.
RUBRICATION: headings in brick red capitals.
SEC. FOL.: 'quam multis'.

Binding

Sewn on four cords, and bound in 18th-cent. Italian(?) parchment over rather
thin pasteboards; with endbands sewn in plain thread; the spine with a red
leather title-piece lettered 'POGGIU. | VARIET | FORT: | MSS.' in the second
compartment, and with a black ink cross inscribed in the compartment below;
marbled pastedowns and plain laid paper flyleaves without visible watermarks;
the edges of the leaves gauffered and gilt, demonstrably pre-dating the present
binding, since the gilding on the fore-edge shows the marks of two straps, of
which no trace remains on the present binding. Prickings in the gutter margin *c.*
21, 52, 116, 178 and 209 mm. from the top (i.e. at the mid-point, and approximately 22 mm. and 53 mm. from both top and bottom, visible e.g. at fol. 24r),
perhaps correspond to the placement of the sewing-stations (kettle-stitches and
three cords) of a previous, perhaps original, binding (cf. MS. Buchanan c. 1, a
contemporary Florentine manuscript in its original binding).

Provenance

1. Written in Florence and dated 1455 by the scribe (fol. 122r): 'DE VARIETATE
FORTVNE LIBER | QVARTVS EXPLICIT :- :- 1455.'; the script is attributable to
the Florentine notary ser Giovanni di Piero da Stia (*c.*1406-74), to whom de la
Mare ('New research', I, 425-6, 499-500) has attributed over forty manuscripts,
two of them signed, and most of them dated; he had previously copied the same
text in 1450 (now Vatican, Ottob. lat. 2134; see Merisalo, *op. cit.,* 27-8 no. 5).
Merisalo suggests that the present manuscript comes probably from the workshop of Vespasiano da Bisticci (*ibid.,* 33), but de la Mare does not include it in
her list of Vespasiano manuscripts (*op. cit.,* I, 555-64).

2. ? Fruosino and/or his son Girolamo da Panzano (see Ullman & Stadter, *The
public library of renaissance Florence,* 43-4): erased inscriptions leave doubt as
to who first owned the manuscript (see below), but if Girolamo died after 1500,
as is probable, then this manuscript, written in 1455, is perhaps more likely to
have been commissioned by his father Fruosino, who seems also to have owned
Florence, Bibl. Laurenziana, MS. San Marco 366, which is signed and dated
1449 by the same scribe (*ibid.,* 44 n. 3; de la Mare, *op. cit.,* 499 no. 10). Ullman
& Stadter, Watson, and Merisalo all give variant readings of the erased inscriptions,
usually supplying Girolomo's name, but inspection under UV, IR, and blue lights
has not clarified the situation. Girolamo bequeathed London, BL, Add. MS. 14798
(written by our scribe), and Harley MS. 2630 to San Marco (Ullman & Stadter, *op.
cit.,* 43-4).

3. The Dominican convent of San Marco, Florence, probably after 1500, since the manuscript does not appear in the San Marco inventory of that date (Ullman & Stadter, *op. cit.*, 44): erased inscriptions on fols. 1r and 1v have been read variously as, e.g. (fol. 1v): 'Iste liber est conuentus s(an)c(t)i Marci de Florentia ord(inis) pred(icatorum) ab heredibus ... de Panzano de[?] Florentia' (this reading based on a note in the hand of R. W. Hunt on the old typescript description of the manuscript).

4. Unidentified 18th-cent. Italian collection: inscribed in an 18th-cent. Italian hand in ink (fol. i verso): 'Codex Saec: XV | Codex iste nitidissimus idem | est, quem Auctor Nicolao V. | obtulit, habemus editum | inter Opera Poggij' (see pl. 12; apparently in the same hand as a similar note in Bodleian Library, MS. Add. C. 139, which was owned by Libri (see below), so presumably they both came from the same source). The inscription is similar to those of Antonio de Santo (on which see J. B. Mitchell, 'Trevisan and Soranzo: some Canonici manuscripts from two eighteenth-century Venetian collections', *BLR* 8 no. 3 (1969), 125-35, esp. pl. XV), one of the librarians of Jacopo Soranzo (1686-1761), many of whose manuscripts passed to Matteo Luigi Canonici (1727-1806), and thence to the Bodleian in 1817; and although the binding resembles some other Canonici bindings, there is no clear evidence that the present manuscript was ever owned by him.

5. ? Guglielmo Libri (1802-1869) (on whom see Marco Mostert and P. Alessandra Maccioni Ruju, *The life and times of Guglielmo Libri (1802-1869), scientist, patriot, scholar, journalist and thief: a nineteenth-century story* (Hilversum, 1995)): inscribed in pencil 'Libri' in the top left corner of fol. i verso in a 19th(?)-cent. hand (pl. 12); not found in his sale catalogues of 1853, 1859, 1862, or 1864.

6. Unidentified 19th-cent. booksellers: inscribed in pencil (fol. i recto) '99' upper left, '72', upper right; (fol. i verso) '<u>elyz</u>', upper left corner; see pl. 12); and (fol. 124r) 'r£m/'(?), centre right, and '41' lower right; an erasure, presumably of an ink inscription, in the upper right corner.

7. Unidentified English 19th-cent. owner: inscribed with an ironic comment in pencil, below the 18th-cent. ink flyleaf inscription (fol. i verso): 'This note is quite correct, with the exception that this is not the copy presented to Nicolas V. and that it is not printed in the works of Poggio.' (pl. 12); the tone is reminiscent of notes inscribed by William Beckford in his books, but the hand is probably not his.

8. William Morris (1834-1896), acquired between *c.*1876 and 1891: the present manuscript does not appear among the medieval manuscripts listed in a catalogue of the former date, but occurs as one of only six western medieval manuscripts in a catalogue of Morris's collection drawn up in 1890-91 (see Needham, 'William Morris: book collector'); it also appears as no. 70 in the inventory drawn up shortly after his death by F. S. Ellis, and has this number inscribed in pencil in the top left corner of fol. i verso (see Introduction, p. xxvi, and pl. 12).

9. Richard Bennett (see Introduction, p. xxvi), with his posthumous Morris book-label on the upper pastedown (cf. MSS. Buchanan c. 1, e. 15); sold in the

'Morris' sale at Sotheby's, 5 December 1898 and five following days, lot 863, bought by Buchanan for £12 12s; inscribed in pencil (fol. i verso): '40.' below and to the right of the Ellis inventory number (see pl. 12), probably by Sotheby's (see Introduction, p. xxv).

10. Rt. Hon. T. R. Buchanan (1846-1911), 1898: bought at the 'Morris' sale; with the description from the sale catalogue pasted to the upper pastedown, inscribed by Buchanan in ink 'Morris Sale | Dec 98.'; given to the Bodleian by his wife, Mrs. E. O. Buchanan, in 1941.

Bibliography

Sotheby, Wilkinson & Hodge, *Catalogue of a portion of the valuable library of manuscripts, early printed books, &c. of the late William Morris, of Kelmscott House, Hammersmith, which will be sold by auction ... 5th of December, 1898 and five following days* (London), lot 863.

Pächt & Alexander, 2, no. 265.

Berthold L. Ullman and Philip A. Stadter, *The public library of renaissance Florence: Niccolò Niccoli, Cosimo de' Medici, and the library of San Marco* (Medioevo e Umanesimo, 10: Padua, 1972), 44.

Paul Needham, 'William Morris: book collector', in *William Morris and the art of the book* (cat. of an exhibition at the Pierpont Morgan Library, New York; London, 1976), 21-47, at 32-33.

Watson, *Dated and datable, British Library*, I, 39 under no. 110.

Watson, *Dated and datable, Oxford*, I, 25 no. 138, 60 under no. 372; II, pl. 524 (upper part of fol. 2r).

Albert Derolez, *Codicologie des manuscrits en écriture humanistique sur parchemin* (Bibliologia, 5-6: Turnhout, 1984), II, 89 no. 561.

Albinia de la Mare, 'New research on humanistic scribes in Florence', in *La miniatura fiorentina del Rinascimento, 1440-1525: un primo censimento* ed. Annarosa Garzelli (Inventari e cataloghi toscani, 18-19: Florence, 1985), I, 395-574, at 500 no. 23.

Kristeller, *Iter italicum*, IV (1989), 673; VI (1992), 560.

Outi Merisalo, ed., *Poggio Bracciolini, De varietate fortunae: edizione critica con introduzione e commento* (Annales Academiae Scientarum Fennicae, Ser. B, 265: Helsinki, 1993), 33 no. 11.

MS. Buchanan e. 2

Book of Hours, Use of Paris, in Latin and French
France, Paris; 14th century, last quarter

Text
[Item 1 occupies quire I]

1. (fols. 1r-12v) Calendar in French, with an entry for every day, major feasts in red; of the type pr. by Paul Perdrizet, *Calendrier Parisien*, for Paris Books of Hours, having all the same major feasts, including Geneviève, patroness of Paris (3 Jan.), Anne (28 July), Louis IX (relics at Paris) (25 Aug.), Denis of Paris (9 Oct.); and in addition George (23 Apr.), Eloi (25 Jun.), Merry (relics at Paris) (29 Aug.), and Matthew (21 Sept.); but with Marcellus of Paris (3 Nov.) given as a minor feast, and Fabian, instead of Sebastian (20 Jan.) also minor; other entries in brown include Ivo Helory (19 May), Germanus of Paris (28 May), Landericus ('Landri') of Paris (10 June), the translation of Marcellus of Paris (26 July), the Crown of Thorns (relic at Paris) (11 Aug.), Cloud, patron of Paris (7 Sept.), Magloire (relics at Paris) (24 Oct.), and Geneviève (26 Nov.).

[Items 2-7 occupy quires II-XII]

2. (fols. 13r-14v) Gospel Pericope from John [John 1:1-14].

3. (fols. 15r-72v) Hours of the Virgin, Use of Paris, with three lessons at Matins.

4. (fols. 73r-77v, rubric on 72v) Hours of the Cross.

5. (fols. 78r-83r, rubric on 77v) Hours of the Holy Spirit.

6. (fols. 83v-97v) The Seven Penitential Psalms [Pss. 6, 31, 37, 50, 101, 129, 142].

7. (fols. 98r-103v, rubric on 97v) Litany and collects: the litany with Columba (of Sens?) (3), and Geneviève (13) among sixteen virgins; followed (fol. 103r-v) by two collects: (i) 'Deus cui proprium est misereri semper et parcere ...' (pr. *Corpus orationum*, no. 1143); (ii) 'Fidelium deus omnium conditor et redemptor ...' (pr. *ibid.*, no. 2684b).

[Item 8 occupies quires XIII-XIX]

8. (fols. 104r-154r) Office of the Dead, Use unidentified (van Dijk calls it 'Romanized Paris use'), the nine lessons at Matins correspond to 'Group 1d', and their responses to numbers 14,72,32; 57,24,68; 28,46,38, in Ottosen, *Office of the Dead*; fols. 154v-155v ruled, otherwise blank.

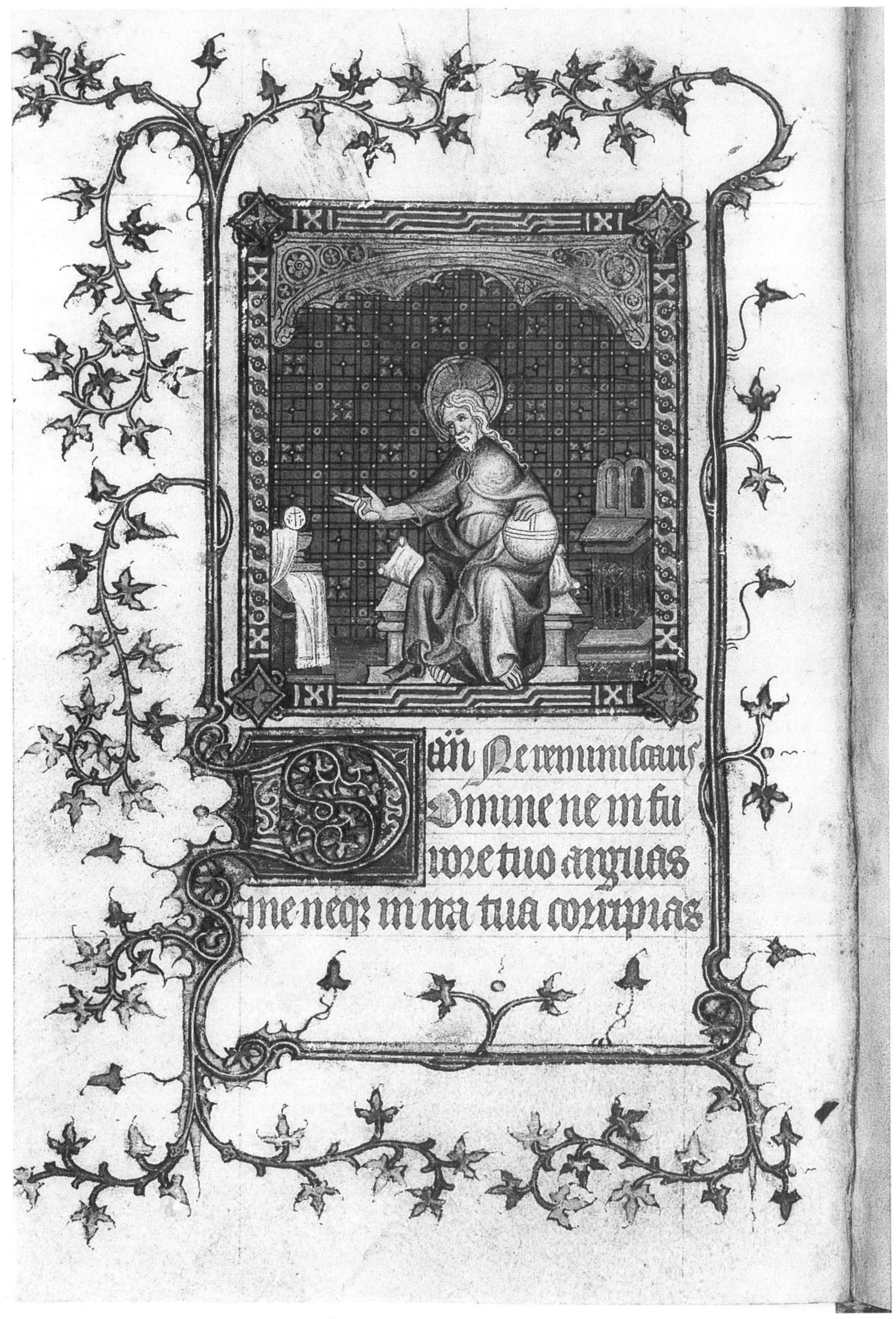

15. *MS. Buchanan e. 2, fol. 83v. [Enlarged]*

[Items 9(i)-(v) occupy quires XX-XXII]

9. (fols. 156r-173v) Prayers to the Virgin and to the Trinity, in Latin and French:
   (i) (fols. 156r-160v) *'Oracio beate marie uirginis. O intemerata ... orbis terrarum ex [sic] te enim ...'* [feminine forms] (pr. Wilmart, *Auteurs spirituels*, 494-5);
   (ii) (fol. 160v-164v) 'Obsecro te ...' [masculine forms] (with similarities to two pr. versions: Wordsworth, *Horae Eboracenses*, 66-7; Leroquais, *Livres d'heures*, II, 346-7);
   (iii) (fol. 165r-166r) 'Ave Maria gracia plena dominus tecum. Martir cum martiribus transgladiata ... contemplacione sine fine frui mereamur. Qui cum patre ...' (also found in Vatican, Ms. Reg. lat. 121; and Karlsruhe, Landesbibliothek, Hs. St. Blasien 77, fol. 142r, see Peter Höhler and Gerhard Stamm, *Die Handschriften der Badischen Landesbibliothek in Karlsruhe, XII: Die Handschriften von St. Blasien* (Wiesbaden, 1991), 123);
   (iv) (fols. 166r-169r) 'E tres certaine esperance ...' (pr. Leroquais, *op. cit.*, II, 332, where it starts with the more common 'O tres ...'; cf. Ker, *MMBL*, I, 260 art 9c; MS. Rawl. liturg. e. 32, fols. 20r-21v; and BL, Harley MS. 2952, fols. 80r-82r, which also start 'E tres ...');
   (v) (fols. 169r-173r) *'Oracio ad sanctam trinitatem. O sancta trinitas atque indiuisa vnitas uera ... gaudiis perfrui mereantur sempiternis. Per dominum.'* (various versions exist; also found in MS. Don. d. 85, fol. 3r-v); fol. 173v ruled, otherwise originally blank.

Decoration

Fourteen miniatures, each above four lines of text; except that for Lauds of the Hours of the Virgin, which is below two lines of text and above three; and that for the *O intemerata*, which is above five lines of text; the figures with grisaille draperies, some in a rudimentary landscape with a groundline and trees, set against a diaper or patterned background; in a rectangular frame with gold bosses at the corners; above a three- or four-line initial, from which sprout ivy-leaf decoration surrounding the text and image on all four sides; there are sewing-holes in the outer margin of the first few miniatures, presumably from protective textile veils.

(fol. 13r) Pericope. St. John the Baptist (*sic*), holding the Agnus Dei set against a reddish ?disc; trees and a rabbit.

(fol. 15r) Hours of the Virgin; Matins. Annunciation: Gabriel kneeling; God above blessing; the Dove flying from his lips to the Virgin's halo; the Virgin holding a book held closed with two clasps.

(fol. 27v) Lauds. Visitation: Elisabeth kneeling; the Virgin holding a book.

(fol. 40r) Prime. Nativity: the Virgin lying on a bed, eyes closed, with hand on an open book on her knee, turned away from Joseph.

(fol. 46v) Terce. Annunciation to the Shepherds: two standing, a third seated, with elaborate bagpipes, and a dog on a leash.

(fol. 51r) Sext. Adoration of the Magi; the Virgin crowned; the middle-aged
Magus pointing to the star, which is painted outside the frame of the miniature;
the Child blessing, his other hand on a chalice(?) offered by the eldest Magus.
(fol. 55v) None. Presentation in the Temple: the handmaid with a basket and
large taper.
(fol. 60v) Vespers. Flight into Egypt: Joseph leading, with a stick over his
shoulder, from which is draped a cloth.
(fol. 68r) Compline. Coronation of the Virgin: her arms crossed at the wrists;
God holding an orb at his knee.
(fol. 73r) Hours of the Cross. Crucifixion: the Virgin with hands clasped; John
with one hand to his face, a book in the other.
(fol. 78r) Hours of the Holy Spirit. Pentecost.
(fol. 83v) Penitential Psalms. God seated, turning away from the Tablets of the
Law (the Old Law), on his left, to bless a covered chalice and wafer (the New
Law), on his right, the latter depicted as if embossed with a representation of the
Crucifixion (pl. 15).
(fol. 104r) Office of the Dead. Funeral Service, with black-clad mourners, and
clerics singing at a lectern, on which an open book is inscribed in minute script
with the Introit of the Mass of the Dead: 'requiem eternam dona eis domine'; six
tapers on the bier, five pots(?) before it.
(fol. 156r) O intemerata. Virgin and Child Enthroned: the Virgin crowned; the
Child kissing her, his hand to her neck; she supports his foot with one hand; a
laywoman kneeling before them (pl. 16).

One three- and one four-line initial sprouting gold ivy-leaf, to the prayers on fols.
160v and 166r; two-line initials alternately gold and blue or red and blue, both
with red and blue filigree penwork, to prayers, psalms, etc.; one-line initials
alternately gold with blue penwork, or blue with red penwork, to verses and
other minor divisions; line-fillers of geometric and other simple forms,
alternately gold and blue or red and blue, usually corresponding to the initial at
the start of the verse.

Pächt & Alexander relate the style to Paris, BnF, mss. fr. 22912-3, a copy of
Augustine, *La Cité de Dieu*, in the translation of Raoul de Presles, datable to
1376-80 (see François Avril and Jean Lafaurie, *La librairie de Charles V* (exhib.
cat: Paris, 1968), 102 no. 177, pls. 3, 20).

Physical Description
MATERIAL: parchment.
DIMENSIONS: the leaves 162-3 x 104-6 mm. (catchwords and marginal
decoration are somewhat cropped).
NUMBER OF LEAVES: ii (modern parchment bifolium) + 174 + ii (modern
parchment bifolium).
FOLIATION: modern, in pencil: i-ii, 1-68a, 68b-175.

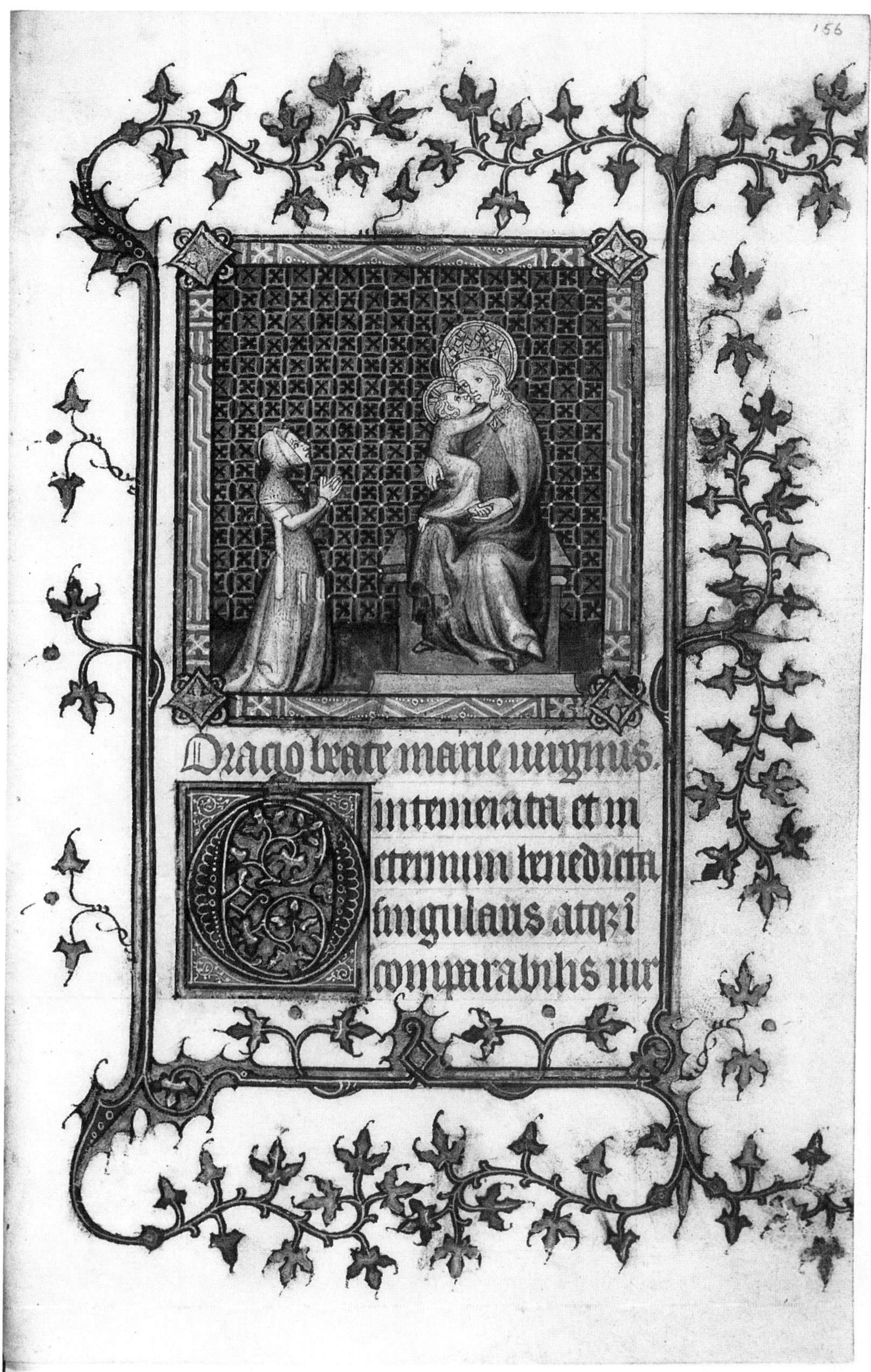

COLLATION: the main text mostly in quires of 8 leaves: I¹² (fols. 1-12) | II¹² (fols. 13-24), III-XII⁸ (fols. 25-103) | XIII-XVIII⁸ (fols. 104-151), XIX⁴ (fols. 152-155) | XX-XXI⁸ (fols. 156-171), XXII² (fols. 172-173); CATCHWORDS survive in all quires except those which contain the end of a major textual unit and quires II, VI, XIII, and XVIII, in the middle of the lower margin at the bottom edge of the page.

RULING: 15 lines ruled in pale brown ink, with single vertical bounding lines extending the full height of the page; the top, and occasionally the bottom one or two horizontals ruled the full width of the page; the ruled area 89-90 x 54-5 mm.; the calendar with 16 lines per page, between single verticals ruled the full height of the page (occasionally in purple ink, e.g. fol. 11r), the top and bottom horizontal ruled the full width, double verticals each side of the column which contains the 'S"/'S'e' abbreviation of Saint/Sainte before the saints' names, the ruled space 92-4 x 52-4 mm.

SCRIPT: written in a fine regular gothic bookhand, with 14 lines of text per page; the written space 88-9 x 52-7 mm.; the script smaller and markedly more angular from the start of the Office of the Dead (fol. 104r), but perhaps all by a single scribe; the shade of ink occasionally changing noticeably from one quire to the next.

RUBRICATION: headings in red; marginal guides to the rubricator occasionally visible (e.g. fol. 81r: 'none').

SEC. FOL.: (Calendar) 'KL Fevrier'; (text, fol. 14) [lumi-]'ne. Erat lux'.

Binding

Sewn on three cords; with green and brown endbands; bound in French 19th-cent. dark brown/black leather over pasteboards, with contemporary pastedowns; the spine with five (false) raised bands, lettered in gilt 'Heures' and 'M. S.' at the top and bottom in 'black letter' characters; one white silk book-mark; the edges of the leaves gilt; the Bodleian shelfmark label at the base of the spine apparently covering an earlier label. Boxed, using funds provided by the Friends of the Bodleian, 1994.

Provenance

1. Unidentified laywoman: presumably made in Paris for the woman depicted on fol. 156r; the prayer which starts on this page uses feminine forms.

2. ? Unidentified German prince-archbishop, 18th cent.: pasted to the upper (19th-cent.) pastedown, is a square armorial bookplate (pl. 17) which may have been transferred from the previous binding; the shield is surmounted by an archbishop's hat, the whole surmounted by a prince's crown, behind which is a crozier and sword.

3. Unidentified 18th/19th-cent. French owner: inscribed '74 [*sic*] feuillets.' (fol. 173v).

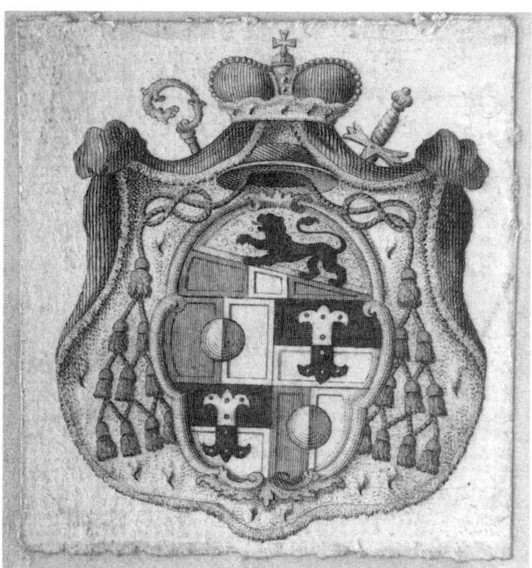

17. MS. Buchanan e. 2, upper pastedown, detail

4. Unidentified 19th-cent. French(?) bookseller: inscribed in ink '1400# [or ff]'
in the upper right corner of the lower pastedown.

5. Messrs. T. & W. Boone, London booksellers (see Introduction, p. xxi):
inscribed in pencil in the upper right corner of the upper pastedown and in
the upper left corner of the lower pastedown (see pl. 5) with their price-code
(cf. MSS. Buchanan e. 3 and g. 1; pls. 3, 4, 6).

6. John (or Thomas?) Buchanan: bought from Boone on 16 April, 1862, for £30
(see Introduction, p. xix); inscribed in pencil with the 'Descriptive list' number,
'2', in the upper left corner of the upper pastedown, and '2.' in the upper left
corner of fol. i verso.

7. Rt. Hon. T. R. Buchanan (1846-1911); given to the Bodleian by his widow,
Mrs. E. O. Buchanan in 1939, when it was accessioned as MS. Lat. liturg. e. 23
(as recorded in pencil in the lower left corner of fol. 1r); re-referenced as MS.
Buchanan e. 2 in 1941.

Bibliography

'Fifteen illuminated *Horae*', *BLR* 1 no. 7 (1939), 115-6, at 115 (cited as MS. Lat.
liturg. e. 23).

van Dijk, *Handlist of Latin liturgical MSS.*, IV, 78.

Pächt & Alexander, 1, no. 609, pl. XLVI.

Rézeau, *Répertoire*, no. 1538.

MS. Buchanan e. 3

Book of Hours, Use of Rouen, in Latin and French
France, Rouen; late 15th or early 16th century

Text
[Item 1 occupies quire I]

1. (fols. 2r-7v) Calendar, in French, with an entry for every day, major feasts in gold, the others alternately red or blue; feasts in gold include the Transfiguration (6 Aug.), Martial (3 July), Denis (9 Oct.), and Romanus of Rouen (23 Oct.); feasts in red or blue include Ansbert of Rouen (9 Feb.), Eustaise of Luxeuil (29 Mar.), Valeric (1 Apr.), Eutropius of Saintes (30 Apr.), Ivo Helory (19 May), Desiderius (23 May), Mellon of Rouen (22 Oct.), Malo (14 Nov., as in Paris Books of Hours: the usual date is 15 Nov.).

[Items 2-5 occupy quires II-VI]

2. (fols. 8r-11r) Gospel Pericopes [John 1:1-14, Luke 1:26-38, Matthew 2:1-12, Mark 16:14-20], John followed by the usual antiphon, versicle, response, and prayer: 'Protector in te sperantium ...' (pr. Wordsworth, *Horae Eboracenses*, 32-4).

3. (fols. 11r-14v) Prayers to the Virgin:
    (i) (fols. 11r-13r) 'Obsecro te ...' [masculine forms] (cf. MS. Buchanan e. 2);
    (ii) (fols. 13r-14v) 'O intemerata ... orbis terrarum. Inclina mater misericordie aures tue pietatis ...' [masculine forms] (pr. Wordsworth, *Horae Eboracenses*, 67-8).

4. (fol. 14v) The Five Joys of the Virgin: '*Quinque gaudia beate marie* Aue cuius conceptio ...' (*Repertorium hymnologicum*, no. 1744), ending imperfect after the fourth verse (at '... nostra fuit purgatio. | |'), thus lacking the fifth verse, and the versicle, response, and prayer, due to the loss of a leaf after fol. 14.

5. (fols. 15r-44v) Hours of the Virgin, Use of Rouen, with three lessons at Matins, with the Hours of the Cross and of the Holy Spirit intermixed.

[Items 6-11 occupy quires VII-XI]

6. (fols. 45r-52r) The Seven Penitential Psalms.

7. (fols. 52r-54v) Litany and collects; the litany with Martial last among fifteen Apostles and Evangelists; followed by All Holy Disciples, All Holy Innocents, and Ursinus (cf. MS. Buchanan e. 14 and MS. Douce 268, Books of Hours of the Use of Evreux and Bayeux respectively, which each have Ursinus between Apostles & Evangelists and Disciples); and including Mellon, Romanus (both of Rouen) (8-9), Hugh (bishop of Rouen), Severus of Avranches (relics at Rouen), Julian, Wulfram, Wandregisil (venerated at Rouen), William (12-17) among seventeen confessors; and Austreberta (8), and Honorina (12) (both venerated at Rouen) among

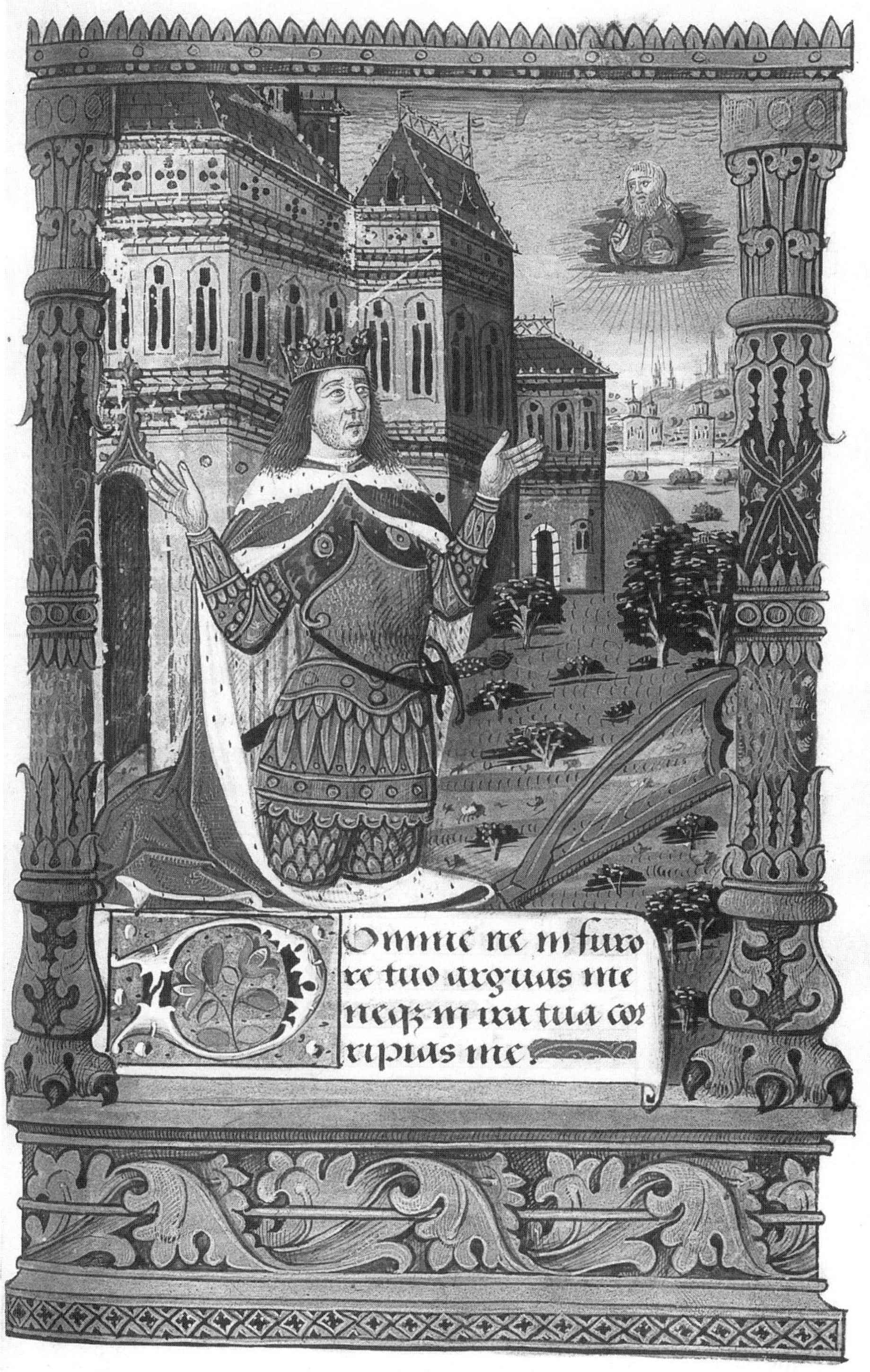

18. *MS. Buchanan e. 3, fol. 45r. [Slightly enlarged]*

sixteen virgins; followed (fol. 54v) by three collects: (i) 'Deus cui proprium est ...'
(pr. *Corpus orationum*, no. 1143), (ii) 'Ure igne sancti spiritus ...' (pr. Bruylants,
Oraisons, no. 1168), and (iii) 'Animabus quesumus domine ...' (pr. *Corpus
orationum*, no. 260).

8. (fols. 55r-71r) Office of the Dead, Use of Rouen; the versicles after the ninth
lesson are 'Dies illa ...', 'Quid ergo ...', and 'Requiem eternam ...'.

9. (fols. 71v-73v, first rubric on 71r) Suffrages to the Trinity and saints:
'*Sequuntur suffragia plurimorum sanctorum et sanctarum. Et primo de sanctissima
trinitate.*'; to (i) the Trinity, (ii) Michael, (iii) John the Baptist, (iv) Sebastian, (v)
Nicholas, (vi) Romanus of Rouen, (vii) Catherine, and (viii) Barbara. (The
prayers are pr. *Corpus orationum*, nos. (i) 3920, (ii) 1198, (iii) 4492, (iv) 1472a,
(v) 1463, (vi) 119b (adapted for Romanus), and (vii) 1521; for (viii) cf. Colker,
Trinity College Dublin cat., II, 863 item 61).

10. (fols. 74r-78r) Prayers, in French and Latin, mostly in verse, to the Virgin,
St. Barbara, and the Guardian Angel:
   (i) (fols. 74r-77r, rubric on fol. 73v) '*Oraison tresdeuote a la vierge marie mere de
   dieu. Mere de dieu qui fustes mise. / Et assise / Lassus en throsne diuin ... Et
   sauuez / En la gloire pardurable.* AMEN.' (Sonet, *Répertoire*, no. 1121; pr.
   Leroquais, *Livres d'heures*, II, 325-8);
   (ii) (fol. 77r-v) '*Aultre oraison tresdeuote. Aduocate pour les pecheurs / Tourne
   vers moy ta doulce face / Et me fais viure tous les iours / En oraison quelque ie
   face / ...*' (Sinclair, *French devotional texts, first supplement*, no. 3927, citing
   only this manuscript; Rézeau, *Répertoire*, states that this is the third stanza of
   Sonet, *Répertoire*, no. 1094);
   (iii) (fol. 77v) '*Aultre oraison de nostre dame. Noble mere du redempteur /
   Fontaine de toute lyesse ... Que tous mes pechez a la fin / Vostre filz iesus me
   pardonne.* AMEN.' (Sonet, *Répertoire*, no. 1241);
   (iv) (fol. 77v) '*Oraison de saincte barbe. Saincte barbe comme ie croy / Que
   siege auez en paradis ... Que garder pouez voz subgictz / De mourir sans
   confession. Amen*' (Sinclair, *French devotional texts, first supplement*, no. 5067,
   citing only this manuscript; Rézeau, *Répertoire*, no. 2306);
   (v) (fols. 77v-78r) '*Aultre oraison de saincte barbe. O uirgo et martyr barbara.
   Quasi pulchra luna plena. Post mariam flos uirginum. Ora pro me ad
   dominum. Amen.*';
   (vi) (fol. 78r) '*Oraison a son bon ange. Angele qui meus es custos pietate
   superna me tibi commissum serua defende guberna. Amen*' (pr. Wordsworth,
   Horae Eboracenses, 35).

11. (fols. 78r-78v) Prayer, in French verse: 'Le chemin de paradis. Qui veult en
paradis aler / Cy en peult le chemin trouuer. ... Ce sont les vertus et la ioye. / Qui
lhomme en paradis enuoye. Amen.' (Sonet, *Répertoire*, no. 1748).

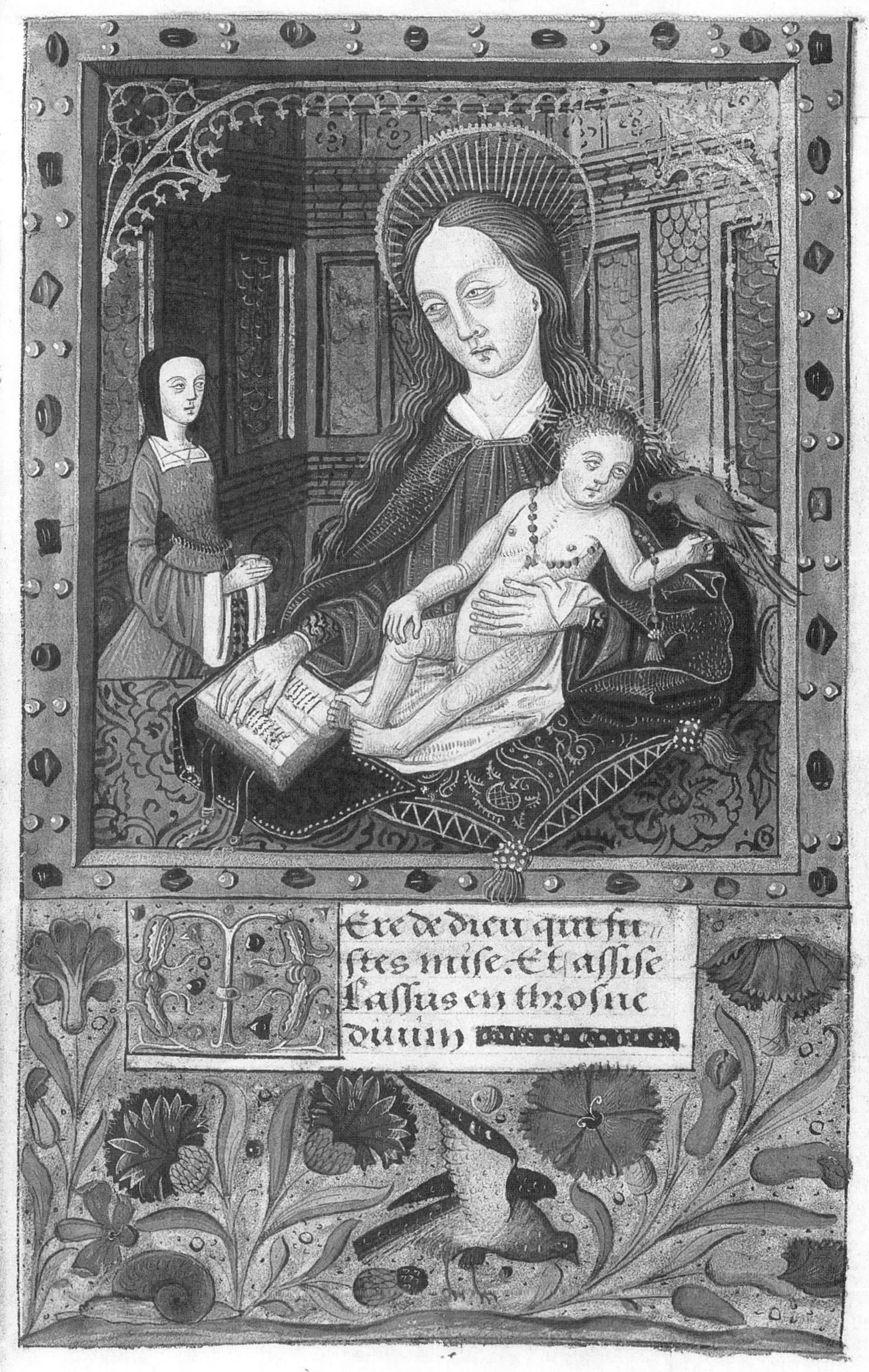

19. *MS. Buchanan e. 3, fol. 74r. [Enlarged]*

Decoration

Four large rectangular miniatures, each above four lines of text, with more-or-less elaborate renaissance architectural framing:

(fol. 15r) Hours of the Virgin, Matins. Annunciation; the lower margin with the Meeting at the Golden Gate, and the Presentation of the Virgin at the Temple (the compositions very similar to those in Watson, *Playfair Hours*, pl. XIII); the framing columns with gold fleurs-de-lis on a blue ground, and crown-shaped elements.

(fol. 29r) Prime. Nativity; the Virgin, Joseph, and two angels all kneeling, adoring the Child; the lower margin with Moses removing his shoes before the Burning Bush (Watson, *Playfair Hours*, fig. 9; the main scene and flanking columns are almost exactly as in Sotheby's, *Western manuscripts … 5 Dec. 1995*, lot 45, pl. on p. 73; the artist appears to be the same).

(fol. 45r) Penitential Psalms. David in Penitence, outside a fine château-like building (pl. 18).

(fol. 55r) Office of the Dead. Job on the Dungheap, tormented by four demons wielding clubs; God and two angels above; a larger miniature with a narrower border.

Ten large gently arched miniatures, each above four lines of text, with four-sided borders of foliage, birds, etc. on a painted gold ground:

(fol. 8r) Gospel Pericopes. St. John on Patmos; buildings and a windmill in the distance.

(fol. 21r) Hours of the Virgin, Lauds. Visitation; two angels behind the Virgin; buildings in the background.

(fol. 27r) Hours of the Cross. Crucifixion (the composition very similar to *Playfair Hours*, frontispiece).

(fol. 28r) Hours of the Holy Spirit. Pentecost (the composition very similar to *Playfair Hours*, fig. 20).

(fol. 32v) Hours of the Virgin, Terce. Annunciation to the Shepherds; two standing shepherds and a seated shepherdess.

(fol. 35r) Sext. Adoration of the Magi (the composition very similar to *Playfair Hours*, pl. XVII).

(fol. 37r) None. Presentation in the Temple.

(fol. 39v) Vespers. Flight into Egypt, from left to right; the Miracle of the Cornfield in the background (this page with a distinctive border, in which the foliage is almost entirely in shades of grey).

(fol. 41v) Compline. Coronation of the Virgin (the composition very similar to *Playfair Hours*, pl. XX).

(fol. 71v) Suffrage. The Trinity; God the Father holding the body of the dead Christ on his lap, the wings of the Dove touching their mouths; beneath a draped canopy lettered 'SAN[C]TAS TRIN', held open by two angels.

One miniature in a nearly square frame (considerably wider than the text column) painted as if set with jewels and pearls, above four lines of text surrounded on the three lower sides by a partial border:

(fol. 74r) Prayer. The Virgin and Child, with a supplicant laywoman; the Virgin with one hand on an open book in a chemise binding with two straps, and supporting the Christ Child with the other hand; the Child, with a coral rosary worn like a baldric, looking at a green parrot perched on his hand (pl. 19).

The iconography of the Virgin and Child with supplicant owner, incorporating both the comparatively common rosary, and the much rarer parrot, perhaps derives ultimately from Jan van Eyck's *van der Paele Madonna*, dated 1436 on the frame (Bruges, Groeninge Museum), or a similar work. (On the iconographic meaning of the parrot, see Carol J. Purtle, *The Marian paintings of Jan van Eyck* (Princeton, 1982), 91-2 and fig. 43, summarising Lawrence Naftulin, 'A note on the iconography of the van der Paele Madonna', *Oud Holland* 86 (1971), 3-8, at 7-8 n. 12). That a version of such an image circulated among Rouen illuminators is suggested by the fact that a closely-related image is present in Lampeter, St. David's University College, MS. 7, also a late 15th- or early 16th-cent. Book of Hours for the Use of Rouen, but without the rosary, by a different artist, and illustrating a different text (see Ker, *MMBL*, III, 11-12; I am grateful to Miss Celia Hewardine for bringing the similarity of the image in the Lampeter manuscript to my attention).

Twenty-four small rectangular miniatures as border panels in the calendar, depicting the Occupations of the Months and Zodiac signs, mostly against naturalistic landscapes or interiors; amid further border panels containing naturalistic flowers on a painted gold ground:
(fol. 2r) Feasting; Aquarius: a naked youth pouring water into a river.
(fol. 2v) Warming by a fire; Pisces.
(fol. 3r) Pruning; Aries.
(fol. 3v) A woman sitting in a meadow holding flowers; Taurus.
(fol. 4r) A man and woman on horseback; Gemini: a naked couple embracing amidst shrubbery.
(fol. 4v) Scything; Cancer: like a crayfish.
(fol. 5r) Reaping; Leo.
(fol. 5v) Winnowing; Virgo, holding a bunch of three flowers.
(fol. 6r) Treading grapes; Libra: a woman, like Virgo, holding scales.
(fol. 6v) Sowing; Scorpio, like Cancer, but with a curled tail.
(fol. 7r) Knocking acorns from trees for pigs; Sagittarius.
(fol. 7v) Killing a pig; Capricorn.

Borders to every text page: a narrow painted gold framing, with a painted border in the outer margin of stylized and naturalistic foliage, flowers, and fruit on a painted gold ground.

Four-line initials of stylized and naturalistic foliage and flowers on a painted gold ground to each hour, major prayer, etc.; similar two-line initials to psalms, lessons, etc.; one-line initials of painted gold on a blue or red ground, alternating, to verses and other minor divisions; similar line-fillers.

Physical Description

MATERIAL: parchment.

DIMENSIONS: the leaves 195 x 125 mm.

NUMBER OF LEAVES: i (paper, conjoint with the pastedown) + i (post-medieval parchment) + 77 + i (post-medieval parchment) + i (paper, conjoint with the pastedown).

FOLIATION: modern, in pencil: i, 1-80.

COLLATION: mostly in quires of 8 leaves: I^{6+1} (1st leaf an added flyleaf) (fols. 1-7) | II^{8-1} (8th leaf excised with scissors(?) after fol. 14) (fols. 8-14), $III-V^8$ (fols. 15-38), VI^6 (fols. 39-44) | $VII-X^8$ (fols. 45-76), XI^{2+1} (3rd leaf an added flyleaf) (fols. 77-79); no catchwords survive.

RULING: 26 lines ruled in pale red ink, with single vertical bounding lines extending the full height of the page, the top and bottom horizontals ruled the full width; the ruled space *c.*115 x 65 mm. (the calendar with 32 lines per page, the ruled space *c.*123 x 63 mm.); no prickings survive.

SCRIPT: written in dark brown ink in *lettre bâtarde* with 25 lines of text per page; the written space c.113 x 65 mm.; in two sizes of script, according to liturgical function.

RUBRICATION: headings in red, capitals touched with a yellow wash.

SEC. FOL.: (Calendar, fol. 3) 'KL Mars.'; (text, fol. 9) 'sed ex deo'.

Binding

Sewn on four cords, with endbands; bound in 18th-cent. speckled brown leather over pasteboards (before 1776, since the last paper flyleaf (fol. 80r) is inscribed with this date (see under Provenance)); the first paper flyleaf apparently with the watermark '1749' (or '1719'?), within an amphora(?)-shaped framing, the last flyleaf with 'P[then a heart-shape]GIIGII'(?); the edges of the leaves — except the paper flyleaves — gauffered and gilt, thus this must pre-date the present binding; the parchment flyleaves (fols. 1, 79) must also belong to a previous binding, and may possibly have been its pastedowns, since fol. 79 shows the impression of a former turn-in around its outer edges.

Provenance

1. Unidentified laywoman: made for the woman depicted on fol. 74r, who, to judge by the suffrage and two prayers to St. Barbara, had a special devotion to her.

2. Gilbert de la Houssay du Trembley, 1776: inscribed (fol. 1r): 'Gibert delahoussaije | Dutrembleij', and '1776' (in paler ink); inscribed very similarly on fol. 80r, where the date is coeval, but the 'gibert' is added in paler ink.

3 Unidentified 18th/19th-cent. collections: the second compartment from the top of the spine with a polygonal paper label printed in blue (for a very similar, perhaps identical, label which has not been covered, see the spine of [pr. bk.] Buchanan c.12), covered by a rectangular paper label printed with a figure (? perhaps a '1' or an 'L' — only the very top is visible), which in turn is obscured by a third paper label, printed '5', which has had this number effaced with ink,

and '3' inscribed next to it. The base of the spine with a paper label printed
'650', and another similar, smaller, paper label pasted to fol. 1r is printed with
the same number. The '650' and '3' may relate to the number '0653' on the
upper pastedown (see below). There are traces of another rectangular paper
label which has been removed from the second compartment from the bottom of
the spine.

4. Unidentified French bookseller, 19th cent.: inscribed on the upper pastedown:
'0653', 'u.m.m.' (perhaps upper-case?), and: '15 grandes miniatures | 12 petites
- les mois'.

5. Messrs. T. & W. Boone, London booksellers (see Introduction, p. xxi): inscribed
in pencil with their price-code in the upper right corner of the upper pastedown
and in the top left corner of the lower pastedown (see pls. 3-4; cf. MSS. Buchanan
e. 2 and g. 1, see pls. 5-6).

6. John (or Thomas?) Buchanan: bought from Boone on 16 April 1862, for £25
(see Introduction, p. xix) and inscribed in pencil 'Boone' on fol. i verso, and with
the 'Descriptive list' number, '3', in the top left corner of the upper pastedown.

7. Rt. Hon. T. R. Buchanan (1846-1911); given to the Bodleian by his widow,
Mrs. E. O. Buchanan, in 1939, when it was accessioned as MS. Lat. liturg. e. 24
(contrary to the pencilled record of accession (fol. 1r): 'D[onated]. 21.vii.1941').

Bibliography

'Fifteen illuminated *Horae*', *BLR* 1 no. 7 (1939), 115-6, at 115 (cited as MS. Lat.
liturg. e. 24).

van Dijk, *Handlist of Latin liturgical MSS.*, IV, 101.

Pächt & Alexander, 1, no. 807, pl. LIX (fol. 74r).

Celia V. Hewardine, 'Symbolic decoration in a fifteenth-century Book of Hours',
Trivium 18 (1983), 49-54, pls. 5-6, at 53 n. 3 (cited as Buchanan liturg. MS. e.3).

Rowan Watson, *The Playfair Hours: a late fifteenth century illuminated manuscript
from Rouen (V&A, L.475-1918)* (London, 1984), 52-3, 73, fig. 9 (fol. 29r).

Rézeau, *Répertoire*, nos. 1094, 1241, 1748, 1804, 2306.

Sotheby's, *Western manuscripts and miniatures ... 5th December, 1995* (London), cited
under lot 45 (many of the miniatures in this manuscript, of which photographs
are in the Conway Library, Courtauld Institute of Art, London, are very similar to
those in the present manuscript).

Sandra Penketh, 'Women and Books of Hours', in *Women and the book: assessing
the visual evidence* ed. Lesley Smith and Jane H. M. Taylor (British Library studies
in medieval culture: London, and Toronto, 1996), 266-80, at 274 fig. 100
(fol. 74r, detail).

Colour filmstrip publication: Bodleian Library, Rolls 431.1 and 431.2, show,
respectively, the calendar (12 frames) and the Hours etc. (15 frames).

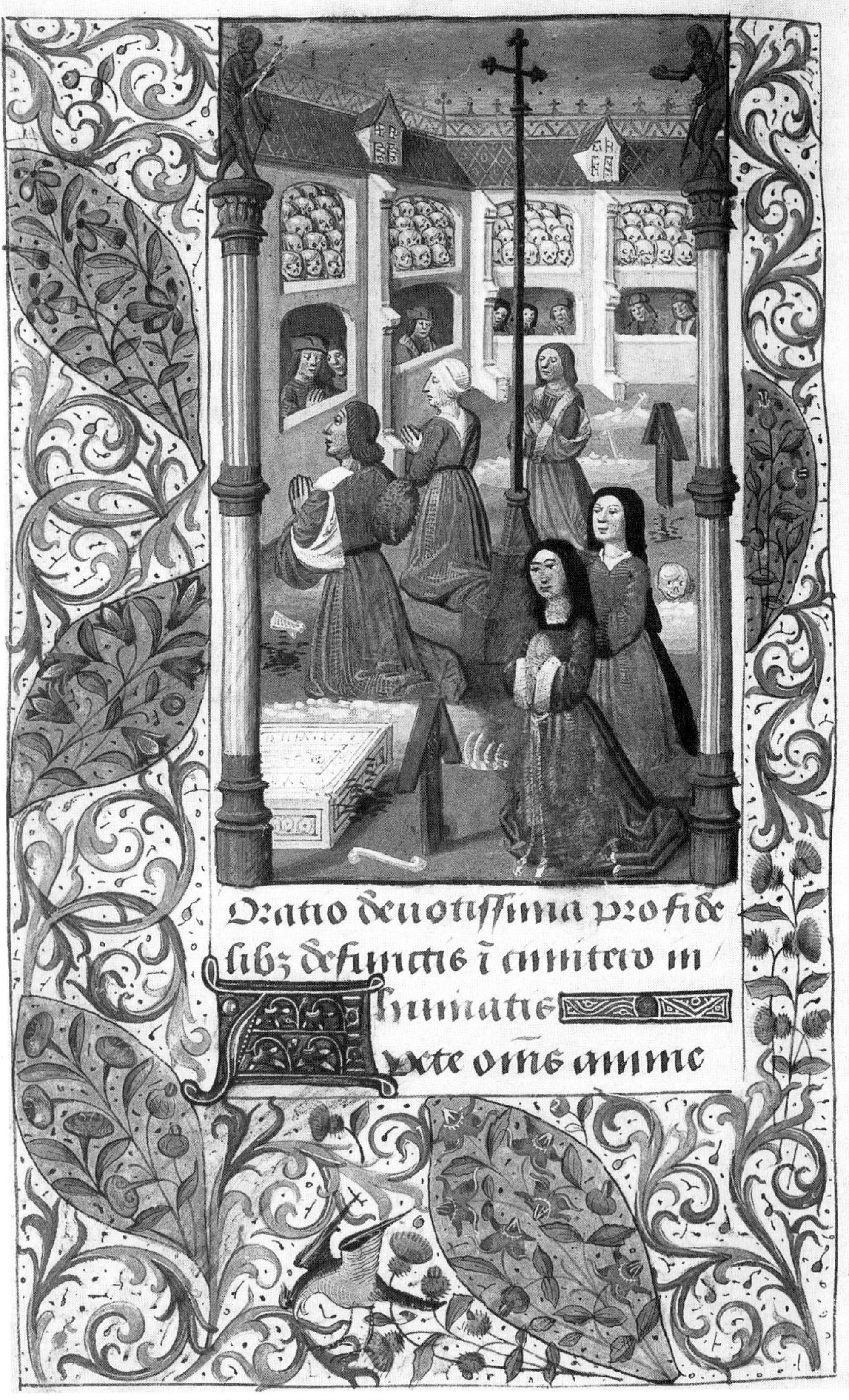

20. MS. Buchanan e. 4, fol. 161v. [Enlarged]

MS. Buchanan e. 4

Book of Hours, Use of Rome, in Latin and French
France; late 15th or early 16th century

Text
[Item 1 occupies quire I]

1. (fols. 1r-6v) Calendar, in French, with an entry for every day, major feasts in gold (none of them local), the others alternately red or blue; neither of the Paris saints, Geneviève (3 Jan.), nor Marcellus (3 Nov.) is in gold; each month headed by a note on the length of the calendar and lunar month in gold.

[Items 2-5 occupy quires II-XII]

2. (fols. 7r-11v) Gospel Pericopes, John followed (fol. 8r-v) by the usual antiphon, versicle, response and prayer: 'Protector in te sperancium ...' (cf. MS. Buchanan e. 3).

3. (fols. 12r-20r) Prayers to the Virgin:
   (i) (fols. 12r-14v, rubric on fol. 11v) '*Deuotissima oratio ad beatam virginem mariam. Obsecro te ...*' [masculine forms] (cf. MS. Buchanan e. 2);
   (ii) (fols. 14v-17v) 'O intemerata ... orbis terrarum de te. De te [*sic*] enim ...' [masculine forms] (pr. Wilmart, *Auteurs spirituels*, 494-5);
   (iii) (fols. 18r-19v) 'Stabat mater dolorosa ...' (pr. Wordsworth, *Horae Eboracenses*, 134-5), followed by a versicle, response, and prayer: 'Interueniat pro nobis quesumus domine ...' (the latter pr. *ibid.*, 147);
   (iv) (fols. 19v-20r) The Five Joys of the Virgin: 'Ave cuius conceptio ...' (*Repertorium hymnologicum*, no. 1744), followed by a versicle, response, and the prayer 'Deus qui nos conceptionis natiuitatis ...'.

4. (fols. 20v-34r, rubric on fol. 20r) The Passion Narrative: '*Passio domini nostri ihesu christi secundum iohannem.*' [John 18:1-19:42; for the divisions of the text, see under Decoration]; followed (fols. 33v-34r) by a versicle, response and the prayer: 'Deus qui manus tuas et pedes tuos ...' (pr. Wordsworth, *op. cit.*, 123-4; Leroquais, *Livres d'heures*, I, p. xxiv) which usually follows the common paraphrased version of the Passion narrative (cf. MS. Buchanan e. 9, fol. 108r-v).

5. (fols. 34v-93v) Hours of the Virgin, Use of Rome, with three lessons at Matins, and (fols. 85r-93v) seasonal variants.

[Items 6-9 occupy quires XIII-XV]

6. (fols. 94r-104v, rubric and antiphon on fol. 93v) The Seven Penitential Psalms.

7. (fols. 104v-111r) Litany and collects: the litany including Lazarus, Martial, and Saturninus between All Holy Apostles & Evangelists, and All Holy Disciples; Paxentius (relics at Paris) last among twenty-five martyrs; Bavo (3) among twenty confessors; Geneviève, Avia, Susanna, Ursula, Rosa, Scholastica, Aldegund, Radegund, Gertrude, Clare (11-20), among twenty-three virgins; followed (fol. 111r-v) by three collects: (i) 'Deus cui proprium est ...' (pr. *Corpus orationum*, no. 1143); (ii) 'Ure igne sancti spiritus ...' (Bruylants, *Oraisons*, no. 1168); and (iii) 'Fidelium deus omnium conditor ...' (pr. *Corpus orationum*, no. 2684b).

8. (fols. 112r-114v) Hours of the Cross.

9. (fols. 115r-117v) Hours of the Holy Spirit.

[Items 10-14 occupy quires XVI-XXV]

10. (fols. 118r-161r) Office of the Dead, Use of Rome; the versicle after the usual ninth lesson and response is (fol. 148v): 'Clamantes et dicentes ...'.

11. (fols. 161v-163r) Prayer for the faithful departed buried in the cemetery: '*Oratio deuotissima pro fidelibus defunctis in cimitero* [sic] *inhumatis*', consisting of an antiphon, 'Avete omnes anime fideles ...', versicle, response, and the prayer 'Domine ihesu christe salus et liberatio fidelium animarum ...' (pr. Leroquais, *op. cit.*, II, 341).

12. (fols. 163v-176v) Suffrages to Saints (i) Michael, (ii) John the Baptist, (iii) John the Evangelist, (iv) Peter & Paul, (v) James, (vi) Laurence, (vii) Christopher ('... michi famulo tuo .N. ...'), (viii) Sebastian, (ix) Roche (fol. 170r-v; as on fols. 185v-186r), (x) Nicholas, (xi) Antony Abbot, (xii) Anne, (xiii) Mary Magdalen, (xiv) Catherine, (xv) Margaret, (xvi) Barbara, and (xvii) Apollonia (prayers pr. in *Corpus orationum* are nos.: (i) 1789, (ii) 4492, (iii) 2416c, (iv) 1158b, (v) 2445c, (vi) 960, (x) 1463, (xi) 1468, (xii) 1366b, (xiii) 3231, (xiv) 1521, and (xv) 1384b).

13. (fols. 177r-182r) Prayers to the Virgin: '*Oratio deuotissima dicenda die sabbati ad honorem intemerate dei genitricis virginis marie. Missus est gabriel angelus ad mariam ... viuos et mortuos et seculum per ignem.*' (as in Leroquais, *op. cit.*, I, 95), with (fol. 178v) interpolated instructions in French (e.g. '*Dictes. dix fois ... Et puis une fois. ...*'); followed (fol. 182v) by the prayer: 'Te deprecor ergo mitissimam piissimam misericordissimam castissimam ... Prestante eodem domino nostro ihesu christo. etcetera. Pater noster. Aue maria.'

[Fol. 183r is ruled, otherwise blank; fol. 183v has a full-page miniature]

14. (fols. 184r-193v) Suffrages to saints, and other prayers in Latin and French, including some on the Holy Tear and the Holy Sudarium:
    (i) (fol. 184r) Suffage to St. Francis; fol. 184v has a full-page armorial design;
    (ii) (fol. 185r-v) Suffrage to St. Martin (the prayer pr. *Corpus orationum*, no. 1497a, adapted for Martin);
    (iii) (fols. 185v-186r) Suffrage to St. Roche (as on fol. 170r-v);

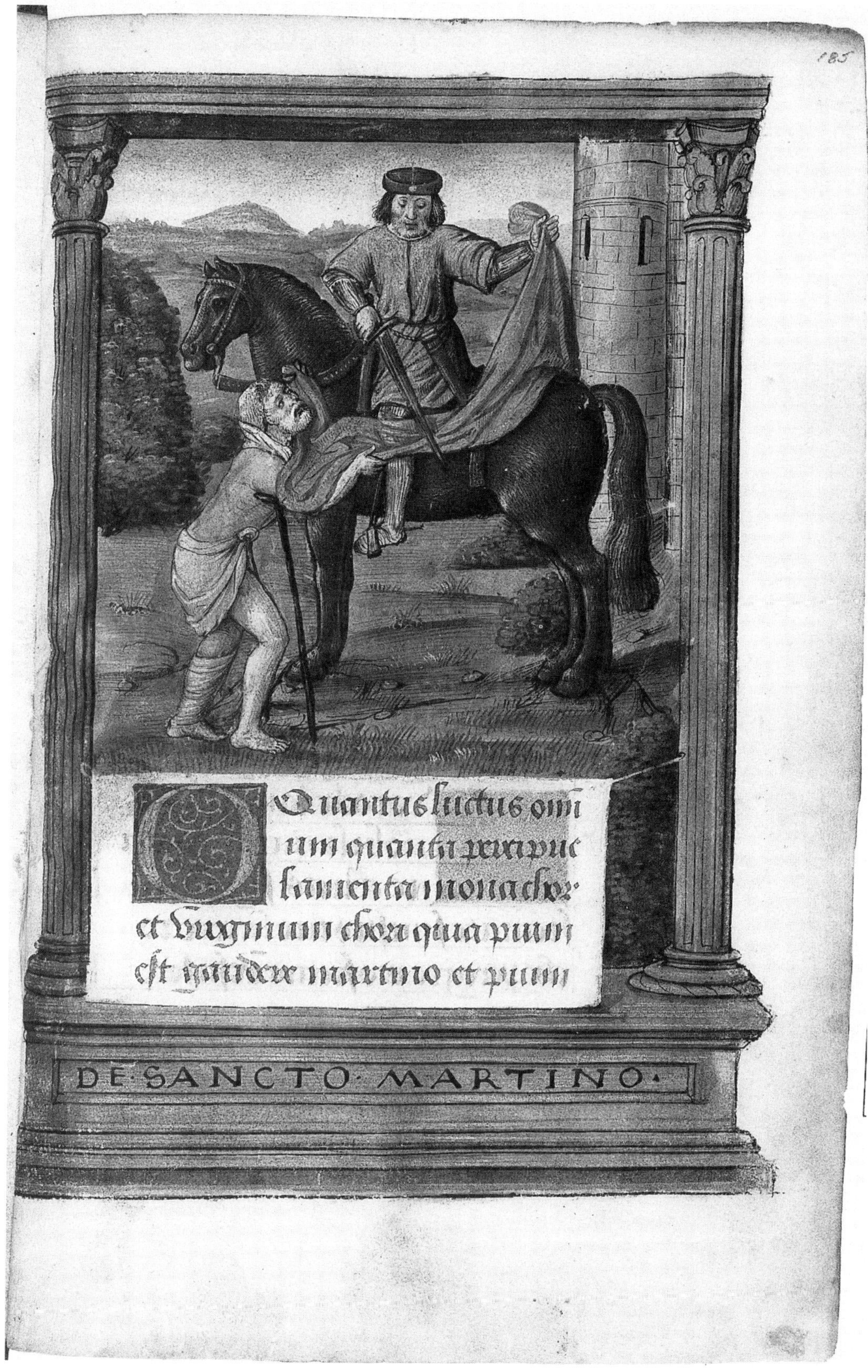

21. *MS. Buchanan e. 4, fol. 185r.*

(iv) (fol. 186v) Prayer to the Virgin: '*Oratio deuota salutifere virginis marie.
O gloriosa domina que filium dei portasti:* ... *tibi supplicare debeo. Per* ...';
(v) (fol. 187r) Suffrage to St. Maxima (rubric on fol. 186v: '*De sancta
maxi | maxima* [sic] *virginis et martyris* [sic]');
(vi) (fols. 187v-188r, rubric starts on fol. 187r) Rhymed prayer to the Five
Wounds of Christ, attributed to and carrying an indulgence of Pope Gregory
[XI] '*Beatus gregorius papa fecit hanc orationem sequentem et dedit deuote
dicentibus eam quingentos annos indul | ciarum.* [sic] Ave dextera manus cristi /
perforata manu tristi. / Nos ad dexteram manum fisti. / Quo per dexteram
redemisti. ... / Ad eternum vite statum. Amen.' (cf. *Repertorium hymnologicum*,
no. 1771); the space left in the last word of the rubric suggests that the
scribe's exemplar was unclear;
(vii) (fol. 188r-v) Prayer attributed to Hugh of St.-Victor, consisting of five
petitions, each beginning 'Dulcissime domine iesu christe ...': '*Hugo de sancto
victore dicit quod quicumque quotidie sequentem orationem diceret ante corpus
domini non moretur in peccato mortali. Dulcissime domine iesu criste ob tui
sacratissimi sacramenti reuerenciam concede michi ... [masculine forms] ...
sanctissimorum tuorum vulnerum passionem Amen.' (cf. Wilmart, *Auteurs
spirituels*, 369 n. 4);
(viii) (fols. 188v-190v) Prayer for help against one's enemies: '*Oratio valde
deuotissima. Domine deus omnipotens pater filius et spiritus sanctus da michi
famulo tuo .N. victoriam ... saluare digneris et ostende misericordiam tuam.
Qui cum patre ...*' (cf. Ker, *MMBL*, I, 47 art. 3);
(ix) (fol. 190v) Prayer for guidance, with rubric in French: '*Deuant ceste
oraison ce doiuent dire ces deus pseaulmes cest a sauoir* Deus in nomine tuo.
[Ps. 53] et Deus misereatur nostri. [Ps. 66] Vias tuas domine demonstra michi
et semitas tuas edoce me. ... ut non moueantur uestigia mea. Gloria patri.'
(cf. James A. Corbett, 'A fifteenth-century Book of Hours from Salisbury',
Ephemerides Liturgicae 71 fasc. iv-v (1957), 293-307, at 297);
(x) (fols. 190v-191v) '*Oratio.* Domine iesu criste fili dei viui quando tu respondisti
... saluum et illesum existam. In nomine patris ... amen. Iesus autem transiens
per medium illorum ibat + cristus vincit ... liberet et deffendat amen.';
(xi) (fols. 191v-192r) Indulgenced devotion to the Passion and Tear of Christ,
here attributed to Pope John XXII: '*Dominus papa iohannes xxii^us. dicentibus
deuote hanc orationem sequentem in memoriam passionis iesu cristi et in
reuerenciam eius sacratissime lacrime concessit trecentum dies indulgentiarum.*',
consisting of an antiphon, 'Fremunt spiritu iesus ... illumina tenebras meas.',
versicle, and the prayer 'Deus cuius unigenitus assumpte humanitatis
probabile argumentum in resuscitatione lazari lacrimando exibuit concede
nobis famulis tuis ut ... et sanitatem conserues oculorum. Per ...' (cf. Leroquais,
Livres d'heures, II, 81);
(xii) (fols. 192v-193r, rubric on fol. 192r) Rhymed prayer in French, on the
Holy Tear of Vendôme: '*Oroison en francoys de la saincte larme. Saincte larme
glorieuse. / De iesu crist nostre pere. / Du ciel pierre precieuse. / ... Es cieulx
perdurablement.*' (Sonet, *Répertoire*, no. 1859; cf. Leroquais, *Sacramentaires*, 183-4);

(xiii) (fol. 193r) 'Domine deus omnipotens qui ad principium huius die ... cogitaciones et opera. Per.'; preceded by a line left blank, presumably intended for a heading (cf. Hoskins, *Sarum and York Primers*, 353);

(xiv) (fol. 193r-v) Prayer on the Holy Sudarium: '*De sancto sudario Oratio. Domine iesu criste qui presentia tui sancti sudarii ... etiam tibi dignus conuersationibus iugiter seruiamus Per cristum.*' (cf. Josef Leisibach and François Huot, *Iter helveticum IV: die liturgischen Handschriften des Kantons Wallis (ohne Kapitelsarchiv Sitten)* (Spicilegii Friburgensis, subsidia, 18: Freiburg, 1984), 164 'i', and pl. 31);

(xv) (fol. 193v) '*Alia oratio* Visita quesumus domine habitacionem istam ... ab omni aduersitate custodi. Per'. (cf. Warner and Gilson, *Royal and King's cat.*, I, 36); fol. 194r-v ruled, otherwise originally blank.

Decoration

Twenty-three large rectangular miniatures (arched on fols. 31v, 33r, 34v), extending above the top ruled line; usually framed by pillars or pilasters painted to resemble marble, or in gold, on which stand angels or other figures related to the main scene, or who carry attributes relevant to the event depicted. Their size is expressed here according to how many lines are left below each miniature for the start of the text.

One miniature above seven lines of text:
(fol. 7r) Pericope of John. John writing on Patmos; the seven-headed beast of the Apocalypse in the background.

The Passion narrative. The first of nine miniatures is above three lines of text, the remainder are above five lines:
(fol. 20v) John 18:1-10. Agony in the Garden; in the background, Judas, holding the bag of money, leading the soldiers into the garden.
(fol. 22r) John 18:11-28. Betrayal, Arrest, and Christ healing Malchus' ear.
(fol. 24r) John 18:29-37. Christ Crowned with Thorns; his two tormenters each in a 'dancing' pose, with one knee raised.
(fol. 25v) John 18:38-19:6. Flagellation: four tormentors; blood on the tiled floor.
(fol. 27r) John 19:6-14. Christ brought before Pilate, who washes his hands.
(fol. 28v) John 19:15-23. Christ Carrying the Cross.
(fol. 30r) John 19:24-31. Crucifixion; the Virgin, John, and other nimbed figures to the left; soldiers to the right.
(fol. 31v) John 19:32-39. Deposition; two figures on ladders lower Christ's body, supporting it under the arms, a third takes his legs.
(fol. 33r) John 19:40-42. Entombment; Mary Magdalen in the foreground; six other figures; Christ heavily repainted.

Hours and other major texts. Most of the thirteen miniatures are above four lines of text:
(fol. 34v) Hours of the Virgin, Matins. Annunciation; Gabriel pointing upward at the Dove.

(fol. 44r) Lauds. Visitation; with Joseph(?) behind the Virgin.
(fol. 55r) Prime. Nativity; the Virgin and Joseph adore the Child.
(fol. 59v) Terce. Annunciation to the Shepherds; one holding bagpipes, another leaning towards a seated shepherdess.
(fol. 64r) Sext. Adoration of the Magi.
(fol. 68r) None. Presentation in the Temple.
(fol. 72r) Vespers. Flight into Egypt, from right to left; the Holy Family accompanied by a maidservant carrying a basket on her head; the Massacre of the Innocents and the Fall of the Idols in the background. [This miniature is above only three lines of text, presumably in error.]
(fol. 79v) Compline. Coronation of the Virgin.
(fol. 94r) Penitential Psalms. David in Penitence, before an altar; a border grotesque is playing a harp.
(fol. 112r) Hours of the Cross. The Man of Sorrows, sitting on the edge of the tomb, surrounded by the Instruments of the Passion.
(fol. 115r) Hours of the Holy Spirit. Pentecost; tongues of fire descend through a window onto the Apostles and Virgin, who kneels at a canopied prie-dieu.
(fol. 118r) Office of the Dead. An emaciated figure draped in a shroud brandishes a spear at a richly-dressed young man with a bird of prey and two dogs; behind them, a casket-like ossuary raised on columns (the composition very similar to that in Cambridge, Fitzwilliam Museum, MS. 85, fol. 71v, which has a woman instead of man; see James, *Fitzwilliam McClean cat.*, 177 item 41, pl. LV; and in other Maître François books such as MS. Canon. Liturg. 43).
(fol. 161v) Prayer. Men and women kneeling in prayer in a cemetery; skulls in upper-storey charnel houses; the foremost woman's face repainted (pl. 20).

Seventeen small miniatures, each eight to ten lines high, narrower than the width of the text, illustrating the suffrages to saints:
(fol. 163v) St. Michael defeating the devil.
(fol. 164r) St. John the Baptist holding the Agnus Dei.
(fol. 164v) St. John the Evangelist with the chalice and serpent.
(fol. 165r) St. Peter & St. Paul.
(fol. 166r) St. James sitting reading a book.
(fol. 166v) St. Laurence reading a large book.
(fol. 167v) St. Christopher carrying the Christ Child across the river.
(fol. 169r) St. Sebastian shot with arrows, watched by the emperor.
(fol. 170r) St. Roche displaying a plague sore on his thigh to the angel.
(fol. 171r) St. Nicholas blessing the three boys in the tub.
(fol. 171v) St. Antony Abbot reading a book outside his hermitage, with his pig.
(fol. 172r) The Virgin writing, left-handed, in a book held by St. Anne.
(fol. 173r) St. Mary Magdalen.
(fol. 173v) St. Catherine reading a book.
(fol. 174r) St. Margaret emerging from the dragon.
(fol. 175r) St. Barbara reading a book.
(fol. 176r) St. Apollonia reading a book.

Two added full-page miniatures:
(fol. 183v) St. Francis receiving the stigmata; with simple architectural framing
in painted gold.
(fol. 184v) A coat of arms: *or*, a mill rind cross *gules*, with helm and mantling of
or and *gules*, and crest of a tree with (?)fir-cones, all supported by a lion and
griffin (see under Provenance).

One added miniature, above five lines of text:
(fol. 185r) Suffrage. St. Martin and the Beggar; with an architectual framing in
painted gold, bearing the rubric 'DE. SANCTO. MARTINO' in square capitals at
the base; the opening five lines of the text on a trompe-l'œuil sheet as if
suspended in front of the plane of the image (pl. 21).

Seven historiated initials, six or seven lines high, illustrating pericopes and prayers:
(fol. 8v) Pericope of Luke. St. Luke writing at a lectern, with the Ox.
(fol. 9v) Pericope of Matthew. St. Matthew writing, the Angel holding his
exemplar open.
(fol. 11r) Pericope of Mark. St. Mark writing, left-handed, with the Lion.
(fol. 12r) Obsecro te. The Virgin of the Apocalypse, holding the Christ Child,
standing on a crescent moon.
(fol. 14v) O intemerata. The Virgin reading a book, watched by Joseph(?).
(fol. 18r) Stabat mater. Pietà, in front of the Cross.
(fol. 177r) Missus est Gabriel. The Annunciation: the Virgin and Gabriel
kneeling either side of her prie-dieu.

Illuminated borders to every page, of stylized foliage and flowers in gold and blue
on a plain parchment ground, and naturalistic plants on variously-shaped
panels of painted gold; the designs the same on each side of the leaf. Borders
around miniatures with partial or complete gold grounds, and containing birds,
insects, hybrid creatures, etc. The foliage in the lower left border of fol. 112r has
been crudely pricked, as if for pouncing.

Four-line foliate initials on a burnished gold ground at major text divisions
(e.g. the first pericope; Matins, Lauds, etc. of the Virgin, etc.); and similar three-line
initials at their major sub-divisions (e.g. passages of the Passion narrative); two-
line initials often containing naturalistic plants on a painted gold ground, to
psalms, prayers, collects, etc.; one-line initials of burnished gold on blue and red
grounds with white tracery to verses, antiphons, etc.; line-fillers similar to the
one-line initials.

The initials and line-fillers at fols. 185r-193v are of a stylistically later type than
in the rest of the book, and use only painted gold on an alternately blue or red
square ground.

At least four main artists worked on the book, the division of their work
corresponding to the sections written by the three main scribes (see under Script):
(i) Most of the main body of the book (up to fol. 182v) was painted and decorated

in one style, having links in style and iconography with the school of Maître François, although several of the miniatures in this section were damaged and have been overpainted at a later date (e.g. the figure of Christ on fol. 33r; the face of the Shepherdess on fol. 59v).
(ii) Within this first section, the miniature at the start of the Hours of the Virgin (fol. 34v), is in slightly later style.
(iii) The border on fol. 184r is of the same general type as those which precede (though with the initials 'E E' - see under Provenance), but the facing miniature appears to be by a later, less able, artist, who was perhaps also responsible for the coat of arms on fol. 184v.
(iv) Finally, the miniature on fol. 185r is by a hand working in the style of Jean Bourdichon: his more sophisticated use of gold highlights, his more subtle modelling, and his treatment of the landscape and the framing architecture set him apart from the miniatures which precede.

Physical Description

MATERIAL: parchment.
DIMENSIONS: the leaves 205 x 135 mm.
NUMBER OF LEAVES: ii (modern parchment bifolium) + 194 + ii (modern parchment bifolium).
FOLIATION: modern, in pencil: i-ii, 1-196.
COLLATION: mostly in quires of 8 leaves: I^6 (fols. 1-6) | II-XI^8 (fols. 7-86), $\mathrm{XII}^{8\text{-}1}$ (8th leaf cancelled, after fol. 93) (fols. 87-93) | XIII-XV^8 (fols. 94-117) | XVI-XXIII^8 (fols. 118-181), $\mathrm{XXIV}^{8\text{-}1}$ (8th leaf cancelled, after fol. 188) (fols. 182-188), $\mathrm{XXV}^{8\text{-}2}$ (7th & 8th leaves cancelled, after fol. 194) (fols. 189-194); it may be that fol. 182, the last leaf written by the first main scribe (see under script), which is now bound as the first leaf of quire XXIV, was previously bound as the last leaf of quire XXIII, and that quire XXIV was therefore originally a ternion; traces of CATCHWORDS survive on fols. 14v, 38v, 125v, written vertically downwards, on the inner vertical ruling line.
RULING: 20 lines ruled in pale red ink, with single vertical bounding lines extending the full height of the page, the top and bottom horizontals extending the full width of the page; the ruled space $c.117$-120×62-72 (usually $c.68$) mm.; the calendar ruled for 33 lines per page, the ruled space $c.127 \times 68$ mm.; PRICKINGS do not survive, except in quire XXV (fols. 189-194).
SCRIPT: written in *lettre bâtarde* with 19 lines of text per page; the written space 115 x 68 mm.; by at least three main scribes: the first up to fol. 182v, with occasional calligraphic flourishes extending from ascenders and descenders (e.g. fols. 47r, 87v); the second on fol. 184r; the third from fol. 185r to the end; the calendar may be by the first or a fourth scribe, but the smaller script and use of coloured inks makes comparison difficult.
RUBRICATION: headings alternately in red or blue, each of the three scribes providing the headings for their own texts.
SEC. FOL.: (Calendar) 'KL Mars.a.xxxi iours'; (text, fol. 8) 'Quotquod autem'.

Binding

Sewn on five cords (all weak or broken at the lower joint); bound in French(?) 19th-cent. dark blue velvet over pasteboards, with a single gilt metal fitting at the fore-edge of each board, the clasp itself (fastening from the lower to the upper board) lacking; the spine with a gilt metal cartouche with the title 'Heures' in relief; yellow and green endbands; cream-coloured watered-silk doublures.

Provenance

1. ? A Franciscan tertiary with the initial(s?) 'E': the St. Francis is the largest miniature (fol. 183v), and the facing page has borders with the initials 'E E' joined by a knotted cord; this same motif is found in other manuscripts, however (most famously those owned by Etienne Chevalier, but also in books probably not owned by him), so it may have some other meaning. The coat of arms on fol. 184v (see under Decoration), perhaps by the same artist, and therefore belonging with the preceding two pages, was identified in the *BLR* (1939) as being of the family of Eylenkirchen of Westphalia, but this is doubtful. The juncture of different scribes and artists around fol. 184, and the repetition of the suffrage to St. Roche, makes it hard to assess whether the images and texts from fol. 183v onwards are likely to have been commissioned by the original owner or a subsequent one.

2. Unidentified 18th/early-19th-cent. French owner: an erased inscription (fol. 194r), partially legible under UV light, starts: 'Ce livre apartiens ...'.

3. Claude François Morlot, O.Cist., Abbot of l'Esclache, near Clermont (Puys de Domes) [according to van Dijk, not verified]: inscribed by him (fol. 194v), signed and dated 22 Feb. 1815, offering a reward for the return of the book if found.

4. Baron de Baussancour[t?]: bought from Morlot in August 1818, according to another inscription (fol. 194v).

5. Unidentified owner/bookseller: inscribed in black ink 'cot/.' in the lower gutter corner of fol. 194v.

6. Messrs. T. & W. Boone, London booksellers, 19th-cent. (see Introduction, p. xxi).

7. John (or Thomas?) Buchanan: bought from Boone on 16 April, 1862, for £20 (see Introduction, p. xix), and inscribed in pencil with the 'Descriptive list' number, '4.', in the top left corner of fol i verso.

8. Rt. Hon. T. R. Buchanan (1846-1911); given to the Bodleian in 1939 by his widow, Mrs. E. O. Buchanan, when it was accessioned as MS. Lat. liturg. e. 25; re-referenced as MS. Buchanan e. 4 in 1941.

Bibliography

'Fifteen illuminated *Horae*', *BLR* 1 no. 7 (1939), 115-6, at 116 (as MS. Lat. liturg. e. 25).

Edmund Craster, *History of the Bodleian Library 1845-1945* (Oxford, 1952, repr. 1981), 296.

van Dijk, *Handlist of Latin liturgical MSS.*, IV, 208.

Pächt & Alexander, 1, no. 777.

Bibliography

'Fifteen illuminated *Horae*', *BLR* 1 no. 7 (1939), 115-6, at 116 (as MS. Lat. liturg. e. 25).

Edmund Craster, *History of the Bodleian Library 1845-1945* (Oxford, 1952, repr. 1981), 296.

MS. Buchanan e. 5

Book of Hours, Use of Rome, in Latin
Flanders/Hainault; 15th century, third quarter, *c.*1460

Text
[Item 1 occupies quires I-II]

1. (fols. 1r-12v) Calendar, about one-quarter full; each month headed by a note on the length of the calendar and lunar month; major feasts (in red) include Amand (6 Feb.), the Translation of Eloi, at Noyon (25 June), Remi & Bavo (1 Oct.), Donatian (14 Oct.), Eloi (1 Dec.), Thomas Becket 'pontifex' (29 Dec.); feasts in plain brown ink include Cuthbert (28 Feb. and 15 Mar. [*sic*]), 'Riti episcopi' (14 Apr.) (perhaps an error for Richard, cf. James A. Corbett, 'A fifteenth-century Book of Hours from Salisbury', *Ephemerides Liturgicae* 71 fasc. iv-v (1957), 293-307, at 295), Alphege (19 Apr.), John (15 May), Dunstan (19 May), Aldhelm (25 May), Arnulf (15 July [*sic*]), Samson (31 July [*sic*]), Bertin (4 [*recte* 5] Sept.), Lambert (18 Sept. [*sic*]), Firmin (25 Sept.), Francis (6 Oct. [*sic*]), Gereon (10 Oct.), Translation of Wulfram (15 Oct.), Malo (15 Nov.), Edmund (20 Nov.).

[Items 2-7 occupy quires III-XII]

[fol.13r blank, fol. 13v with a miniature]

2. (fols. 14r-19v) Hours of the Cross.

[fol. 20r blank, fol. 20v with a miniature]

3. (fols. 21r-26r) Hours of the Holy Spirit; fol. 26v ruled, otherwise blank.

[fol. 27r blank, fol. 27v with a miniature]

4. (fols. 28r-32v) Mass of the Virgin.

5. (fols. 33r-37r) Gospel Pericopes (cf. MS. Buchanan e. 3; without the antiphon, versicle, response and prayer after John); fol. 37v ruled, otherwise blank.

[fol. 38r blank, fol. 38v with a miniature]

6. (fols. 39r-91v) Hours of the Virgin, Use of Rome, '... *Secundum consuetudinem romane ecclesie ...*', with three lessons at Matins; fols. 58v, 73v, 78v, 86v ruled, otherwise blank; fols. 48, 59, 64, 69, 74, 79, 87 blank on the recto and with a miniature on the verso.

7. (fols. 92r-99v) Prayers to the Virgin:
    (i) (fol. 92r-v) The Salve Regina: '*Salutacio ad mariam virginem* Salue regina misericordie vita. ...' (pr. Wordsworth, *Horae Eboracenses*, 62), followed (cf. MS. Buchanan e. 18, fols. 77v-78r) by the usual versicle, response and prayer: 'Omnipotens sempiterne deus qui gloriose virginis ...' (pr. *ibid.*, 63);
    (ii) (fols. 93r-96r) '*Deuotissima oratio ad mariam* Obsecro te ...' [masculine forms] (cf. MS. Buchanan e. 2);

(iii) (fols. 96v-98v) '*Alia oratio deuota ad mariam* O intemerata ... orbis
terrarum Inclina mater misericordie ...' [masculine forms] (pr. *ibid.*, 67-8);
(iv) (fol. 99r-v) The Five Joys of the Virgin, '*Salutationes ad honorem beate marie*
Ave cuius conceptio solempni plena gaudio ... auxiliatricem sentiamus. Per ...'
(*Repertorium hymnologicum*, no. 1744).

[Items 8-10 occupy quires XIII-XIX]

[fol. 100r blank, fol. 100v with a miniature]

8. (fols. 101r-110v) The Seven Penitential Psalms.

9. (fols. 111r-119v) Litany and collects; the litany including Erasmus (7) and
Lupus (18) among twenty-three martyrs; Louis, Donatian, Amand, Eloi, and
Ghislain (4-8) among eight bishops; Amalberga (11) and Ursula (15) among
twenty-four virgins; followed (fols. 118r-119v) by the usual ten collects (cf. MSS.
Buchanan e. 7, f. 4, g. 1, and g. 3):
   (i) 'Deus cui proprium est misereri semper et parcere suscipe deprecationem
   nostram. ...' *Corpus orationum*, no. 1143);
   (ii) 'Exaudi quesumus domine supplicum preces et confitentium tibi parce
   peccatis. ...' (pr. *ibid.*, no. 2541);
   (iii) 'Ineffabilem misericordiam tuam ...' (pr. *ibid.*, no. 3129);
   (iv) 'Deus qui culpa offenderis ...' (pr. *ibid.*, no. 1511);
   (v) 'Omnipotens sempiterne deus. miserere famulo tuo ministro ...' (pr. *ibid.*,
   no. 3859, with 'ministro' in place of 'illi');
   (vi) 'Deus a quo sancta desideria ...' (pr. *ibid.*, no. 1088a);
   (vii) 'Ure igne sancti spiritus renes nostros ...' (pr. Bruylants, *Oraisons*, no. 1168);
   (viii) 'Fidelium deus omnium conditor et redemptor ...' (pr. *Corpus orationum*,
   no. 2684b);
   (ix) 'Actiones tuas quesumus domine ...' (pr. *ibid.*, no. 74; Bruylants, *op. cit.*,
   no. 18);
   (x) 'Omnipotens sempiterne deus. qui viuorum dominaris simul et
   mortuorum ...' (pr. *ibid.*, no. 4064), ending incomplete at '... corpore suscepit.
   intercedentibus||'.

[fol. 120r blank, fol. 120v with a miniature]

10. (fols. 121r-158v) Office of the Dead, Use of Rome.

Decoration
Thirteen full-page miniatures, with gently arched tops, and gold and coloured
framing; all inserted on unruled single leaves, blank on the recto; each with
sewing holes clustered at the centre of the upper margin (presumably indicating
the previous presence of protective textile veils), the sewing threads having
caused indentations in the adjacent leaves.

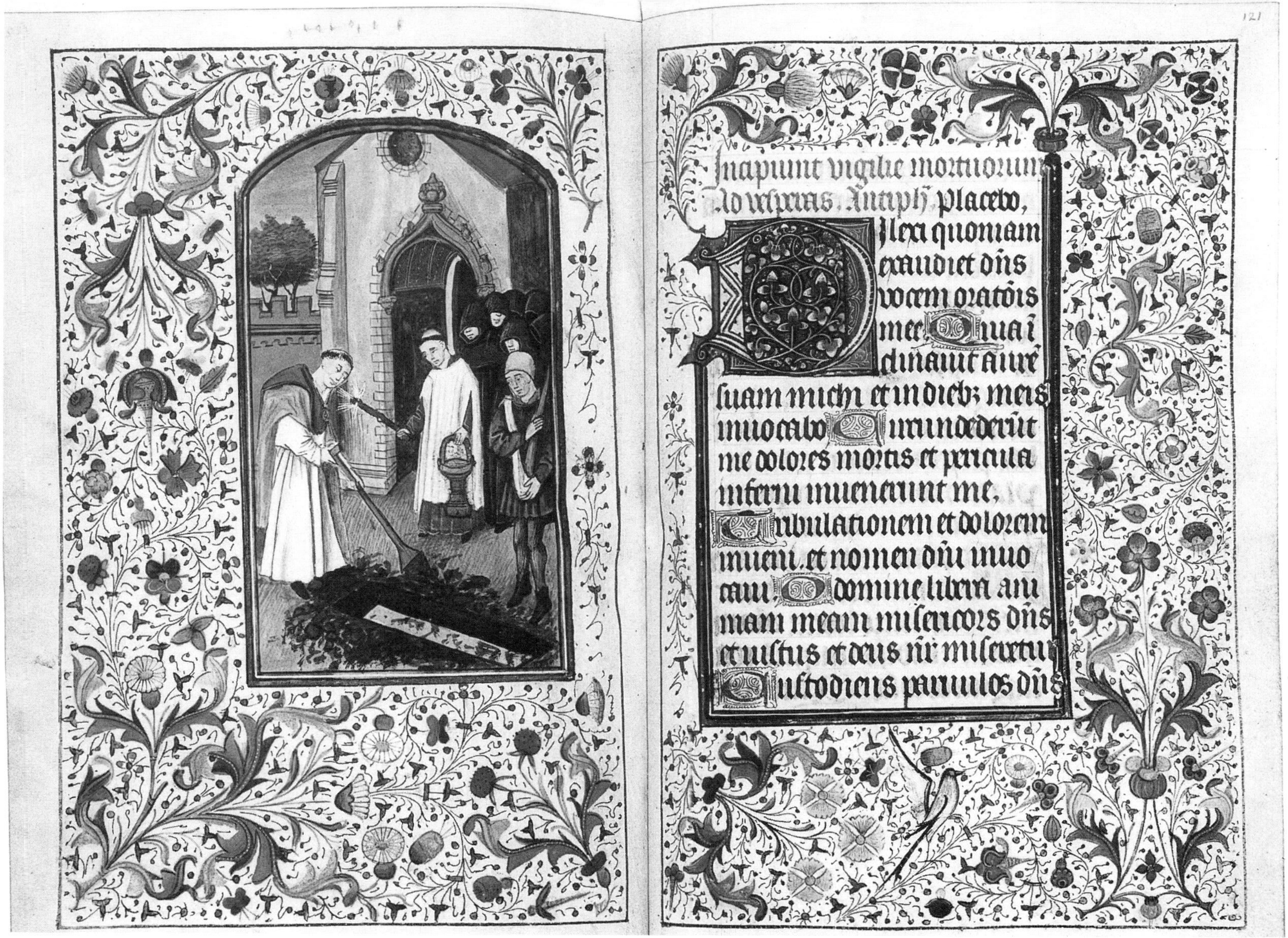

22. MS. Buchanan e. 5, fols. 120v–121r. [Slightly reduced]

The subjects of the miniatures are:

(fol. 13v) Hours of the Cross. Crucifixion; John supporting the swooning Virgin to the left, soldiers to the right.

(fol. 20v) Hours of the Spirit. Pentecost; the Apostles surrounding the Virgin.

(fol. 27v) Mass of the Virgin. Virgin and Child; the Child reaching up to touch the Virgin's cheek; the Virgin holding a red berry(?); a rose(?)-garden in the background.

(fol. 38v) Hours of the Virgin, Matins. Annunciation; the Virgin at a prie-dieu beneath an architectural canopy.

(fol. 48v) Lauds. Visitation (Pächt & Alexander, 1, pl. XXVI).

(fol. 59v) Prime. Nativity; the Virgin and Joseph adoring the Child.

(fol. 64v) Terce. Annunciation to two Shepherds; their flock grazing.

(fol. 69v) Sext. Adoration of the Magi.

(fol. 74v) None. Presentation in the Temple.

(fol. 79v) Vespers. Massacre of the Innocents; a woman and her infant are siezed by a soldier, watched by Herod and his advisors.

(fol. 87v) Compline. Flight into Egypt.

(fol. 100v) Penitential Psalms. Last Judgement; Christ above the Virgin and John, arrows fall from an area of darkened sky on Christ's left, towards some of the figures rising from their graves.

(fol. 120v) Office of the Dead. A burial: in front of the porch of a church, a priest shovels earth onto a coffin in a grave, watched by a cleric with aspergill and aspersory, a taperer/crucifer, and mourners (pl. 22).

Offsets of colour on fol. 33r suggest that an inserted miniature may once have faced the start of the Gospel Pericopes, but there is no indentation in the upper margins of the adjacent leaves (see above).

Each miniature with a four-sided border of painted stylized and naturalistic floral and foliate decoration, with occasional birds, vases, etc., all within a gold framing line; the facing pages each with a similar border and a five-line initial in blue with a red field, or *vice versa*, containing foliage on a gold ground; five-line initials in gold, on a red and blue ground, with delicate white tracery, at the start of the prayers on fols. 93r and 96v, each with partial painted and gilt borders; similar initials for the prayers on fol. 92r (three-line) and fol. 99r (four-line), with some painted and gilt foliate sprays, and for the KL monograms (three-line) in the calendar; similar two-line initials to psalms, prayers, etc.; one-line initals alternately gold with blue penwork, or red with blue penwork, to verses and other minor textual divisions; occasional line-fillers in blue, or blue and gold, especially in the litany.

Gregory Clark kindly informs me that the miniatures in the present manuscript can probably be attributed to the Master of the Lee Hours. Named after a Book of Hours formerly in the collection of R. A. Lee, London (present location unknown), the artist was a follower of the Master of Wauquelin's Alexander. Closely related miniatures are found in three other Books of Hours: Los Angeles, J. Paul Getty Museum, MS. 2; Madrid, Biblioteca Nacional, Vit. 25-4; and Biblioteca Vaticana Apostolica, Barb. lat. 444.

Physical Description

MATERIAL: parchment, of fine, even quality.

DIMENSIONS: the leaves *c*.194-6 x 131-2 mm.

NUMBER OF LEAVES: i (marbled paper, conjoint with the pastedown) + 158 + i (marbled paper, conjoint with the pastedown).

FOLIATION: modern, in pencil: i, 1-159.

COLLATION: mostly written on quires of 8 leaves, with miniatures on single inserted leaves: I-II^6 (fols. 1-12) | III^{8+2} (1st & 8th leaves inserted, fols. 13 & 20) (fols. 13-22), IV^{8+1} (5th leaf inserted, fol. 27) (fols. 23-31), V^{8+1} (7th leaf inserted, fol. 38) (fols. 32-40), VI^{8+1} (8th leaf inserted, fol. 48) (fols. 41-49), VII^8 (fols. 50-57), VIII^{8+2} (2nd & 7th leaves inserted, fols. 59 & 64) (fols. 58-67), IX^{8+2} (2nd & 7th leaves inserted, fols. 69 & 74) (fols. 68-77) X^{8+1} (2nd leaf inserted, fol. 79) (fols. 78-86), XI^{8+1} (1st leaf inserted, fol. 87) (fols. 87-95), XII^4 (fols. 96-99) | XIII^{8+1} (1st leaf inserted, fol. 100) (fols. 100-108), XIV^8 (fols. 109-116), XV^{8+1} (4th leaf inserted, fol. 120) (fols. 117-125), XVI-XVIII^8 (fols. 126-149), XIX^{8+1} (9th leaf an original addition, fol. 158) (fols. 150-158); traces of CATCHWORDS survive on fols. 133v, 157v.

RULING: 18 lines ruled in pale red ink, with single vertical bounding lines extending the full height of the page, the top and bottom horizontal lines extending the full width of the page; the ruled space *c*.100-1 x 62-3 mm. (both calendar and text); no prickings visible.

SCRIPT: written in a fine regular gothic bookhand, with 17 lines of text per page; the written space *c*.98 x 62 mm.

RUBRICATION: headings in purplish red, not the same red as the pen-flourishing of initials; capitals touched with yellow wash.

SEC. FOL.: (calendar) 'KL Februarius habet'; (text, fol. 15) 'deus. per omnia'.

Binding

Sewn on five cords, with endbands; bound in early 19th-cent. English(?) brown leather over pasteboards, with onlays of red leather dotted in gilt: semi-circular ones around the edges, and heart-shaped ones at the corners (the latter resembling strawberries), with gilt foliate decoration around their edges; the spine without raised bands, but divided into seven compartments, with gilt foliate ornament and a red title-piece lettered 'PRÆCES | PIÆ'; pale blue marbled endpapers conjoint with pastedowns; the edges of the leaves and boards gilt (pl. 1).

Provenance

1. Probably made in Flanders/Hainault for export to England: several saints in the calendar are not identifiable in standard reference works, others are recognizable but are entered on the wrong days; Donatian in red is suggestive of Bruges, but the presence of both feasts of Eloi in red in the calendar, and of Ghislain in the litany, point to Hainault; the presence of Cuthbert, Dunstan, Aldhelm, etc., suggest that the English market was intended.

2. ? Adolphe Labitte, 19th-cent. Paris bookseller (see Introduction, pp. xxiv-xxv): inscribed in brown ink 'obb' above 'Lss.', separated by a horizontal line, probably his pricecode, in the top right corner of fol. 159r (cf. MS. Buchanan e. 7, lower pastedown, and MS. Buchanan e. 14, fol. 72r).

3. Thomas Buchanan (d. 1864): bought in Paris in October 1857, with other books, for 800 francs (Introduction, p. xix); a partially erased pencil inscription at the top left of fol. i verso reads 'Tho Buchanan | Oct 1857' (only the numerals are absolutely clear, but a comparison with the inscription on the front flyleaf of [pr. bk] Buchanan e.136 (see next catalogue entry) leaves little room for doubt); with other semi-legible pencil markings; presumably bequeathed to his brother John Buchanan.

4. John Buchanan (see Introduction, xix): inscribed in pencil, with the 'Descriptive list' number, '5', in the upper left corner of fol. i verso.

5. Rt. Hon. T. R. Buchanan (1846-1911); given to the Bodleian by his widow, Mrs. E. O. Buchanan, in 1939, when it was accessioned as MS. Lat. liturg. e. 26; re-referenced as MS. Buchanan e. 5 in 1941.

Bibliography

'Fifteen illuminated *Horae*', *BLR* 1 no. 7 (1939), 115-6, at 116 (as MS. Lat. liturg. e. 26).

S. J. P. van Dijk, *Latin liturgical manuscripts and printed books: guide to an exhibition held during 1952* (Bodleian Library: Oxford, 1952), 52 no. 109 (cited as MS. Buchanan c. 5 [*sic*]).

van Dijk, *Handlist of Latin liturgical MSS.*, IV, 290.

Pächt & Alexander, 1, no. 329, pl. XXVI.

Barbara A. Shailor, *Catalogue of medieval and renaissance manuscripts in the Beinecke Rare Book and Manuscript Library, Yale University*, I (Medieval and Renaissance Texts and Studies, 34: Binghamton, NY, 1984), 299.

Gerard Achten, *Das christliche Gebetbuch im Mittelalter: Andachts- und Stundenbücher in Handschrift und Frühdruck*, 2nd edn. (Staatsbibliothek Preubischer Kulturbesitz, Berlin, Ausstellungskataloge, 13: Wiesbaden, 1987), 98.

MS. Buchanan e. 6

This is a vacant shelfmark, formerly occupied by an illuminated copy of the
Book of Hours of the Use of Rome printed on parchment at Paris *c.*1518 by
Gilles Hardouyn for Germain Hardouyn. It is inscribed in pencil on fol. i recto
'Tho Buchnanan', presumably by Thomas Buchanan (d. 1864), uncle of
T. R. Buchanan (d. 1911) (see Introduction, p. xix).

The volume was acquired by the Bodleian in 1939 with the fourteen manuscript
Books of Hours catalogued here, and shelfmarked as MS. Lat. liturg. e. 27; when
the remaining Buchanan manuscripts and printed books were received in 1941
it was re-referenced as MS. Buchanan e. 6; and was finally re-referenced once
more, as a printed book, as Buchanan e.136. It is mentioned in 'Fifteen
illuminated *Horae*', *BLR* 1 no. 7 (1939), 115-6 at 116.

MS. Buchanan e. 7

Book of Hours, Use of Rome and the Carmelites(?), in Latin
Italy, Florence; late 15th century

Text
Original(?) leaf signatures (see under Physical Description), and worm-holes in
fols. 184-193, suggest that the texts enumerated here were previously bound in
the following order: 6, 1, 5, 3, 4, 2.

[Item 1 occupies quires I-IX]

1. (fols. 1r-80v) Hours of the Virgin, Use of Rome, with three lessons at Matins;
with (fols. 66v-71r) weekly, and (fol. 71r-80v) seasonal variants; Matins lacking
from near the start of the hymn 'Quem terra pontus ...' to Ps. 8:3 (from '...
regentes machinam. | |' to '| | lactentium [*sic*] perfecisti ...') due to the loss of a
leaf after fol. 3, and lacking Ps. 18:7-14 (from '... ad summum eius. | |' to
'[domi] | | nati tunc immaculatus ...') due to the loss of a leaf after fol. 5; also
lacking from the weekly variant psalms to the seasonal variants (from Ps. 45:3,
'... Propterea non timebimus dum | |' to Ps. 97:1 '| | quia mirabilia fecit ...') due
to the loss of probably six leaves after fol. 69; and lacking from the rubric for
Lauds in Advent to the rubric for Prime in Advent (from '... *Ad laudes et per* | |' to
'[*in?*] | | *fra ad benedictus. ...*') due to the loss of a leaf after fol. 76.

[Item 2 occupies quires X-XIII]

2. (fols. 81r-108v) Long Hours of the Cross, with three lessons at Matins;
misbound (fols. 91-95 should follow fol. 106); Vespers ending imperfect and
Compline starting imperfect (from the prayer 'Domine iesu christe | |' to Ps. 150
'| | Laudate dominum ...') due to the loss of a leaf after fol. 94 .

[Items 3-4 occupy quires XIV-XVI]

3. (fols. 109r-118r) The Seven Penitential Psalms; lacking Ps. 37:5-19 (from '...
sunt caput | |' to '[cogi] | | tabo pro peccato ...') due to the loss of a bifolium after
fol. 112; lacking Ps. 50:14-21 and Ps. 101:1-2 (from '... principali con | |' to '| |
orationem meam ...') due to the loss of a leaf after fol. 114; lacking Ps. 101:9-26
(from '... mihi inimici | |' to '[manu] | | um tuarum sunt ...') due to the loss of two
leaves after fol. 115; lacking Ps. 129:6-8 and Ps. 142:1-5 (from '... A c- | | [ustodia]'
to '[an] | | tiquorum meditatus ...') due to the loss of a leaf after fol. 116.

4. (fols. 118r-129r) Litany and collects; the litany very short, the petitions
lacking the 'A'/'Ab' and 'Per' petitions (from '... Propitius esto. parce nobis
domine. | |' to '| | Peccatores. te rogamus ...') due to the loss of a leaf after fol.
120; followed (fol. 125v-129r) by the usual ten collects (cf. MS. Buchanan e. 5,
where they are listed, with refs.), the fifth with '... famulo tuo papa nostro ...';
fol. 129v ruled, otherwise blank.

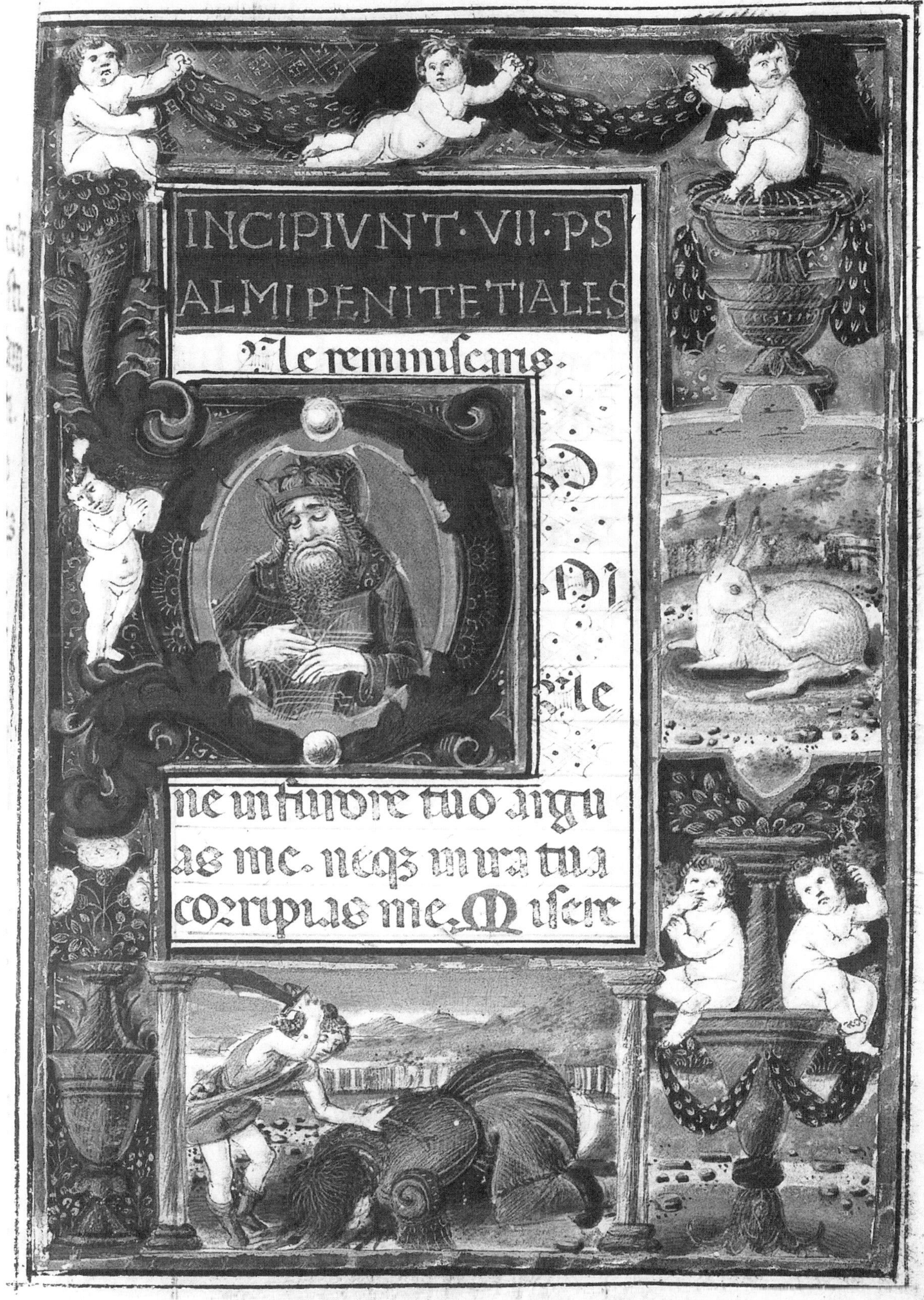

23. *MS. Buchanan e. 7, fol. 109r. [Considerably enlarged]*

[Item 5 occupies quires XVII-XXII]

5. (fols. 130r-183v) Office of the Dead, Carmelite(?) Use; Vespers lacking Ps.
129:3-8 and Ps. 137:1-8 (from '... quis sustinebit | |' to '[despi]| |cias. Requiem.
...') due to the loss of two leaves after fol. 133; also lacking part of the *Magnificat*
and Ps. 145:1-5 (from '... Esurientes imple-| |' [i.e. Luke 1:35] to '[ad]| |iutor
eius. spes eius ...') due to the loss of a leaf after fol. 134; Matins lacking Ps. 26:4-8
(from '... ego sperabo. | |' to '| | domine requiram. ...'), Ps. 39:4-9 (from '...
gressus meos. | |' to '| | uolui et legem ...'), Pss. 40:14-41:6 (from '... fiat fiat.
Re| |' to '[confite]| |bor illi salutare ...') due to the loss of single leaves after fols.
153, 158, and 162, respectively; the responses of the nine lessons are Ottosen,
Office of the Dead, numbers 14,72,24; 32,57,28; 68,82,38: he assigns books
with this series to a wide variety of places, mostly French, but also Sarum and
the Carmelite Order, which is the most likely in the present context.

[Item 6 occupies quire XXIII]

6. (fols. 184r-195v) Calendar, very sparse, major feasts in red, none of them
local; each month headed by a note on the length of the calendar and lunar
month; feasts in brown ink include Fortunatus (6 Mar. [*sic*]), Romanus (31 Mar.
[*sic*]; perhaps the roman martyr who d. 258, usually venerated on 9 Aug., a relic
of whose arm was in Arezzo cathedral; the year '258' was added in pencil in the
18th/19th-cent. next to his name), Antony of Padua (13 June), Donatus of
Arrezzo (7 Aug.), Antoninus of ?Florence (2 Sept. — the usual date for different
saints of the same name; Antoninus of Florence died on 2 May), Francis (4 Oct.),
Reparata (8 Oct.), and Gallus (16 Oct.).

Decoration

Four seven-line historiated initials; each below a coloured panel with the heading
of the text, mostly in square capitals of humanistic style; and surrounded by a
four-sided border containing further scenes in panels framed in gold:
(fol. 1r) Hours of the Virgin. Initial D[omine]: the Virgin and Child, half-length;
a bird on the Virgin's hand; the upper border with putti flanking the Redeemer,
and seraphim at the corners; the lower border with two putti flanking a coat of
arms (see under Provenance), with a vase of flowers and an angel at the corners;
the right border with a deer lying on the ground, with a putto above and below;
with some flaking and rubbing (Pächt & Alexander, 2, pl. XXIX no. 325a).
(fol. 81r) Hours of the Cross. Initial D[omine]: the Man of Sorrows, standing in
the tomb; the upper border with two putti holding the flaming 'yhs' roundel of
St. Bernardino of Siena; the lower border with Christ on the Cross in a landscape,
bleeding profusely; the right border with Mary Magdalen mourning, and further
putti; with some smudging.
(fol. 109r) Penitential Psalms. Initial D[omine]: King David playing the psaltery,
held at his chest; the borders with several putti; the lower border with David
beheading Goliath; the right border with a deer lying on the ground (pl. 23).

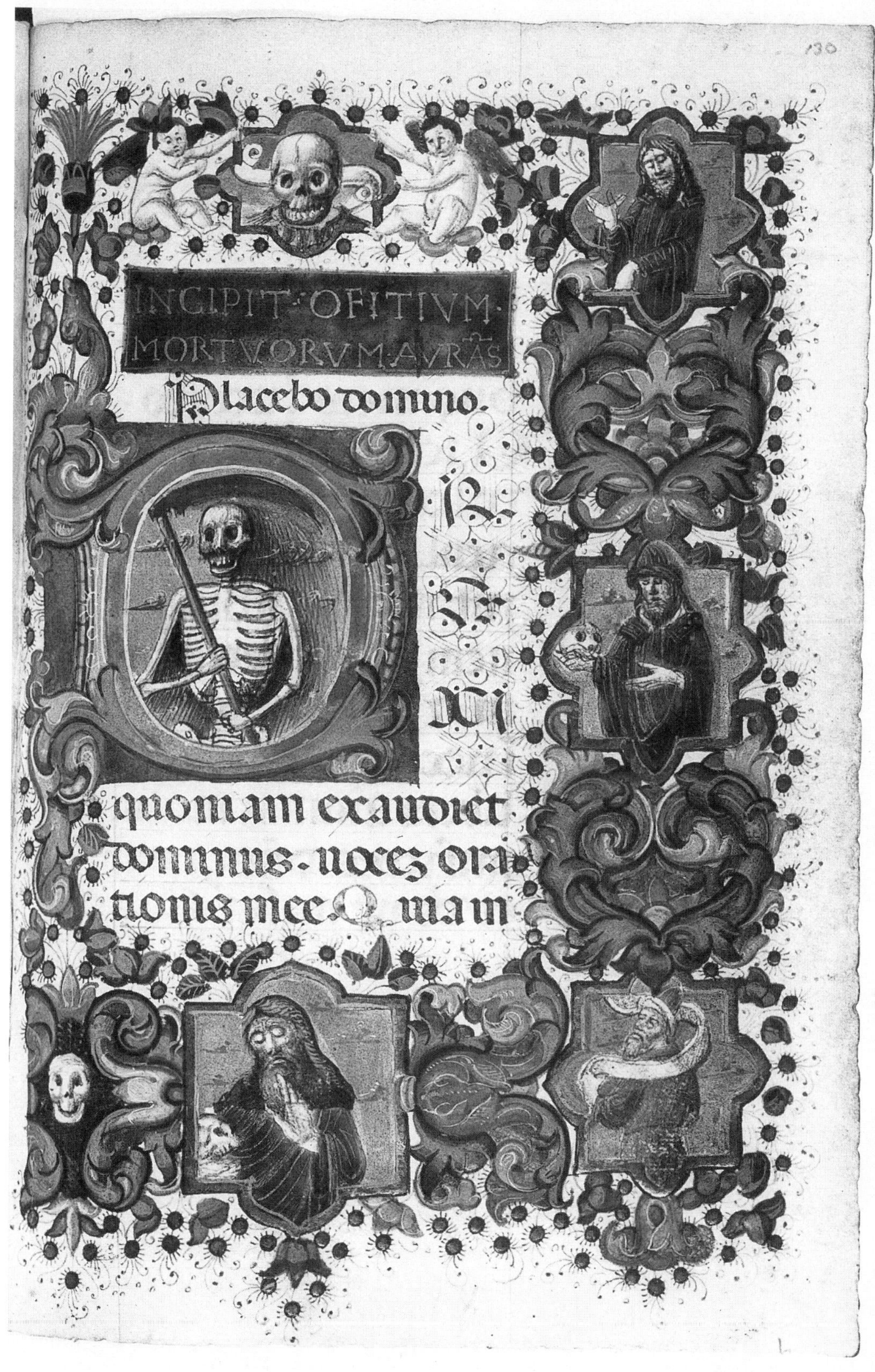

24. MS. Buchanan e. 7, fol. 130r. [Considerably enlarged]

(fol. 130r) Office of the Dead. Initial D[ilexi]: a half-length skeleton holding a scythe (the silver blade oxidised); the borders with several skulls and putti, and four other figures, two of them each holding a skull, another holding a scroll; the border in a different style to the others, having lush acanthus foliage, without gilt framing, but with individual gilt-framed panels for the figures and one skull (pl. 24).

Four-line painted foliate initials with burnished and painted gold, at the start of each hour from Prime to Compline in the Hours of the Virgin (fols. 29r, 35r, 41ar, 45r, 50v, 61r); similar three-line initials to the same hours in the Hours of the Cross (fols. 92r, 98r, 100v, 103r, 105v); three-line initials in gold with blue penwork, or blue with red penwork, respectively, to Lauds of the Hours of the Virgin and the Cross (fols. 13v, 90r); two-line initials alternately gold with blue penwork, or blue with red penwork, to psalms, lessons, KL monograms in the calendar, etc.; one-line initials alternately in gold or blue, to verses and other minor textual divisions.

The illumination is attributed by Garzelli to Mariano del Buono di Jacopo (1433-1504?) (on whom see Levi d'Ancona, *Miniatura e miniatori a Firenze*, 175-81; and Garzelli, 'Le immagini ...', I: 189-215).

Physical Description
MATERIAL: parchment; the lower margin of fol. 158 cut away.
DIMENSIONS: the leaves 137-9 x 91-4 mm. (the calendar somewhat smaller).
NUMBER OF LEAVES: i (paper) + 196 + ii (paper).
FOLIATION: modern, in pencil: i, 1-41a, 41b-197.
COLLATION: mostly in quires of 10 leaves, but with numerous leaves missing: I$^{10-2}$ (4th & 7th leaves, a bifolium, missing, after fols. 3 & 5) (fols. 1-8), II-VII^{10} (fols. 9-67), VIII$^{10-6}$ (3rd to 8th leaves missing, after fol. 69) (fols. 68-71), IX$^{10-1}$ (6th leaf missing after fol. 76) (fols. 72-80) | X^{10} (fols. 81-90), XI$^{6-1}$ (5th leaf missing after fol. 94; this whole quire belongs after fol. 106) (fols. 91-95), XII^{10} (fols. 96-105), XIII^{10+1-6} (the 2nd to 5th, and 7th leaves of the original quire are now fols. 91-95; the last leaf is an original insertion, fol. 108) (fols. 106-108) | XIV$^{10-3}$ (5th, 6th, and 9th leaves missing, after fols. 112 and 114) (fols. 109-115), XV$^{10-4}$ (1st, 2nd, 4th, & 9th leaves missing, after fols. 115, 116, & 120) (fols. 116-121), XVI^{8} (fols. 122-129) | XVII$^{10-3}$ (5th, 6th, & 8th leaves missing, after fols. 133 & 134) (fols. 130-136), XVIII^{10} (fols. 137-146), XIX$^{10-1}$ (8th leaf missing, after fol. 153) (fols. 147-155), XX$^{10-2}$ (4th & 9th leaves missing, after fols. 158 & 162, respectively) (fols. 156-163), XXI-XXII^{10} (fols. 164-183) | XXIII^{12} (fols. 184-195); horizontal CATCHWORDS are in the centre of the lower margin, between dots or short dashes, except quires containing the end of a major textual unit (i.e. quires IX, XIII, XVI, XXII, XXIII); early (original?) leaf signatures survive in most quires, taking the form e.g. [v1], 'v2' - 'v5', 'v6+' (quire XII, fols. 96-105), the letters of the alphabet are in the order [a]-i, t-[w/x], q-s, and k-p, indicating the original sequence of the main texts (see under Text); 19th(?)-cent. quire numbers in pencil, in arabic numerals, in the centre of the lower margin on the first recto of each quire, according to the present (incorrect) sequence of the quires.

RULING: 14 lines ruled partly in pale grey-blue ink (quires I-VIII, XIV-XX), and partly in pale brown (the remainder), between single vertical bounding lines extending the full height of the page (the calendar with 18 ruled lines, for 17 lines of text per page; with five verticals ruled in leadpoint, all extending the full height of the page); the ruled space 68-9 x 41-2 mm.; single prickings are present in the fore-edge margin, *c*.4-5 mm. below the bottom ruled line.
SCRIPT: written in a rounded gothic bookhand, in two sizes of script according to liturgical function; with 13 lines of text per page; the written space *c*.66 x 41 mm.
RUBRICATION: headings in red, guides to rubrics and coloured initials in a tiny cursive script; capitals touched in pale yellow wash.
SEC. FOL.: (calendar, now fol. 185) 'KL Februarius habet'; (text, fol. 2) 'iubilemus deo'.

Binding

Sewn on three cords, with pink silk endbands; bound in brown leather with gilt tooling over pasteboards, almost entirely obscured by 19th(?)-cent. red velvet; the spine flat; the pastedowns, and the first and last flyleaves, are lined with pink silk; the last flyleaf (fol. 197) with a large watermark 'h'; the edges of the leaves gilt and gauffered. Boxed, using funds provided by the Friends of the Bodleian, 1994.

Provenance

1. A member of the Florentine Bellacci (?) family, with Carmelite links: with their(?) coat of arms (fol. 1r): *vert*, a bend *argent* (now oxidized to black), with three uncertain five-pointed objects *gules*, the shield within a wreath held by two putti (Pächt & Alexander, 2, pl. XXIX no. 325a); this matches the Bellacci arms if the five-pointed objects were intended to represent cinquefoils (see Michel Popoff, *Florence (1302-1700)* (Répertoires d'héraldique italienne: Paris, 1991), 163 no. 467; cf. 48 no. D 301), or roses (Rietstap, *Armorial général*, I, 156, and *Planches*, I, pl. CLXVII; Crollalanza, *Dizionario storico-blasonico*, I, 108; Angelo M. G. Scorza, *Enciclopedia araldica italiana* (Genoa, [1953?-]), IV, 112; also illustrated as such in MS. Ital. d. 25, fol. 105v). The Use of the Office of the Dead is probably Carmelite (see under Text).

2. Adolphe Labitte, 19th-cent. Paris bookseller (see Introduction, pp. xxiv-xxv): the lower silk pastedown-lining inscribed in brown ink 'Baa' 'Uss' separated by a horizontal line, presumably his pricecode (pl. 9; cf. MS. Buchanan e. 5, fol. 159r, and MS. Buchanan e. 14, fol. 72r).

3. ? Thomas Buchanan (d. 1864) (see Introduction, p. xiv): perhaps bought with MS. Buchanan e. 5 and [pr. bk.] Buchanan e.136 in Paris in October 1857 (see Introduction, p. xix).

4. John Buchanan (see Introduction, p. xix): inscribed in pencil with the 'Descriptive list' number, '7.', in the top left corner of fol. i verso.

5. Rt. Hon. T. R. Buchanan (1846-1911); given to the Bodleian by his widow, Mrs. E. O. Buchanan, in 1939, when it was accessioned as MS. Lat. liturg. e. 28; re-referenced as MS. Buchanan e. 7 in 1941.

                    Bodleian Library, Oxford

Bibliography

'Fifteen illuminated *Horae*', *BLR* 1 no. 7 (1939), 115-6, at 116 (as MS. Lat. liturg. e. 28).

van Dijk, *Handlist of Latin liturgical MSS.*, IV, 254.

Pächt & Alexander, 2, no. 325, pl. XXIX.

L. M. J. Delaissé, James Marrow, and John de Wit, *The James A. de Rothschild Collection at Waddesdon Manor: illuminated manuscripts* (Fribourg, 1977), 346.

Annarosa Garzelli, 'Le immagini, gli autori, i destinatari', in *La miniatura fiorentina del Rinascimento, 1440-1525: un primo censimento* ed. Annarosa Garzelli (Inventari e cataloghi toscani, 18-19: 2 vols., Florence, 1985), I, 5-391, at 214.

MS. Buchanan e. 8

Book of Hours, Use of Paris, in Latin and French
France, Paris; late 15th or early 16th century

Text
[Item 1 occupies quire I]

1. (fols. 1r-3v) Hymns, added 16th/17th-cent.:
   (i) 'Veni sancte spiritus, et emitte celitus ... da perenne gaudium, Amen'
   (*Repertorium hymnologicum*, no. 21242);
   (ii) 'Veni creator spiritus mentes tuorum visita ... carisma sancti spiritus,
   Amen.' (*ibid.*, no. 21204);
   (iii) 'Vexila regis prodeunt ... salua rege per secula, Amen,' (*ibid.*, no. 21481);
   (iv) 'Veni redemtor gentium ... fideque iugi luceat, Amen.' (*ibid.*, no. 21234).

[Item 2 occupies quires II-III]

2. (fols. 4r-15v) Calendar, in French, with an entry for every day, major feasts in
gold, the remainder alternately red or blue; each month headed by a note on the
length of the calendar month in lines of gold and blue; feasts in gold include
Denis (9 Oct.), Anne (28 July), and Marcellus (3 Nov.); feasts in red or blue
include Geneviève (3 Jan. and 26 Nov.), Ivo Helory (19 May), Germain of Paris
(28 May), Landericus (10 June), the Translation of Marcellus (26 July), Louis IX
(25 Aug.), Aurea (4 Oct.), and Magloire (24 Oct.).

[Items 3-4 occupy quires IV-V]

3. (fols. 16r-21v) Gospel Pericopes (cf. MS. Buchanan e. 3; without the
antiphon, versicle, response and prayer after John).

4. (fols. 21v-25r) Prayer to the Virgin: '*Oratio ad beatam mariam. Obsecro te ...*'
[masculine forms] (cf. MS. Buchanan e. 2); fol. 25v ruled, otherwise blank.

[Items 5-6 occupy quires VI-XI]

5. (fols. 26r-71v) Hours of the Virgin, Use of Paris, with three lessons at Matins.

6. (fol. 72r) Prayer: '[Omnipotens sempiterne deus qui] gloriose uirginis ...' (pr.
Wordsworth, *Horae Eboracenses*, 63) starting imperfect at the fifth word due to
the loss of a leaf after fol. 71; this prayer often follows the *Salve regina* with a
response and versicle (cf. MSS. Buchanan e. 5, e. 18, and f. 4), and these are
therefore likely to have been on the missing leaf; fol. 72v ruled, otherwise blank.

[Items 7-8 occupy quire XII]

7. (fols. 73r-76v) Hours of the Cross.

8. (fols. 77r-80r, title on fol. 76v) Hours of the Holy Spirit; fol. 80v ruled, otherwise blank.

[Items 9-10 occupy quires XIII-XIV]

9. (fols. 81r-91v) The Seven Penitential Psalms; starting imperfect in Ps. 6:8 (at '| | meus inueteraui ...') due to the loss of a leaf before fol. 81.

10. (fols. 91v-96r) Litany and collects; the litany including Denis last among thirteeen martyrs; Fiacre (3) among eight confessors; Geneviève (8) and Avia (15) among fifteen virgins; followed (fol. 95v) by three collects:
(i) 'Deus cui proprium est ...' (*Corpus orationum*, no. 1143); (ii) 'Inclina domine aurem tuam ad preces nostras ...' (cf. version pr. Bruylants, *Oraisons*, no. 644); (iii) 'Fidelium deus omnium conditor et redemptor ...' (pr. *Corpus orationum*, no. 2684b); fol. 96v ruled, otherwise blank.

[Items 11-13 occupy quires XV-XXII]

11. (fols. 97r-136v) Office of the Dead, Use of Paris, starting imperfect in Vespers before the start of Ps. 119 (at '[Re-]| |quiem *antiphona* Placebo domino ...'), due to the loss of a leaf before fol. 97.

12. (fols. 136v-137v) Devotion, with a heading in French: '*Pour les trespassez*', consisting of an antiphon 'Auete omnes anime fideles ...', versicle, response, and the prayer 'Domine iesu christe salus et liberacio fidelium animarum ...' (pr. Leroquais, *Livres d'heures*, II, 341).

13. (fols. 138r-150r) Suffrages and other prayers: suffrages to (i) the Trinity; and (ii) St. Michael; followed by (iii) a rhyming prayer to one's guardian angel, with a heading in French: '*A son bon ange. Angele qui meus es custos ... guberna ut valeam tecum scandere celestia regna*' (a line longer than the version pr. in Wordsworth, *Horae Eboracenses*, 35); suffrages to saints (iv) John the Baptist; (v) John the Evangelist; (vi) Peter & Paul; (vii) Stephen; (viii) Sebastian; (ix) Nicholas; (x) Anne; (xi) Mary Magdalen; (xii) Catherine; (xiii) Margaret; (xiv) Barbara; (xv) Geneviève; (xvi) All Saints; followed by (xvii) a prayer for one's enemies: '*Pro inimicis suis*' (prayers pr. in *Corpus orationum* are nos. (i) 3920, (ii) 1798, (iv) 4492, (v) 2416c, (vi) 1158b, (vii) 4032, (ix) 1463, (x) 1366a, (xi) 3231, (xii) 1521, (xiii) 1384a, (xvi) 3134, and (xvii) 1293).

[Item 14 occupies the last leaf of quire XXII, which was originally ruled, otherwise blank, and an added leaf]

14. (fols. 151r-152v) Hymns, added 16/17th-cent.:
    (i) 'Christe redemptor omnium ex patre patris ... hymnum nouum concinnimus. Gloria tibi ...' (*Repertorium hymnologicum*, no. 2960);
    (ii) 'Christe qui lux es et dies ... adesto nobis domine, Deo patri sit gloria ...' (*ibid.*, no. 2934);

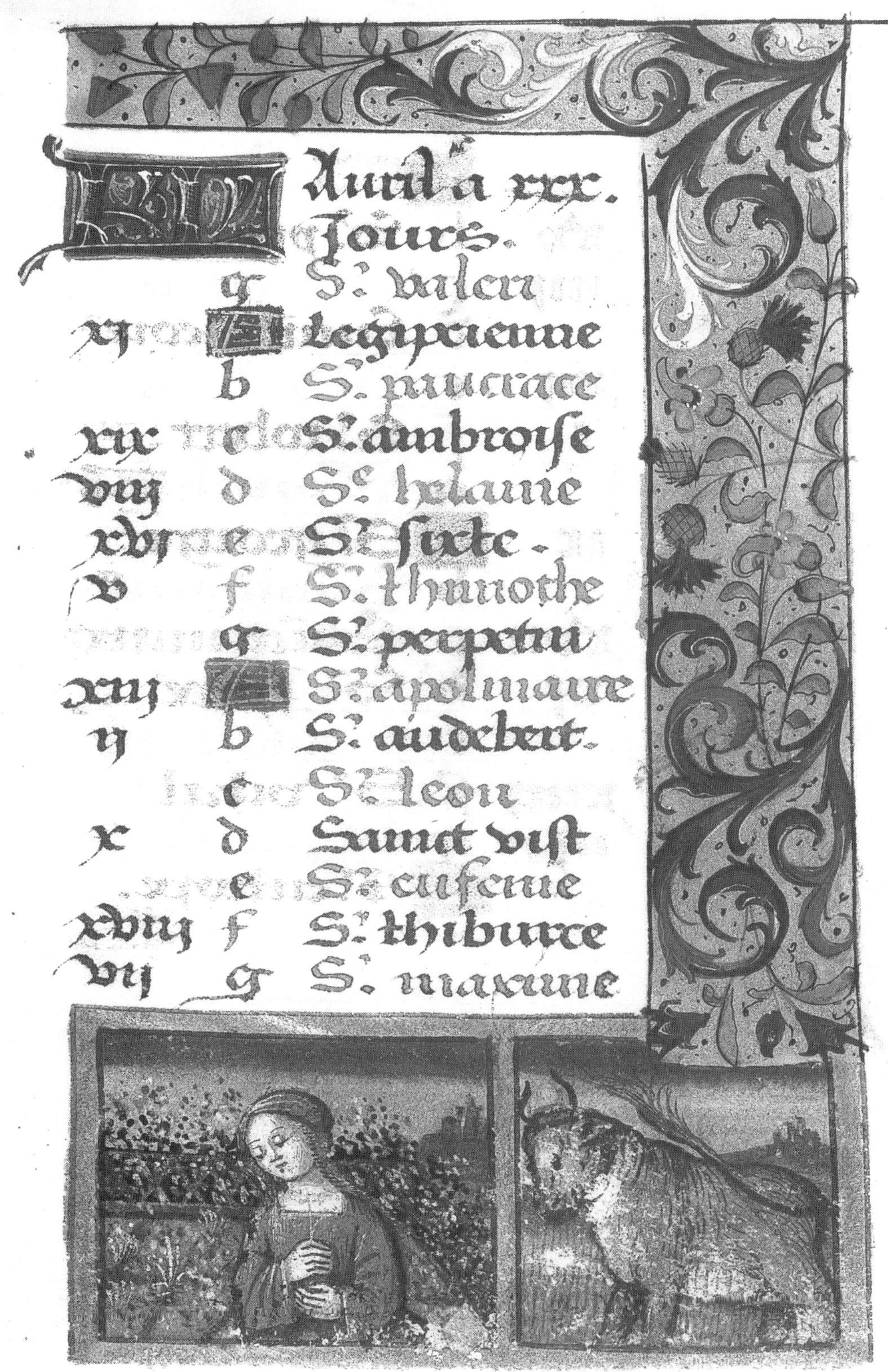

25. MS. Buchanan e. 8, fol. 7r. [Enlarged]

(iii) 'Christe redemptor omnium, conserua tuos famulos: ...' (*ibid.*, no. 2959) ending imperfect (at 'Vates eterni iudicis apo- | |') due to the loss of a leaf or leaves after fol. 152.

Decoration

Four large miniatures with arched tops, above three (fol. 138r), four (fol. 73r), or five (fols. 26r, 77r) lines of text:

(fol. 26r) Hours of the Virgin, Matins. Annunciation.

(fol. 73r) Hours of the Cross. Crucifixion: the Virgin and John to the left; soldiers, including Longinus, to the right.

(fol. 77r) Hours of the Holy Spirit. Pentecost; the Apostles around the Virgin (pl. 26).

(fol. 138r) Suffrage to the Trinity. The Trinity: the Father and Son seated together, holding an open book between them.

Twenty-five (of an original twenty-six?) small miniatures, framed in liquid gold on the upper three sides; six to nine lines high, mostly eight lines high, narrower than the width of the column:

(fol. 16r) St. John on Patmos.

(fol. 17r) St. Luke painting the Virgin, on a panel on an easel.

(fol. 18v) St. Matthew and his angel, each holding a book.

(fol. 20v) St. Mark writing.

(fol. 21v) *Obsecro te.* The Virgin praying.

(fol. 36r) Lauds. Visitation; an angel behind the Virgin.

(fol. 46v) Prime. Nativity; the Virgin and Joseph adoring the Child.

(fol. 52r) Terce. Annunciation to two Shepherds.

(fol. 56r) Sext. Adoration of the Magi.

(fol. 59r) None. Presentation in the Temple.

(fol. 62v) Vespers. Massacre of the Innocents: a woman holding a dead infant before Herod and two attendants, but no soldiers.

(fol. 67v) Compline. Coronation of the Virgin.

(fol. 139r) St. Michael and the dragon.

(fol. 140r) St. John the Baptist holding the Agnus Dei on a book(?).

(fol. 140v) St. John the Evangelist blessing the poisoned chalice.

(fol. 141r) St. Peter and St. Paul.

(fol. 142r) St. Stephen.

(fol. 142v) St. Sebastian shot with arrows.

(fol. 144r) St. Nicholas and the three boys in the tub.

(fol. 144v) St. Anne teaching the Virgin to read.

(fol. 145v) St. Mary Magdalen.

(fol. 146r) St. Catherine.

(fol. 147r) St. Margaret emerging from the dragon.

(fol. 147v) St. Barbara.

(fol. 149r) St. Geneviève; an angel preventing a devil from extinguishing her taper.

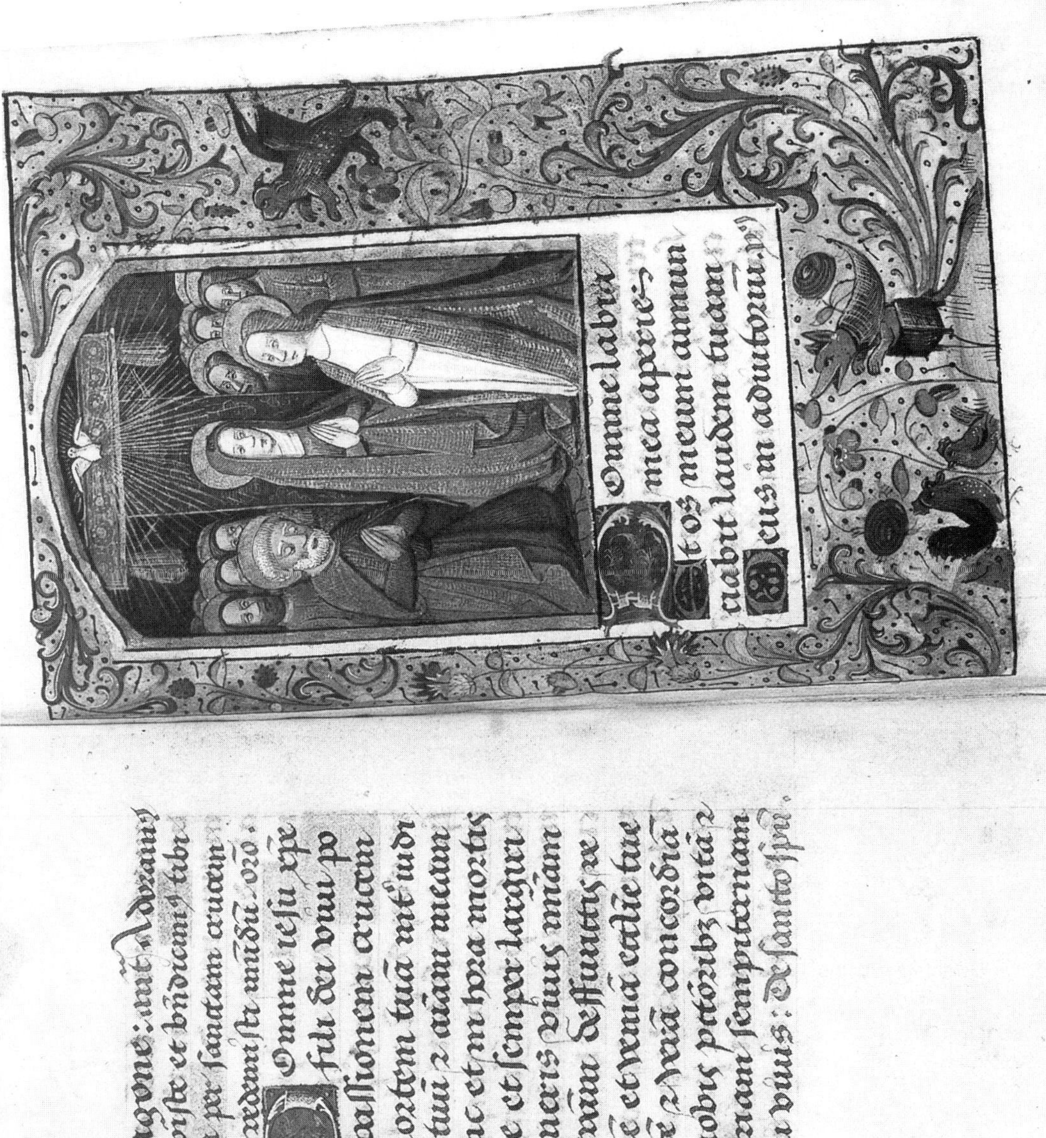

25. *MS. Buchanan e. 8, fols. 76v–77r.* [Slightly enlarged]

Offsets on fol. 71v suggests that there was another miniature, probably for the prayer *Salve regina*, on the missing leaf before fol. 72 (see description of item 6 under Text).

Twenty-four small miniatures illustrating the Occupations of the Months and Zodiac signs, mostly set in landscapes, in the lower margin of the calendar:
(fol. 4r) Feasting; Aquarius.
(fol. 5r) Warming; Pisces.
(fol. 6r) Pruning; Aries.
(fol. 7r) Woman in a garden holding a flower; Taurus (pl. 25).
(fol. 8r) Man with a branch; Gemini: a naked couple embracing (smudged).
(fol. 9r) Scything (? - only the handle visible); Cancer: a crayfish-like creature.
(fol. 10r) Hay-making; Leo.
(fol. 11r) Reaping; Virgo: a woman next to a wheat-sheaf.
(fol. 12r) Grape-treading; Libra: a pair of scales.
(fol. 13r) Sowing; Scorpio.
(fol. 14r) Knocking acorns from trees to feed hogs; Saggitarius.
(fol. 15r) Killing a hog; Capricorn.

Four-sided borders to pages with miniatures, two-sided borders in the calendar, one-sided borders in the fore-edge margin of pages with a two- or three-line inital. All these borders of stylized foliage and flowers on a plain parchment or painted ground, and naturalistic foliage and flowers on geometrically-shaped panels of painted gold, occasionally containing hybrid creatures (e.g. fol. 26r) and/or animals, some of them engaged in human activities, e.g. a hybrid carrying an infant (fol. 16r), an animal playing a pipe and drum (fol. 21v), a caped fox in a pulpit preaching to a congregation of chickens (fol. 77r; pl. 26), and a Pelican in her Piety (fol. 56r), birds, insects, etc.

Two- or three-line initials in red, blue and white, with painted gold decoration, at the start of the hours, psalms, capitula, etc.; one-line initials in painted gold on a brown or red ground, alternating (red, brown and blue grounds used on fols. 26v-31v, brownish red and blue only on fols. 134r-150v), to verses and other minor textual divisions; similar line-fillers in the litany.

By two main artists: the larger miniatures are by an artist working in a late gothic style, while the illustrations of the calendar and suffrages are by an artist working in an essentially renaissance style. The borders in the calendar (which appear to be consistent in style with the borders throughout the rest of the volume) seem to have been executed before the calendar miniatures, which they abut somewhat awkwardly (see pl. 25).

Physical Description
MATERIAL: parchment.
DIMENSIONS: the leaves 134-6 x 94-7 mm.
NUMBER OF LEAVES: ii (modern paper, the first conjoint with the pastedown) + 152 + ii (modern paper, the second conjoint with the pastedown).

FOLIATION: modern, in pencil: i-ii, 1-154.
COLLATION: mostly on quires of 8 leaves: I^{2+1} (3rd leaf inserted, all three leaves a
later addition) (fols. 1-3) | II-III^6 (fols. 4-15) | IV^8 (fols. 16-23), V^2 (fols. 24-25) |
VI-X^8 (fols. 26-65), XI$^{8-1}$ (7th leaf missing, after fol. 71) (fols. 66-72) | XII^8 (fols.
73-80) | XIII$^{8-1}$ (1st leaf missing, before fol. 81) (fols. 81-87), XIV^{8+1} (9th leaf
added, fol. 96) (fols. 88-96) | XV$^{8-1}$(1st leaf missing, before fol. 97) (fols. 97-103),
XVI^6 (fols. 104-109), XVII-XX^8 (fols. 110-141), XXI^8 (fols. 142-149), XXII^2 (fols.
150-151), XXIII$^{2-1(?)}$ (an added leaf, contemporary with fols. 1-3, perhaps a
bifolium of which the second leaf is now missing) (fol. 152); CATCHWORDS
present throughout, except in quires with the end of a major textual unit, plus
quire XX where a heading rendered one unnecessary, and quires II, IV, and XXI; in
the centre of the lower margin, usually followed by two dots like a colon ':'; modern
pencil quire signatures in arabic numerals in the upper left corner of first rectos.
RULING: 19 lines ruled in pale red ink (17 ruled lines in quire XIX, fols. 126r-133v)
between single vertical bounding-lines extending the full height of the page, the
top and bottom horizontal line ruled the full width of the page; the ruled space
79-82 x 47-50 mm.; the added leaves (fols. 1-3, 152) ruled with 19-21 lines in pale
leadpoint, and frame-ruled in pale red ink, extending towards the edges of the page,
the ruled space 101-5 x 61-4 mm.; prickings occasionally survive at the fore-edge.
SCRIPT: written in *lettre bâtarde*, in two different sizes of script, according to
liturgical function, for 18 lines of text per page (16 lines of text in quire XIX);
the written space *c.*77 x 47 mm.; the added leaves with 18-20 lines of text per
page; by at least three main scribes, responsible respectively for: (i) fols. 16r-125v;
(ii) fols. 126r-133v (quire XIX, with different ruling, as noted above); and
(iii) fols. 134r-150v (with different one-line initials, as noted under Decoration);
the attribution of the calendar to one of these hands, perhaps the third, is uncertain;
and the added leaves (fols 1r-3v & 151r-152v) are by a much later hand in rounded
humanistic script, perhaps imitating books printed in Roman type.
RUBRICATION: headings in blue.
SEC. FOL.: (added leaves, fol. 2) 'corporis virtute'; (calendar, fol. 5) 'KL Fevrier a';
(text, fol. 17) 'testatem filios dei'.

Binding

Modern sewing probably on five cords, without endbands; re-cased in 16/17th-
cent. French limp parchment over parchment 'boards'; the covers tooled in gilt
with foliate and interlace designs within framing lines (the gilt mostly rubbed
away); the spine with four (of an original six) thin parchment sewing supports
(no longer functional) emerging from the spine at the joints, and then passing
back under the boards; the spine decorated with dense interlace designs in gilt;
modern flyleaves without watermarks conjoint with the pastdowns; the edges
of the leaves gilt.

Provenance

1. Presumably written and decorated in Paris *c.*1500, but with no indications of the original owner.

2. Unidentified French(?) owner, 16th/17th cent.: the added leaves with hymns at the beginning and end of the volume were probably added at the time of the present binding.

3. John Buchanan (see Introduction, pp. xiv, xix): inscribed in pencil with the 'Descriptive list' number, '8.', in the top left corner of the upper pastedown.

4. Rt. Hon T. R. Buchanan (1846-1911); (the volume was perhaps re-cased for him or at the Bodleian, since the flyleaves and pastedowns show no evidence of having passed through booksellers' hands); given to the Bodleian in 1939 by his widow, Mrs. E. O. Buchanan, when it was accessioned as MS. Lat. liturg. e. 29; re-referenced as MS. Buchanan e. 8 in 1941.

Bibliography

'Fifteen illuminated *Horae*', *BLR* 1 no. 7 (1939), 115-6, at 115 (as MS. Lat. liturg. e. 29).

van Dijk, *Handlist of Latin liturgical MSS.*, IV, 82.

Pächt & Alexander, 1, no. 797.

Susan Groag Bell, 'Medieval women book owners: arbiters of lay piety and ambassadors of culture', *Signs: Journal of Women in Culture and Society* 7 no. 4 (1982), 742-68, pls. 1-14, at n. 84 (repr. in *Sisters and workers in the Middle Ages* ed. Judith M. Bennett (Chicago & London, 1989), 135-61).

MS. Buchanan e. 9

Book of Hours, Use unidentified, in Latin and French
North(?) France; 15th century, second quarter

Text
[Item 1 occupies quire I]

1. (fols. 1r-12v) Calendar, in French, with an entry for every day, major feasts in
gold (none of them local), the others alternately red or blue; each month headed
by a note on the length of the calendar month in gold, and of the lunar month in
blue, and with a note at the end of each month on the length of the night and day
in red; feasts in gold include Eloi (1 Dec.), and his translation (24 [*recte* 25] June).

[Items 2-3 occupy quires II-III]

2. (fols. 13r-17r) Gospel Pericopes (cf. MS. Buchanan e. 3; without the antiphon,
versicle, response and prayer after John).

3. (fols. 17r-25v) Prayers to the Virgin, each with the rubric: '*Oratio beate marie
uirginis.*':
    (i) (fols. 17r-20r) 'Obsecro te ...' [masculine forms] (cf. MS. Buchanan e. 2);
    (ii) (fols. 20r-23v) 'O intemerata ... orbis terrarum de te enim ...' (pr. Wilmart,
    Auteurs spirituels, 494-5);
    (iii) (fols. 23v-25v) 'Salue mater dolorosa. / Iuxta crucem lacrimosa. / ...'
    (*Repertorium hymnologicum*, no. 18018; on this version, starting 'Salve'
    instead of 'Stabat', see *Lyell cat.*, 359 no. 352, giving further references, and
    Wilmart's statement that this is the older version).

[Items 4-5 occupy quires IV-X]

4. (fols. 26r-75r) Hours of the Virgin, Use unidentified (the antiphon and
capitulum at Prime are: 'Quando natus es', and 'Ab inicio'; and at None: 'Ecce
maria genuit' and 'Per te dei'); Prime, Sext and None each start imperfect (at
'| | festina. Gloria patri ...'; '[mor-]| | |tis suscipe. Gloria tibi ...'; and '[prote-]| | |ge
et in hora mortis suscipe.' respectively), due to the loss of single leaves after fols.
47, 57 and 60.

5. (fol. 75r-v) Added texts relating to Sens:
    (i) a response: 'O mirum syroneum senonensis ecclesie. sit presulum. ...', and
    versicle 'O deus pontificum et honor certantium ...'; and
    (ii) a suffrage to Sts. Sabinianus and Potentianus of Sens, consisting of an
    antiphon: 'Orbis senonensium gemma splendet pontificum sauinianus
    inchtus et martir potencianus ...', versicle, and prayer: 'Concede quesumus
    omnipotens et misericors deus ut qui beati potenciam martiris tui atque
    pontificis ...' (the latter an adaptation of the prayer pr. *Corpus orationum*, no. 783).

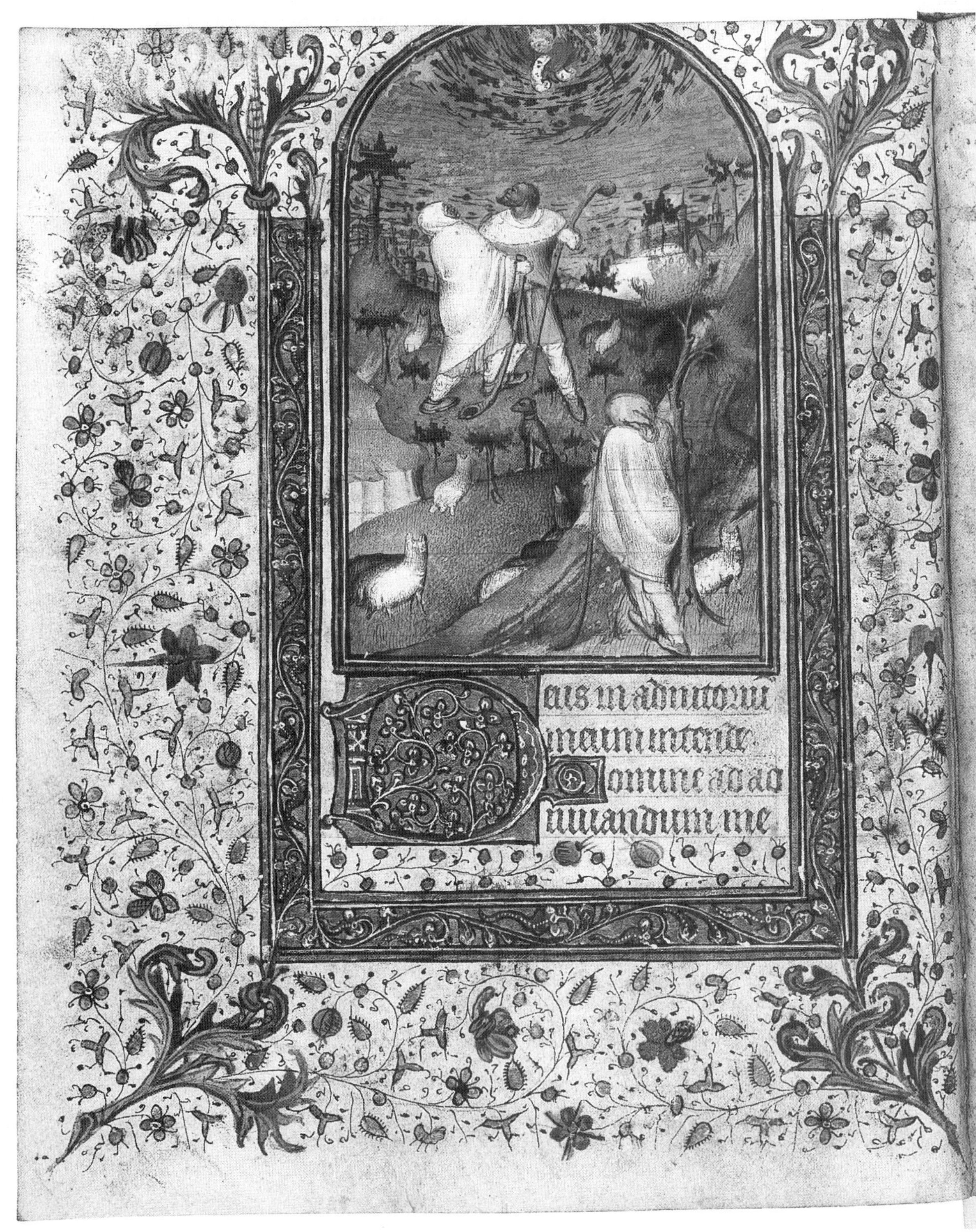

27. *MS. Buchanan e. 9, fol. 53v. [Enlarged]*

[Items 6-9 occupy quires X-XIV]

6. (fols. 76r-87v) The Seven Penitential Psalms.

7. (fols. 88r-94r, rubric on fol. 87v) Litany and collects: the litany including 'Sylea' (Silas?), and Martial (17-18) among eighteen apostles and evangelists; Vincent twice (9, 20) among twenty-six martyrs; Vigor, Germanus, Omer, Bertin, Alexius, Bertin (i.e. repeated), Silvinus, Basil, Piatus, Eloi, and Giles (14-24) among 24 confessors; followed (fol. 94r) by two collects: (i) 'Deus cui proprium est ...' (pr. *Corpus orationum*, no. 1143), (ii) 'Fidelium deus omnium conditor ...' (pr. *ibid.*, no. 2684b).

8. (fols. 94v-101r, rubric on fol. 94r) Hours of the Cross.

9. (fols. 101v-107v, rubric on fol. 101r) Hours of the Holy Spirit.

[Items 10-14 occupy quires XV-XVI]

10. (fols. 108r-113r) The Fifteen Joys of the Virgin, in French: 'Doulce dame de misericorde ...' (pr. Leroquais, *Livres d'heures*, II, 310).

11. (fols. 113v-116r, rubric on fol. 113r) The Seven Requests of Our Lord, in French: '*Ci apres commence les cinq* [sic] *plaies*. Doulx dieu doulx pere sainte trinite ...' (pr. Leroquais, *Livres d'heures*, II, 309).

12. (fol. 116r-v) Prayer to the Holy Cross, in French, in rhyming verse, written out as prose: 'Sainte uraie crois aouree / Qui du corps dieu fus a ornee ... Et en paradis paruenir. Amen.' (a version is pr. in Perdrizet, *Calendrier Parisien*, 32).

13. (fols. 116v-118v) Devotion to the Passion of Christ, consisting of (fols. 116v-118r): '*Passio domini nostri ihesu christi secundum iohannem.*' (actually a paraphrase, mainly of John 19:1-34, but incorporating John 18:4 and Matthew 27:30 & 27:34), 'In illo tempore. Apprehendit pylatus ihesum et flagellauit eum ...' (pr. Wordsworth, *Horae Eboracenses*, 123), followed (fol. 118r-v) by the usual prayer: 'Deus qui manus tuas et pedes tuos ...' (pr. *ibid*, 123-4; Leroquais, *Livres d'heures*, I, xxiv).

14. (fols. 118v-119v) The Verses of St. Bernard: '*Les .vii.* [sic] *vers saint bernart.*', written, as often, as eight verses in the following order:
    (i) 'Illumina oculos meos ... aduersus eum.' [Ps. 12:4-5]
    (ii) 'In manus tuas domine ... deus ueritatis.' [Ps. 30:6]
    (iii) 'Locutus sum in lingua mea ... finem meum.' [Ps. 38:5]
    (iv) 'Et numerum dierum meorum ... desit michi.' [Ps. 38:5]
    (v) 'Disrupisti domine uincula mea ... inuocabo.' [Ps. 115:16-17]
    (vi) 'Periit fuga a me ... animam meam.' [Ps. 141:5]
    (vii) 'Clamaui ad te domine ... terra uiuencium'. [Ps. 141:6]
    (viii) 'Fac mecum signum ... consolatus es me.' [Ps. 85:17];
(*Repertorium hymnologicum*, no. 27912; cf. Leroquais, *Livres d'heures*, I, p. xxx; also found in MS. Buchanan g. 4; cf. MSS. Buchanan e. 11 and e. 18, which have

slight variants); followed (fol. 119r-v) by the usual prayer: 'Omnipotens
sempiterne deus qui ezechie regi ... misericordiam tuam inuenire. Per ...' (cf. Ker,
MMBL, I, 412 art 2, etc.).

[Items 15-16 occupy quires XVII-XXII]

15. (fols. 120r-161r) Office of the Dead, Use unidentified: the responses at the
nine lessons correspond to Ottosen, *Office of the Dead*, numbers 14,72,24;
32,57,68; 83,46,38, but this sequence does not occur in his tables.

16. (fols. 161v-162v) Suffrage to St. Barbara, a contemporary addition.

[Items 17(i)-(l) occupy quires XXIII-XXVI]

17. (fols. 163r-188r) Suffrages, an unusually long series: to the (i) Trinity, (ii)
Holy Spirit, and (iii) the Virgin; and to Saints (iv) Michael, (v) John the Baptist,
(vi) Peter, (vii) Paul, (viii) Andrew, (ix) James, (x) Bartholomew, (xi) John the
Evangelist, (xii) Matthew, (xiii) Thomas, (xiv) Philip & James, (xv) Simon & Jude,
(xvi) Matthias, (xvii) Barnabas, (xviii) Mark, (xix) Luke, (xx) Stephen, (xxi)
Clement, (xxii) Vincent, (xxiii) Lawrence, (xxiv) Denis, (xxv) Christopher, (xxvi)
George, (xxvii) Blaise, (xxviii) Quentin, (xxix) Nicasius, (xxx) Victor, (xxxi)
Sebastian, (xxxii) Hippolytus, (xxxiii) Maurice, Exuperius, Candidus, Victor, and
Innocent, (xxxiv) Eustace, (xxxv) Eutropius, (xxxvi) Lazarus, (xxxvii) the Holy
Innocents, (xxxviii) Martin, (xxxix) Nicholas, (xl) Germain, (xli) Augustine, (xlii)
Gregory, (xliii) Ambrose, (xliv) Jerome, (xlv) Antony, (xlvi) Giles, (xlvii) Claudius
of Besançon, (xlviii) Anne, ending imperfect in the prayer (at '... ut mariam
matrem tuam in | |'), followed by the very end of an unidentified suffrage ('| |
per consolatione gaudere. Per christum ...'), both imperfect due to the excision of
two leaves after fol. 186, (xlix) Geneviève, and (l) Agnes; fol. 188v, ruled, and
with decorated borders, as on preceding pages, but otherwise originally blank
(prayers pr. in *Corpus orationum* are nos. (i) 3920, (iii) 706, (iv) 1798, (v) 4492,
(vi) 1411, (vii) 1808, (viii) 3290b (Gregorian recension), (x) 4872 (adapted for
Bartholomew), (xi) 2416c, (xiv) 1841, (xv) 1906 (with Simon & Jude's names
inserted), (xvi) 1459, (xvii) 4872 (adapted for Barnabas), (xviii) 1458, (xix)
3180, (xx) 4039, (xxi) 1843 (adapted for Clement), (xxiv) 1472b, (xxvi) 1860,
(xxviii) 141 (adapted for Quentin), (xxix) 1874a (adapted for Nicasius), (xxx)
3135 (adapted for Victor), (xxxi) 1472a, (xxxii) 925a (adapted for Hypolitus),
(xxxiii) 289 (omitting Vitalis), (xxxiv) 1443 (including mention of his wife and
sons, Theopista, Agapius, and Theopistus), (xxxvi) 1990 (a version), (xxxvii)
1168, (xxxviii) 1497a (adapted for Martin), (xxxix) 1463, (xl) 2504, (xli) 182
(adapted for Augustine), (xliv) 2423, (xlv) 1486, (xlviii) 1366a, and (l) 3929b).

Decoration
Twelve (of at least an original fifteen) large fine miniatures; all but three (noted
below) above four lines of text; most with ogee-curved tops, though many are
cropped at the top, one is trefoil-shaped (fol. 94v), and one is rounded (fol. 101v);

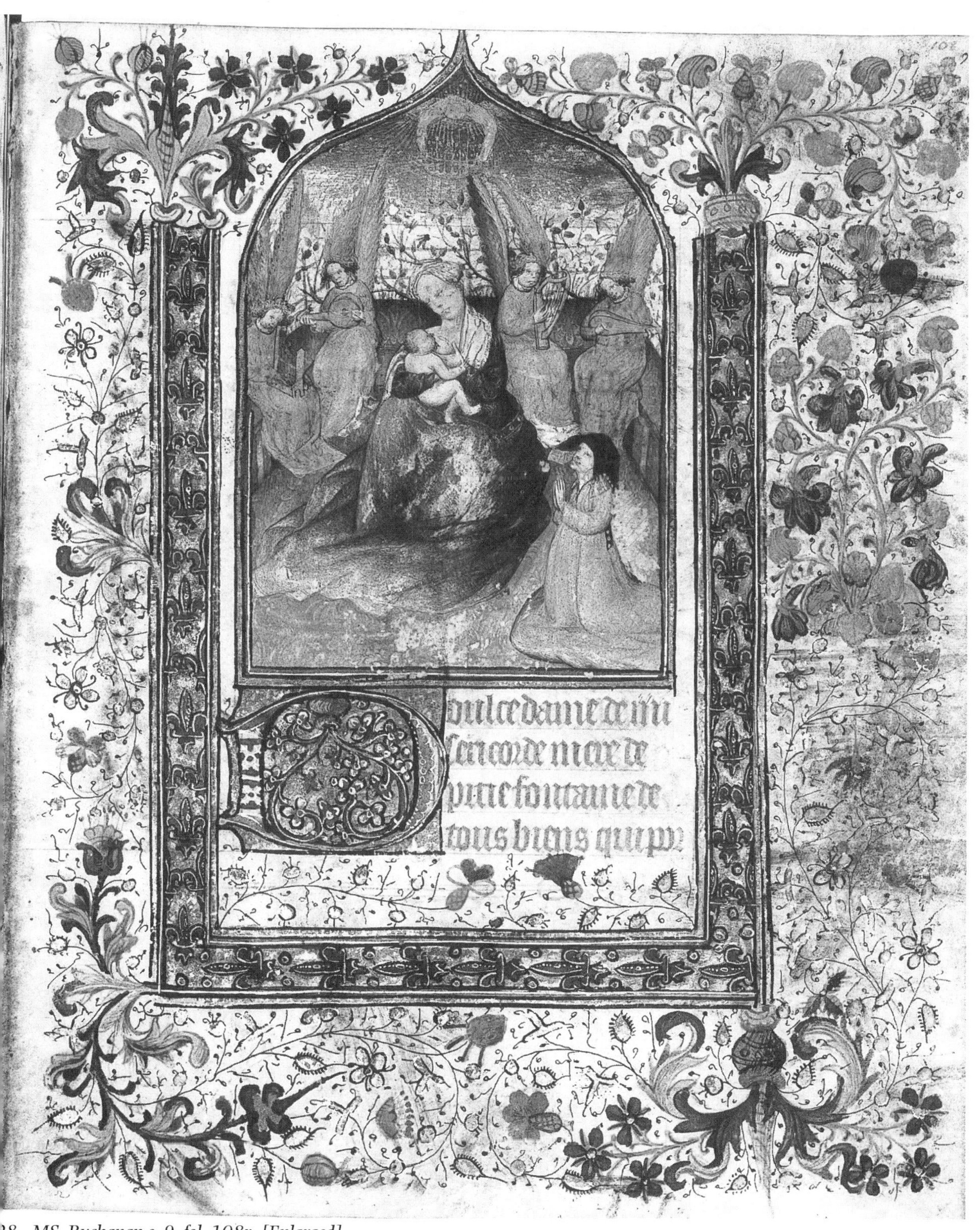

28. *MS. Buchanan e. 9, fol. 108r.* [Enlarged]

each with a three-sided frame (open at the top) usually of gold and painted foliage; most of the miniatures damaged by considerable rubbing, smudging, and/or flaking of the pigments and gold, causing underdrawing to be visible in some places (e.g. David's garments, fol. 76r); silver and white have usually oxidised: (fol. 13r) Pericopes. St. John writing on Patmos, his eagle beside him, a large demon behind him stealing his pen-case and upsetting his inkpot; the sky and water presumably once silver, now oxidised. [Above three lines of text].
(fol. 26r) Hours of the Virgin, Matins. Annunciation; the architectural setting very like that in Paris, BnF, ms. lat. 9471, fol. 21r (ill. in Meiss and Thomas *The Rohan Hours* (see below), pl. 27), but reversed.
(fol. 37v) Lauds. Visitation; the Virgin holding a book.
[Prime miniature missing: offset on fol. 48r].
(fol. 53v) Terce. Annunciation to three Shepherds, each holding a long curved houlette (pl. 27).
[Sext and None miniatures missing: offsets on fols. 57v and 60v respectively].
(fol. 63v) Vespers. Flight into Egypt; the Holy Family leave a city gate; the landscape largely oxidised.
(fol. 70r) Compline. Coronation of the Virgin; the faces largely oxidised. [Above three lines of text].
(fol. 76r) Penitential Psalms. David in Penitence, in a landscape.
(fol. 94v) Hours of the Cross. Crucifixion; a crowded composition, with the Good and Bad Thieves, and numerous figures standing or on horseback.
(fol. 101v) Hours of the Holy Spirit. Pentecost; the Apostles around the Virgin; diaper background.
(fol. 108r) Fifteen Joys. The Virgin nursing the Child in a rose-garden, flanked by music-making angels, another angel holding a crown above her head; a supplicant lay-woman in the foreground, wearing a black head-dress lined(?) and edged in gold; the gold framing filled with blue fleurs-de-lis (pl. 28).
(fol. 113v) Seven Requests. The Last Judgement; the Virgin and John the Baptist(?) either side of the Redeemer; a sword and lily either side of his mouth; below them, angels sound the last trump, figures rise from graves, with the Blessed led by an angel to Christ's right, the Damned dragged by a demon into a hell-mouth at his left; the sky oxidised.
(fol. 120r) Office of the Dead. Funeral Service; in a chapel, with a priest celebrating a requiem mass at an altar, with an altarpiece depicting the Crucifixion; black-clad mourners(?) in stalls to the left of the bier, nuns(?) to the right, wearing white/grey habits and black head-dresses, one following the text with her finger in an open book. [Above three lines of text.]

Vertical borders to every page, to both sides of the text, with stylized and semi-naturalistic plants amongst gold ivy-leaf decoration and four-petalled flowers.

Three- or four-line initals in red, pink, blue and white on a gold ground at the start of major textual units, hours, etc.; similar two-line initials to psalms, capitula, lessons, etc.; similar one-line initials to verses and minor divisions; line-fillers throughout.

The miniatures are in the style of the Master of the Rohan Hours (on whom see
— not mentioning the present manuscript — Millard Meiss and Marcel Thomas,
The Rohan Book of Hours: Bibliothèque nationale, Paris (MS. latin 9471) (London,
1973); and Millard Meiss, *French painting in the time of Jean de Berry: the
Limbourgs and their contemporaries* (2 vols., New York and London, 1974)); they
were published as being by the Rohan Master by Porcher, based on information
provided by Otto Pächt.

Physical Description

MATERIAL: parchment, originally of very fine quality.
DIMENSIONS: the leaves 171-3 x 136-8 mm., some miniatures considerably
cropped at the top and cropped close to the border decoration at the fore- and
lower edges.
NUMBER OF LEAVES: i (modern paper) + 189 + i (modern paper).
FOLIATION: modern, in pencil: i, 1-160a, 160b-189.
COLLATION: mostly on quires of 8 leaves: I^{12} (fols. 1-12) | II^8 (fols. 13-19), III^6
(fols. 20-25) | $IV-V^8$ (fols. 26-41), VI^{8-1} (7th leaf excised, leaving a stub after fol.
47) (fols. 42-48), VII^8 (fols. 49-56), VIII^{8-2} (2nd & 6th leaves excised, leaving stubs
after fols. 57 & 60) (fols. 57-61), IX^8 (fols. 62-69), X^6 (fols. 70-75) | $XI-XIV^8$ (fols.
76-107) | XV^8 (fols. 108-115), XVI^4 (fols. 116-119) | $XVII-XXI^8$ (fols. 120-159),
XXII^4 (fols. 160a-162) | $XXIII-XXV^8$ (fols. 163-186), XXVI^{4-2} (1st & 2nd leaves
excised, leaving stubs before fol. 187) (fols. 187-188); no catchwords visible.
RULING: 16 lines ruled in pale red ink (the calendar with 18 lines ruled) between
single vertical bounding lines extending the full height of the page, the first and
last horizontal extending the full width of the page; the ruled space 89-90 x 61-3
mm.; no prickings visible.
SCRIPT: written in gothic bookhand, in two sizes according to liturgical function,
probably by a single main scribe; with 15 lines of text per page (the calendar with
17 lines); the written space *c.*88 x 60 mm.; text items 5(i)-(ii) (fol. 75r-v) added
in 15th-cent. gothic bookhand; text item 16 (fols. 161v-162v) is written in a
finer 15th-cent. gothic bookhand, but presumably in a lower-quality ink, since it
has largely powdered away.
RUBRICATION: most headings in red, rather brown in text item 16, rather purple
from fol. 163r to the end.
SEC. FOL.: (calendar) 'KL Fevrier a'; (text, fol. 14) 'illuminat omnem'.

Binding

Sewn on three cords, with head- and (detached) tail-bands, (five(?) previous
sewing stations are perhaps visible, but the gutter fold is damaged and dirty);
bound in 17th(?)-cent. parchment over thin pasteboards, stamped in gilt with an
oval wreath in the centre of each cover; the spine divided into three compartments
by four horizontal gilt bars, each compartment stamped in gilt with a small five-
petalled rose; remains of the upper of two pairs of leather ties at the fore-edge;
the edges, especially of the upper cover, damaged (perhaps largely by rodents)

and repaired; the bottom edge of the upper cover repaired with later parchment;
modern flyleaves conjoint with the pastedowns (without watermarks); the edges
of the leaves gilt.

Provenance

1. Unidentified laywoman, depicted on fol. 108r; van Dijk implies that a
prayer at the end of the Office of the Dead, 'Deus venie largitor ...' (fol. 160b r-v)
indicates that 'the volume was written for a member of a religious community',
presumably because it includes '... ut nostre congregationis fratres familiares
benefactores nostros ...', but this textual evidence is weak (cf. the versions in MS.
Buchanan e. 10, fols. 109v-110r and Wordsworth, *Horae Eboracenses*, 111), and
appears to be refuted by the visual evidence. The Use of the Hours of the Virgin
and of the Office of the Dead are unidentified; they do not correspond with
Troyes, Angers, or Paris, the three identified Uses for which the Rohan Master
produced Books of Hours. Several saints in the litany point rather strongly to St.-
Omer/St.-Bertin and the surrounding region: Sts. Bertin (twice), Omer, Silvinus
(relics once at St.-Omer), Piatus (relics once at St.-Omer).

2. Unidentified near-contemporary owner, diocese of Sens (?): the added texts
on fol. 75r-v suggest that a 15th-cent. owner made additions appropriate to use
in or around Sens. The suffrage to Barbara (fols. 161v-162v) was perhaps added
at about the same time, on leaves which would have been left blank at the end of
quire XXII, but which, like fol. 188v, had had the borders supplied by the original
decorators.

3. Symeon de Roussel, 1694(?); inscribed: 'Ces p(resents?) heures a | partienne
à s(ieu)r | Symeon de - | Roussel S(ieu)r decz [?] | Tauxsellecz qui | le(s)
trouuoiront | le(s) Renderont | au[?]ds S(ieu)r decz | Tauxsellecz qui | poira[?]
Le Tiy[?] | Comme Il faut | de sa[?] Ligne de | Roussel' followed by an elaborate
paraph sign; and, in darker ink with a thinner-nibbed pen, '1694' and '[S.?]
Roussel [followed by an elaborate paraph sign] | La prairie 1694.' (fol. 188v).
The binding may date from Roussel's ownership of the volume.

4. Unidentified 19th-cent. French owner; inscribed: 'Les 7. alegresses de la
Ste Vierge.' (fol. 107v).

5. John Buchanan (see Introduction, pp. xiv, xix): inscribed in pencil with the
'Descriptive list' number, '9.', in the upper left corner of the upper pastedown.

6. Rt. Hon. T. R. Buchanan (1846-1911); given to the Bodleian in 1939
by his widow, Mrs. E. O. Buchanan, when it was originally accesssioned as
MS. Lat. liturg. e. 30; re-referenced as MS. Buchanan e. 9 in 1941.

Bibliography

'Fifteen illuminated *Horae*', *BLR* 1 no. 7 (1939), 115-6, at 116 (as MS. Lat. liturg. e. 30).

Jean Porcher, *The Rohan Book of Hours* (The Faber Library of Illuminated Manuscripts: London, 1959), 32 n. 11.

van Dijk, *Handlist of Latin liturgical MSS.*, IV, 113.

Pächt & Alexander, 1, no. 678, pl. LII.

MS. Buchanan e. 10

Book of Hours, Use of Paris, in Latin and French
France, Paris; late 15th or early 16th century

Text
All except item 2 have rubrics in French.

[Item 1 occupies quire I]

1. (fols. 2r-13v) Calendar, in French, an entry for almost every day, major feasts
in gold (none of them local), the others alternately red or blue; each month
headed by a note on the length of the calendar month in gold; feasts include
'Dedicace saint eustace' (6 Oct.), but lack most of the feasts characteristic of
Paris, such as Germanus (28 May), Marcellus (3 Nov.) and Geneviève (26 Nov.).

[Items 2-3 occupy quires II-IV]

2. (fols. 14r-19v) Gospel Pericopes; John followed (fol. 15v) by the usual
antiphon, versicle, response, and the prayer 'Protector in te sperantium ...'
(cf. MS. Buchanan e. 3).

3. (fols. 19v-25r) Prayers to the Virgin:
   (i) (fols. 19v-22v) '*Deuote oraison de nostre dame* Obsecro te ... [masculine
   forms]' (cf. MS. Buchanan e. 2)
   (ii) (fols. 23r-25r, rubric on fol. 22v) '*Aultre oraison de nostre dame.* O
   intemerata ... orbis terrarum. Inclina aures tue pietatis ... [feminine forms]',
   the second word mis-written and partially corrected by erasure (pr. Wilmart,
   Auteurs spirituels, 488-90); fol. 25v ruled, otherwise blank.

[Item 4 occupies quires V-XIII]

4. (fols. 26r-91v) Hours of the Virgin, Use of Paris, with nine lessons at Matins;
fol. 70v ruled, otherwise blank.

[Items 5-13 occupy quires XIV-XXV]

5. (fols. 92r-104v) The Seven Penitential Psalms.

6. (fols. 104v-110v) Litany and collects: the litany with Martial last among the
Apostles, and including Lubin and Sulpice (14-15) among sixteen confessors,
and Geneviève (8) among thirteen virgins; followed (fol. 109v) by four collects:
(i) 'Deus cui proprium est ...' (*Corpus orationum*, no. 1143); (ii) 'Deus qui nos
patrem et matrem ...' (*ibid.*, no. 1903); (iii) 'Deus venie largitor ...' (*ibid.*, no.
2205, but mentioning '... sorores parentes amicos benefactores et
recommandatos nostros ...' after 'fratres', and '... beata maria semper uirgine ...'
in place of '... beato illi patrono nostro ...'; cf. MS. Buchanan f. 2, text item 8(iv),
and MS. Buchanan e. 9, under Provenance); (iv) 'Fidelium deus omnium
conditor ...' (*ibid.*, no. 2684b).

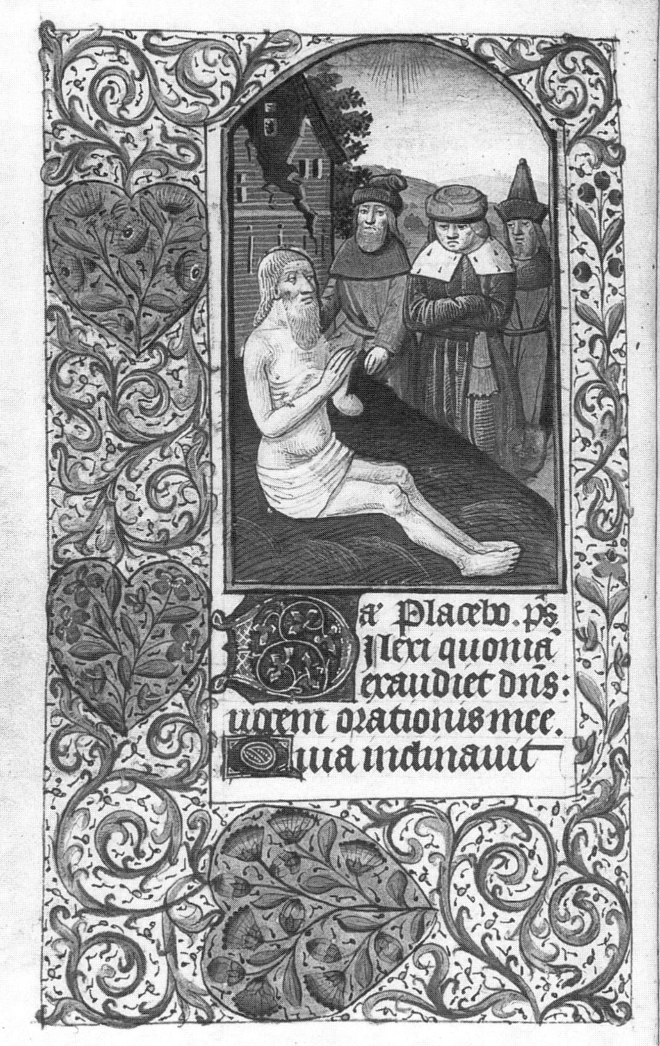

aurem suam michi: z in
diebus meis inuocabo.
Circundederunt me
dolores mortis: z pericula
inferni inuenerunt me.
Tribulatione z dolore
inueni: et nomen dni
inuocaui.
Domine libera ani
mam mea misericors
dominus et iustus: et
deus noster miseretur.
Custodiens paruulos
dominus: humiliatus
sum et liberauit me.
Conuertere anima
mea in requiem tua:
quia dominus benefe

29. MS. Buchanan e. 10, fols. 123v-124r.

7. (fols. 111r-117v, rubric on fol. 110v) Hours of the Cross.

8. (fols. 118r-123r, rubric on fol. 117v) Hours of the Holy Spirit.

9. (fols. 123v-166r) Office of the Dead, Use of Paris.

10. (fols. 166v-171r, rubric on fol. 166r) The Fifteen Joys of the Virgin, in French: '*Les xv. ioyes nostre dame.* Doulce dame de misericorde: ... mercy et vray repos. Amen Aue maria ...' (pr. Leroquais, *Livres d'heures*, II, 310-11).

11. (fols. 171v-174v, rubric on fol. 171r) The Seven Requests of Our Lord, in French: '*Les sept requestes nostre seigneur.* Doulx dieu doulx pere saincte trinite. ...' (pr. Leroquais, *Livres d'heures*, II, 309-10); followed (fol. 174r-v) by the usual rhymed verse devotion in French: 'Saincte vraie croix aouree. Qui du corps dieu fus aournee. ...' (pr. Perdrizet, *Calendrier Parisien*, 32).

12. (fols. 174v-182v) Suffrages to (i) the Trinity, and Sts. (ii) Michael, (iii) John the Baptist, (iv) James, (v) Christopher ('... michi famulo tuo ...'), (vi) Antony Abbot, (vii) Sebastian, (viii) Nicholas, (ix) Catherine, (x) Geneviève, and (xi) Barbara (the prayers pr. in *Corpus orationum* are nos. (i) 3920, (ii) 1798, (iii) 4492, (iv) 2445d, (vi) 1486, (viii) 1463, (ix) 1521, and (x) 1368); fols. 183r-184v ruled, otherwise originally blank.

13. (fols. 183r-184r) Communion prayers, added in a small 16th-cent. cursive hand:
    (i) (fol. 183r) '[title partly cropped, perhaps: Quant on veult recevoir le corps] de nostre seigneur', 'Domine non sum dignus ut intres sub tectum meum ... remissionem peccatorum meorum qui viuis et regnas ...';
    (ii) (fol. 183v) 'quant on la receu', 'Vera preceptio corporis et sanguinis tui ... vitam presentem et eternam introductio per ...';
    (iii) (fols. 183v-184r) 'oraizun apres la communium [*sic*]', 'Gratias tibi ago domine. sancte pater omnipotens eterne deus qui me indignum peccatorem ... dignatus es corpore' [ends incomplete];
the first two of these prayers frequently occur together; for all three together see e.g. Ker, *MMBL*, II, 197 arts. 13b-d; Leroquais, *Livres d'heures*, II, 232.

Decoration
Fourteen large miniatures with arched tops, all but one (fol. 92r) above five lines of text:
(fol. 14r) Pericopes. St. John writing on Patmos, with the Eagle holding his ink-pot and pen-case; some flaking of pigment, especially in the sky.
(fol. 26r) Hours of the Virgin, Matins. Annunciation; the Virgin with an open book on her lap.
(fol. 60r) Prime. Nativity; the Virgin and Joseph adore the Child.
(fol. 66r) Terce. Annunciation to the Shepherds, one with bagpipes.
(fol. 71r) Sext. Adoration of the Magi.
(fol. 75v) None. Presentation in the Temple.
(fol. 80r) Vespers. Flight into Egypt, from right to left; Joseph's face and the sky flaking.

(fol. 86v) Compline. Coronation of the Virgin.
(fol. 92r) Penitential Psalms. King David in Penitence; some striations of pigment.
[Above six lines of text].
(fol. 111r) Hours of the Cross. Crucifixion, with the Virgin and John to the left,
the centurian Longinus and other soldiers to the right.
(fol. 118r) Hours of the Spirit. Pentecost.
(fol. 123v) Office of the Dead. Job on the Dungheap, with his three friends (pl. 29).
(fol. 166v) Fifteen Joys. The Virgin and Child enthroned, adored by angels.
(fol. 171v) Seven Requests. The Trinity: the Son holding the Cross, the Father
wearing a papal tiara and holding an orb, seated together, both holding an open
book between them, the Dove above.

Ten small miniatures to the suffrages, mostly seven lines high:
(fol. 175r) St. Michael (eight-line).
(fol. 175v) St. John the Baptist.
(fol. 176r) St. James the Greater.
(fol. 176v) St. Christopher; the hermit in the background.
(fol. 178r) St. Antony Abbot.
(fol. 179r) St. Sebastian.
(fol. 180r) St. Nicholas and the three boys in the tub.
(fol. 180v) St. Catherine.
(fol. 181r) St. Geneviève, with an angel preventing a devil from extinguishing
her taper.
(fol. 181v) St. Barbara.

One six-line historiated initial:
(fol. 49r) Hours of the Virgin, Lauds. Visitation.

Two five-line historiated initials:
(fol. 19v) *Obsecro te.* Virgin and Child enthroned; the Virgin holding a red fruit(?).
(fol. 23r) *O intemerata.* Pietà.

The large miniatures and the Lauds initial are surrounded by four-sided framed
borders of stylised foliage on a plain parchment ground, and variously-shaped
panels of naturalistic plants on a painted gold ground; the small miniatures and
five-line historiated initials surrounded by similar three-sided borders (in the outer
margins); similar one-sided border panels on all pages with a two-line initial.

Four- or three-line initials in blue and red, enclosing foliage, on a gold ground, at
the start of each text with a large miniature; two-line initals in gold, on a blue
and red ground with white tracery, to psalms, capitula, lessons, etc. and the KL
monograms in the calendar; similar one-line initials to verses and other minor
divisions; similar line-fillers throughout.

Fol. 1 is an inserted leaf of parchment printed on the recto with a 16th-cent.
German(?) engraving of the Crucifixion, signed 'G.N.'; gilded and hand-coloured.

Physical Description

MATERIAL: parchment.

DIMENSIONS: the leaves 157-8 x 105 mm.

NUMBER OF LEAVES: ii (modern paper, the first conjoint with the pastedown) + 184 + ii (modern paper, the second conjoint with the pastedown).

FOLIATION: modern, in pencil: i-ii, 1-186.

COLLATION: mostly on quires of 8 leaves: I^{12+1} (1st leaf added, fol. 1) (fols. 1-13) | II^6 (fols. 14-19), III^4 (fols. 20-23), IV^2 (fols. 24-25) | V-XII^8 (fols. 26-89), XIII^2 (fols. 90-91) | XIV-XVII^8 (fols. 92-123), XVIII^4 (fols. 124-127), XIX-XXIV^8 (fols. 128-175), XXV^{10-1} (10th leaf cancelled, after fol. 184) (fols. 176-184); a trace of a catchword survives at fol. 127v.

RULING: 19 lines ruled in red ink (in both calendar and text), between single vertical bounding lines extending the full height of the page, the top and bottom horizontal lines extending the full width of the page; the ruled space 90-2 x 47-9 mm.; no prickings visible.

SCRIPT: written in a gothic liturgical bookhand in two sizes, according to liturgical function; with 18 lines of text per page; the written space approx. 88 x 48 mm.

RUBRICATION: headings in red, capitals touched with a yellow wash.

SEC. FOL.: (calendar, fol. 3) 'KL Feurier a', (text, fol. 15) 'venientem in'.

Binding

Sewing not visible; tightly rebound between 19th-cent. pasteboards, re-using panels of 16th-cent. brown leather with gilt tooling à la fanfare, Paris *c.*1580-90, in the style associated with Clovis Eve (pl. 1; of the bindings ill. in Hobson, *Les reliures à la fanfare*, the boards are closest in general design to pl. XXI b); the centre of each cover inlaid with a 17th-cent. oval medallion of red leather tooled in gilt (perhaps replacing the identifying mark of a previous owner); the spine similarly tooled, without raised bands or title-piece (similar in design to *ibid.* pl. XIXa); coloured endbands; the edges of the leaves and boards gilt. Boxed.

Provenance

1. Perhaps made for use in Paris, and presumably still there when bound in the late 16th cent.; fol. 1 was perhaps added at the same time.

2. Unidentified English 19th-cent. owner: no markings characteristic of booksellers survive, since the endleaves have been replaced, but 'Small office of the | Virgin' has been written in pencil below the image on fol. 1r.

3. John Buchanan (see Introduction, pp. xiv, xix); inscribed in pencil with the 'Descriptive list' number, '10.', in the top left corner of the upper pastedown.

4. Rt. Hon. T. R. Buchanan (1846-1911); given to the Bodleian in 1939 by his widow, Mrs. E. O. Buchanan, when it was accessioned as MS. Lat. liturg. e. 31; re-referenced as MS. Buchanan e. 10 in 1941.

Bibliography

'Fifteen illuminated *Horae*', *BLR* 1 no. 7 (1939), 115-6, at 115 (as MS. Lat. liturg. e. 31).

S. Gibson, 'Bookbindings in the Buchanan Collection', *BLR* 2 no. 16 (1941), 6-12, at 9-10.

van Dijk, *Handlist of Latin liturgical MSS.*, IV, 90.

Pächt & Alexander, 1, no. 798.

MS. Buchanan e. 11

Book of Hours, Use unidentified, in Latin and French
French Flanders; early 15th century

Text
Short added texts, which occur intermittently throughout the manuscript, are
listed following the original texts, as sections [II]-[IV] below.
Most of the texts in section [I] have rubrics with spellings characteristic of
French Flanders (e.g. 'tierche', 'lichon').

[I]

[Item 1 occupies quires I-II]

1. (fols. 2r-7v) Calendar, in French, rather sparse; lacking Feb., Mar., May,
June, Sept., and Oct. due to the loss of two leaves after each of fols. 2, 3, and 5;
each month headed by a note on the length of the calendar and lunar month;
major feasts (in red) include Nicasius of Rheims (14 Dec.); other feasts include
Aldegundis ('Audegone') (30 Jan.), 'Patris' (16 Apr.), 'Rufin' (19 Apr.), Thomas
the apostle (3 July), Milburga (10 July [*sic*]; perhaps an error for Mildred, whose
feast-day is 13 July), Vincent, abbot of Soignies (14 July), 'Rufin' (27 Aug.),
Hubert, of Liège (3 Nov.), 'Claudin' (8 Nov.), Livin (12 Nov.), Linus (26 Nov.),
Alexander (18 Dec.), 'Paulin' (23 Dec.); with 15th-cent. additions, in various
hands, including Peter ('saint piere le martir prescheur') (29 Apr.), Arnulf of Metz
(18 July), Dominic (5 Aug.), Roche, in plummet (16 Aug.), and Fiacre (30 Aug.).

[Items 2-5 occupy quires III-VII]

2. (fols. 8r-10v) Hours of the Cross.

3. (fols. 11r-13v) Hours of the Holy Spirit.

4. (fols. 14r-46v) Hours of the Virgin, Use unidentified, with three lessons at
Matins; the antiphon and capitulum at Prime are: 'O admirabile ...', and 'Ego
mater pulcre dilectionis ...'; at None they are: 'Germinavit radix ...', and 'Per te
dei genitrix ...'.

5. (fol. 47r-v) Hymn: 'Veni creator spiritus mentes tuorum uisita ...' (*Repertorium
hymnologicum*, no. 21204; pr. *Analecta Hymnica*, II (1888), 93-4 no. 132).

[Items 6-8 occupy quires VIII-XI]

6. (fols. 48r-56v) The Seven Penitential Psalms.

7. (fols. 56v-59v) Litany and collects, the litany with no local saints, followed
(fol. 59r-v) by two collects: (i) 'Deus qui [*sic*] proprium est misereri ...' (pr. *Corpus
orationum*, no. 1143); and (ii) 'Fidelium deus omnium conditor et redemptor ...'
(*ibid.*, no. 2684b).

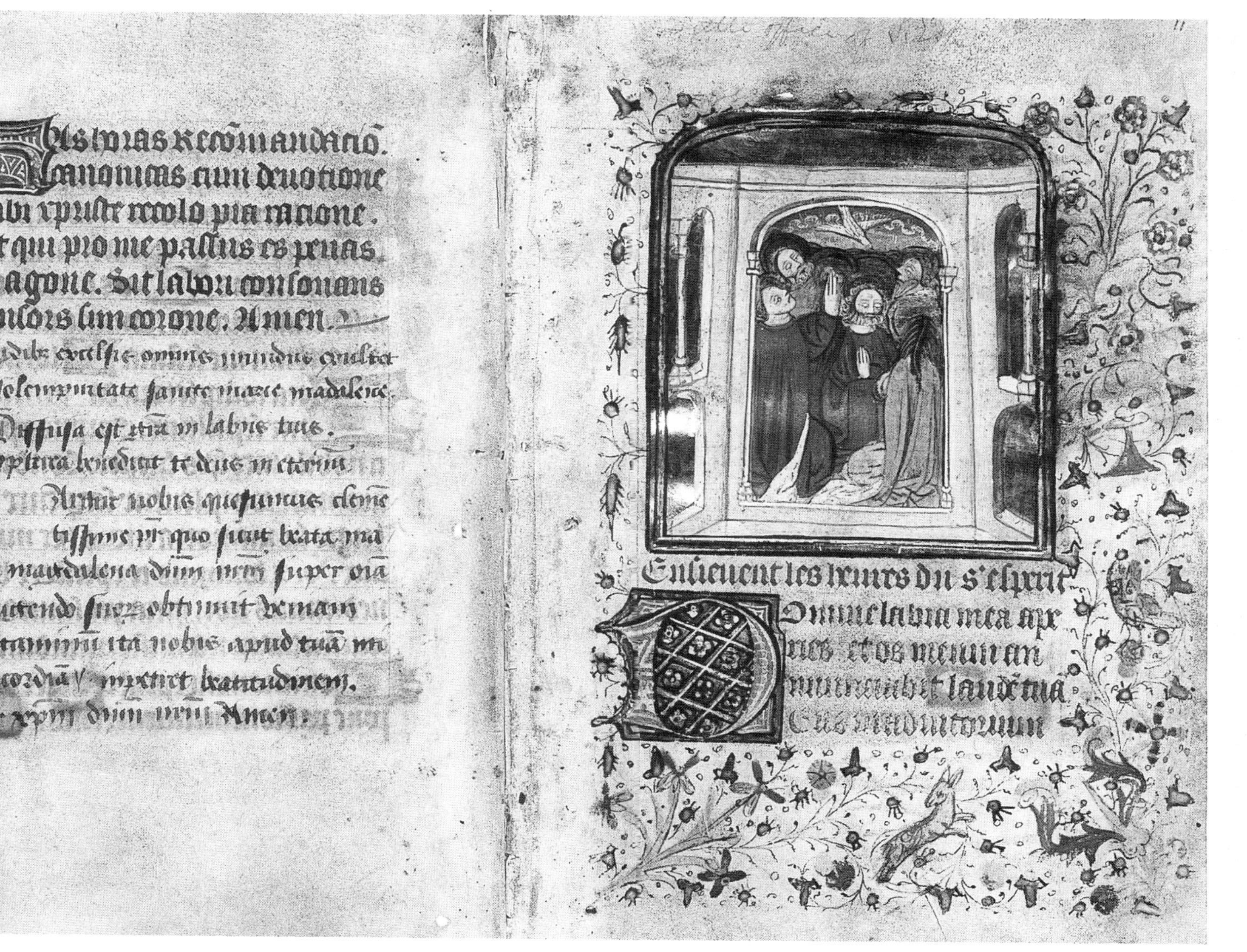

30. *MS. Buchanan e. 11, fols. 10v-11r.*

8. (fols. 60r-78v) Office of the Dead, Use unidentified, with three lessons at Matins; with the following lessons, responses, and versicles: I 'Parce michi ...', 'Credo quod ...', 'Quem uisurus ...'; II 'Tedet animam ...', 'Qui lazarum ...', 'Qui uenturus ...'; III 'Manus tue ...', 'Libera me domine de morte ...', 'Dies illa ...'.

[II]

9. (fols. 79r-84r) Three prayers to the Virgin added at the end of the main text, by a near-contemporary scribe, for a female supplicant:

 (i) (fols. 79r-81r) '[O] intemerata ... orbis terrarum Inclina aures tue pietatis ... [feminine forms]' (pr. Wilmart, *Auteurs spirituels*, 488-90);

 (ii) (fol. 81r) Suffrage to the Virgin, with antiphon, versicle, and the prayer '[D]eus qui in sancta cruce pro salute nostra pendens ... in uitam eternam introducant Per ...';

 (iii) (fols.81v-84r) '[O]bsecro te ... [feminine forms]' (pr. Wordsworth, *Horae Eboracenses*, 66-7); fol. 84v originally blank.

[III]

10. Suffrages to saints, added in the 15th cent. in blank spaces throughout the main texts, by perhaps two scribes, one of them responsible only for (i):

 (i) (fol. 7v) Suffrage to St. Fiacre (the prayer perhaps a version of that pr. as *Corpus orationum*, no. 3374);

 (ii) (fol. 10v) Suffrage to Mary Magdalen (the prayer pr. *ibid.*, no. 3231);

 (iii) (fol. 13v) Suffrage to St. Hubert (the prayer a version of that pr. *ibid.*, no. 1999);

 (iv) (fols. 46v and 78v) Suffrage to St. Margaret (the prayer a version of that pr. *ibid.*, no. 3125b).

11. (fol. 47v) The Verses of St. Bernard: '[I]llumina oculos. ... Ora pro nobis beate bernarde.', the first two verses given by cue only; the verses in the same order as in MS. Buchanan e. 9, fols. 118v-119r but with verses (iii) and (iv) as listed there run together as one; followed (fol. 59v) by the usual prayer: '[O]mnipotens sempiterne deus qui ezechie regi Iude ... misericordiam tuam impetrare. Per ...'.

[IV]

12. Various prayers and verses in French, added in the 16th(?) cent., probably by a single scribe, on the final leaves:

 (i) (fol. 84r) a letter 'M' surrounded by four comma-shaped marks, above '[O?] bien doret [...?] le coeur[?] mary femme ... cest dure destinee', followed by 'laet drushet | varen', and 'kf hfs mbxkf'(?), the latter presumably in code (for example, if each letter is replaced by the preceding letter of the alphabet, one may decode it as 'je ger la vie');

 (ii) (fol. 84v) three quatrains:

  (a) 'Bien te doy hain[?] et blasmer ...' ('bien te doy' repeated at the bottom of the page);

  (b) 'Ma joie nest que de pleurer ...';

  (c) 'Mon vieng amor[?] fin[?] ...';

(iii) (fol. 85v) a quatrain, 'Argent faict raige | Amour faict mariaige | ...'; with 'Le present'(?) written above, in lighter ink; and '1567 29 Juin [?]' written below, in darker ink.

Decoration

Five large miniatures of mediocre quality, gently arched, above five lines of text, within a gold framing line, above a four-line initial, and surrounded by a four-sided border (see below):

(fol. 8r) Hours of the Cross. Crucifixion, with the Virgin and John.

(fol. 11r) Hours of the Holy Spirit. Pentecost; depicted as if seen through the doorway of a building with two arcades of arches to each side (pl. 30).

(fol. 14r) Hours of the Virgin. Annunciation; the border incorporating a lily-pot, peacock, and crown.

(fol. 48r) Penitential Psalms. Last Judgement.

(fol. 60r) Office of the Dead. Funeral Service, with the bier before an altar, three grey-clad mourners, and two clerics at a lectern.

Four-sided borders surrounding miniatures and other pages with a four-line initial, of gold ivy-leaf, stylized and naturalistic foliage, occasional animals and birds e.g. a rabbit(?) (fol. 11r), a crane(?) (fol. 21v), a peacock (fols. 31v, 43r), a cat with a mouse (fol. 48r), and a crown (fols. 14r, 60r); four-line foliate initials at the start of the main texts and each hour in the Hours of the Virgin; two-line initials in gold against blue and red grounds with white tracery, to psalms, canticles, lessons, the KL monograms in the calendar, etc.; similar one-line initials to verses and other minor divisions; line-fillers in the litany.

Physical Description

MATERIAL: parchment; the margins around the text frequently marked, as if by attempted washing.

DIMENSIONS: the leaves 169-70 x 119-21 mm.

NUMBER OF LEAVES: iii (paper, the first marbled, originally conjoint with the pastedown) + i (parchment, apparently added, 16th-cent.(?)) + 83 + i (parchment, apparently added, 16th(?)-cent.) + iii (paper, the last marbled, conjoint with the pastedown).

FOLIATION: modern, in pencil: i-iii, 1-88.

COLLATION: mostly on quires of 8 leaves: the structure of the first two quires is uncertain, but there are at least six leaves missing from them (see under Text): I$^{?6-4+1}$ (? 2nd & 3rd leaves missing after fol. 2; 5th & 6th leaves missing after fol. 3; 1st leaf added, fol. 1) (fols. 1-3), II$^{?6-2}$ (? 3rd & 4th leaves missing, after fol. 5) (fols. 4-7) | III-VII^8 (fols. 8-47) | VIII-XI^8 (fols. 48-79) | XII^{6-1+1} (6th leaf cancelled, another leaf added in its place, fol. 85) (fols. 80-85); the leaves containing the miniatures were excised, and re-attached on parchment strips (that on fol. 14v has traces of writing), as were fols. 38 and 80; no catchwords visible; 18th/19th-cent. quire signatures in arabic numerals, in ink: 1-12, in the upper gutter margin of the first recto of each quire.

RULING: 18 lines ruled in pale red ink, between single vertical bounding lines extending the full height of the page, the top and bottom horizontals extending the full width of the page; quire XII is ruled with only 17 lines, and the bottom horizontal does not extend the full width; the ruled space 102-4 x 72-4 mm.; no prickings visible.

SCRIPT: written in a spiky gothic bookhand; for 17 lines of text per page; the written space *c.* 102 x 71 mm.; quire XII with 16 lines of text; item 9 in a near-contemporary more rounded gothic bookhand, text items 10-12 in 15th- and 16th-cent. *lettre bâtarde* scripts (see pl. 30).

RUBRICATION: headings in red.

SEC. FOL.: (calendar, fol. 3) 'KL Avril'; (text, fol. 9) 'nobis peccatoribus'.

Binding

Sewn on five cords (some sewing stations of a previous binding visible), with endbands; bound in 19th-cent. brown leather over pasteboards; the covers, edges, and turn-ins of the boards roll-tooled in blind all over with foliate wave-patterns and geometric designs; the body of the book detached from the binding at the upper joint; the pastedowns and their conjoint leaves marbled; fol. ii with a bunch of grapes as a watermark; one green silk bookmark; the edges of the leaves gilt. At some time after the book had had its excised leaves re-inserted, rough holes were crudely stabbed through the gutter margin—presumably rudimentary stab-stitching for a previous binding.

Provenance

1. Unidentified original owner: the Picard(?) French and some of the saints in the calendar (Aldegund, Hubert, Livin, etc.) suggest that the book was made for use in French Flanders, perhaps for someone with Dominican interest (Peter Martyr, Dominic); text item 9 was added for a woman, who may have been the original owner.

2. Anthoine Hanvbeel, Ghent, 16th cent.; inscribed (fol. 1r): 'A dieu Lhonneur | 1570 [the date erased but visible under UV light] | Antoine Hanvbeel [read by van Dijk as Hautbeel] | advocat au conseil | de Flandres | A Gand'; below this, in another hand, six lines mentioning '... Mʳ Floreins Hanvbeel ...'; also inscribed with the start of another 16th-cent. ownership(?) inscription in another hand (fol. 85v): 'Le present [   ]'.

3. Unidentified English bookseller, 19th cent.; inscribed in the top left corner of the last flyleaf (fol. 88r) with a price-code(?) in pencil: 'h v m', vertically, each letter separated from the next by a horizontal line; other pencil notes erased, but including (fol. i verso): '[Interesting?] early MS' and '£4 11s 6'; inscriptions in pencil in English (now largely illegible) identify the major texts, e.g. fols. 8r, 11r, etc.

4. John Buchanan (see Introduction, pp. xiv, xix): inscribed in pencil with the 'Descriptive list' number, '11.', in the top left corner of fol. i verso.

5. Rt. Hon. T. R. Buchanan (1846-1911); given to the Bodleian in 1939 by his widow, Mrs. E. O. Buchanan, when it was accessioned as MS. Lat. liturg. e. 32; re-referenced as MS. Buchanan e. 11 in 1941.

Bibliography

'Fifteen illuminated *Horae*', *BLR* 1 no. 7 (1939), 115-6, at 115 (as MS. Lat. liturg. e. 32).

van Dijk, *Handlist of Latin liturgical MSS.*, IV, 131.

Pächt & Alexander, 1, no. 303.

Avril Henry, ed., *Biblia Pauperum: a facsimile and edition* (Aldershot, 1987), 160.

MS. Buchanan e. 12

Book of Hours, Use of Bayeux, in Latin and French
France, Normandy; late 15th or early 16th century

Text

[I]

[Item 1 occupies quire I]

1. (fols. 1r-3v) Calendar, about half-full, major feasts in red, laid out in two columns with two months per page; feasts, several of them characteristic of Bayeux (cf. Leroquais, *Bréviaires*, I, 105-8 no. 72), include: William of Donjeon (10 Jan.), Ivo (25 Feb., 19 Apr., and 19 May), Honorina (27 Feb.), the translation of the relics of Ragnobert, bishop of Bayeux (16 May), Ursinus (12 June and 30 Dec.), Manvoeus, bishop of Bayeux (28 May and 15 July), the feast of the relics of Bayeux (1 July), Arnulf of Metz (18 July), Vivianus of Saintes (27 Aug.), and Gerald of Aurillac (13 Oct.); 'S. Boni' occurs on 17 Feb., 19 Mar., and 5 May.

[Items 2-7 occupy quires II-VI]

2. (fols. 4r-5v) Gospel Pericopes; John followed by the usual antiphon, versicle, response, and the prayer 'Protector in te sperantium ...' (cf. MS. Buchanan e. 3).

3. (fols. 5v-8r) Prayers to the Virgin:
  (i) (fols. 5v-6v) *'De nostra domina. Obsecro te ...'* [masculine forms] (cf. MS. Buchanan e. 2);
  (ii) (fols. 6v-8r) 'O intemerata ... orbis terrarum. De te enim ...' [masculine forms] (pr. Wilmart, *Auteurs spirituels*, 494-5).

4. (fols. 8v-24r) Hours of the Virgin, Use of Bayeux, with three lessons at Matins; with the Hours of the Cross intermixed; Prime starting imperfect in Ps. 2:5 (at '| | Tunc loquetur ...') due to the loss of a leaf before fol. 18; None ending imperfect in Ps. 127:2 (at '... manducabis | |') and Vespers starting imperfect at the cue for Ps. 123 ('| | Nisi quia dominus.'), due to the loss of a leaf after fol 21; fol. 15v ruled, otherwise blank; fol. 17r-v also ruled, otherwise blank, after Matins of the Hours of the Cross, at the end of quire III.

5. (fols. 24v-28v) The Seven Penitential Psalms.

6. (fols. 28v-29v) Litany and collects; the short litany (fols. 28v-29r) with Uriel last among four angels; and including Silvester, Leo, Antony and Ivo as the only confessors; followed (fol. 29r-v) by two collects: (i) 'Deus cui proprium ...' (pr. *Corpus orationum*, no. 1143); (ii) 'Fidelium deus omnium conditor ...' (pr. *ibid.*, no. 2684b);

7. (fols. 30r-40v) Office of the Dead, Use of Bayeux.

benedictio tua . Ps
Laudate dñm oēs
gentes laudate
eum omnes populi.
Qia confirmata est
super nos mia eius et
veritas dñi manet ie
ternum.
Gloria. ã Beata mr
et intacta virgo glori
osa regina mundi iter
cede pro nobis ad dñm
Ab inicio et antese
cula creata sum
et usqz ad futuri secz
non desinam et in ha
bitatione sancta cora
ipso ministraui. Deo
gratias. R Aue maria
gratia plena. Dñs tecū.
Aue maria. V Benedi
cta tu in mulieribz et
bñdictus fructus ventris
tui. Dñs te. Gloria pa.
Aue maria. V Sancta
dei genitrix virgo sep
maria. R Intercede p
nobis ad dñm deū no
stri. Dñe exaudi. Et.

Concede quesumus
omnipotens et mi
sericors deus fragilitati
nostre presidium ut qui
sancte dei genitricis et vir
ginis marie memoria
agimus intercessionis ei
auxilio a nostris iniqui
tatibz resurgamus. Per.
Deus in adiutorium.
Ora prima dictus
est ihesus ad pila
tum. falsis testimonijs
multum accusatuin.
In collo percutiunt ma
nibz ligatum. Vultum
dei conspuunt lumen celi
gratiam. ã Adoramus
domine ihesu criste.
Deus in adiutorium.
Dż virtute maria
cristus fuit natus
Crucifixus mortuus
atqz tumulatus. Resur
gens discipulis fuit de
monstratus. Et ipse
cernentibz celis eleuatz
ã Veni sancte spūs. oro
Omnipotens sempet.

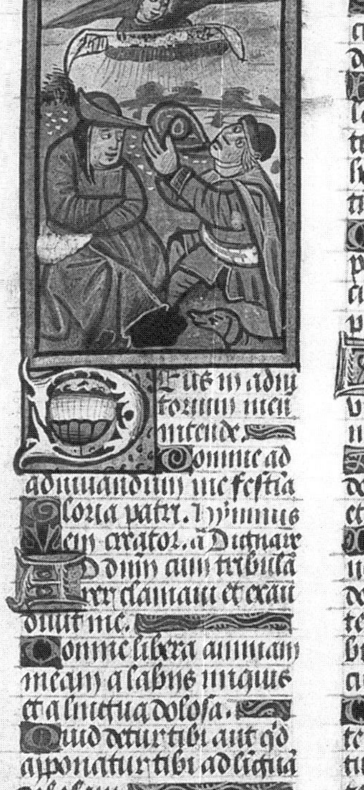

Eus in adiu
torium meū
intende.
Domine ad
adiuuandum me festina
Gloria patri. Hymnus
Veni creator. ã Dignare
Domine cum tribula
rer clamaui et exau
diuit me.
Domine libera animam
meam a labijs iniquis
et a lingua dolosa.
Quid detur tibi aut qd
apponatur tibi ad linguā
dolosam.

Sagitte potentis ac
ute cum carbonibus
desolatorijs.
Heu michi quia inco
latus meus prolonga
tus est habitaui cum
habitantibz cedar mul
tū incola fuit aīa mea.
Qui his qui oderūt
pacem eram pacificus
cum loquebar illis i
pugnabant me gratis.
Leuaui oculos
meos in montes
unde veniet auxiliū
michi.
Auxilium meum a
domino qui fecit celū
et terram.
Non det in comotio
nem pedem tuū neqz
dormitet qui custodit
te. Ecce non dormita
bit neqz dormiet qui
custodit israel.
Dominus custodit
te dominus protectio
tua super manū dex
teram tuam

31. MS. Buchanan e. 12, fols. 18v-19r.

[II]

[Item 8 occupies quire VII]

8. (fols. 41r-43v) Rhyming Verse Devotion in French, in ten nine-line stanzas, an addition of the early 16th cent.: 'Uecy lhome saint innocent et iuste. / A moy preuost dessoubz cezar auguste / Par les faulx iuifz faulcement accuse. / Uecy lhomme qui fut fort et robuste. ... Contemplatifz regardes uecy lhomme' (cf. Sonet, *Répertoire*, no. 2343).

Decoration

Three (of an original five?) large miniatures, each with an arched top, framed by a band of painted gold, above a six- or seven-line initial on a painted gold ground, in one column, containing a flowering plant; surrounded by a full border of naturalistic and stylised foliage, flowers, fruit, birds, etc., on painted gold grounds (that on fol. 8v in compartments of various shapes, some on coloured grounds):
(fol. 8v) Hours of the Virgin, Matins. Annunciation.
[Prime miniature on the recto of the missing leaf excised before fol. 18; offsets on fol. 17v appear to show a full border, and the bottom of the miniature seven lines from the bottom of the page, more than one column wide.]
[Vespers miniature on the verso of the missing leaf excised after fol. 21; offsets on fol. 22r indicate that it had a full border.]
(fol. 24v) Penitential Psalms. David in Penitence, in a landscape.
(fol. 30r) Office of the Dead. Burial of a shroud-wrapped corpse; with several black-clad mourners, and two coped priests, one with an aspergill(?), reading from a book held by an attendant.

Seven smaller miniatures, twelve or thirteen lines high, one column wide, at the start of each hour from Lauds to Compline, each with a four-line initial (five-line on fol. 4r) alternately in red and white, or blue and white, against a painted gold ground, each containing a flower:
(fol. 4r) Pericopes. St. John on Patmos.
(fol. 12r) Hours of the Virgin, Lauds. Visitation.
(fol. 16r) Hours of the Cross. Crucifixion; the Virgin to Christ's right, two men (not St. John) to his left.
(fol. 19r) Hours of the Virgin; Terce. Annunciation to two Shepherds (pl. 31).
(fol. 20r) Sext. Adoration of the Magi.
(fol. 21r) None. Flight into Egypt, from right to left.
(fol. 22v) Compline. Coronation of the Virgin.

Two-line initials alternately in blue and white, or red and white, on a painted gold ground, containing a flower design, to psalms, capitula, prayers, the KL monograms in the calendar, etc.; two-line initials in blue and white against a painted gold ground, containing a flower, in a different style, at the start of each stanza on fols. 41v-43v; one-line initials to verses, in gold on an alternately blue or red ground, each at the start of a new line; line-fillers comprising patterns in painted gold on panels of blue and red.

One large added 16th-cent. miniature, with an arched top, above four lines of text and a three-line initial in lilac against a painted gold ground, containing a foliate design, surrounded by a four-sided border of flowers against a very thin painted gold ground, a banderole in the lower border inscribed 'SA(N)S FOY FAILLIR'; considerably cropped at each edge:
(fol. 41r) Vecy l'homme. Christ before Pilate; a banderole next to Pilate's mouth inscribed 'ECCE HOMO'.

Physical Description

MATERIAL: parchment.

DIMENSIONS: the leaves 162-3 x 111-3 mm.

NUMBER OF LEAVES: i (parchment, conjoint with the pastedown) + 43 + i (parchment, conjoint with the pastedown).

FOLIATION: 19th/20th-cent dark grey ink, occasionally clarified or entirely supplied in modern pencil: i, 1-44; an earlier pagination (18th-cent.?), in arabic numerals in pale brown ink, starting with '1' at fol. 4r, is largely erased but still visible on many leaves.

COLLATION: mostly on quires of 8 leaves: I^{4-1} (1st leaf cancelled, before fol. 1) (fols. 1-3) | II^6 (fols. 4-9), III^8 (fols. 10-17) | IV^{8-2} (1st leaf excised before fol.18, 6th leaf excised after fol. 21, the latter excision causing fol. 22 also to be partly cut) (fols. 18-23), V^8 (fols. 24-31), VI^{8+1} (9th leaf added, fol. 40) (fols. 32-40) | VII^{4-1} (4th leaf cancelled, after fol. 43) (fols. 41-43); no catchwords visible.

RULING: 31 lines ruled in pale red ink, in two columns, each with single vertical bounding lines extending the full height of the page, the top and bottom horizontal extending the full width of the page; the ruled space 100-2 x 67-70 mm., each column 31-2 mm. wide, the intercolumnar space 6-7 mm.; the calendar ruled with 32 lines per page, in two columns, each column 31-3 mm. wide, the ruled space 104-6 x 67-70 mm.; the intercolumnar space 6-7 mm. wide; fols. 41r-43v ruled with 21 lines in a single column, between single vertical bounding lines extending the full height of the page, the top and bottom horizontals extending the full width of the page, the ruled space c.113 x 82 mm.; prickings survive only at the fore-edge of fol. 3.

SCRIPT: written in *lettre bâtarde*, with 30 lines of text per page, in two columns; the written space of each column 100 x 30 mm.; the calendar with 31 lines of text per page, and because the names of the months are the first written line of each column, months with 31 days extend below the bottom ruled line; fols. 41r-43v with 20 lines of text per page, in a single column.

RUBRICATION: headings in red.

SEC. FOL.: (calendar) 'KL Mayus'; (text, fol. 5) 'impossibile apud'.

Binding

Sewn on three cords (further sewing-stations from a previous binding also visible) with blue endbands; bound c.1810-40 in red velvet over pasteboards, the spine with a red leather titlepiece lettered 'HORÆ | B.V.M. | MS. MEMB | SÆC. XV.'; a damaged area at the bottom of the spine is probably evidence of another label; parchment flyleaves conjoint with the pastedowns; the edges of the leaves gilt. The present binding must presumably postdate Collier's ownership, and predate the 1841 inscriptions on the flyleaves (see under Provenance).

Provenance

1. Unidentified original owner, Bayeux.

2. Unidentified owner, of Bayeux?, with the motto 'Sans foy faillir' (fol. 41r). There is an early(?) erased inscription, nineteen lines long, not legible even under UV light (fol. 15r).

3. John Payne Collier (1789-1883), the Shakespeare scholar and forger (on whom see *DNB*), before 1841: signed 'J. Payne Collier' in the upper right margin of fol. 1r, the inscription subsequently cropped in binding.

4. Unidentified English owner, 1841: inscribed (fol. i verso): 'Ms. N°. [the number obliterated with ink] | 1. Horae B.V.M. | 2. Ecce homo - Gallicè.'; and with a note (fol. 44r), dated 1841, headed 'Mus. Brit. 1072. a. | 1. [the '1' directly below the 'a', separated by a horizontal line] small 8°. lit. goth.', concerning a devotion comparable to text item 8. It has not been possible to identify the British Library volume referred to.

5. Unidentified English bookseller, 19th cent.: a cutting from a catalogue is pasted to the upper pastedown; the pastedown is also inscribed in pencil 'N/O/-' and with the price '38/0'; an erased inscription below these is illegible, even under UV light.

6. John Buchanan, bought for 38 shillings (see Introduction, pp. xiv, xix): inscribed in pencil with the 'Descriptive list' number, '12.' (subsequently crossed through in pencil), in the top right corner of fol. i recto.

7. Rt. Hon. T. R. Buchanan (1846-1911); given to the Bodleian in 1939 by his widow, Mrs. E. O. Buchanan, when it was accessioned as MS. Lat. liturg. e. 33; re-referenced as MS. Buchanan e. 12 in 1941.

Bibliography

'Fifteen illuminated *Horae*', *BLR* 1 no. 7 (1939), 115-6, at 116 (as MS. Lat. liturg. e. 33).

van Dijk, *Handlist of Latin liturgical MSS.*, IV, 35.

Pächt & Alexander, 1, no. 803.

MS. Buchanan e. 13

Book of Hours, Use of Rouen, in Latin and French
France, Rouen; 15th century, last quarter

Text
[Item 1 occupies quire I]

1. (fols. 1r-12v) Calendar in French, about half-full, major feasts in gold, the remainder alternately red or blue; feasts in gold include Gervase (19 June), Eloi (25 June), Martial (3 July), Louis IX (25 Aug.), Denis (9 Oct.), Romanus of Rouen (23 Oct.); feasts in red or blue include William of Donjeon (10 Jan.), Severus (relics at Rouen) (1 Feb.), Ansbert of Rouen (9 Feb.), Austreberta (10 Feb.), Thomas Aquinas (7 Mar.), Patrick (17 Mar.), Leodegar (27 Mar.), Hugh of Rouen (9 Apr.), the translation of Ouen (5 May), Wandrille (19 May [sic]), Hildebert (27 May), Ursinus and his translation (12 June, 30 Dec.), the translation of Romanus of Rouen (17 June), Evodius (8 July), the translation of Clarus (18 July), Fiacre (30 Aug.), Nicholas of Tolentino (10 Sept.), Lubin (15 Sept.), Francis (4 Oct.), Nicasius of Rouen (11 Oct.), Malo (15 Nov.), 'S. candre.' (19 Nov.), and Gatianus (18 Dec.).

[Items 2-3 occupy quires II-III]

2. (fols. 13r-18r) Gospel Pericopes; John followed by the usual antiphon, versicle, response, and prayer: 'Protector in te sperancium ...' (cf. MS. Buchanan e. 3), and by the prayer: 'Ecclesiam tuam quesumus domine benignus ...' (cf. Bruylants, *Oraisons*, II, no. 520).

3. (fols. 18r-26r) Prayers to the Virgin:
   (i) (fols.18r-21v) '*Oraison tres deuote de nostre dame.* Obsecro te ...' [masculine forms] (cf. MS. Buchanan e. 2);
   (ii) (fols. 21v-22v) 'Sancta maria mater domini nostri ihesu christi in manus filii tui ... in perpetuum separari. In manus tuas domine commendo spiritum meum redemisti me domine deus ueritatis.' (cf. version pr. in Lilli Gjerløw, *Adoratio crucis, the Regularis Concordia, and the Decreta Lanfranci: manuscript studies in the early medieval church of Norway* (Norwegian Universities Press, 1961), 116);
   (iii) (fols.22v-26r) '*De nostre dame.* O intemerata ... orbis terrarum. de te enim ...' [masculine forms] (pr. Wilmart, *Auteurs spirituels*, 494-5); fol. 26v ruled, otherwise blank.

[Item 4 occupies quires IV-IX]

4. (fols. 27r-49r) Hours of the Virgin, Use of Rouen, with three lessons at Matins; suffrages (fols. 46v-50r) after Lauds with rubrics in French ('*Du saint esperit.*', '*De saint nicolas*', etc.), to (i) the Holy Spirit, to Sts. (ii) Nicholas,

(iii) Catherine, (iv) Barbara, (v) for Peace, and (vi) All Saints; these followed (fols. 49v-50r, rubric on fol. 49r) by a contemporary added suffrage to (vii) St. Adrian (whose rubric is worded differently from those which precede it: '*Memoire de saint adrien.*') (the prayers pr. in *Corpus orationum* are nos. (ii) 1464, (iii) 1521, (iv) 1159, (v) 1088a, and (vi) 3134); fols. 50v and 72v ruled, otherwise blank.

[Items 5-8 occupy quires X-XII]

5. (fols. 73r-84v) The Seven Penitential Psalms.

6. (fols. 84v-89v) Litany and collects; the litany including Christopher (2), and Adrian (10) among eleven martyrs; Martin (1) among twelve confessors; and Mastidia of Troyes (12) among fifteen virgins; followed (fol. 89r-v) by three collects: (i) 'Deus cui proprium est ...' (pr. *Corpus orationum*, no. 1143); (ii) 'Deus qui nos patrem et matrem ...' (pr. *ibid.*, no. 1903); and (iii) 'Fidelium deus omnium conditor ...' (pr. *ibid.*, no. 2684b).

7. (fols. 90r-93r) Hours of the Cross; fol. 93v ruled, and with offsets from the facing page, otherwise blank.

8. (fols. 94r-96v) Hours of the Holy Spirit.

[Item 9 occupies quires XIII-XVI]

9. (fols. 97r-124v) Office of the Dead, Use unidentified: the lessons, responses and versicles at Matins, and the antiphons at Lauds, are all the same as those of the Use of Rouen, with the exceptions that here the response and versicle of lesson VI are: 'Ne recorderis ...' and 'Dirige ...', and of Lesson VIII they are: 'Domine secundum ...' and 'Amplius lava ...' (the responses are Ottosen, *Office of the Dead*, numbers 14,72,24; 32,57,57; 68,28,38, but this series is not found in his tables); the final three prayers given by cue only; fol. 125r-v ruled, otherwise blank.

Decoration
Twelve miniatures with arched tops, each above three lines of text with a three-line initial containing foliage, on a gold ground, surrounded by a full border of stylized and naturalistic foliage, flowers, and fruit (that on fol. 27r with birds, an archer, and a centaur-like hybrid):
(fol. 27r) Hours of the Virgin, Matins. Annunciation.
(fol. 37r) Lauds. Visitation; a supplicant angel behind the Virgin.
(fol. 51r) Prime. Nativity; the Child adored by the Virgin and Joseph.
(fol. 56r) Terce. Annunciation to three Shepherds; one playing bagpipes, another with a pipe at his feet.
(fol. 59r) Sext. Adoration of the Magi.
(fol. 62r) None. Presentation in the Temple.
(fol. 65r) Vespers. Flight into Egypt, from right to left; Joseph carrying a bundle on a stick.

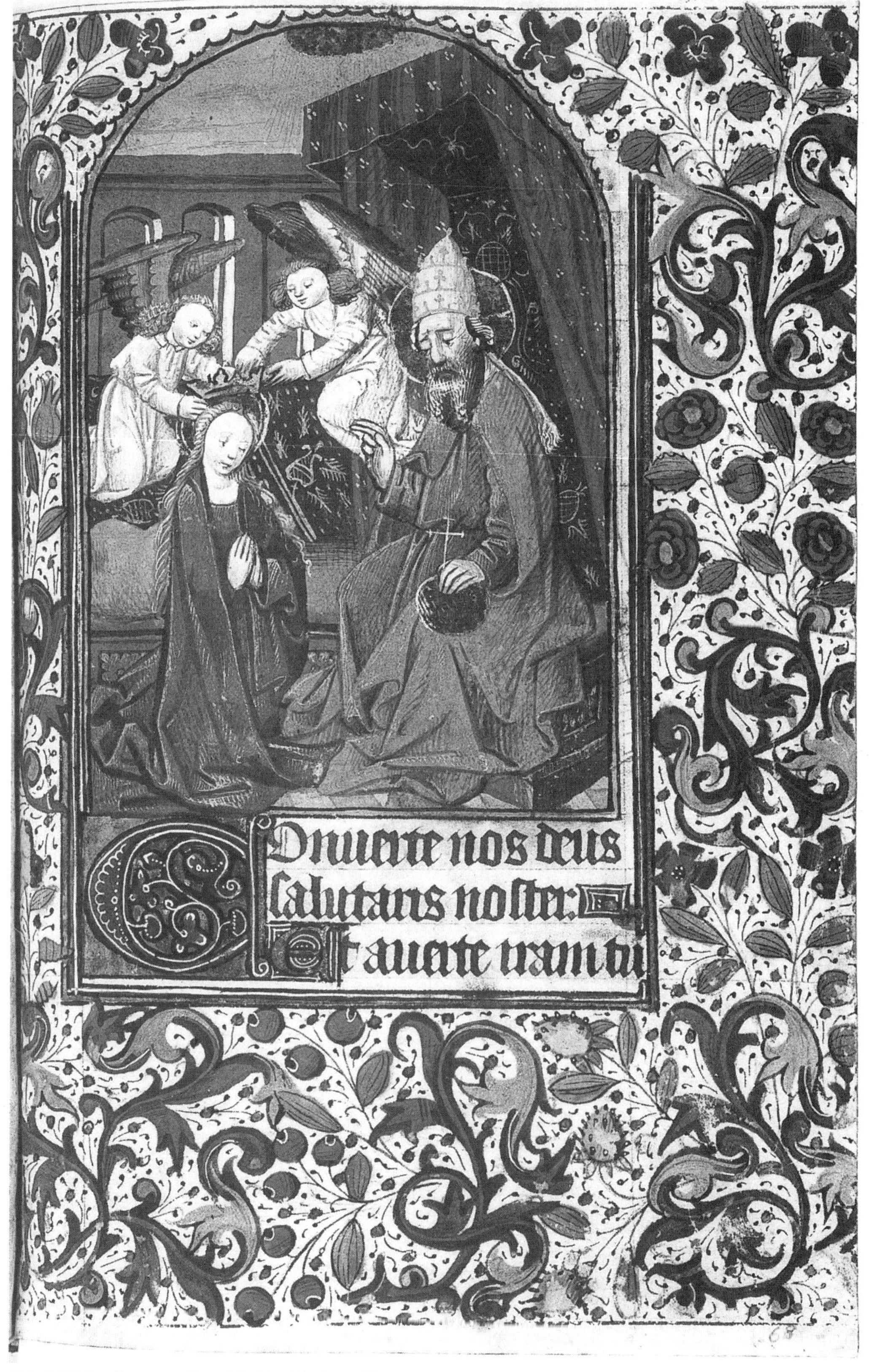

32. MS. Buchanan e. 13, fol. 68r. [Enlarged]

(fol. 68r) Compline. Coronation of the Virgin by two angels, before God wearing a papal tiara (pl. 32).
(fol. 73r) Penitential Psalms. David in Penitence, kneeling before an altar(?) on which is his harp, and above which is an angel wielding a sword.
(fol. 90r) Hours of the Cross. Crucifixion; the Virgin, John, and a nimbed woman to the left, Joseph of Arimathea(?) and soldiers to the right.
(fol. 94r) Hours of the Holy Spirit. Pentecost.
(fol. 97r) Office of the Dead. Burial of a shrouded corpse (Watson, *Playfair Hours*, fig. 28; Virgoe, *Private life*, col. pl. on p. 152).

One eight-line historiated initial, with a full border:
(fol. 18r) *Obsecro te*. The Virgin and Child of the Apocalypse, standing on a crescent moon.

One three-line initial in blue and red with white tracery, on a gold ground with painted foliage, with a three-sided border open at the right, at the start of the Pericopes (fol. 13r); one similar two-line initial and three-sided border open at the right to the prayer on fol. 22v; two-line initials in gold on a blue and red ground with white tracery, to psalms, lessons, hymns, etc. (the blue and red perhaps slightly paler on fol. 49v, in the added suffrage to Adrian); similar one-line initials to the KL monograms in the calendar, and to verses, and other minor textual divisions; similar line-fillers throughout.

Physical Description
MATERIAL: parchment.
DIMENSIONS: the leaves 155-6 x 103 mm. (painted borders around the miniatures are cropped at the fore-edge, and the margins above and below the borders on these pages are very narrow).
NUMBER OF LEAVES: i (marbled paper, conjoint with the pastedown) + 125 + i (marbled paper, conjoint with the pastedown).
FOLIATION: modern, in pencil: i, 1-126.
COLLATION: mostly on quires of 8 leaves: I^{12} (fols. 1-12) | II^8 (fols. 13-20), III^6 (fols. 21-26) | IV-VIII^8 (fols. 27-66), IX^6 (fols. 67-72) | X-XII^8 (fols. 73-96) | XIII-XV^8 (fols. 97-120), XVI$^{6-1}$ (6th leaf cut out after fol. 125) (fols. 121-125); no catch-words visible.
RULING: 16 lines ruled in pale red ink, between single vertical bounding lines extending the full height of the page, the top and bottom horizontals usually extending the full width of the page; the ruled space 95-6 x 61-2 mm.; no prickings visible.
SCRIPT: written in dark brown ink in a gothic bookhand, in two sizes according to liturgical function; with 15 lines of text per page; the written space 93-4 x 59-65 mm.; apparently by a single scribe throughout, except for the suffrage to Adrian (fols. 49r-50r) which is by a different but contemporary hand, perhaps in the same workshop.
RUBRICATION: headings in red.
SEC. FOL.: (Cal.) 'KL Fevrier.', (text, fol. 14r) 'uerbum caro'.

Binding

Sewn on four cords, with green and yellow endbands; bound in 19th-cent. undecorated brown-black leather over pasteboards; the spine divided into five compartments by four raised bands; marbled pastedowns and conjoint endleaves; the edges of the leaves red. The leaves have been re-folded a few mm. to the side of the previous sewing stations: the old spine-fold and four sewing-stations (for two cords plus kettle-stitches) are sometimes clearly visible (e.g. fols. 15, 95). Boxed, using funds provided by the Friends of the Bodleian, 1994.

Provenance

1. The liturgical evidence of the volume falls into two groups: the calendar and Hours of the Virgin point very strongly to Rouen, as does the style of the miniatures; but the Office of the Dead seems to contradict this, as does the litany, which has none of the usual Rouen saints; the suffrage to Adrian, and his mention in the litany, may perhaps indicate that the original owner was a soldier. Marks and holes in the lower half of fol. 26v, and abrasion to the facing page (the start of the Hours of the Virgin) may perhaps have been caused by the sewing-in of a large pilgrim badge or other votive image.

2. ? Unidentified 19th-cent. collection: the lowest compartment of the spine with a paper label inscribed in brown ink with a large 'I'; the middle compartment with a small vestige of what may have been another such label.

3. ? Unidentified 19th-cent. French(?) owner; inscribed in pencil (fol. 126r): '1480 a 1500', possibly by the same hand that inscribed MS. Buchanan e. 14, fol. iii verso.

4. John Buchanan (see Introduction, pp. xiv, xix): inscribed in pencil with the 'Descriptive list' number, '13.', in the upper left corner of fol. i verso.

5. Rt. Hon. T. R. Buchanan (1846-1911); given to the Bodleian in 1939 by his widow, Mrs. E. O. Buchanan, when it was accessioned as MS. Lat. liturg. e. 34; re-referenced as MS. Buchanan e. 13 in 1941.

Bibliography

'Fifteen illuminated *Horae*', *BLR* 1 no. 7 (1939), 115-6, at 115 (as MS. Lat. liturg. e. 34).

van Dijk, *Handlist of Latin liturgical MSS.*, IV, no. 112.

Pächt & Alexander, 1, no. 752.

Rowan Watson, *The Playfair Hours: a late fifteenth century illuminated manuscript from Rouen (V&A, L.475-1918)* (London, 1984), 8 and fig. 28.

Roger Virgoe, *Private life in the fifteenth century: illustrated letters of the Paston family* (London, 1989), col. pl. on p. 152 (fol. 97r).

MS. Buchanan e. 14

Book of Hours, Use of Evreux, in Latin and French
France, Normandy; late 15th or early 16th century

Text
[Item 1 occupies quire I]

1. (fols. 1r-6v) Calendar, in French, about half-full, major feasts in red, each month headed by a note in red on the number of days in the calendar month; feasts, many of them characteristic of Evreux (cf. Leroquais, *Bréviaires*, II, 95-6), include: Gaudus of Evreux (31 Jan.), Ansbert of Rouen (9 Feb.), Aquilinus of Evreux and his translation (15 Feb., 18 July), Benedict of Nursia and his translation (21 Mar., 11 July), Benedict (12 Apr. [*sic*]), Maximus and Venerandus (25 May), Leufred (21 June), Swithun (2 July), Thuriaf (13 July), the invention of Taurinus of Evreux (5 Sept.), Michael (16 Oct.), King Edmund (20 Nov.), Ursinus (30 Dec.).

[Items 2-5 occupy quires II-VIII]

2. (fols. 7r-33v) Hours of the Virgin, Use of Evreux, with the Hours of the Cross and the Hours of the Holy Spirit intermixed; Lauds of the Hours of the Virgin followed by six collects (fol. 16r-v), for (i) the Virgin, (ii) the Holy Spirit, (iii) John the Evangelist, (iv) Nicholas, (v) Catherine, and (vi) Peace (those pr. in *Corpus orationum*, are nos. (i) 706, (iii) 2416a, (iv) 1463, (v) 1521, and (vi) 1088a).

3. (fols. 34r-39r) The Seven Penitential Psalms.

4. (fols. 39r-42r) Litany and collects: the litany including Uriel last among four angels and archangels, Martial last among sixteen Apostles and Evangelists; Ursinus between All Apostles and Evangelists and All Disciples (cf. MS. Buchanan e. 3); the confessors ending with Mellon, Romanus, Ouen, Ansbert, Eloi, Giles, Taurinus, Nicholas, Benedict, Benedict (i.e. twice), Theobald, Maurus, Lubin, Sulpicius, Gorgonius (8-22); the petitions followed (fol. 42r) by three collects (i) 'Deus cui proprium ...' (pr. *Corpus orationum*, no. 1143); (ii) 'Ure igne sancti spiritus ...' (pr. Bruylants, *Oraisons*, no. 1168); and (iii) 'Consciencias nostras quesumus domine visitando purifica ...' (pr. *Corpus orationum*, no. 800d); fol. 42v ruled, otherwise blank.

5. (fols. 43r-61r) Office of the Dead, use of Evreux; followed (fol. 61r-v) by a memorial for the Dead: 'Auete omnes anime fideles ...' (pr. Leroquais, *Livres d'heures*, II, 341); fols. 62r-63v ruled, otherwise blank.

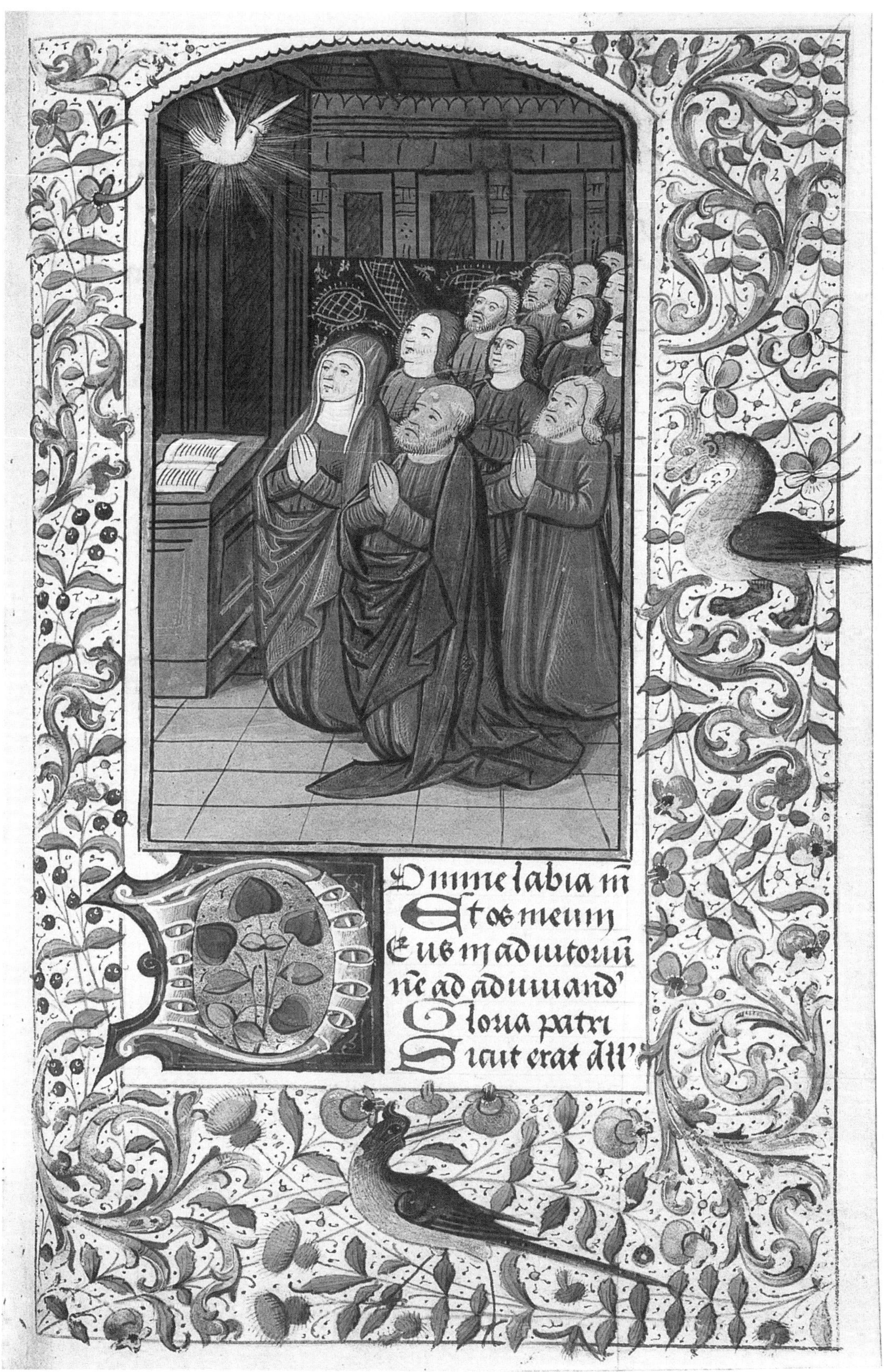

33. MS. Buchanan e. 14, fol. 18r. [Slightly enlarged]

Decoration
Twelve miniatures, each with an arched top, above six lines of text to fol. 22r,
and above seven lines of text thereafter, except for fol. 34r which has a line left
blank for a rubric, and seven lines of text:
(fol. 7r) Hours of the Virgin, Matins. Annunciation.
(fol. 12r) Lauds. Visitation; an angel with folded arms behind the Virgin.
(fol. 17r) Hours of the Cross. Crucifixion, with the Virgin and St. John.
(fol. 18r) Hours of the Holy Spirit. Pentecost; the Virgin and disciples all kneel,
facing the Dove (pl. 33).
(fol. 19r) Hours of the Virgin, Prime. Nativity; the Virgin and Joseph adore the
Child.
(fol. 22r) Terce. Annunciation to four Shepherds.
(fol. 24r) Sext. Adoration of the Magi. [Above seven lines of text].
(fol. 26r) None. Presentation in the Temple.
(fol. 28r) Vespers. Flight into Egypt, from right to left; with a handmaid.
(fol. 31r) Compline. Coronation of the Virgin.
(fol. 34r) Penitential Psalms. David in Penitence.
(fol. 43r) Office of the Dead. Job on the Dungheap, with his three friends.

Each miniature above a six- to eight-line decorated initial in shades of grey,
against a field of red or brown and gold, and enclosing naturalistic flowers
against a gold ground; the miniatures each surrounded by a full border of
naturalistic and stylised foliage, and various animals including a frog (fol. 7r),
a squirrel (fol. 26r), a snail (fol. 34r), a butterfly(?) (fol. 24r), a peacock (fol. 43r),
and other birds (e.g. fol. 12r), and various hybrid creatures (e.g. fol. 17r); two-
line initials to psalms, hymns, etc. alternately in red or blue; similar one-line
initials to verses and other minor divisions; line-fillers in red and blue, especially
in the litany; occasional paraphs in blue.

Physical Description
MATERIAL: parchment.
DIMENSIONS: the leaves 208-12 x 137-140 mm.
NUMBER OF LEAVES: iii (paper, the first marbled, conjoint with the pastedown),
vi (parchment) + 63 + vi (parchment), iii (paper, the last marbled, conjoint with
the pastedown); fols. iv-ix and 64-9 are blank parchment flyleaves, of a similar
quality and weight to fols 1-63: they may be original.
FOLIATION: modern, in pencil: i-ix, 1-72.
COLLATION: mostly written on quires of 8 leaves: I⁶ (fols. iv-ix) | II⁶ (fols. 1-6)
| III-IX⁸ (fols. 7-63) | X⁶ (fols. 64-69); no catchwords visible.
RULING: 28 lines ruled in pale red ink, between single vertical bounding lines
extending the full height of the page, the top and bottom horizontal extending
the full width of the page; the ruled space 143-5 x 72-4 mm.; in the calendar,
months with 30 days have 32 ruled lines, those with 31 days have an extra line
ruled at the bottom of the column to accommodate the extra day; the ruled space
166-74 x 72-4 mm.; prickings frequently survive at the fore-edge.

SCRIPT: written in *lettre bâtarde* in two sizes according to liturgical function, with 27 lines of text per page; the written space *c.* 142 x 72 mm.; the calendar with up to 31 lines of text per page.

RUBRICATION: headings alternately in red or blue, but frequently omitted.

SEC. FOL.: (calendar) 'KL Mars a xxxi iour'; (text, fol. 8) 'vestri; probauerunt'.

Binding

The sewing not clearly visible; endbands missing; bound in late-18th-cent. French mottled brown leather over pasteboards; the spine with five raised bands, and a red title-piece lettered 'PSAUME | DE | DAVID' in the second compartment, gilt ornament and a flower motif in each of the other five; watermarks of flyleaves are unclear, but perhaps (fol. ii): 'M [then a lozenge shape] H.[?] M.', and, lower down: a backward-leaning 'D R.'(?), and (fol. 70): 'F.I.N 1788' (the last two numerals unclear, perhaps alternatively '99' or '83'?) and a bunch of grapes; blue silk bookmark; the edges of the leaves and boards gilt; the parchment flyleaves (fols. iv-ix, 64-69) may be original, or belong to an intermediate previous binding.

Provenance

1. Unidentified original owner; the three feasts of Benedict in the calendar, and the repetition of his name in the litany, perhaps suggest someone with Benedictine links.

2. Unidentified owner: six paste deposits in a cruciform arrangement (fol. 67v), one of them apparently with traces of torn paper, perhaps from a pasted-in votive image.

3. Unidentified 18th/19th-cent. owner or bookseller: inscribed in pencil (fol. 72r), in indistinct characters, possibly: 'B^t £5 6s. 8^d' if read as a purchase record with an English price, but probably closer to: 'L^t L9 678^4' (perhaps a shelfmark?).

4. ? Adolphe Labitte, 19th-cent. Parisian bookseller (see Introduction, pp. xxiv-xxv): inscribed in ink 'Ira | Bos', separated by a horizontal line, probably a bookseller's price-code, near the top right corner of fol. 72r (see fig. 10; cf. MSS. Buchanan e. 5 and e. 7); also inscribed in pencil (fol. iii verso): 'vers [crossed through] 1450', possibly by the same hand that inscribed MS. Buchanan e. 13, fol. 126r.

5. John Buchanan (see Introduction, pp. xiv, xix): inscribed in pencil with the 'Descriptive list' number, '14', in the top left corner of fol. i verso.

6. Rt. Hon. T. R. Buchanan (1846-1911); given to the Bodleian by his widow, Mrs. E. O. Buchanan, in 1939, when it was accessioned as MS. Lat. liturg. e. 35; re-referenced as MS. Buchanan e. 14 in 1941.

Bibliography

'Fifteen illuminated *Horae*', *BLR* 1 no. 7 (1939), 115-6, at 116 (as MS. Lat. liturg. e. 35).

van Dijk, *Handlist of Latin liturgical MSS.*, IV, no. 51.

Pächt & Alexander, 1, no. 804.

MS. Buchanan e. 15

Ps.-Fenestella, *De Romanorum magistratibus*, in Latin
Italy, Venice; 15th century, third quarter

Text
(fols. 1r-42v) Ps.-Fenestella, *De Romanorum magistratibus*: '*PLINIVS.DE.MAGI-*
| stratibus Romanorum. et primum de | Lupercis. Omnium deorum uetus
Romanorum religio excoluit ... et omnes prouincias regentes licet senatores sint:
Praesides appellantur. *.P.E. F.A.*' (no modern edition found; pr. in numerous early
editions, under the name of Lucius Fenestella, for which see *Gesamtkatalog der
Wiegendrucke* VIII (Stuttgart, Berlin, New York, 1978), cols. 496-500); fols. 43r-44v
ruled, otherwise blank.

Andrea di Domenico Fiocchio (or Floccus) (d. 1452) wrote a tract in two books
titled *De potestatibus Romanorum* (or *Romanis*), probably in the 1420s (see
Giovanni Mercati, 'Andreas de Florentia, segretario apostolico: alcune notizie e
varie lettere di Andrea Fiocchi, canonico fiorentino', in *Ultimi contributi alla storia
degli umanisti, fascicolo I: Traversariana* (Studi e testi, 90: Vatican City, 1939), 97-
131, at 97-101, 130-1). Incipits are [preface:] 'Cum per hos dies ...' (Bertalot,
Initia humanistica, II/I, no. 3757), [tract:] 'Omnium deorum quas vetus
Romanorum superstitio ...'. This work circulated under his name (e.g.
MS. D'Orville 50, fols. 1-31v), and anonymously (e.g. Sotheby & Co., *Important
western and oriental miniatures ... 11 December, 1961* (London), lot 170 and pl. 15,
dated 5 Nov. 1465).

Perhaps in Fiocchio's lifetime, however, and at least as early as 1469 (see R.
Sabbadini, *Le scoperte dei codici latini e greci ne' secoli XIV e XV: nuove ricerche col
riassunto filologico dei due volumi* (Biblioteca storica del rinascimento, 5: Florence,
1914), 222), an abridged one-book version without the preface appeared,
attributed to the Augustan historian, Fenestella, who had indeed written a
work about Roman magistrates. The 'Fenestella' version is titled *De Romanorum
magistratibus*, and opens: 'Omnium deorum quos uetus Romanorum religio
excoluit ...'. It is the 'Fenestella' which was first printed (Venice, 1474) (see
John Monfasani, 'Calfurnio's identification of pseudepigrapha of Ognibene,
Fenestella, and Trebizond, and his attack on renaissance commentaries',
Renaissance quarterly 41 no. 1 (1988), 32-43, esp. 36).

The present manuscript is a copy (with errors) of the Ps.-Fenestella redaction.
The attribution in the rubric to 'Plinius' must refer to Pliny the Elder, who
referred to the real Fenestella in his *Natural History*.

Decoration
One five-line facetted initial O[mnium] (fol. 1r) in red and gold, on a square blue
ground, containing a bust in *camaïeu d'or* of a male youth in profile, and, in the

centre of the lower border of the same page, a coat of arms (see under Provenance) within a green laurel wreath (pl. 34); two- or three-line square capitals, alternately red or blue, at the start of each section, with guide letters usually visible.

The illumination is attributed by Armstrong to the Master of the Putti or his workshop, *c.*1471-3, to whom she also attributes the Huntington and Vienna manuscripts written by the same scribe (see under Provenance).

Physical Description

MATERIAL: parchment, of good quality, but with occasional natural flaws at the edges (e.g. fols. 7, 8, 14, etc.), and some repaired holes (e.g. fol. 13), sometimes within the text area (e.g. fol. 25).
DIMENSIONS: the leaves 214-5 x 143-4 mm.
NUMBER OF LEAVES: i (modern parchment, conjoint with the pastedown) + i (fol. ii, original(?) parchment) + i (18th(?)-cent. paper, glued to the *recto* of fol. ii; see under Provenance) + 44 + i (original(?) parchment) + i (modern parchment, conjoint with the pastedown).
FOLIATION: modern, in pencil: i-iii, 1-46.
COLLATION: mostly on quires of 10 leaves: I^{10+1} (1st leaf inserted, fol. ii) (fols. ii, 1-10), II-IV^{10} (fols. 11-40), V^{4+1} (5th leaf inserted, fol. 45) (fols. 41-45); quires arranged flesh side outermost; CATCHWORDS in the hand of the main text, between horizontal dashes, to the right of the centre of the lower margin.
RULING: 27 lines ruled in very pale brown ink, virtually invisible in places, between single vertical bounding lines extending the full height of the page; the ruled space 138-9 x 83-4 mm.; each leaf with a single PRICKING near the fore-edge, about 5 mm. below the bottom line of text, and another near the lower gutter corner, to the left of the vertical bounding line.
SCRIPT: written in a good, regular, humanistic bookhand, perhaps by Paolo Erizzo (see under Provenance), with 27 lines of text per page, written above the top ruled line; the written space 138-41 x 85-8 mm.
RUBRICATION: headings by the scribe, in pink (not the same as the red of the painted initials).
SEC. FOL.: 'aptius stragula'.

Binding

Contemporary blind-tooled binding (pl. 1). Sewn on three double straps, with endbands; bound in polished brown leather over wood boards, the edges of their inner faces bevelled; both covers blind-tooled with ropework designs in rectangular panels around a central cruciform design; originally with two clasps, now lacking, but the impressions left by their mountings indicate that those on the upper board were rectangular, and those on the lower were trefoil-shaped (cf. MS. Buchanan c. 1), their nail-holes skilfully repaired; the edges of the leaves gauffered and gilt; rebacked by 1898, with new parchment pastedowns and conjoint flyleaves, probably by Messrs. Leighton, *c.*1889 (see under Provenance; advertisements in their catalogues state: 'Old Books and Engravings carefully cleaned, mended,

PLINIVS·DE·MAGI

stratibus Romanorum, et primum de
Lupercis.

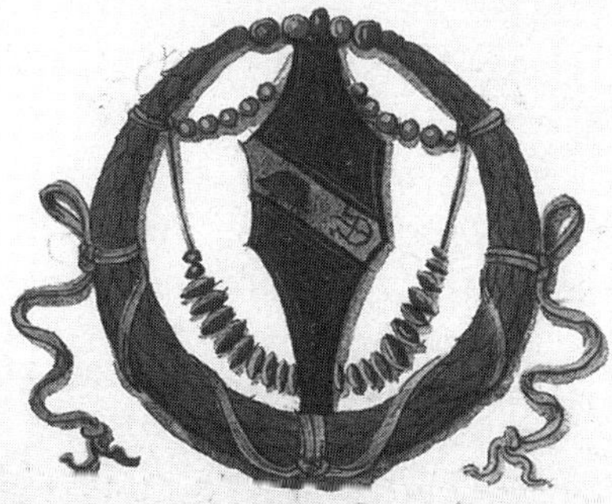

Mnium deorum uetus Romanorum religio excoluit. Primum Pani Liceo seu Ianu̅ illu̅ seu potius Siluanum uocari placet. Per Lupercos rem diuina̅, Lupercalesq; ludos fecisse apud uetustatis assertores constat. Ea quidem sacrorum genera t ab Euandro rege qui ex Archadia profugus in eum locum uenerat, qui tandem Romanę presuit ara, ad nostros primum delata ac celebrata fuisse feruntur. Hunc Pana nudos͛ pastores quorum tunc precipuum nume̅ fuit ac deum sumos etiam uiros uenerari mos fuit. loresq; pro manibus ferre quibus obuios t quosq; redderent. Lauiuiq; facies tectas portare. Cur autem nudi hunc deum collerent, pleraq; e articialo uetustatis ad nos usq; delapsa referuntur. Siue enim q'ipsi deo qui aliquis fingitur sue celeritati eo pacto longe aptior͛ nudos etiam habere ministros placeat. Siue quidem Archades omnium populorum qui Greciam coluerunt longe uetustissimi feris adhuc similem uitam siluis ac montibus age̅

34. MS. Buchanan e. 15, fol. 1r.

restored, and deficiencies made up in exact facsimile'); the upper joint weak, with
the lowest strap broken; the spine lettered in gilt, probably for William Morris (see
under Provenance; cf. the spine of MS. Buchanan c. 1): 'PLINIVS | DE | MAGIST-
|RATIBVS | ROMAN-|ORVM | | MS. | IN | MEMBRANIS', and with a saltire
pattern in blind in each compartment. Matching pairs of nail(?)-holes in the
bevelled fore-edges of of both the upper and lower boards, near the top, bottom
(and perhaps middle?), possibly indicate that thin ties were once used to secure
the volume closed.

Provenance
1. Made for a member of the Erizzo family, of Venice; with their coat of arms
(fol. 1r): *azure*, on a bend *or* a hedgehog and a reversed gothic initial E *sable*
(cf. Rietstap, *Armorial général*, I, 621, and *Planches*, II (1909), pl. CCLXXIV;
but closer to the design in Marco Vicenzo Coronelli, ed., *Arme, blasoni, ò insegne
gentilitie delle famiglie patritie esistenti nelle serenissime republica di Venetie* ([Venice?,
1694?]; the arms also appear in a slightly earlier manuscript, sold at Sotheby's,
London, 11 Dec. 1961, lot 169, ill. in pl. 14). The initials, presumably of the
scribe, occur in pink roman square capitals at the end of the text (fol. 42v):
'.P.E.F.A.'. The same scribe copied San Marino, Huntington Library, HM 1031
(see Dutschke, *Huntington cat.*, I, 293-4), and Vienna, ÖNB, Cod. 3180 (see
Hermann, *Verzeichnis der illuminierten Handschriften in Österreich*, n.F., VI/2,
19-20, Taf. VII.2), both of which also have the coat of arms of the Erizzo family,
and both of which contain the initials 'P.E.A.F.'; de Ricci *Census*, I, 81 (followed
by Dutschke) proposed that the initials may stand for 'Paulus Erizzo Antonii
Filius' (fl. 1473-1503?). Dutschke transcribes the following inscription in the
Huntington manuscript: '1658 24 Decembre. Questo manoscrito fu comparato
da me Marsilio Papafava con molti altri da Messer Paolo Fasolati per ducenti
venti.'; it is possible that the Buchanan manuscript was also among those sold
by Fasolati to Papafava.

2. Unidentified Italian library, 18th(?) cent.: fol. iii is a small sheet of laid paper,
pasted to the recto of fol. ii, inscribed on the present recto: 'Falsò in hoc Codice
Plinio | inscribitur Opus de Magistratibus | Romanorum | Cum sit Lucij
Fenestellæ, ut ex impressis | apparet | Codex iste nitidissimus Saec: XV ad
| illustrem familiam Erizzo de | Venetijs pertinuit ut | ex Stemmate in fronte
Codicis | adposito apparet.'; the configuration of worm-holes in this leaf and in
the following parchment leaves indicate that it was previously inserted slightly
higher up, with its present recto as the verso; and traces of glue(?) along the
present gutter edge of the present verso suggest that it was originally pasted
along this edge to the board, or to a previous pastedown.

3. Messrs. J. & J. Leighton, London book-binders and -sellers (on whom see
David Pearson, *Provenance research in book history: a handbook* (The British Library
Studies in the History of the Book: London, 1994), 161): included in their *A list
of interesting books* (1889) item 727, priced £5 15s. ('in the original Venetian
binding, nice specimen'); Messrs. Leighton and other, unidentified, 19th-cent.

bookseller(s) are presumably responsible for various pencil inscriptions: in the top left corner of the upper pastedown is '2239', and in the bottom gutter corner 'il/t/-'(?) above '6/SS' (?); and in the top right corner of fol. i recto: 'xc'(?).

4. William Morris (1834-1896); presumably bought from Messrs. Leighton (binders of the Kelmscott Press books) in 1889 or shortly thereafter; the manuscript is no. 42 in the inventory of Morris' library drawn up shortly after his death by F. S. Ellis (see Introduction, p. xxvii): the upper pastedown inscribed in pencil with this number in the top left corner.

5. Richard Bennett, of Manchester (see Introduction, p. xxvii): with his posthumous Morris book-label on the upper pastedown; sold in the 'Morris' sale at Sotheby's on 5 December 1898 and five following days, lot 297; inscribed in pencil below and to the right of the Ellis inventory number: '87', encircled, presumably by Sotheby's (see Introduction, p. xxv).

6. Rt. Hon. T. R. Buchanan (1846-1911): bought by Buchanan at the 'Morris' sale for £13; given to the Bodleian by his widow, Mrs. E. O. Buchanan, 28 May 1941.

Bibliography
Sotheby, Wilkinson & Hodge, *Catalogue of a portion of the valuable library of manuscripts, early printed books, &c. of the late William Morris, of Kelmscott House, Hammersmith, which will be sold by auction ... 5th of December, 1898 and five following days* (London), item 727.

A list of interesting books, many in fine bindings ... offered for sale by J. & J. Leighton (London, 1889)

S. Gibson, 'Bookbindings in the Buchanan Collection', *BLR* 2 no. 16 (1941), 6-12, at 8.

Pächt & Alexander, 2, no. 558, pl. LI (fol. 1r, detail).

Lilian Armstrong, *Renaissance miniature painters & classical imagery: the Master of the Putti and his Venetian workshop* (London, 1981), 6, 117 no. 26, ill. 57 (fol. 1r).

Dutschke, *Huntington cat.*, I, 293.

MS. Buchanan e. 18

Book of Hours, Use of Rome, in Latin and Netherlandish
Flanders, Bruges; 15th century, third quarter, after 1461

Text
[Item 1 occupies quires I-II]

1. (fols. 1r-12v) Calendar, about one-third full, each month headed by a note on
the length of the calendar and lunar months; major feasts (in red) include:
Amand (6 Feb.), Basil (14 June), Remi & Bavo (1 Oct.), Eloi and his translation
(1 Dec., 25 June), Nicasius of Rheims (14 Dec.); feasts in plain ink include:
Milburga (23 Feb.), the translation of Augustine (28 Feb.), Adrian (4 Mar.),
Patrick (17 Mar.), Quentin (Quintinus), in error for Quirinus (30 Mar.), Peter
Martyr (29 Apr.), Gervase, in error for Servatius (Gervasii for Servacii) (13 May),
Brendan (17 May), Dominic (5 Aug.), Clare (12 Aug.), Magnus (19 Aug.), Bertin
(5 Sept.), Humbert (6 Sept.), Lambert (17 Sept.), Francis (4 Oct.), Quentin
(31 Oct.), Livin (12 Nov.), Malo (15 Nov.), and Elisabeth of Thuringia (19 Nov.).

[Items 2-5 occupy quires III-V]

2. (fols. 13r-18v) Hours of the Cross.

3. (fols. 19r-23r) Hours of the Holy Spirit; fol. 23v ruled, otherwise blank.

4. (fols. 24r-28v) Mass of the Virgin.

5. (fols. 28v-32v) Gospel Pericopes (cf. MS. Buchanan e. 3; without the versicle,
response, and prayer after John).

[Item 6 occupies quires VI-XI]

6. (fols. 33r-78r) Hours of the Virgin, Use of Rome, with three lessons at Matins;
Compline followed (fols. 77v-78r) by the hymn 'Salve regina ...' (pr. Wordsworth,
Horae Eboracenses, 62), with a versicle and the usual prayer: 'Omnipotens
sempiterne deus qui gloriose uirginis ...' (pr. *ibid.*, 63; cf. MS. Buchanan e. 5, fol.
92r-v); fols. 51v, 63v, 67v, 78v, ruled, otherwise blank.

[Items 7-8 occupy quires XII-XIII]

7. (fols. 79r-88r) The Seven Penitential Psalms.

8. (fols. 88r-94v) Litany and collects; the litany: '*Letania sanctorum*', with its list
of doctors and confessors ending with: Bernard, Francis, Louis, Eloi, Giles,
Dominic, Livin, and Amand (11-18); followed by five collects (fols. 93r-94v):
(i) 'Deus cui proprium est ...' (pr. *Corpus orationum*, no. 1143); (ii) 'Deus a quo
sancta desideria ...' (pr. *ibid.*, no. 1088a); (iii) 'Ure igne sancti spiritus ...'
(pr. Bruylants, *Oraisons*, no. 1168); (iv) 'Fidelium deus omnium conditor ...'

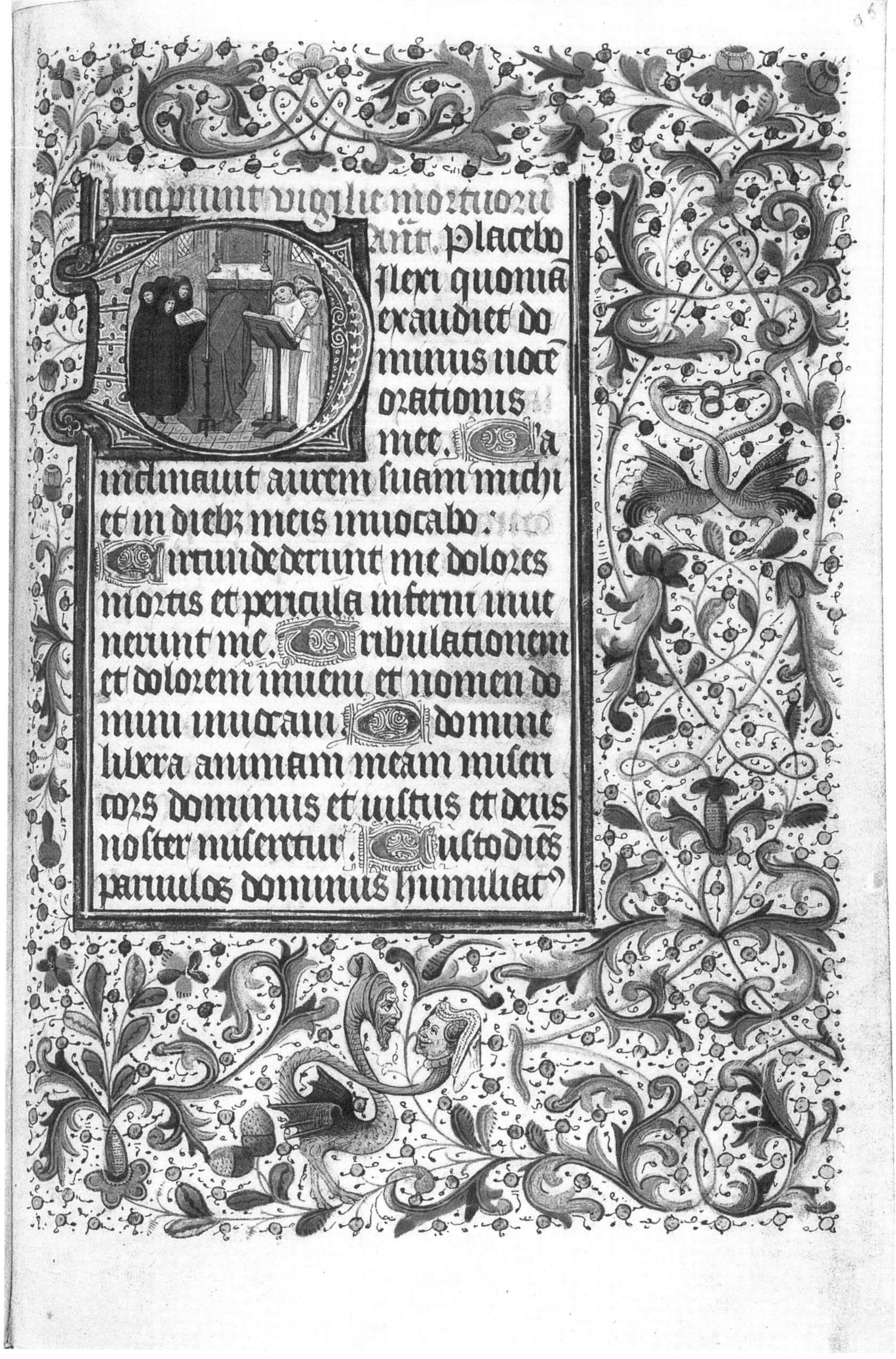

35. *MS. Buchanan e. 18, fol. 95r. [Enlarged]*

(pr. *Corpus orationum*, no. 2684b); (v) 'Omnipotens sempiterne deus qui viuorum dominaris ...' (pr. *ibid.*, no. 4064).

[Items 9-14 occupy quires XIV-XX]

9. (fols. 95r-130v) Office of the Dead, Use of Rome.

10. (fols. 131r-136r) Prayers to the Virgin:
   (i) (fols. 131r-134r) '*Oratio de sancta maria* Obsecro te ...' [masculine forms] (cf. MS. Buchanan e. 2);
   (ii) (fols. 134r-136r) '*Alia oratio de sancta maria.* O intemerata ... orbis terrarum. Inclina mater misericordie aures tue pietatis ...' [masculine forms] (pr. Wordsworth, *Horae Eboracenses*, 67-8; Wilmart, *Auteurs spirituels*, 488-90).

11. (fols. 136v-137v) Hymns, the first with a rubric in Netherlandish:
   (i) (fols. 136v-137v) '*Vanden heilighen sacrament.* Pange lingua gloriosi corporis misterium ... procedenti ab utroque comparsit laudatio' (*Repertorium hymnologicum*, no. 14467), with a versicle and the prayer 'Deus qui nobis sub sacramento mirabili ...' (the latter pr. Bruylants, *Oraisons*, II, no. 393);
   (ii) (fol. 137v) 'O salutaris hostia. que celis pandis hostium ... future glorie nobis pignus datur.' (*Repertorium hymnologicum*, no. 13680).

12. (fols. 137v-142v) Suffrages, predominantly to Dominican saints, in Latin and Netherlandish, with rubrics in Netherlandish (most consisting of an antiphon, versicle and response, followed by a rubric '*Te benedictus*' and a second antiphon, versicle and response, before the collect) to: (i) Dominic, (ii) Peter Martyr ('*Van sinte pieter van melaene.*'), (iii) Thomas Aquinas, (iv) Vincent Ferrer (canonised in 1455), (v) Catherine of Siena ('*Van sinte kath' vand' predicaers*') (canonised in 1461), (vi) Donatian ('*Van sinte donaes. Archebijscop*'), (vii) Elisabeth of Thuringia, the latter (fol. 142r-v) entirely in Netherlandish: '*Van Sinte lysebette van dueringhen* O werde vrauwe sinte lisabette Ionc pogedi ondeuweghe vreden ... Doet my beseffen. van huwen loone. Amen' (prayers pr. in *Corpus orationum* are nos. (i) 1559, and (iii) 1562).

13. (fol. 143r-144r) The Verses of St Bernard: '*Incipiunt septem versus sancti bernardi abbatis. O bone ihesu* Illumina oculos meos ...', the verses in the same order as in MS. Buchanan e. 9, fols. 118v-119r, but omitting verse (vi) as listed there; followed (fols. 143v-144r) by a versicle, response, and the usual prayer: 'Omnipotens sempiterne deus qui ezechie regi iude ... misericordiam consequi merear. Per ...'.

14. (fols. 144r-145r) Prayer to Christ: '*Oracio deuota ad christum ihesum.* Da nobis quesumus omnipotens deus. velle. cogitare. facere. ... et perseuerancia mundicie. sine fine Amen.'; fol. 145v ruled, otherwise blank.

Decoration
Sixteen historiated initials, each six lines high (except those on fols. 56r and 60r
which are five-line), each accompanied by a full border (see below):
(fol. 42r) Hours of the Virgin, Lauds. Visitation.
(fol. 52r) Prime. Nativity; the Virgin and Joseph adoring the Child; Joseph
holding a candle.
(fol. 56r) Terce. Annunciation to two Shepherds; the border with a wolf(?) with
a sheep in its jaws.
(fol. 60r) Sext. Adoration of the Magi.
(fol. 64r) None. Presentation in the Temple.
(fol. 68r) Vespers. Massacre of the Innocents; with only one mother and her
nimbed infant; the border with a half-length soldier wielding a sword.
(fol. 74r) Compline. Flight into Egypt; with the Fall of the Idols in the background
(Cardon, fig. 169).
(fol. 95r) Office of the Dead. Funeral Service; a bier before an altar, with mourners
to the left, one holding an open book, and clerics singing at a lectern to the right
(pl. 35).
(fol. 131r) *Obsecro te.* Pietà, with another figure (Mary Magdalen or St. John ?)
supporting Christ's head; the Cross in the backbround.
(fol. 136v) Hymn. Two angels holding the Host in a monstrance on an altar cloth.
(fol. 139r) Suffrage. St. Thomas Aquinas (his face damaged) holding and pointing
to an open book.
(fol. 139v) Suffrage. St. Vincent Ferrer holding a book, the cover with a large
gold cross.
(fol. 140v) Suffrage. St. Catherine of Siena (her face damaged), with a crown
atop her halo, a twisted wreath about her head, holding a heart in her hand.
(fol. 141r) Suffrage. St. Donatianus, holding a cross-staff and a wheel set round
with candles (Pächt & Alexander, 1, pl. XXVI).
(fol. 142r) Suffrage. St. Elisabeth of Thuringia, wearing a crown, holding another
crown in each hand.
(fol. 143r) Verses of St. Bernard. St. Bernard, holding a crozier and the chain
of a demon, on which he stands.

The borders of stylised and naturalistic foliage on a plain parchment ground,
often containing animals, birds, human-headed grotesques (e.g. Cardon, fig. 169),
etc., some apparently inspired by the subject of the adjacent initial (see above),
and including a finely-dressed woman feeding a squirrel on a leash (fol. 19r),
a youth playing a lute, emerging half-length from foliage (fol. 33r), a mermaid
combing her hair and looking in a mirror (fol. 60r), and two birds with entwined
necks, holding interlocked rings in their beaks, and a grotesque with a male
human head, looking at its own tail, which terminates in a female human head
(both on fol. 95r; pl. 35).

Six-line initials in red or blue, infilled with painted flowers and foliage on a gold
ground, the whole within a square field in red or blue with a gold edge, and full

borders, at the start of the Hours of the Virgin and Penitential Psalms (fols. 33r, 79r
—both with their fore-edge margin cut away; see under Physical Description);
similar five-line initials and full borders at the start of the Hours of the Cross and
of the Holy Spirit, and the Mass of the Virgin (fols. 13r, 19r, 24r; fore-edge border
of 13r cut away, see below); a similar three-line initial with partial borders at the
start of the *O intemerata* (fol. 134r); three-line initials in gold on red and blue
grounds with white tracery, with ivy-leaf sprays, to the KL monograms in the
calendar; a similar three-line initial at the final prayer (fol. 144r); similar two-
line initials to psalms, hymns, lessons, etc.; one-line flourished initials alternately
in gold with blue penwork, or blue with red penwork (often with the penwork
jutting sharply out into the margins when they occur at the edge of the text
area) to verses and other minor textual divisions; line-fillers in blue and gold,
especially in the litany.

The decorative hierarchy and common Flemish practice suggest that it was
originally intended to insert a full-page miniature before fol. 33, and it is also
likely that miniatures were intended for the start of each of the other major
texts; but there is no clear physical evidence that such miniatures were ever
inserted.

The decoration has been attributed to the artist Willem Vrelant: documentary
evidence indicates that he was born in Utrecht, was active in Bruges as a miniaturist
from 1445, and died in 1481. (See Dogaer, 98-105, and Bousmanne, *passim*, for
a discussion of Vrelant's school and a list of books attributed to it, including the
present manuscript.)

Physical Description
MATERIAL: parchment; the fore-edge borders of fols. 13, 33, 42, 43, 52, 53, 79,
131 cut away (cf. under Provenance), and repaired with secondhand parchment
(some of it ruled, e.g. fols. 42v, 43r); traces of paste and penwork decoration (e.g.
fol. 52r) suggest that decoration from other manuscripts was pasted onto this
parchment to decorate the otherwise blank borders, but this was later removed.
DIMENSIONS: the leaves 175 x 125 mm.
NUMBER OF LEAVES: iii (a leaf of marbled paper, conjoint with the pastedown,
followed by a bifolium of modern parchment) + 145 + iii (a bifolium of modern
parchment, followed by a leaf of marbled paper, conjoint with the pastedown),
with protective sheets of tissue bound in to face pages with decoration before fols.
13, 19, 24, 33, 42, 52, 56, 60, 64, 68, 74, 79, 95, 131.
FOLIATION: modern, in pencil: i-iii, 1-148 (the protective tissue interleaves are
not foliated).
COLLATION: mostly in quires of 8 leaves: I-II⁶ (fols. 1-12) | III-IV⁸ (fols. 13-28),
V⁴ (fols. 29-32) | VI-X⁸ (fols. 33-72), XI⁶ (fols. 73-78) | XII-XIII⁸ (fols. 79-94) | XIV⁸⁻¹
(7th leaf cancelled, after fol. 100) (fols. 95-101), XV-XIX⁸ (fols. 102-141), XX⁸⁻⁴
(5th to 8th leaves cancelled, after fol. 145) (fols. 142-145); no catchwords or
quire/leaf signatures visible.

RULING: 19 lines ruled in very pale red ink (fols. 15r-20v ruled with only 18 lines), between single vertical bounding lines extending the full height of the page, the top and bottom horizontal lines extending the full width of the page; the ruled space *c.*93 x 60 mm.; no prickings visible.

SCRIPT: written in fine gothic bookhands, with 18 lines of text per page (fols. 15r-20v with 17 lines per page); the written space *c.*92 x 61 mm.; by probably three scribes, responsible for (i) fols. 1r-12v, (ii) fols. 13r-136r, and (iii) fols. 136v-145r, respectively.

RUBRICATION: each scribe was apparently responsible for his own rubrics: pale red is used in the calendar (fols. 1r-12v), perhaps slightly deeper red for the headings of the main texts (fols. 13r-134r), and bright red for those from fol. 136v to the end.

SEC. FOL.: (calendar) 'KL Februarius habet dies'; (text, fol. 14r) 'Deus in'.

Binding

Sewing not clearly visible; bound probably in the first half of the 19th cent., probably in England, in 'tree-calf' over pasteboards tooled with a gilt twisted-wreath border pattern within an outer frame; the spine without raised bands, but divided into six compartments by gilt ornament, with traces of a paper label at the bottom; red and white endbands; brick-coloured marbled pastedowns and conjoint flyleaves; one blue silk bookmark; the edges of the leaves gilt; fol. 1r is discoloured and marked, suggesting that the upper board of a previous binding may have been detached for some time.

Provenance

1. Unidentified original owner: the calendar, litany, and style of decoration suggest that the book was made in Bruges, and the inclusion of a suffrage to Catherine of Siena (canonized in 1461) provides a *terminus post quem* for its production. The suffrages to Dominican saints, and their presence in the calendar, suggest that the original owner may have been a member of the Dominican Third Order. Deposits of paste on fols. 1r, 12v, and 145r may have been caused by the insertion of votive images.

2. Unidentified 19th-cent. English owner(s) and bookseller(s): inscribed in pencil (fol. i verso): '15 ornamented Pages of which 10 contain | miniature Paintings [?] (7 pages are cut) | 7 miniatures without other ornaments'; it appears that an ownership(?) inscription has been erased at the top right of fol. ii recto. Various booksellers are presumably responsible for the pencil notes on fol. i verso: 'G 9893', upper left and: 'ti/.', bottom left; and the the pencil price-code: 'xa/u'(?) in the top left corner of fol. 148r; the bottom gutter corner of fol. 147v inscribed in pencil 'L' or 'I.' (?); another erased price(?) in pencil is in the upper right corner of fol. 148r.

3. William Stuart (1798-1874), of Tempsford Hall, Bedfordshire, and Aldenham Abbey, Hertfordshire (on whom see John Burke, *A genaeological and heraldic history of the commoners of Great Britain and Ireland ...*, I (London, 1833), 427-8);

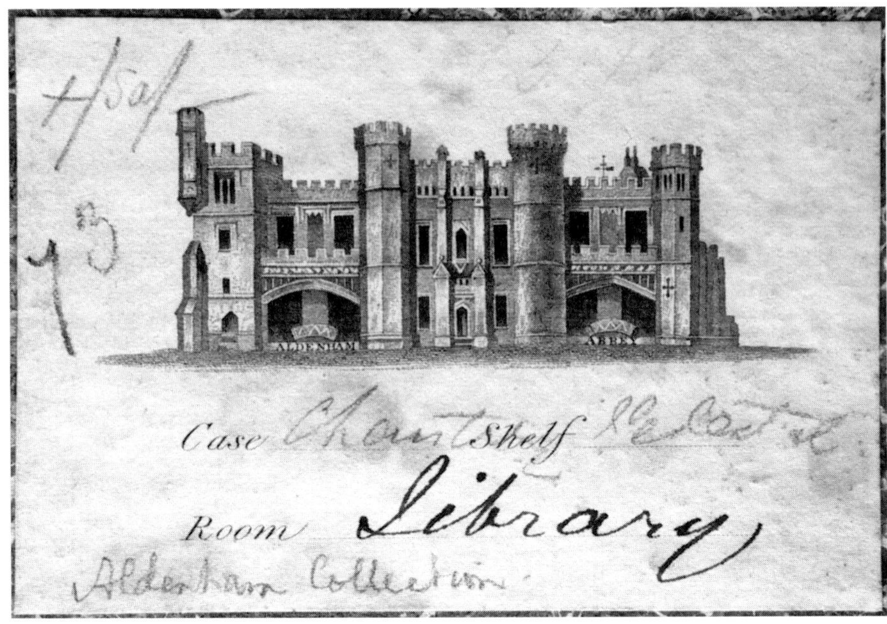

36. *MS Buchanan e.18, upper pastedown, detail [Enlarged]*

with the bookplate of Aldenham Abbey glued to the upper pastedown
(cf. Gambier Howe, *Franks bequest*, III, no. 28457 or no. 28458; see fig 36)
incorporating the words 'ALDENHAM ABBEY' in very small capitals, and printed
'Case..... Shelf..... | Room.....', the first two spaces inscribed in pencil 'Chantrey'
and 'Pedestal' respectively, the third space inscribed in ink 'Library'. It is perhaps
likely that this William Stuart, son of William Stuart (1755-1822), Archbishop
of Armagh, Primate of all Ireland, was responsible for the mutilation of some
leaves, as recorded in a pencil inscription: 'German Missal Fine as to | Border &
Initials 1433. [this number/date perhaps not coeval with the rest of the
inscription] | Several of the Borders are withdrawn | on account of their
voluptuous Images' (fol. ii recto).

4. William Stuart (1825-93), of Tempsford Hall, Bedfordshire, and Aldenham
Abbey, Hertfordshire, son of William Stuart (b. 1798); sold at Sotheby's, 17 June
1875, lot 88; bought by Arthur for £3 12s.; Sotheby's were presumably responsible
for the pencil number '595', encircled, on fol. i verso (see Introduction, p. xxv).

5. Thomas Arthur, London bookseller (see Introduction, pp. xxii-xxiv): the
manuscript was in his *Catalogue*, pt. 76 (Nov. 1875), item 73, priced £5 15s. 6d.
[I am grateful to Claudine Lemaire of the Bibliothèque royale Albert Ier, Brussels,
for supplying me with a photocopy of the relevant pages of this catalogue]; the
bookplate (see above) inscribed in pencil with the catalogue item number and
price: '73', '£5-15[-6 (erased)]', 'Aldenham Collection', and Arthur's price-code:
'x/sa/-' (i.e. £3 12s; see above).

6. Rt. Hon. T. R. Buchanan (1846-1911), November 1875: the gutter margin
of fol. ii recto with a pasted-in cutting from Arthur's catalogue (see above),
inscribed by Buchanan 'Arthur | Nov 75'; a note in pencil on fol. i verso
concerning the Flemish origin of the manuscript was added perhaps during
Buchanan's ownership. Given to the Bodleian by his widow, Mrs. E. O.
Buchanan, in 1941.

Bibliography

Sotheby, Wilkinson & Hodge, *Catalogue of an important and a valuable portion of
the library of the late William Stuart, Esq., removed from Aldenham Abbey, Herts.,
comprising very choice manuscripts, excessively rare Bibles & liturgies (several with
MS. illuminations) ... which will be sold by auction ... 17th day of June, 1875* (London),
lot 88.

Thomas Arthur, *Catalogue of a valuable collection of books, many dating from the
infancy of printing ... manuscripts on vellum from the twelfth century, beautifully
illuminated, including Bibles, liturgies, Missals, Horæ, ...* (Early Printed Books and
MSS, pt. 76: London, Nov. 1875), item 73.

van Dijk, *Handlist of Latin liturgical MSS.*, IV, 284.

Pächt & Alexander, 1, no. 327, pl. XXVI.

Georges Dogaer, *Flemish miniature painting in the 15th and 16th centuries*
(Amsterdam, 1987), listed at 105.

Bert Cardon, *Manuscripts of the* Speculum Humanae Salvationis *in the Southern
Netherlands (c. 1410 - c. 1470)* (Corpus of Illuminated Manuscripts, 9: Louvain,
1996), 273, 277, fig. 169 (cited as 'Buchanon e.18' and 'Ms. Buchanon c. 18').

Bernard Bousmanne, *Guillaume Wielant ou Willem Vrelant, miniaturiste à la cour de
Bourgogne au XVe siècle [exposition organisée à la Bibliothèque royale de Belgique,
Chapelle de Nassau, du 5 décembre 1997 au 18 janvier 1998]* (Brussels, 1997), 8, 64.

Bernard Bousmanne, *"Item a Guillaume Wyelant aussi enlumineur". Willem Vrelant:
un aspect de l'enluminure dans les Pays-Bas méridionaux sous le mécénat des ducs de
Bourgogne, Philippe le Bon et Charles le Téméraire* (Turnhout, 1997), 43, 79, 82,
115, 136, 165, 284-5, 377. At 284-5 is a description of the manuscript, which is
in a few respects more detailed than that given here; for example, it gives the
entire calendar and litany.

Colour filmstrip publication: Bodleian Library, Roll 221.3, consisting of 17 frames,
shows all the historiated initials (fol. 60r occurs twice).

MS. Buchanan f. 1

Book of Hours, in Dutch, mainly in the translation of Geert Grote
Northern Netherlands, Enkhuizen(?); 15th century, last quarter, after 1471

Text
[Item 1 occupies quires I-II]

1. (fols. 1r-9v) Calendar, with an entry for every day, each month headed by a
note on the length of the calendar month and lunar month in red; written
continuously, such that two months occupy three pages; major feasts (in red)
include: Pontianus (14 Jan.), Gertrude of Nivelles (17 Mar.), Servatius (13 May),
Boniface (5 June), Odulph (12 June), Adalbert (25 June), Lambert (17 Sept.),
Remi & Bavo (1 Oct.), Gereon & Victor (10 Oct.), Gummar (11 Oct.), 11,000
Virgins (21 Oct.), Willibrord (7 Nov.), Lebuin, and his translation (12 Nov., 25
June). The calendar has all the saints listed in Saenger, *Newberry cat.*, 114
(Newberry MS. 61).

[Items 2-5 occupy quires III-VIII]

[fol. 10r blank, fol. 10v with a miniature]

2. (fols. 11r-38r, rubric on fol. 9v) Hours of the Virgin: '*Hier beghinnen onse
vrouwe ghetiden*' (pr. N. van Wijk, ed., *Het Getijdenboek van Geert Grote: naar het
Haagse Handschrift 133 E 21* (Leidsche Drukken en Herdrukken: Kleine Reeks, III:
Leiden, 1940), 36-70, without the prologue on p. 36).

3. (fol. 38r-v) Prayer to the Guardian Angel: '*Tot dinen heilighen enghel. ghebet*
Heilighe enghel godes den ic beuolen bin ... verweerdighen moet mi te gheuen die
vader die zoen ...', with a versicle and the collect: 'God ouermits wies godliker ...
becuddinghe werde beschermet. ouermits ousen here ihesum christum. Amen'.

[fol. 39r blank, fol. 39v with a miniature]

4. (fols. 40r-56r, rubric on fol. 38v) Hours of Eternal Wisdom: '*Hier beghinnen die
ewige wijsheit ghetiden*' (pr. *ibid.*, 92-112).

5. (fol. 56r-v) Prayers with indulgences:
    (i) (fol. 56v, rubric on fol. 56r) '*Item sixtus die vierde* [1471-84] *heest ghegheuen
    alle die in penitencie ... .xi^m. iaer aflaets. ghebet* Wes ghegruet alre heilichste
    maria moeder godes. coninghinne des hemels ... ende bidt voer mijn sonden.
    Amen' (as in Maria Meertens, *De godsvrucht in de Nederlanden naar
    handschriften van gebedenboeken der XVe eeuw* I-III, VI [all published] (Leuvense
    Studieën en Tekstuitgaven: Brussels, 1930-4), VI, 94 item 7.a.);
    (ii) (fol. 56v) '*Item soe wie na maeltijtspreket dit ghebet die verdient .xl. daghen
    aflaets* God gheue den leuendighen gracie ende ontfarmherticheit ... ewighe
    leuen ende blijscap. Amen' (as in *ibid.*, 96 item 22.a.; with the same rubric as
    the present manuscript).

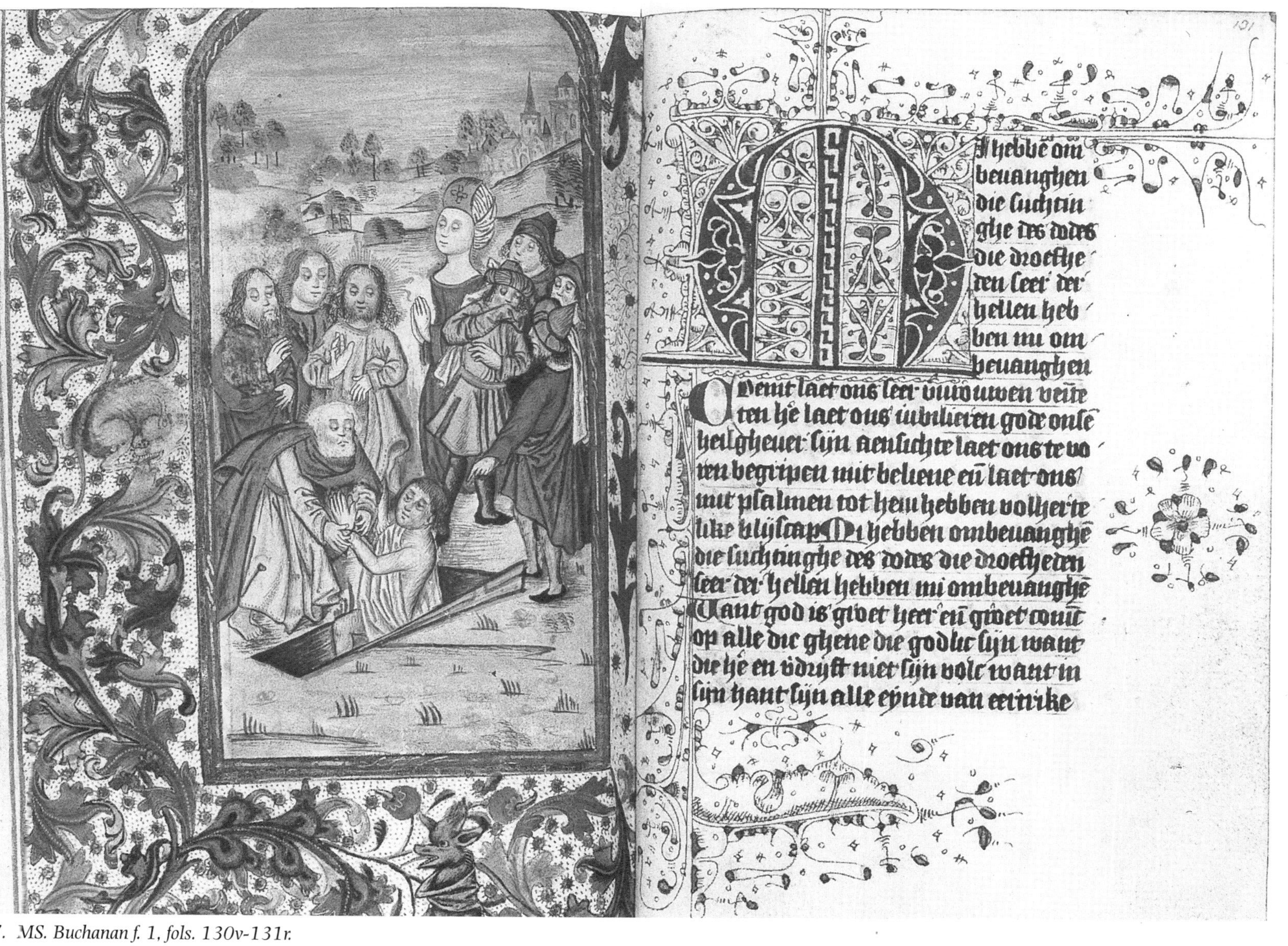

37. *MS. Buchanan f. 1, fols. 130v–131r.*

[Items 6-8 occupy quires IX-XII]

[fol. 57r blank, fol. 57v with a miniature]

6. (fols. 58r-75v, rubric on fol. 56v) Long Hours of the Cross: '*Hier beghinnen die langhe cruus ghetiden*' (pr. van Wijk, *op. cit.*, 113-38), preceded by the prayer: 'O here ihesu christe des leuendighen godes ...' (pr. *ibid.*, 113 n. 1).

[fol. 76r blank, fol. 76v with a miniature]

7. (fols. 77r-90r, rubric on fol. 75v) Hours of the Holy Ghost: '*Hier beghinnen die heilighe gheest ghetiden*' (pr. *ibid.*, 71-86).

8. (fol. 90r-v) Two indulgenced devotions to the Name of Christ:
   (i) (fol. 90r-v) '*Item soe wie na dat in wat guets gedaen heest leset dit ghebet die verdienst xl. daghen aflaets* Die soete naem ons heren ihesu christi ...' (as in Meertens, *op. cit.*, VI, 94 item 7.d.);
   (ii) (fol. 90v) '*Item soe wie wanneer hi die honichuloyname* Ihesus ... *verdient van paeus iohan xl. daghen aflaets ...* O scepper alre creaturen du biste ontfarmhertich van naturen doer dine grondelose barmherticheit soe verghif mi here mine crancheit. ende ouermits iv heilighe vijf wonden soe verghif mi lieue here al mine sonden. Amen'.

[Items 9-12 occupy quires XIII-XVII]

9. (fols. 91r-108v, rubric on fol. 90v) Hours of All Saints: '*Hier beghinnen alle heilighen ghetiden*' (cf. R.-A. Parmentier, 'Een vijftiendeeuwsch getijdenboek uit het voormalig bisdom Utrecht (Handschrift van Zuylen)', *Annales de la Société d'Emulation de Bruges* 76 (1934), 95-136, at 108-12).

[fol. 109r blank, fol. 109v with a miniature]

10. (fols. 110r-116v, rubric on fol. 108v) The Seven Penitential Psalms: '*Hier beghinnen die seuen psalmen*' (pr. van Wijk, *op. cit.*, 139-45).

11. (fols. 116v-123v) Litany and collects; the litany substantially as pr. in *ibid.*, 145-50; among the differences are the inclusion of Valerianus, 'Panciaes', Ivo, Poncianus, Bavo, 'Geliis', Gummar, Alexius, Spes, Barbara, Martha, Justina, and Juliana, and the omission of Pancras and Brice; followed (fols. 122v-123v) by three collects: (i) 'Wi bidden di here verhore die bede ...' (pr. *ibid.*, 153); (ii) 'Onutfarme [*sic*] di onser here ontfarme di onser barmliker ...' (pr. *ibid.*, 153-4 line 4); (iii) 'Verlosse ons vanden dode totten leuen ...' (pr. *ibid.*, 154 ll.4-25; i.e. the long collect in van Wijk is divided in the present manuscript by a one-line red initial and the rubric '*collect*').

12. (fols. 124r-129v, rubric on fol. 123v) Hours of the Cross: '*Hier beghinnen die corte cruus ghetiden*' (pr. *ibid.*, 87-91); followed (fols. 127v-129v) by a Cross-related prayer and indulgenced devotions:
   (i) (fol. 127v) '*Tot sinte andries* Doe sinte andries quam totter stede daer dat cruce bereit was ... o heilighe cruus ... in die ghehanghen heest', with versicle

and the collect: 'O here wi bidden di seer ynnichlike ende deuotelike … lieuer
brienden ziclen. Amen' (as in Meertens, *op. cit.*, VI, 95 item 19.b.);
(ii) (fol. 128r-v) a version of the Seven Prayers of St. Gregory: *'Dic dese seuen
ghebedekijn leset mit .vij. pater noster ende aue maria al knielende voer die wapenen
ons heren die verdient .xlvi^m. iaer. ende xl. daghen aflaets* O here ihesu christe ic
aenbede di hanghende anden cruce. ende op dijn hoest draghende … wes
ghenadich mijn ziele in haer intuaert' (cf. Meertens, *op. cit.*, II, 86-7);
(iii) (fol. 128v-129v) Gospel Pericope from John, followed by two rubrics
detailing indulgences of Clement V: *'Item soe wie sinte ians ewangeli* Inden
beghinne *hoert of leset … die verdient van paeus clemens die vijste een iaer. ende xl.
daghen aflaets'*, and *'Item soe wie onser vrouwen lof sanc leset in latijn of in
duytsche. dat is* Magnificat *die verdient elkes daghes .xxxiij. iaer aflaets ende alsoe
vele weken'*.

[Items 13-16 occupy quires XVIII-XXII]

[fol. 130r blank, fol. 130v with a miniature]

13. (fols. 131r-158v, rubric on fol. 129v) Office of the Dead: *'Hier beghint die
vigeli. Invitatorium'* (pr. van Wijk, *op. cit.*, 156-95 n. 10; i.e. beginning on the
second page of the printed text, and omitting the end of the last pr. collect); with
(fol. 158r-v) an extra collect at the end: 'Ontfarmhertighe ende almachtighe
vader wi bidden ontfarme der zielen dinen … alle dinen heilighen van ewen tot
ewen sonder eynde Amen Here ghif here die ewighe rust ende dat ewighe licht
moet here licht Si moeten rusten in breden Amen'.

14. (fols. 158v-162r) Prayers before communion: *'Alsmen ten heilighen
sacramente gaen willen les dit'*:
   (i) (fols. 158v-159v) 'Wes ghegruet o alre heilichste lichaem ons heren
   onthouden inden heilighen sacramente … lesten een salich wtgans moet
   ghegheuen werden Amen' (cf. Meertens, *op. cit.*, III, 63-4);
   (ii) (fols. 159v-160v) 'O leuende vrucht du suete gheminde paradijs. du suete
   dropel … openbaerliken sien moghen inder ewigher saliche Amen' (cf.
   Meertens, *op. cit.*, III, 61; VI, 110 item 31.d.);
   (iii) (fols. 160v-161v) 'O here der enghelen glorie ic arme sondighe … in dien
   name daer di ontfenc dijn ghebenedide moeder maria Amen' (cf. Meertens, *op.
   cit.*, III, 51-52);
   (iv) (fols. 161v-162r) 'O almachtighe ende ghenadighe god ic onwaerde
   sondighe mensche … moet daer di die enghen louen ende eren Amen'.

15. (fols. 162r-v) Prayer during communion: *'Alstu dat sacrament ontfanges les dit'*
Heer ic en bins niet waerdich dattu comest onder mijn dac … alle eertsche minne
veronweerdighet' (cf. Meertens, *op. cit.*, VI, 160 item 6.c.).

16. (fols. 162v-164v) Prayers after communion: *'Nader ontfanghenisse les dit'*:
   (i) (fols. 162v-163r) 'Danc segghe ic di o almachtighe god dattu mi onwaerde
   … werscappe der ewigher vrouden ende bliiscap Amen';

(ii) (fol. 163r-v) 'O here ihesu christe die alle tijt voer onsen sculden wordes
gheoffert ...' (pr. Meertens, *op. cit.*, III, 88);
(iii) (fols. 163v-164r) 'Ic bidde dij lieue ghenadighe here dat dese
ontfanghenisse ... ende leues ende reguiers van ewen tot ewen Amen';
(iv) (fol. 164r) 'O here ihesu christe lof si dijnre onsprekeliker minnentliker
goedertierenheit ... ghecomen der heilighen heilicheit Amen' (pr. *ibid.*, 89 ll.18-25);
(v) (fol. 164r-v) '*Item die dit ghebet leset alsmen dat heilighe sacrament op boert
die verdient .ccc. daghen aflaets* Wes ghegruet waerachtich lichaem gheboren
vander ioncfrouwe marien ...' (as in Meertens, *op. cit.*, VI, 76 item 18.b.);
(vi) (fol. 164v) '*Tot onse here ghebet* Gods ziel heilighe mi. Gods lichaem behoede
mi. Gods bloet drinke mi ... mitten enghelen ewelike. Amen' (cf. Meertens, *op. cit.*,
III, 31).

Decoration

Six very fine full-page miniatures, each with an arched top, taller than the ruled
text area (122-30 mm. high including the arched top, but not the framing),
framed by blue and gold lines (pink and gold on fols. 39v, 57v) and a full painted
border of stylized foliage, with birds, animals, and grotesques, etc., framed by a
double gold fillet (where not cropped), the interstices filled with small gold dots (a
similar border is illustrated in colour in the frontispiece to the Sotheby's catalogue referred to below); on single leaves of thicker parchment than the rest,
blank on the recto, cropped especially severely at top and bottom, inserted into
the manuscript (see also under Provenance):
(fol. 10v) Hours of the Virgin. Annunciation, in a vaulted interior; the border
with a Wild Man.
(fol. 39v) Hours of Eternal Wisdom. The Virgin and Joseph find Christ among
the Doctors.
(fol. 57v) Long Hours of the Cross. Crucifixion; with the Virgin and John to the
left; the Magdalen embracing the Cross; Longinus on horseback, piercing Christ's
side; and other soldiers, also mostly on horseback; the border with a Pelican in
her Piety (see colour frontispiece).
(fol. 76v) Hours of the Holy Spirit. Pentecost; the Apostles seated around the
Virgin (Pächt & Alexander, 1, pl. XVII).
(fol. 109v) Penitential Psalms. Last Judgement; the Redeemer's head flanked by
lilies and a sword; below are the Virgin and John, and figures rising from graves.
(fol. 130v) Office of the Dead. Raising of Lazarus; St. Peter unties Lazarus's
hands (pl. 36). (The composition is very similar to that in the The Hague,
Koninklijk Bibliotheek, 135 E 45, illustrated in the Sotheby's catalogue referred
to below, pl. facing p. 56.)

The miniatures have been attributed to the Bezborodko Master(s), who also
painted Amsterdam, Bibliotheca Philosophica Hermetica (J.R. Ritman Library)
MS. BPH 2 (dated 1491); Antwerp, Museum Plantin-Moretus, MS. 14.7 (dated
1489); Bloomington, Ind., Indiana University, Lilly Library, MS. Ricketts 133
(dated 1491); and The Hague, Koninklijk Bibliotheek, 135 E 45 (dated 1490;

this is the eponymous manuscript, named after a former owner, sold at Sotheby's, 11 December 1979, lot 50.)

Seven mostly ten-line initials (nine-line on fols. 110r, 131r, see pl. 36) opposite the miniatures, and also at fol. 91r: each composed of a 'puzzle' initial in red and blue pigments, containing, and surrounded by, penwork in red and blue inks, with green and pale yellow washes, usually in all four margins; three-line initials in blue with red penwork and green wash touches at the start of each hour from Lauds to Compline; plain two-line initials alternately in red or blue, at psalms, hymns, lessons, the KL monograms in the calendar, etc.; plain one-line initials alternately in red or blue, at verses and other minor divisions.

Hülsemann, in 'Sets of codicological characteristics', states that the penwork decoration in a group of eight manuscripts, all probably from Enkhuisen or the surrounding area, was probably supplied by two hands (she illustrates each in her figs. 6 and 9).

Note

It is possible that the miniatures were added to the volume at some time after it was first written, but if they did originally belong in the present volume, they are likely to have been included when the book was bound for the first time, and therefore of approximately the same date; other manuscripts with miniatures attributed to the same artist are dated 1489, 1490, 1490, and 1491 (see Broekhuijsen, 'The Bezborodko Masters') suggesting a date in the 1480s or 1490s for the present manuscript. The great difference in the size of the miniatures and the text space, however, combined with the fact that the miniatures are bound in on paper guards of uncertain date, makes the original relationship between the miniatures and text somewhat uncertain.

To complicate matters further, each leaf with a miniature has evidence to suggest that it was not always bound into the volume: most have deposits of paste at the top and bottom of their recto, and most have one or both of two types of pin-hole, either (i) at or very close to the upper edge of the leaf, i.e. before trimming (see Fontispiece); or (ii) somewhat lower (sometimes within the area of the miniature) and often showing a rust stain (see Frontispiece). This suggests that the leaves (a) were at some stage pasted to a surface, (b) were at some stage pinned to a surface (presumably wooden), and at some subsequent time, after the edges of the leaves were cropped, (c) were again pinned to a surface with ferrous tacks, before (d) they were eventually re-inserted in the manuscript.

Physical Description

MATERIAL: parchment.
DIMENSIONS: the leaves 159-60 x 116-8 mm., penwork decoration somewhat cropped, the outer borders of the inserted leaves considerably cropped.
NUMBER OF LEAVES: ii (paper, the first marbled) + 164 + ii (paper, the second marbled).

FOLIATION: modern, in pencil: i-ii, 1-166.
COLLATION: mostly in quires of 8 leaves, with miniatures on inserted single leaves: I (two singletons) (fols. 1-2), II^{6+1} (6th leaf a half-sheet, fol. 8) (fols. 3-9) | III^{8+1} (1st leaf inserted, fol. 10) (fols. 10-18), IV-V^8 (fols. 19-33), VI^{8+1} (6th leaf inserted, fol. 39) (fols. 34-42), VII^8 (fols. 43-50), VIII^6 (fols. 51-56) | IX^{8+1} (1st leaf inserted, fol. 57) (fols. 57-65), X^8 (fols. 66-73), XI^{8+1} (3rd leaf inserted, fol. 76) (fols. 74-82), XII^8 (fols. 83-90) | XIII^8 (fols. 91-98), XIV^6 (fols. 99-104), XV^{8+1} (5th inserted, fol. 109) (fols. 105-113), XVI-XVII^8 (fols. 114-129) | XVIII^{8+1} (1st leaf inserted, fol. 130) (fols. 130-138), XIX-XXI^8 (fols. 139-162), XXII (two half sheets) (fols. 163-164); CATCHWORDS in the bottom gutter corner of most quires other than those at the end of a major textual unit; no quire/leaf signatures visible.
RULING: 22 lines ruled in pale brown ink, between single vertical bounding lines, usually so faint as to be almost invisible; the ruled space 95-6 x 65-6 mm.; prickings frequently visible in upper and lower margins, also occasionally at the fore-edge, e.g. fol. 162.
SCRIPT: written in gothic bookhand, with 21 lines of text per page; the written space *c.*93 x 65 mm.; the litany of saints written (but not ruled) in two columns.
RUBRICATION: headings, occasional paraphs and underlinings in red, capitals touched in red; guides for rubrics often visible, e.g. fols. 66r, 67r, 69r, etc.
SEC. FOL.: (calendar) 'd Helena coninghinne', (text, fol. 12r) 'hoert sine stemme'.

Binding

Sewn on five cords, with endbands; bound in 18th(?)-cent. mottled brown leather over pasteboards, the covers undecorated, the spine with five raised bands and dense gilt ornament in all six compartments; marbled endleaves; one green silk bookmark; the edges of the leaves red with some green speckling; the corners and upper joint rather worn.

Provenance

1. Written at or for Enkhuizen(?), as suggested by the calendar and litany, after 1471 (the date of the election of Pope Sixtus IV, who is mentioned on fol. 56r). See also the Note under Decoration.

2. Unidentified, presumably post-medieval, owner(s): the characteristic Enkhuizen feasts in red in the calendar were marked by a group of three black dots arranged in a triangle; for reasons now obscure, in the 18th/19th(?) cent. the numbers '132', '131', and '134' were written against the entries for Eulalia, Gabinius, and Romanus (13 [*recte* 12], 19, and 28 Feb., respectively), with a letter 'H'(?) immediately after Romanus's name, and 'I _P RCO'(??) in the lower margin (fol. 2r), perhaps just a pen-trial.

3. Unidentified 19th-cent. owner(s): inscribed in pencil 'N° 1' towards the upper left corner of fol. i verso; to the left of this a circular label has been removed.

4. John Buchanan (see Introduction, pp. xiv, xix): inscribed in pencil with the 'Descriptive list' number, '15.', in the top left corner of fol. i verso.

5. Rt. Hon. T. R. Buchanan (1846-1911); given to the Bodleian by his widow, Mrs. E. O. Buchanan, in 1939, when it was accessioned as MS. Dutch f. 1; re-referenced as MS. Buchanan f. 1 in 1941.

Bibliography

'Fifteen illuminated *Horae*', *BLR* 1 no. 7 (1939), 115-6, at 116 (as MS. Dutch f. 1).

van Dijk, *Handlist of Latin liturgical MSS.*, IV, 309 (mentioned, not described).

Pächt & Alexander, 1, no. 245, pl. XVII (fol. 76v).

Friedrich Gorissen, *Das Stundenbuch der Katharina von Kleve: Analyse und Kommentar* (Berlin, 1973), 802 (cited as 'Buch. 245', i.e. the no. in Pächt & Alexander).

Sotheby, Parke Bernet & Co., *Catalogue of western manuscripts and miniatures ... which will be sold by auction ... 11th December 1979* (London), mentioned at p. 56, under lot 50.

Martin Breslauer, *Books, MSS. & autographs selected for exhibition at the 9th International Antiquarian Book Fair, October 2-4, 1980* (New York), mentioned under item 1.

A. S. Korteweg and C. A. Chavannes-Mazel, *Schatten van de Koninklijke Bibliotheek: acht eeuwen verluchte handschriften* (The Hague, 1980), 193; and, *Treaures of the Royal Library, The Hague* [translation by H. S. Lake of the former into English] (The Hague, 1980), 104.

Avril Henry, ed., *Biblia Pauperum: a facsimile and edition* (Aldershot, 1987), 147 n. 2.

James H. Marrow, Henri L. M. Defoer, Anne S. Korteweg, and Wilhelmina C. M. Wüstefeld, *The golden age of Dutch manuscript painting* (New York, 1990), 290.

A. S. Korteweg and K. H. Broekhuijsen, 'Twee boekverluchters uit de Noordelijke Nederlanden in Duitsland: een Zwarte-ogen-meester, Johannes Ruysch en het Graduale van de abdij Gross St. Martin te Keulen uit het jaar 1500', in *Annus quadriga mundi: opstellen over middeleeuwse kunst opgedragen aan Prof. Dr. Anna C. Esmeijer* ed. J. B. Bedaux and A. M. Koldeweij (Clavis Kunsthistorische Monografieën, 8: Zutphen, 1989), 49-76, at 66.

Klara Broekhuijsen, 'The Bezborodko Masters and the use of prints', in *Masters and miniatures: proceedings of the Congress on Medieval Manuscript Illumination in the Northern Netherlands (Utrecht, 10-13 December 1989)* ed. Koert Van Der Horst and Johann-Christian Klamt (Studies and Facsimiles of Netherlandish Illuminated Manuscripts, 3: Doornspijk, 1991), 403-12, at 403 nn. 4, 6.

Klara Broekhuijsen, *De Zwarte-Ogen-Meesters: een onderzoek naar de stijl en iconografie van een groep Noordnederalndse miniaturisten rond 1500*, unpublished disseration, Universiteit van Amsterdam (1997), 21-3, 101. [Not consulted.]

Margriet Hülsmann, 'Sets of codicological characteristics and their overlapping areas: various aspects of book production', in *Sources for the history of medieval books and libraries* ed. Rita Schlusemann, Jos M. M. Hermans, and Margriet Hoogvliet (Boekhistorische reeks, 2: Groningen, 1999), p. 264 n. 9.
[I am grateful to the author for sending me a pre-publication copy].

MS. Buchanan f. 2

Bridgettine Breviary, in Latin
Netherlands, Diocese of Liège, Mariënwater; 15th century, last quarter

Text
[Item 1 occupies quires I-II]

1. (fols. 1r-10v) Calendar, about half-full, major feasts in red, feasts fully graded
from memoriae and commemorations up to IX lessons and *totum duplex*; written
continuously, so that most months do not start on a new page; each month
headed by a note on the length of the calendar and lunar month in red, most
pages with a note at the bottom on the length of the night and day, also in red;
feasts in red include: Servatius, 'duplex' (13 May), Lambert, 'totum duplex' (17
Sept.), the canonisation of Bridget, 'totum duplex' (7 Oct.), Hubert, 'duplex' (3
Nov.); other *duplex* feasts, not in red, include: Gertrude (17 Mar.), the translation
of Lambert (28 Apr.), the translation and nativity of Bridget (28 May, 23 July),
Augustine, 'totum duplex' (28 Aug.), Remacle (3 Sept.), Madelberta (7 Sept.),
Theodard (10 Sept.), Maternus (19 Sept.), the octave of Lambert (24 Sept.), the
'Triumphus' of Lambert (13 Oct.), Barbara (4 Dec.); these, and other feasts in the
present manuscript, are almost identical with those listed in the descriptions of
three other Bridgettine breviaries: by Leroquais, *Livres d'heures*, II, no. 287 (Paris,
BnF, ms. n.a.l. 688); by Schutzner, *Library of Congress cat.*, 198 (Library of
Congress, MS. 30); and by the British Museum [now Library] *Cat. of additions to
the MSS. 1936-1945* (1970), 370-1 (Egerton MS. 3271); (on these three
manuscripts see under Provenance); fol. 11r-v blank except for slight offsets from
facing pages.

[Items 2-4 occupy quires III-XXIV]

2. (fols. 12r-166v) Psalms 1-150; the ten-part divisions marked by large initials;
with (fols. 138v-140v) the Athanasian Creed (*Quicumque vult*) between Ps.
118:32 and 118:33, preceded by a heading in blue (fol. 138r): '*Canticum
Anastasii.*' (sic).

3. (fols. 166v-179r) The six ferial canticles, followed by the *Benedicite*, with (fol.
176v): '*Repeticio.* Pro honore et gloria dignissime creature virginis marie matris
dei ... commendare digneris virgo maria mater dei.', *Te deum* (headed '*Canticum
ambrosii et augustini*'), *Benedictus*, *Magnificat*, and *Nunc dimittis*.

4. (fols. 179r-184v) Litany and collects; the litany including Lambert (24)
among thirty-one martyrs; Hubert (9), and Severinus (19) among twenty
confessors; Bridget of Sweden ('birgitta') (4), Elizabeth (6), Walburga (19),
Gertrude (23), Dympna (28), Bridget of Ireland ('brigida') (30), and Ursula (31)
among thirty-one virgins; the petitions (fols. 181r-183v) including (fol. 182r):
'Ut ordinem nostrum beatissime virgini marie dedicatum tua inolita pietate
exaltare et conseruare digneris.'; and four collects (fols. 183v-184v):

(i) 'Exaudi quesumus domine supplicum preces ...' (*Corpus orationum*, no. 2541);
(ii) 'Ineffabilem misericordiam tuam domine ...' (*ibid.*, no. 3129);
(iii) 'Omnipotens eterne deus edificator et custos ...' (*ibid.*, no. 3787);
(iv) 'Pietate tua quesumus domine nostrorum solue uincula peccatorum
omnium. ... eternam concede. Per ...' (pr. A. Jefferies Collins, ed., *The
Bridgettine Breviary of Syon Abbey: from the MS. with English rubrics F.4.II at
Magdalene College Cambridge* (Henry Bradshaw Society, 96: Worcester, 1969),
151; differing from *Corpus orationum*, no. 4227).

[Item 5 occupies quires XXV-XXXVIII]

5. (fols. 185r-297v) Office of the Virgin for each day of the week, with three
lessons at Matins, and with variations for major feasts and seasons, as translated
from Swedish into Latin for St. Bridget by Peter Olovsson (*alias* Peter the Venerable
of Skänninge (d. 1378)): (fols. 185r-202v) Sunday; (fols. 203r-216v, rubric on
fol. 202v) Monday; (fols. 216v-230v) Tuesday; (fols. 230v-243v) Wednesday;
(fols. 244r-258v, rubric on fol. 243v) Thursday, starting imperfect at Ps. 57
(at '| | *psalmus* Si vere utique ...') due to the loss of a leaf before fol. 244; (fols.
258v-275v) Friday; (fols. 275v-291r) Saturday; with (fols. 291r-297v) variations
for major seasons and feasts (substantially the same as pr. by Collins, *op. cit.*, 13-131;
and by Tryggve Lundén, ed., *Den heliga Birgitta och den helige Petrus av Skänninge:
Officium parvum beate Marie Virginis* (Acta Universitatis Upsalensis; Studia
Historico-Ecclesiastica Upsaliensia, 27-28: 2 vols., Uppsala, 1976), in Latin and
parallel Swedish translation (the Latin on even-numbered pages): I, 2-139
(Sunday-Tuesday); II, 6-169 (Wednesday-Saturday)).

[Items 6-9 occupy quires XXXIX-XLII]

6. (fol. 298r-v) Prayers to be said by the hebdomadaries: '*Lectrix ad mensam in
die dominica ter dic* Domine labia mea aperies. ...', '*Ebdomadarie coquinarie ter ante
altare* Benedictus es domine deus meus ...', '*Ebdomadarie coquinarie.* Deus in
adiutorium meum intende. ...'; with rubrics indicating parts to be said by the
'*chorus*' and '*horista*', and collects (cf. Library of Congress, MS. 30, fol. 147r-v
(see Schutzner, *op. cit.*, 199); and Liverpool, University Library, MS. F. 2. 2, fol.
132r-v (see Ker, *MMBL*, III, 273)).

7. (fols. 299r-307v) Office of the Holy Spirit (pr. Lundén, *op. cit.*, II, 184-209),
starting imperfect in the capitulum before the hymn *Veni creator* (at '| | datus est
nobis.', *ibid.*, 184), due to the loss of a leaf before fol. 299.

8. (fols. 307v-317r) Office of the Dead, '*Pro fidelibus defunctis*', Use of the
Brigittines (pr. *ibid.*, 210-35) followed (fols. 315r-317v) by eleven collects:
    (i) '*Pro una defuncta.* Quesumus domine pro tua pietate miserere anime
    famule tue .N. [feminine forms] ...' (pr. *Corpus orationum*, no. 4843);
    (ii) '*Collecta pro parentibus* Deus qui nos patrem et matrem ...' (pr. *ibid.*, no. 1903);
    (iii) '*pro uno defuncto* Omnipotens sempiterne deus cui nunquam sine spe
    misericordie ...' (pr. *ibid.*, no. 3809);

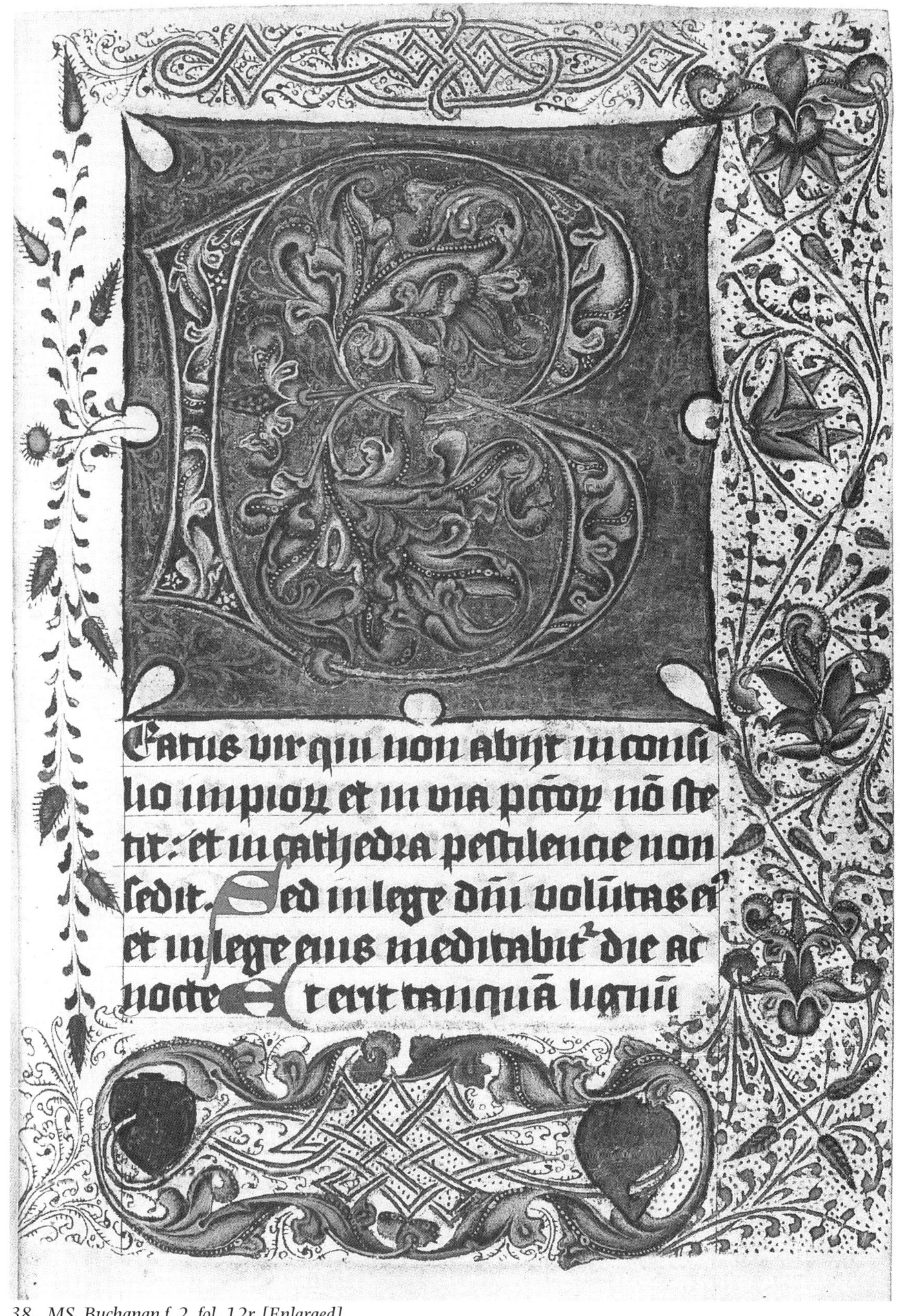

38. MS. Buchanan f. 2, fol. 12r. [Enlarged]

(iv) '*Pro congregacione.* Deus venie largitor ...' (pr. *ibid.*, no. 2205, with 'et sorores' inserted after 'fratres', and 'beata maria semper uirgine' instead of 'beato illo patrono nostro', cf. MS. Buchanan e. 10, text item 6);

(v) '*Pro sacerdote.* Presta quesumus omnipotens deus ut anima famuli tui .N. sacerdotis ...' (similar to that pr. *ibid.*, no. 4467);

(vi) '*Pro benefactoribus.* Deus cuius misericordie non est numerus, suscipe propicius preces humilitatis nostre. ...' (pr. *ibid.*, no. 1178);

(vii) '*Pro viuis et mortuis* Omnipotens sempiterne deus qui viuorum dominaris ...' (pr. *ibid.*, no. 4064);

(viii) '*Animabus desolatis. collecta.* Miserere obsecro domine misereris animabus seruorum tuorum et ancillarum tuarum ...';

(ix) '*Collecta generalis.* Inclina domine aurem tuam ad preces nostras ...' (pr. *ibid.*, no. 3116b);

(x) '*Collecta generalis.* Miserere quesumus domine clementer animabus omnium benefactorum nostrorum defunctorum ...' (pr. *ibid.*, no. 3366);

(xi) '*Collecta generalis* Fidelium deus omnium conditor ... Per ihesu christe saluator mundi ... Requiescat in pace Amen.' (pr. *ibid.*, no. 2684b).

9. (fol. 317v) A short confession: 'Confiteor deo omnipotenti et beatissime semper virgini marie beate birgitte beato augustino et omnibus sanctis dei ... virginem mariam beatam birgittam beatum augustini [*sic*] et omnibus dei [*sic*] et te patrem orare pro me.'

10. (fol. 317v) A short prayer: '*Ante vesperas* Ave maria ... Indulgete nobis propter deum et piissimam matrem eius mariam ...' (pr. Collins, *op. cit.*, 29).

Decoration
Three (of an original four?) large fourteen- (fols. 131r, 185r) or twelve-line (fol. 12r) painted initials, containing foliage and flowers, on a patterned gold ground; each with a four-sided gold and painted border of stylised and naturalistic foliage and flowers (fol. 185r also with fruit):
(fol. 12r) Psalm 1. Initial B[eatus]; the lower border with two gold heart shapes joined by interlace decoration (pl. 38).
(fol. 131r) Psalm 109. Initial D[ixit] (Pächt & Alexander, 1, pl. XVII, no. 247).
(fol. 185r) Office of the Virgin. Initial T[rinum]; the lower border with the letters 'b l' (or 'b i'?) joined by interlace decoration (see also under Provenance).

An offset on fol. 243v suggests that a similar initial with a full border may have originally decorated the start of the Office for Thursday, for no apparent reason.

One might expect that the removal of the first leaf of the Office of the Holy Spirit was on account of its being decorated, but there is little visible offset on fol. 298v which might support this.

Eight- or nine-line 'puzzle' initials in red and blue, with reserved designs, enclosing and surrounded by penwork in red and purple inks, extending into the margins, partially filled with blue, green and yellow, at major divisions of

the Psalms: Ps. 26 (fol. 36v), Ps. 38 (fol. 52r), Ps. 52 (fol. 66r), Ps. 80 (fol. 97v),
Ps. 97 (fol. 113v) and the start of the Offices for Monday to Saturday (fols. 203r,
216v, 230v [pl. 39], [leaf for Thursday missing before fol. 244,] 258v, 275v);
similar six- or seven-line initials at the other major divisions of the Psalms: Ps. 51
(fol. 65r), Ps. 68 (fol. 79v), and Ps. 101 (fol. 116r), but with the body of the
initial in blue only; three-line initials, many with reserved designs, alternately in
red with purple penwork, or blue with red penwork, to psalms, the start of each
hour from Lauds to Compline in the offices, lessons, etc.; plain two-line initials,
alternately red or blue, to hymns, collects, the KL monograms in the calendar,
etc.; plain one-line initials, alternately red or blue, to verses and other minor
textual divisions; line-fillers in red and blue in the litany.

On decorated manuscripts from Mariënwater see A. van Veenendaal,
'Gedecoreerde handschriften van Mariënwater', in *In Buscoducis 1450-1629.
Kunst uit de Bourgondische tijd te 's-Hertogenbosche: de cultuur van late
Middeleeuwen en Renaissance*, 2, ed. A. M. Koldeweij (Maarssen, etc., 1990),
497-500, 613; and de Beer, 'Noorde-Brabant', esp. 154-6, 160-2 nos. 151-5.

Physical Description
MATERIAL: parchment.
DIMENSIONS: the leaves 158-61 x 107-9 mm., the decoration cropped in all outer
margins.
NUMBER OF LEAVES: an original pastedown + i (modern paper) + 317 + i (modern
paper) + an original pastedown.
FOLIATION: modern, in pencil: i, 1-318; older markings number fols. 299r-303r
from '4' to '12', and fols. 298v, 303v, and 304r as '(I)', '(III)', and '(IV)' respectively.
COLLATION: mostly in quires of 8 leaves: I$^{6-1}$ (4th leaf cancelled, leaving a stub
after fol. 3) (fols. 1-5), II^{6-1+1} (3rd leaf cancelled, leaving a wide stub after fol. 7;
7th leaf an inserted blank, fol. 11) (fols. 6-11) | III-XIV^8 (fols. 12-107), XV^{8-1+1}
(2nd leaf cancelled after fol. 108, leaving a wide stub, and replaced with fol. 109;
see the *Note*, below) (fols. 108-115) | XVI^8 (fols. 116-123), XVII^{8-1+1} (8th leaf
cancelled after fol. 130, leaving a wide stub, and replaced with fol. 131; see the
Note, below) (fols. 124-131), XVIII$^{10-1}$ (10th leaf cancelled, after fol. 140) (fols.
132-140), XIX-XXII^8 (fols. 141-172), XXIII^6 (fols. 173-178), XXIV^6 (fols. 179-184)
| XXV^{10} (fols. 185-194), XXVI-XXXI^8 (fols. 195-242), XXXII$^{8-1}$ (2nd leaf missing,
after fol. 243) (fols. 243-249), XXXIII-XXXVI^8 (fols. 250-281), XXXVII^{8-1+1} (7th
leaf cancelled after fol. 287, leaving a wide stub, and replaced with fol. 288)
(fols. 282-289), XXXVIII^8 (fols. 290-297) | XXXIX$^{8-1}$ (2nd leaf missing, after fol.
298) (fols. 298-304), XL^8 (fols. 305-312), XLI$^{4-1}$ (4th leaf cancelled, after fol. 315)
(fols. 313-315), XLII^2 (fols. 316-317) | the lower pastedown appears to have been
the fourth leaf of a quire of six: three very narrow stubs of the first half of the
quire survive, and parts of the fifth and sixth leaves are visible under the
pastedown; CATCHWORDS are largely cropped, but traces occasionally survive,
in small, less formal script, in pale brown ink (e.g. fols. 202v, 265v, 273v).

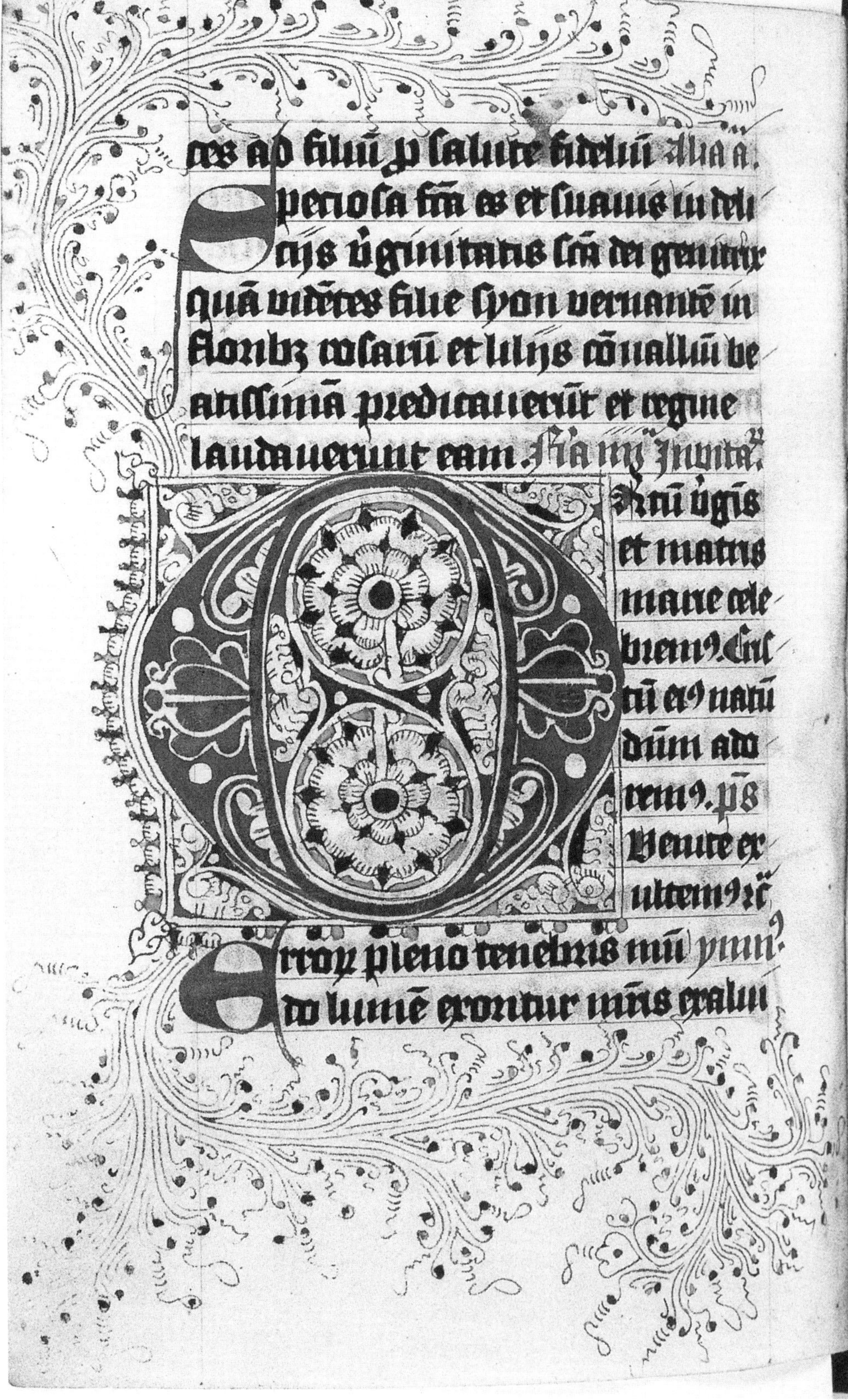

39. *MS. Buchanan f. 2, fol. 230v. [Enlarged]*

RULING: 19 lines ruled in brown ink, between single vertical bounding lines extending the full height of the page, the litany in two columns with double vertical ruling lines each side of each column, extending the full height of the page; the ruled space 101-4 x 68-70 mm.; the calendar with 21 lines ruled in purple, with 6 verticals, 5 of them extending the full height of the page, the ruled space 101-3 x 80-4 mm.; prickings are frequently visible in the lower margin, and occasionally at the fore-edge.

SCRIPT: written in a good, regular, gothic bookhand, with 18 lines of text per page; the written space 97-100 x 70-6 mm.; the calendar with 20 lines of text per page.

RUBRICATION: headings in red (occasionally in blue, e.g. fols. 140v, 175v), with guides occasionally visible in the gutter margin in cursive script (e.g. fols. 140v, 141r, 306r); capitals, when not painted, touched in red; marginal colour notes in plummet for two-line initials, apparently in the vernacular: 'b' for blue (i.e. blauw?), 'r'(?) for red (i.e. rood?) (e.g. fols. 4r, 5r, 25r, 28v).

SEC. FOL.: (calendar) 'v c vij'; (text, fol. 13r) 'in celis'.

Note

The structure of quires XV and XVII deserves brief comment. The stub of the cancelled leaf between fols. 108 and 109 is wide enough to preserve traces of script and decoration, and therefore shows that this leaf had been written on both sides, and decorated on the recto with a three-line initial in red, pen-flourished in purple, like the initial which now replaces it in the same position on fol. 109. Elsewhere, the pen-flourishing of three-line initials overlaps one-line initials, demonstrating that the latter were executed first. This suggests that, exceptionally, the leaf must have been cancelled and replaced not only after the (whole?) book had been written, but after at least two stages of its decoration were also complete.

The stub between fols. 130 and 131 preserves traces of script, evidence of its having been written on the verso (and therefore also on the recto) before being cancelled. The leaf which now replaces the cancelled leaf, fol. 131, is the last leaf of the quire, and contains the major decorated initial to Psalm 109; this suggests that the scribe did not leave enough space for the initial when he/she first wrote out the text of Psalm 109, but that this mistake was noticed and rectified before she/he started to write the following quire.

Binding

Early 16th-cent.(?) stamped leather binding in the style commonly attributed to the the van Gavere family of binders of Ghent (pl. 2). Originally sewn at four sewing-stations (double cords or split straps?); bound in brown leather over bevelled wood boards; each cover with a rectangular blind-stamped panel surrounded by framing fillets and consisting of two narrow vertical rectangles, separated by a zig-zag design with three-petal flowers in the interstices, each rectangle containing four angels facing inwards, blowing trumpets, within foliate scrolls with bunches of grapes, all surrounded by the text 'veni·creator·spi(ri)t(u)s | mentes tuorum visita imple | :superna:gracia: | que tu creasti pectora'

(*Repertorium hymnologicum*, no. 21204) starting at the top left, in gothic letters, with floral designs at each corner, and a palmette motif separating each word on the left and right sides; the spine with simple horizontal lines in the top and bottom compartments; two pairs of brass clasp fittings at the fore-edge (fastening from bottom to top), traces of the leather straps remaining; with original pastedowns, the lower pastedown ruled as for the main textblock. Resewn on four straps (visible between fols. 131 and 132), without endbands; rebacked, with the earlier spine leather relaid; modern laid paper flyleaves, that at the back with part of a watermark: 'Ch[...]' in English 'black-letter' style. The upper pastedown has a stub before fol. i, in the gutter fold of which one can see the original sewing-stations, which correspond approximately to the present sewing; that the book has been re-sewn, however, is shown by the fact that this stub, in its present position, would have prevented the offset of the 'KL' monogram on fol. 1r onto the upper right corner of the pastedown, so the stub must originally have been hooked around the first quire; in addition the singletons appear to be sewn on modern laid paper guards.

The binding has been noticed by Duff and Prideaux, and mentioned by Gibson; the binding panel is apparently identical with one represented by a rubbing in the Victoria and Albert Museum, described in Weale, *Bookbindings in the National Art Library*, II, 181 no. 370 ('Flanders. Ghent. Van Gavere'); and one until 1914 in the Louvain Universitaatsbibliothek, on a printed book of 1520, described and illustrated in L. Indestege, 'Paneelstempels met musicerende engelen op Vlaamse boekbanden uit de late Middeleeuwen', in *Dr. L. Reypens-Album: opstellen aangeboden aan Prof. Dr. L. Reypens s. j. ter gelegenheid van zijn tachigste veraardag op 26 februari 1964* ed. Albert Ampe (Antwerp, 1964), 173-85, at 182-3 'Type VIII', afb. 8. Through the kindness of Dr. Rowan Watson a photocopy of the V&A rubbing is available at the Bodleian.

Provenance
1. Made for the Bridgettine nunnery of Mariënwater, at 's Hertogenbosch (founded 1434): the calendar is of Liège (having four feasts of Lambert as well as other Liège saints), and Bridgettine (having three feasts of Bridget, all highly graded); the only Bridgettine house in the diocese of Liège was Mariënwater (about which see Tore Nyberg, *Birgittinische Klostergründungen des Mittelalters* (Bibliotheca Historica Lundensis, 15: Lund, 1965), esp. ch. V, 'Die Niederlande').

2. Unidentified 18th/19th-cent. owner: inscribed in black ink in the top left corner of the upper pastedown 'N°. 12.' (the same hand wrote 'N°. 19.' in the same place in London, BL, Egerton MS. 3271; and 'N°. 31.' in MS. Lat. liturg. e. 4, on both of which see below).

3. D.-C. and J.-J. van Voorst, Amsterdam, before 1859: almost certainly the manuscript described as lot 113 in the auction catalogue of the books and manuscripts of D.-C. and J.-J. van Voorst, sold in Amsterdam by Frederik Muller, 27 Jan. 1859. The catalogue states (p. 13) that the Books of Hours, lots 111-141,

'... proviennent pour une grande partie du monastère de Brigittines *S. Marien water* près de Bois-le-Duc [i.e. 's Hertogenbosch], fondé en 1434'; the brief description of lot 113 is close to the present manuscript in its reported date, contents, size, number of leaves, type of decoration, and binding. Three other Bridgettine Breviaries from Mariënwater, lots 111, 122, and 126 in this sale, are now Washington, D.C., Library of Congress, MS. 30; Paris, BnF, ms. n.a.l. 688; and London, BL, Egerton MS. 3271; lot 124 was resold in London at Sotheby's, 1 December 1987, lot 38, and is now Schøyen Collection, London and Oslo, MS. 39; and lot 140, another Brigittine MS., is now Bodleian, MS. Lat. liturg. e. 4.

4. M. A. van der Linde, before 1864: in the auction catalogue of his library, sold in Brussels by G.-A. van Trigt, 7-16 April, 1864, lot 202 [I am grateful to Ulla Sander Olsen for this reference].

5. Unidentified 19th-cent. continental owner(s) and/or bookseller(s); inscribed in pencil, above the centre of the upper pastedown: 'XIVe S^cle' (presumably this owner did not know that the book came from Mariënwater, or else did not know that the house was founded in the 15th cent.); the upper pastedown inscribed in pencil '280' (? - the final digit obscured by the remains of a pasted-in piece of paper, now removed); the lower pastedown inscribed in pencil: 'me.-' in the upper right corner, and '72..'' (perhaps a price in francs) below this.

6. Raguin, bookseller, Paris (see Introduction, p. xxiv); the lower pastedown inscribed in pencil: 'bms. ok' in the upper left corner.

7. Rt. Hon. T. R. Buchanan (1846-1911), probably after 1874, but before 1891 (when it was exhibited at the Burlington Fine Arts Club); given to the Bodleian by his widow, Mrs. E. O. Buchanan, in 1941.

Bibliography

Frederik Muller, *Catalogue raisonné de la précieuse collection de manuscrits et d'autographes de MM. D.-C. van Voorst, père, et J.-J. van Voorst, fils, pasteurs evangéliques à Amsterdam ... vendue le 27 Janvier 1860 et les jours suivants ...* (Amsterdam, 1859), lot 113.

G.-A. van Trigt, *Catalogue de la bibliothèque de M. A. van der Linde, Docteur en philosophie: la vente aura lieu du 7 au 16 avril 1864* (Brussels), lot 202.

E. Gordon Duff and S. T. Prideaux, *Burlington Fine Arts Club: exhibition of bookbindings* (London, 1891), no. 5.

S. Gibson, 'Bookbindings in the Buchanan Collection', *BLR* 2 no. 16 (1941), 6-12, at 9.

S. J. P. van Dijk, *Latin liturgical manuscripts and printed books: guide to an exhibition held during 1952* (Bodleian Library: Oxford, 1952), no. 107.

van Dijk, *Handlist of Latin liturgical MSS.*, IV, 15.

Pächt & Alexander, 1, no. 247, pl. XVII (fol. 131r).

Ulla Sander Olsen, *Et klosterbibliothek, Mariënwater, fra ca. 1434-1713: forsog på en rekonstruktion.*, Copenhagen, Danmarks Biblioteksskole, 110 no. 119 (unpublished, but the locations of several copies are listed in the same author's 1995 article (see below); through the kindness of the author, a photocopy of the entry relating to MS. Buchanan f. 2 is available at the Bodleian.

Sotheby, Parke Bernet & Co., *Catalogue of western manuscripts and miniatures ... which will be sold by auction ... 22nd June 1982* (London), cited under lot 84.

Judith Oliver, ed., *Manuscripts sacred and secular: from the collections of the Endowment for Biblical Research and Boston University* (Boston, 1985), 48-50 no. 85, at 50.

Richard W. M. de Beer, 'Noorde-Brabant', in *Kriezels, aubergines en takkenbossen: randversiering in Noordnederlandse handschriften uit de vijftiende eeuw* ed. A. S. Korteweg (The Hague, 1992), 154-65, at 155.

Ottosen, *Office of the Dead*, pp. xxiv, 107, 238 (cited as 'OXF2').

Ulla Sander Olsen, 'Handschriften uit het Birgittinessenklooster Mariënwater te Rosmalen bij 's- Hertogenbosch', in *Serta devota in memoriam Guillelmi Lourdaux, pars posterior: Cultura Mediaevalis*, ed. Werner Verbeke *et al.* (Mediaevalia Lovaniensia, Series I, 21, 1995), 225-54, at 233, 244.

MS. Buchanan f. 3

Book of Hours, in Dutch, mainly in the translation of Geert Grote
The Netherlands, diocese of Utrecht(?), for use in the diocese of Cologne(?); 15th
century, second quarter

Text
[fols. 1r-2v are described last, under II]

[I]

[Item 1 occupies quires I-II]

1. (fols. 4r-15v) Calendar, with an entry for almost every day of the year; each
month headed by a note in red, usually relating the seasonal occupation to the
length of the calendar month ('*Januarius Ioemaent*'; '*Sporkelle heuet xxviij dage*';
'*Hert maent heuet xxxi dage*'; etc.); major feasts (in red) include several saints
whose relics were at Cologne, including Pantaleon (28 July), Gereon, Victor
(10 Oct.), 11,000 virgins (21 Oct.), and Severinus (23 Oct.). Compared to the
major feasts in the Cologne calendar (i.e. those printed in bold type by Grotefend,
Zeitrechnung des deutschen Mittelalters, II pt.1, 82-6), the present manuscript
has the following differences: the following are in black: Fabian & Sebastian
(20 Jan.), Gregory (12 Mar.), and Mark (25 Apr.); the following, whose relics
were at Cologne, are in red: Albinus and 10,000 martyrs (22 Jun.), and Cunibert
(12 Nov.); the following are omitted: translation of the Three Kings (relics in
Cologne) (23 July), dedication of Cologne Cathedral (27 Sept.), Presentation of
the Virgin (21 Nov.); fols. 3r-v and 16v originally blank, fol. 16r is ruled only
with the left-hand vertical lines of the calendar.

[Item 2 occupies quires III-IX]

2. (fols. 17r-74v) Hours of the Virgin: '*Hier beghint onser vrouwe ghetide.*'
(pr. N. van Wijk, ed., *Het Getijdenboek van Geert Grote: naar het Haagse Handschrift
133 E 21* (Leidsche Drukken en Herdrukken: Kleine Reeks, III: Leiden, 1940),
36-70, the present manuscript without the prologue on p. 36); with rubrics
giving the Latin incipits of texts which are here in Dutch (e.g. '*Deus in adiutorium
God wilt dencken in mijn hulpe. ...*'), other rubrics are in Dutch (e.g. '*die eerste
lesse.*'); fols. 39v, 45v ruled, but blank except for the rubrics to Prime and Terce
respectively; fols. 40r, 46r, 55r, 60r blank, with miniatures on the versos.

[Item 3 occupies quire X]

3. (fols. 75r-80v) Hours of the Cross: '*Hier beghint theilich cruus ghetide.*'
(pr. *ibid.*, 87-91).

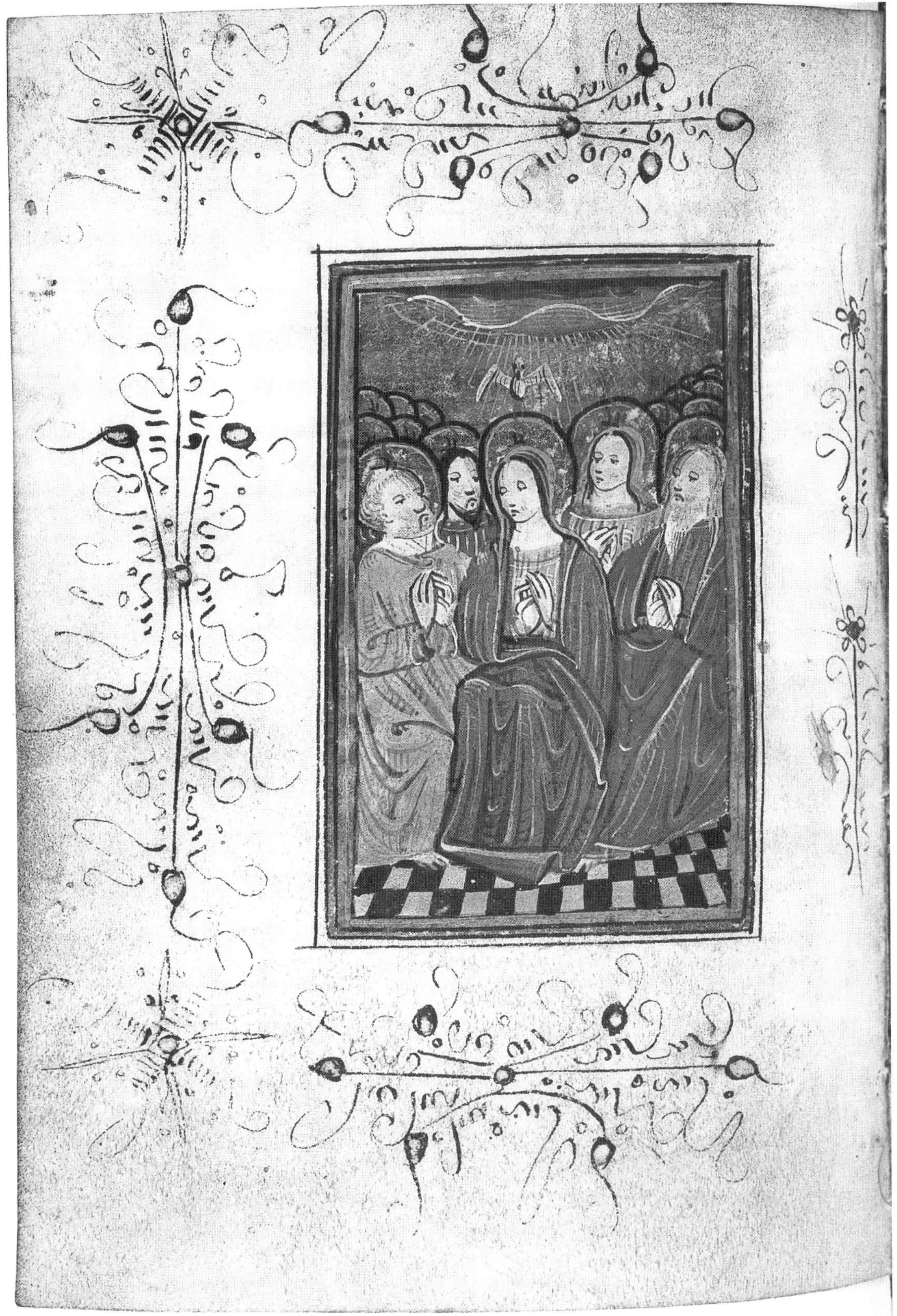

40. MS. Buchanan f. 3, fol. 104v. [Enlarged]

[Items 4-5 occupy quires XI-XIII]

[fol. 81r blank, fol. 81v with a miniature]

4. (fols. 82r-95r) The Seven Penitential Psalms: '*Hier beghint die .vij. psalm.*'
(pr. *ibid.*, 139-45).

5. (fols. 95r-103v) Litany, a prayer, and collects; the litany with Augustine (1),
Lubin, and Odulf (18-19) among nineteen confessors; Mary Magdalen (1),
Walburga, Gertrude (10-11), Ursula and Elizabeth (15-16) among sixteen virgins;
followed (fols. 101v-102v) by a prayer: '*preces.* Ic hebbe gheseit here ontferme
mijns. ... Die heer si mit v. Ende mit uwen gheest. Laet ons bidden.'; and three
collects, each headed '*Collecte.*': (i) (fols. 102v-103r) 'Wi bidden di heer verhoer
die bede ...' (pr. *ibid.*, 153); (ii) (fol. 103r) 'God dient properlike toe behoert ...
goedertierenheit bi onsen heer ihesum christum. Amen.'; (iii) (fol. 103r-v)
'O heer openbaer ons goedertierenlike dine onsprekelike ... ouermits dese sonden
verdienen bi onsen heer ihesum christum dinen soen ... zielen moeten rusten in
vreden. A.M.E.N. Heer verhoer mijn ghebet. Ende mijn roepen come totti.'

[fol. 104r blank, fol. 104v with a miniature]

[Item 6 occupies quires XIV-XIX]

6. (fols. 105r-152v) Short offices for each day of the week:
   (i) (fols. 105r-116r) for Sunday, devoted to the Trinity: '*Des sonnendages
   vander heyligher drieuoudicheit te metten.*';
   (ii) (fols. 116v-125r, rubric on fol. 116r) for Monday, devoted to All Souls:
   '*des manen daghes voer die zielen te metten.*';
   (iii) (fols. 125v-131r, rubric on fol. 125r) for Tuesday, devoted to the Baptism:
   '*Des dinxdaghes vander dopen ons heren. Te metten.*';
   (iv) (fols. 131v-137r, rubric on fol. 131r) for Wednesday, devoted to the
   Betrayal of Christ: '*Des woensdaghes van dat onse heer vercost wert te metten.*';
   (v) (fols. 137v-142r, rubric on fol. 137r) for Thursday, devoted to the Holy
   Sacrament: '*des donre daghes vanden heilighen sacrament. te metten*';
   (vi) (fols. 142v-149r, rubric on fol. 142r) for Friday, devoted to the Passion:
   '*Des vridages vander passien ons heren. Te metten tijt.*';
   (vii) (fols. 149v-152v, rubric on fol. 149r) for Saturday, devoted to the Virgin:
   '*Des saterdages van onser vrouwen.*'

[Item 7 occupy quires XX-XXIII]

7. (fols. 153r-185v) Office of the Dead: '*Hier beghint die vighelie in duutsch*', with
only three lessons at Matins (pr. *ibid.*, 156-95, i.e. starting on the second page of
the pr. text, at 'Mi hebben ombeuanghen die suchten des doots. ...'; and with only
the first three lessons at Matins); fol. 186r-v ruled, otherwise blank.

[Items 8-14, by a different scribe, occupy quires XXIV-XXVII]

8. (fols. 187r-190v) Devotion to the Seven Last Words, here attributed to Bede:
'*Hier beghint die bedinge des eersamen vaders beda vanden lesten souen woerden ...*
Pater noster. O here ihesu christi [*sic*] die inden lesten daghe ... een salich eynde
ende die moeder gades in mijnre lester noet Amen' (cf. Maria Meertens, *De*
godsvrucht in de Nederlanden naar handschriften van gebedenboeken der XVe eeuw I-
III, VI [all published] (Leuvense Studieën en Tekstuitgaven: Brussels, 1930-4), II
(1931), 111, not found in *ibid.*, VI), each of the eight sections with a Latin cue
for the Pater noster.

9. (fols. 191r-193r, rubric on fols. 190v-191r) Indulgenced prayer on the
Passion, here attributed to Pope John XXII: '*Men seget dat pauwes Iohannes die*
tweentwintichste die dit nae gescreuen gebet makede ... inder missen of inder
tegenwoerdicheit des heiligen sacraments alsoe menigen dach aflaets ... Ic bidde di alre
mildeste heer ihesu christi omme die sonderlinghe hoge ...' (as in *ibid*, VI, 197
item 19), followed by a collect: 'O Almechtige god ic bidde di omme dine heilige
vijf wonden ... lichaem noch sonder uwen heiligen olye Die leues ende regniers ...
Amen.'

10. (fols. 193v-195r, rubric on fol. 193r-v) A long indulgenced version of the
Anima Christi, here attributed to Pope John [XXII?]: '*Die pauwes iohannes heest*
gegeuen drie dusent dage aflaets van dootliken sunden Ende dusent iaer van daghelixen
sunden soe wie dit gebet leest onder missen mit ynnicheit. O Alre heilichste siele
christi heilige mi O ghebene dide ende gloriose lichaem christi in dinen wil soe
bewaert my ... heues gegeuen blijtscap in onsen herten', followed by the collect:
'God die ons daer bewijst menichuoldicheit ... moet ghedelicht werden Amen'.

11. (fols. 195r-212r) Three Communion prayers, the first two here attributed to
St. Thomas (Becket?) and St. Bernard, respectively:
   (i) (fols. 195r-196v) '*Dit ghebet heest ghemaect sancte Thomas in sinen lesten*
eynde vanden heiligen sacrament Ic aenbede di verborghen waerheit ...' (as in
ibid., VI, 47 item 14c);
   (ii) (fols. 197r-198v, rubric on fols. 196v-197r) '*Dit gebet heest gemaect sancte*
bernaert vanden heilighen sacrament O leuende vrucht du suete gheminde ...
openbaer liken gebruken in ewicheit der ewicheiden Amen.' (as in *ibid.*, VI,
47 item 14d);
   (iii) (fols. 198v-201r) '*Dit salmen lesen als men dat heilige sacrament ontfangen*
heest O here ihesu christe lof si dijnre onspreliker minnentliker
guedertierenheit ...' (pr. *ibid.*, III, 89-90; the present manuscript with an extra
eleven lines:) '... O minlike here ihesu christe wi bidde ic di om die minlike ...
Ende allen gelouigen sielen dat leuen dijnre ewicheit Amen.'

12. (fols. 201r-202r) Prayers and suffrages:
   (i) a prayer to one's Guardian Angel: '*Een gebet van minen lieuen heiligen engel*
O mijn alre liefste engel claer blinckende sterre ...' (as in Meertens, *op. cit.*, VI,
15 item 9c);

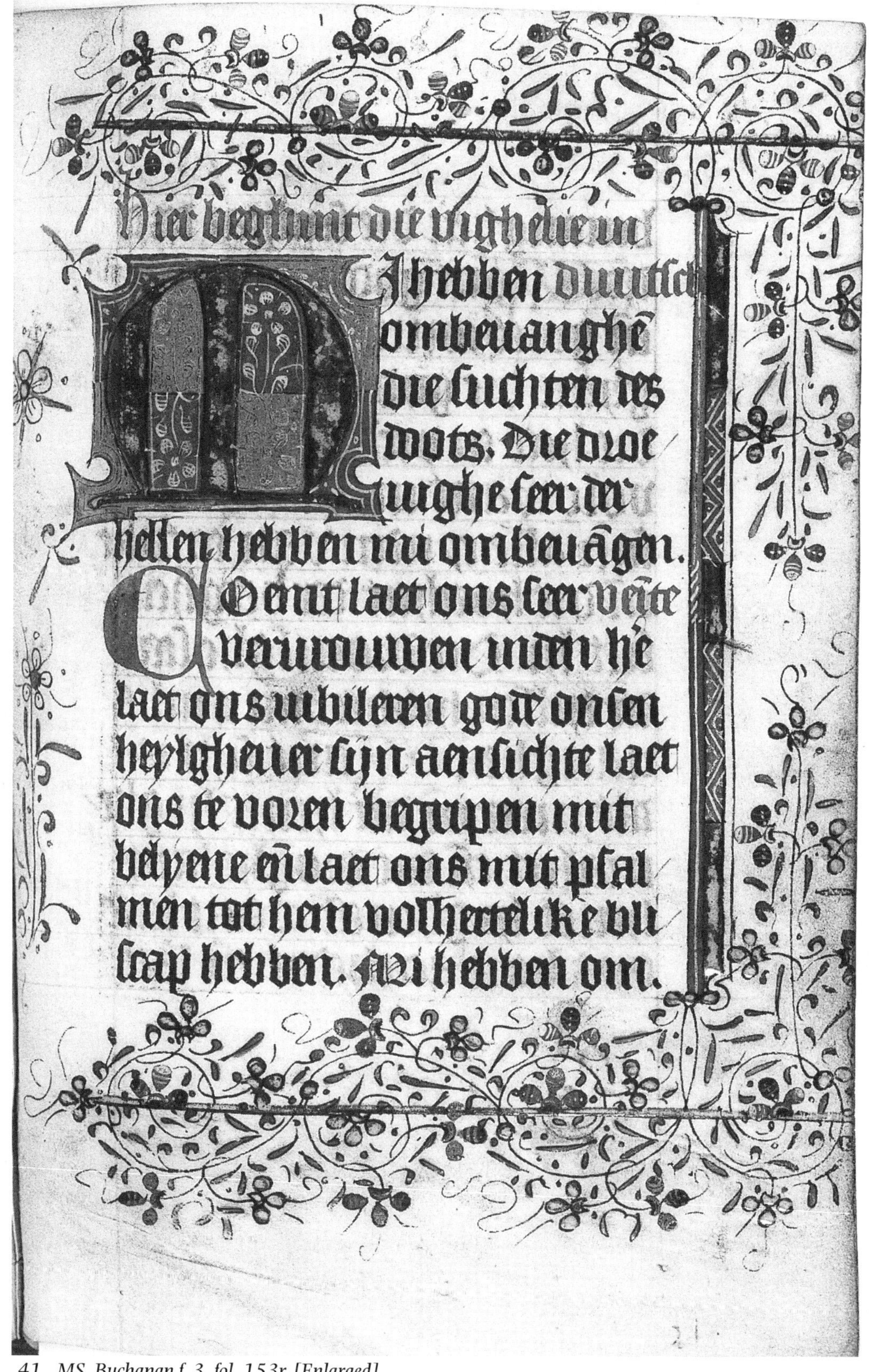

41. MS. Buchanan f. 3, fol. 153r. [Enlarged]

(ii) (fols. 202r-205v) suffrages to Sts. Philip & James, Antony Abbot, Catherine, and Barbara;
(iii) (fols. 205v-206r) a prayer to Our Lord: '*Een gebet van onsen lieuen here* O alre guedertierenste here ihesu christi sich op mi mitten oghen dijnre barmherticheit ... mordaner inden hemelschen paradise di ewelic te bescouwen';
(iv) (fols. 206r-212r) a long prayer to Our Lord: '*Een guet gebet van onsen lieuen here* O here ihesu hemelsche coninc guedertieren ontfermhertige gads soen ... mitten ewigen lichte uwer ewiger salicheit Amen'.

13. (fols. 212v-213v) Devotion to the Virgin: '*Van onser lieuer vrouwen.*', consisting of a prayer: 'O heilige maria sterne des meers verluchtende alle der werlt verluchte mijn herte ... maget ende moeder marien ende inder ewiger glorien mitti te besitten die ewige blijscap Amen.', and seven invocations, the first: 'O du vlietende borne der ewicheit woe bistu wi aldus verseghen', each followed by a Latin cue for the *Ave Maria*.

14. (fols. 213v-215v) Devotion to St. Erasmus: '*Van sancte herasme* O heilige herasme martelaer christi die op den heiligen sonnendach ... ende mi tot enen troest O heilige herasme di beuele ... ghescien hier om O heilige herasme ontfanck mi ... tot enen troest O heilige erasme oet beuele ... ende ewelic Amen Kyrieleison ... werden der belaesten ons heren ihesu christi', with a collect: 'O Almechtige god wi bidden verleen ... wederspoet werden verloest bi onsen here ihesum christum Amen'; fol. 216r-v ruled, otherwise originally blank.

[II]

(fols. 1r-2v) A bifolium of a 14th-cent. Netherlandish portable Breviary, in Latin, the Use unidentified; an unfinished, presumably discarded, central bifolium of a quire, containing from the end of the versicle of lesson IV to the start of lesson IX (from '| | aurem tuam. Quia. ...' to '... viuere cum christo. Actualis | |'), perhaps part of Matins of the feast of the Assumption of the Virgin (15 Aug.).

Decoration
Six (of an original thirteen?) full-page miniatures, in the general style of the Masters of Otto van Moerdrecht (on which see James H. Marrow, *et al.*, *The golden age of Dutch manuscript painting* (New York, 1990), 14 and cat. nos. 21-5), less fine than the historiated initial, smaller than the text-area, each on a gold ground, framed by coloured and gold lines and with sketchy black penwork and gold dots in the margins; on inserted single leaves, blank on the recto; several cut out, leaving stubs:
[Hours of the Virgin, Matins and Lauds: miniatures missing, leaving stubs before fols. 17 & 28 respectively.]
(fol. 40v) Prime. Betrayal of Christ; Malchus's Ear.
(fol. 46v) Terce. Christ before Pilate.

[Sext miniature missing, leaving a stub before fol. 51.]
(fol. 55v) None. Christ Carrying the Cross.
(fol. 60v) Vespers. Deposition; Joseph of Arimathaea supporting Christ's body.
[Compline miniature missing, leaving a stub before fol. 69.]
[Hours of the Cross miniature missing, leaving a stub before fol. 75.]
(fol. 81v) Penitential Psalms. Last Judgement; a lily and a sword either side of
Christ's head; figures rising from graves.
(fol. 104v) Daily Hours. Pentecost (pl. 40).
[Office of the Dead miniature missing, leaving a stub before fol. 153.]
[Seven Last Words miniature missing, leaving a stub before fol. 187, and an
offset on fol. 187r.]

There is no sign of the small ink stamps sometimes found on inserted leaves
painted in this style (see James Douglas Farquhar, 'Identity in an anonymous
age: Bruges manuscript illuminators and their signs', *Viator* 11 (1980), 371-83,
figs. 1-12).

One seven-line historiated initial on a gold ground, the margins of the page with
a foliate and floral border in colours and gold on all four sides, overlaid on three
intersecting gold fillets, one in each of the outer margins:
(fol. 17r) Hours of the Virgin, Matins. Virgin and Child, the Virgin crowned,
half-length; damaged by abrasion.

Five-line initials in gold on a cusped square 'quartered' ground in pink and blue,
with white tracery, with a painted and gilt bar-border in the outer margin,
a gold fillet in the upper and lower margins, and gold and painted foliage and
flowers in all four margins, at the start of the Hours of the Cross (fol. 75r), the
Penitential Psalms (fol. 82r), the first of the Daily Offices (fol. 105r), and the
Office of the Dead (fol. 153r; pl. 41); similar initials, but without the gold fillets,
and with simpler foliage ornament, to the other Daily Offices (fols. 116v, 125v, etc.);
similar four-line initials with a bar border the height of the text area, sprouting
foliage into the upper and lower margins at the start of each canonical hour
except Matins in the Hours of the Virgin (fols. 28r, 41r, etc.); similar three-line
initials and borders at each canonical hour except Matins in the Hours of the
Cross (fols. 76v, 77v, etc.); similar three-line initials without borders, but with a
simple daisy-like design in the margin alongside at each hour of the Daily Offices
except Matins (fols. 106v, 108v, etc.); one five-line penwork initial in blue with
reserved designs containing and surrounded by penwork in red ink, partially
filled-in with green wash (fol. 187r: the start of the section by the third scribe);
plain two-line initials, alternately red or blue, to psalms, hymns, lessons, etc.; plain
one-line initials, alternately red or blue, to verses and other minor textual divisions.

Comparable border decoration can be found in manuscripts with illumination in
the style the Masters of Zweder van Culemborg, e.g. Utrecht, University Library,
MS. 1037 (2.E.19), illustrated in van der Horst, *University Library, Utrecht, cat.*,
no. 37, col. pl. F, figs. 155-8.

Physical Description

MATERIAL: parchment.

DIMENSIONS: the leaves 152-3 x 106-9 mm.; the decoration cropped in the upper and fore-edge margins.

NUMBER OF LEAVES: ii (14th-cent. parchment bifolium) + 214 + 1 (modern paper).

FOLIATION: modern, in pencil: 1-217; a 17th?-cent. hand has numbered fols. 100r, 201r, and 216r as '100', '200', and '215', suggesting that at least some of the missing miniatures were already lacking by that date.

COLLATION: mostly in quires of 8 leaves, with miniatures on inserted single leaves: I^8 (fols. 3-10), II^6 (fols. 11-16) | III^{8+1-1} (1st leaf inserted, later excised, leaving a stub before fol. 17) (fols. 17-24), IV^{8+1-1} (4th leaf inserted, later excised, leaving a stub before fol. 28) (fols. 25-32), V^{8+1} (8th leaf inserted, fol. 40) (fols. 33-41), VI^{8+1} (5th leaf inserted, fol. 46) (fols. 42-50), VII^{8+1} (5th leaf inserted, fol. 55) (fols. 51-59), VIII^{8+1} (1st leaf inserted, fol. 60) (fols. 60-68), IX^{6+1-1} (1st leaf inserted, later excised, leaving a stub before fol. 69) (fols. 69-74) | X^{6+1-1} (1st leaf inserted, later excised, leaving a stub before fol. 75) (fols. 75-80) | XI^{8+1} (1st leaf inserted, fol. 81) (fols. 81-89), XII^8 (fols. 90-97), XIII^{6+1} (7th leaf inserted, fol. 104) (fols. 98-104) | XIV-XIX^8 (fols. 105-152) | XX^{8+1-1} (1st leaf inserted, later excised, leaving a stub before fol. 153) (fols. 153-161), XXI-XXIII^8 (fols. 162-186) | XXIV^{8+1-1} (1st leaf inserted, later excised, leaving a stub before fol. 187 and the wrap-around after fol. 194) (fols. 187-194), XXV-XXVI^8 (fols. 195-210), XXVII^6 (fols. 211-216) ('inserted' leaves are blank on the recto, with a miniature on the verso); CATCHWORDS visible in most quires except (i) in the calendar, (ii) at the end of each major textual unit, and (iii) quires XXIV-XXVII; alphanumeric LEAF SIGNATURES (ai, aii, aiii, etc.), from quires III to XXIII, with two forms of the letter 'r' (normal, and '2'-shaped), and two forms of the letter 's' (upright, and round).

RULING: 16 lines ruled in pale purple ink (a brighter tone in the calendar), between single vertical bounding lines extending the full height of the page, the top two and bottom two horizontal lines ruled the full width of the page; the ruled space 87-90 x 60-1 mm. (the calendar 94-5 x 81-2 mm., with all five verticals ruled the full height of the page); prickings frequently survive in all margins, about 10 mm. from the lower edge in the lower margin, the penultimate horizontal ruled line with a double pricking at the fore-edge.

SCRIPT: written in gothic bookhand, with 15 lines of text per page; the written space *c.*86 x 61 mm.; by two main scribes, responsible for (i) 17r-185v, and (ii) 187r-215v; the calendar appears to be by the second of these, or a third scribe.

RUBRICATION: headings in red, capitals and some abbreviations touched in red.

SEC. FOL.: (endleaves, fol. 2) 'te dilecto'; (calendar, fol. 5) 'KL Sporkelle heuet'; (text, fol. 18) 'sijn volc want'.

The front endleaves (fols. 1-2) are ruled in brown ink with single vertical bounding lines extending the full height of the page, but horizontal lines are not visible (not ruled?), the 'pricked height' is 103 mm., the written height 100 mm., the ruled width 63 mm.; pricked with five regularly-spaced prickings in the fore-edge margin (alongside the notional bottom horizontal ruled line, and, counting from the bottom, the sixth, twelfth, eighteenth, and twenty-fourth lines), perhaps indicating the (intended?) use of a six-nibbed ruling implement; written with 23 lines of text per page, in gothic bookhand, with headings in red, capitals touched in red, guide letters for one- and two-line painted initials which were never supplied, guides for rubrics in the outer margins; the letter 'a' in the lower margin of fol. 2r. Similar endleaves may have been used at the back of the volume, to judge by what appear to be offsets of rubrics on the inner face of the lower board.

Binding

Contemporary sewing and blind-stamped binding. Sewn on four split tawed straps, with cord endbands; bound in brown leather over bevelled wood boards: the four straps regularly spaced, and laced and pegged into staggered horizontal channels (the first and third longer than the second and fourth in both boards), the endbands secured in channels angled at about 45 degrees; each cover with a large central blind-stamped panel (that on the lower board very indistinct) representing the Man of Sorrows, standing in his tomb, surrounded by the Instruments of the Passion, enframed by the legend: 'O v[os om]nes qui transitis | per viam attendite | et : videt[e] si est [dolor similis] | sicut dolor m[eus]' (Lamentations 1:12) in gothic letters, starting at the lower left corner; framed by roll-tooled foliate scrollwork (using two different rolls) within blind fillets; the spine with four pronounced raised bands, the leather of the spine folded and stitched over the endbands; the top compartment inscribed in black ink '470' (cf. under Provenance) the fore-edges of both boards with marks from two pairs of metal clasp fittings, each with three nail-holes, parts of some of which are still visible on the inner face of the boards, which have been crudely gouged-out at these points; repaired, especially at the joints and corners, the leather of the upper joint weak, but the straps sound; with a bifolium of a breviary used as upper pastedown (now lifted) and endleaf (fols. 1-2); a similar pastedown (and endleaf?) are presumably missing at the end (see the note above).

The panel stamps are similar to, but not the same as, those in Weale, *Bookbindings in the National Art Library*, II, 186-7 nos. 387-8, each of which he describes as a Netherlandish 'Image of Pity' stamp, and are rubbings taken from manuscript Books of Hours in Dutch.

Provenance

1. Made for an unidentified Dutch-speaking patron, perhaps living in or near Cologne (possibly an exile during the Utrecht Schism of 1423-50?): the decoration and the litany suggest that the main texts of the book were made in the diocese of Utrecht, while the calendar (on a separate quire, as usual, and by a different scribe; but also in Dutch, not German or Latin) indicates that it was tailored to the needs of a client in the city or diocese of Cologne, who presumably also requested the inclusion of the non-standard devotions from fol. 187r to the end (on separate quires, perhaps by the scribe of the calendar); since one of the inserted miniatures originally faced fol. 187r, the miniatures were presumably

inserted after the writing of these textual additions. Patterns of holes and rust or other marks in fols. 39-40r, 45-46r, 186-187r suggest that pilgrim badge(s) or other votive image(s) may have been pinned/sewn in at these points, i.e. blank pages preceding miniatures.

2. Unidentified 17th(?)-cent. owners: the upper cover of the binding inscribed (apparently by the hand responsible for the foliation numbers on fols. 100r, 201r, and 216r): 'i5.' or 'is.' (possibly an abbreviation of 'ihesus', who is represented below?); inscribed by another hand in the upper margin of fol. 2r: 'fautis wal val slieri' (??).

3. Unidentified 18th/19th-cent. collection(s): inscribed in the top right corner of fol. 1r: '470' in a large bold hand (crossed through in ink), and in the top compartment of the spine (cf. under Binding); there is an erased inscription before this number on fol. 1r, apparently ending with a 'p'(?), but otherwise illegible even under UV light.

4. Unidentified 19th-cent owner: inscribed in pencil (fol. 3v): 'Cöllnischer [?] Kalender'.

5. Thomas Arthur, or William Ridler, London booksellers, *c.*1875-85 (see Introduction, pp. xxii-xxiv): the inner face of the upper board with a clipping from one of their catalogues, affixed sideways, in which the present manuscript was item 1, priced £8 8s.; inscribed in pencil on fol. 1r with the price-code 'd/s/-' (i.e. £5 10s) in the upper left margin, and on the wood of the inner face of the upper board, towards the centre of the fore-edge, sloping upwards; a pencil inscription is largely obscured by the catalogue clipping except for the word 'Pages', '[Cen]tury'(?), and a '£' sign.

6. Rt. Hon. T. R. Buchanan (1846-1911), after 1874 (see Introduction, pp. xix-xx); given to the Bodleian by his widow, Mrs. E. O. Buchanan, in 1941.

Bibliography
S. Gibson, 'Bookbindings in the Buchanan Collection', *BLR* 2 no. 16 (1941), 6-12, at 9.

van Dijk, *Handlist of Latin liturgical MSS.*, IV, 309 (listed, not described).

Pächt & Alexander, 1, no. 207.

Avril Henry, ed., *Biblia Pauperum: a facsimile and edition* (Aldershot, 1987), 160.

Klara Broekhuijsen, *De Zwarte-Ogen-Meesters: een onderzoek naar de stijl en iconografie van een groep Noordnederalndse miniaturisten rond 1500*, unpublished dissertation, Universiteit van Amsterdam (1997), 51. [Not consulted.]

MS. Buchanan f. 4

Rubricated Breviary, Use of Rome, in Latin
Italy, Milan, S. Giovanni in Conca, signed by the priest Dionisius de Castello;
dated 1464 and 1465

Text
[Item 1 occupies quire I]

1. (fols. 1r-6v) Ambrosian calendar ('*Incipit kalendarium secundum morem sancti
Ambrosii episcopi Mediolanensis*'), with an entry for almost every day of the year;
each month headed by a verse on the unlucky days in brown ink (pr. S. J. P. van
Dijk, ed., *Sources of the modern Roman liturgy: the ordinals of Haymo of Faversham
and related documents (1243-1307)* (Studia et Documenta Franciscana: 2 vols.,
Leiden, 1963), II, 365-76), and a note on the length of the calendar and lunar
month, and the length of the night and day, in red; Feb. to Dec. also headed by
notes on the Hebrew and Greek names of the months in brown; a note on the
length of the year at the end of Jan., the other months with calendrical verses
(pr. *ibid.*, 366-76); major feasts (in red) include Antony Abbot (17 Jan.), Matthias
(7 Feb.), Ambrose '*de uictoria*' (21 Feb.), the finding of the head of John the
Baptist (24 Feb., in place of Matthias), the deposition of Ambrose (5 Apr.), John
the Evangelist '*in oleo feruenti*' (6 May), Bernard (20 Aug.), the dedication of the
monastery of S. Salvatore (27 Aug. [dedicated to S. Radegund from the 12th cent.]),
the beheading of John the Baptist (29 Aug.), Eustorgius of Milan (18 Sept.), Tecla
(24 Sept.), the Dedication of Milan Cathedral (the Sunday after 15 Oct.: at 15 Oct.
is: '*Dedicatio ecclesie sequenti dominica.*'), Andrew, and the Baptism of Ambrose
(30 Nov.), Castritianus 'et Iacet in sancto Iohanne ad concham. in porta romana.'
(1 Dec.), the ordination of Ambrose (7 Dec.), Mary '... *fabrice mundi.*' (19 Dec.),
and the ordination of James the Greater (29 Dec.).

[Item 2 occupies quire II]

2. (fols. 7r-12v) Roman calendar, with an entry for almost every day; each
month headed by a note on the length of the calendar and lunar month in red;
in the body of the calendar are indicated the unlucky days and hours, the *duplex*
and *semiduplex* feasts, various seasonal information including indications of the
zodiac signs, equinoxes, notes on blood-letting, etc.; major feasts (in red) include
Bernardino of Siena (canonized 1450) (20 May), Antony of Padua (13 June),
the dedication of the basilica of S. Salvatore, *duplex* (9 Nov.), the dedication of
the basilica of SS. Pietro e Paolo, *duplex* (18 Nov.), Ambrose, *duplex* (7 Dec.); early
additions in plain brown ink, by more than one hand, are Mamertus (7 [*recte* 11]
May), Hermagorus & Fortunatus (12 July; cf. fol. 481r), Herculanus of Perugia
(7 Nov.), Pontianus, subsequently erased (19 Nov.)

[Item 3 occupies quires III-XX]

3. (fols. 13r-192v) Temporale: '*Incipit breuiarium secundum consuetudinem romane curie.*', from the first Saturday in Advent to the fourth Sunday in November (pr. *ibid.*, 17-114); with (fols. 30v-33r) tables of the antiphons before Christmas (pr. *ibid.*, 401-8).

[Items 4-11 occupy quire XXI]

4. (fols. 193r-194v) General Rubrics (pr. *ibid.*, 114-20), ending imperfect in the list of feasts with octaves (at '... *Apostolorum petri et pauli. Visitationis marie.* | |') due to the loss of a leaf after fol. 194.

5. (fol. 195r-v) Table of scriptural readings for September, in red, beginning imperfect in the list of readings for years when the kalends of September fall on a Monday (at '| | *sancti mathei apostoli quando cadet eodem die ...*') due to the loss of a leaf after fol. 194.

6. (fols. 195v-197r) New Rubrics, in the order of the months: '*Incipiunt rubrice noue per ordinem. Additiones et earum declarationes que in libris defectuose reperiuntur.*'

7. (fol. 197r-v) Form of absolution from excommunication: '*Absolutio ab excommunicatione maiori.*'

8. (fols. 197v-198r) Lists of fast days, vigils, days of obligations, and movable feasts, a rubric concerning feasts during Advent, and a list of *semiduplex* feasts, from Nicholas to Antony Abbot.

9. (fol. 198v) Rubric for feasts during the octave of Corpus Christi, here attributed to Pope John XII; fol. 199r blank.

10. (fols. 199v-200r) Hymn: 'Verbum caro factum est. | De uirgine maria. | In hoc anni circulo | Uita datur seculo ... honor uirtus et gratia. maria.' (*Repertorium hymnologicum*, no. 21347); fol. 200v ruled, otherwise blank.

[Items 11-17 occupy quires XXII-XXXI]

11. (fols. 201r-277r) Ferial Psalter: '*Incipit psalterium secundum consuetudinem romane curie.*'

12. (fols. 277r-279r) Litany: '*Letanie maiores*', followed (fols. 278v-279r) by the usual ten collects (listed under MS. Buchanan e. 5, *q.v.*); the fifth (fol. 279r) mentioning '... famulo tuo .N. pontifici nostro ...'.

13. (fol. 279v, rubric on fol. 279r) The Seven Penitential Psalms, consisting of the usual antiphon and only the cues to the psalms: '*Inferi sunt septem psalmi penitentiales qui dicuntur ante predictas letanias.*'; the psalm cues numbered in the margin by a later hand.

Incipit comune scōz.
in nat aplōz ī pmis
uespis ā Mox est īcepti
meuz. cuz rel de laud.
pS. Dixit dō?. pS Cōfi-
tebōz. pS. Btūs uir. pS.
Laudate pueri dō. pS.
Laud. dō. o. gts. Capit

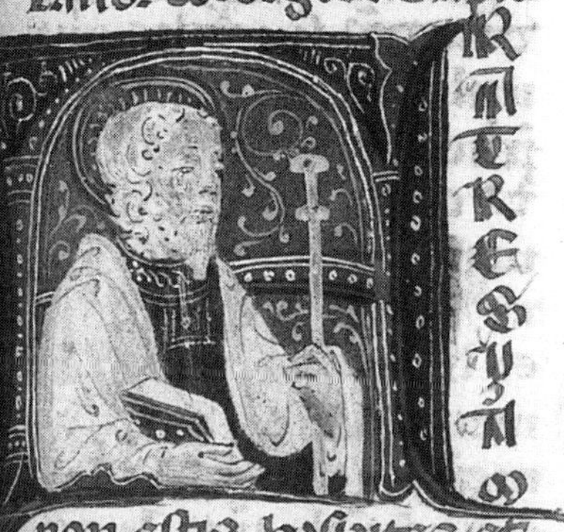

non estis hospites et
aduene? sed estis ciues
scōz et domestici dei/
sup hedificati sup fun-
damtuz aplōz/ 7 pro
phetaz. R. Deo gr. v?
Exultet celuz lau. V.
In ōem terraz exiuit so-
nus eoz. R. Et i fines
orbis tic uba eoum.
Ad mag. aī. Tradent
emz nos ī cōciliis/ 7 in

sinagogis suis flagellabt
nos. et aū reges/ī pfides
ducemī pp me ī testimo
niuz illis. et gētibz. pS.
Magnificat aīa. Oro.
Quesum? omps
deus/ut btūs. N.
apls/tuuz pro nob im
ploret auxiliuz. ut a
nostris reatibz absoluti
a cūctis etiaz piculis
eruam?. P do. Alia oro
plurimōz apostolōz.
Deus qui nos an-
nua aplōz tuōz
N. 7 N. sollēnitate leti
ficas. pia qs/ut quoz
gaudem? meritis istru
amur exēplis. P do.
Ad mat. inuit? Regē
aplōz dūm. uenite adore
mus. pS. Uenite exul.
Seqns inuit dī ī festis
scōz mathie bānabe/
Jacobi bartholomei -
mathei luce/7 aplōz
simois/7 iude. Inuit.
Gaudete 7 exultate. Qm
noīa uīa sēpta sūt ī celis.

42. MS. Buchanan f. 4, fol. 432r. [Enlarged]

14. (fols. 279v-280v) The Pater Noster ('*Oratio dominica.*'), Ave Maria ('*Salutatio marie.*'), Gloria in excelsis ('*Laus angelorum.*'), Apostles' Creed ('*Simbolum apostolorum.*'), Nicene Creed ('*Simbolum sanctorum patrum.*'), and the Invitatory Psalm [Ps. 94] in two slightly different versions, the first headed: '*In epiphania domini dicitur iste psalmus.*', the second: '*Iste psalmus dicitur per totum annum ad matutinas.*'

15. (fols. 281r-291v) Hymnal for proper and common feasts, from the first Saturday in Advent: '*Incipiunt hymni per totum annum. ...*'; with the date '*.1464.*' at the end, in the same red ink as the rubrics.

16. (fol. 292r) Prayers:
> (i) '*Salutatio uirginis marie. Aue regina celorum. Aue domina angelorum. ...*' (*Repertorium hymnologicum*, no. 2070; pr. Daniel, *Thesaurus hymnologicus*, II, 319, no. X, very close to version B);
> (ii) '*Oratio quando ministratur eucaristia. Domine sancte pater omnipotens eterne deus. te fideliter deprecamur ...*', with alternative readings for '*... fratri nostro uel sorori nostre. fratribus uel sororibus nostris. ...*' (similar to that pr. *Corpus orationum*, no. 2373);
> (iii) '*Oremus Oratio. Omnipotens sempiterne deus. qui gloriose uirginis matris marie ...*' (pr. Wordsworth, *Horae Eboracenses*, 63).

17. (fol. 292r-v) Miscellaneous notes: calendrical rubrics, on how to find the dates of Septuagesima, Easter, and the Ember Days; followed (fol. 292r) by verses on the properties of fennel: '*proprietas feniculi* Bis duo dat maratrum. [glossed by the scribe in cursive script: 'id est feniculum'] febres fugat. atque uenenum. Et purgat stomacum. lumen quoque reddit acutum.' (also found in a 14th-cent. collection of anonymous Dominican sermons, Avignon, Bibliothèque du Musée Calvet, ms. 606, fol. 126r; see M. L.-H. Labande, *Avignon*, I (Catalogue général des manuscrits des bibliothèques publiques de France: départements, 27: Paris, 1894), 338); '*Feniculum quasi fenum oculorum* Semen feniculi fugat spiramina.'; and (fol. 292v) '*Prima die martis lune mensis februarij celebratur carnis priuium secundum curiam.*'.

[Items 18-19 occupy quires XXXII-XLV]

18. (fols. 293r-425r) Sanctorale: '*Incipit proprium sanctorum per anni circulum.*', from the feast of St. Saturninus (29 Nov.) to St. Catherine (25 Nov.) (pr. van Dijk, *op. cit.*, II, 121-73); lacking part of Matins of the feast of St. Laurence (from '*... experire certe utrum | |*' in the versicle 'Quid in me ...' in the second nocturn; to '*| | regira aliam et manduca. Nam. ...*' at the end of the third nocturn), due to the loss of a leaf after fol. 381.

19. (fols. 425v-431r) Extra offices and prayers:
> (i) (fols. 425v-428v) Office of the Transfiguration, instituted by Pope Calixtus III (1455-8): '*Incipit officium transfigurationis domini nostri yhesu christi institutum de nouo per sanctissimum dominum nostrum Calixtum papam tertium sollemniter et duplex celebrandum.*';

(ii) (fols. 428v-431r) Office of St. Anne: '*In festo sancte \anne/ matris marie matris domini.*';
(iii) (fol. 431r) three short prayers of St. Anastasia, to be said after the octave of Epiphany: '*Orationes sancte Anastasie festum cuius celebrari debet post octauam epiphanie id est officium suum. ...*'; fol. 431v ruled, otherwise blank.

[Items 20-28 occupy quires XLVI-L]

20. (fols. 432r-458r) Common of Saints (pr. van Dijk, *op. cit.*, II, 173-85).

21. (fols. 458r-460r) Order of Grace before and after meals (pr. *ibid.*, 199-203).

22. (fols. 460r-465r) Office of the Virgin, Use of Rome (pr. *ibid.*, 185-91).

23. (fols. 465r-468v) Office of the Dead, Use of Rome (pr. *ibid.*, 191-95).

24. (fols. 468v-476v) Ritual of the Last Sacraments, including (fols. 470v-471r) the '*... letanie breues ...*' (pr. *ibid.*, 387-97); and (fol. 476v) general absolution: '*Ista est forma absolutionis generalis indulgentie a pena et a culpa in articulo mortis. ordinata in consistorio apostolico.*'.

25. (fols. 477r-478v, rubric on fol. 476v) Forms for blessing: (i) (fols. 477r-478r) salt and water; (ii) (fol. 478r) an altar; (iii) (fol. 478v) incense; and (iv) bread.

26. (fols. 478v-480v) Additional lections for the Common of Saints.

27. (fol. 480v) Dated '*1465*', with a scribal colophon (see under Provenance).

28. (fols. 480v-481r) Contemporary additional commemorations, by two or three different hands, of:
>   (i) (fol. 480v) St. Thomas Aquinas: '[D]eus qui ecclesiam tuam beati thome confessoris tui eruditione clarificas et sancta operatione fecundas ...' (pr. *Corpus orationum*, no. 1562);
>   (ii) (fol. 481r) Sts. Hermagoras and Fortunatus: '*Commemoratio sanctorum hermacore et fortunati. ...* Prothopresul Italie hermacora aquilegie pastor mentis nostre ...';
>   (iii) the Holy Cross: 'Nos autem gloriari oportet in cruce domini nostri ihesu christi ...'; fol. 481v ruled, otherwise blank.

Decoration

Five historiated initials, of varying size, depicting mostly half-length figures; the letter maroon on a blue ground, each with a red foliage extension descending down the margin, and a green one rising up it:
(fol. 13r) Temporale. Seven-line initial F[ratres]: St. Paul(?) in profile, holding a sword and book; the bottom margin of the page with a shield, now overpainted with an 'IHS' monogram of S. Bernardino (see under Provenance).
(fol. 201v) Psalm 1. Nine-line initial B[eatus]: King David playing the psaltery in a landscape (Pächt & Alexander, 2, pl. LXX no. 731, detail).

     Bodleian Library, Oxford

(fol. 265v) Psalm 109. Five-line initial D[ixit]: God the Father, holding an orb.
(fol. 293r) Sanctorale. Six-line initial D[eus]: St. Saturninus(?), holding a palm of
martyrdom (Watson, *Dated and datable, Oxford*, pl. 626, showing most of the page).
(fol. 432r) Common. Nine-line initial F[ratres]: an Apostle holding a staff and
book (pl. 42).

Seven similar smaller painted foliate initials, to the first hymn of the ferial
Psalter, and the remaining eight-part divisions of the psalms (fols. 201r, 221v,
230r, 236r, 242r, 250v, 257r).

Three- and four-line initials in red with purple penwork, or blue with red
penwork, to major feasts in the temporale and sanctorale; similar two-line
initials, alternating, to prayers, lessons, psalms, etc.; one-line initials alternately
in red or blue, to verses and other minor textual divisions; paraphs in blue.

Physical Description
MATERIAL: parchment.
DIMENSIONS: the leaves 144-5 x 99-102 mm.
NUMBER OF LEAVES: iii (modern paper, the first marbled on both sides) + 481 + iii
(modern paper, the last marbled on both sides).
FOLIATION: modern, in pencil: ii-iii, 1-483 (fols. i and 484, because they are
marbled on both sides, are not physically foliated); a previous modern pencil
foliation on every tenth leaf was out of sequence after fol. 330, and has now
been corrected, according to Bodleian practice, by encircling the error, e.g. fol.
340 has '341' encircled the photograph in pl. 42 was taken some years before
the erroneous foliation was encircled).
COLLATION: mostly in quires of 10 leaves: I^6 (fols. 1-6) | II^6 (fols. 7-12) | III-XX^{10}
(fols. 13-192) | XXI^{10-2} (a bifolium, the 3rd and 8th leaves, missing, after fols. 194
and 198, the latter perhaps blank) (fols. 193-200) | XXII-XXX^{10} (fols. 201-290),
XXXI^2 (fols. 291-292) | XXXII-XXXIX^{10} (fols. 293-372), XL^{10-1} (10th leaf missing,
after fol. 381) (fols. 373-381), XLI-XLV^{10} (fols. 382-431) | XLVI-L^{10} (fols. 432-481);
CATCHWORDS by the original scribe, written horizontally, half-way down the
lower margin, below the right-hand side of the right-hand column of text,
present throughout, except in those quires which contain the end of a major
textual unit (i.e. quires I, II, XXI, XXXI, and XLV); in red if the next quire starts with
a rubric; modern QUIRE SIGNATURES in pencil in arabic numerals in the lower
gutter margin of the first recto of each quire (cf. MS. Buchanan g. 1, also bound
by Simier), skipping quire XVI.
RULING: 30 lines ruled in very faint (often invisible) grey or brown ink, in two
columns, each with single vertical bounding lines, ruled in plummet, extending
the full height of the page; the ruled space 97-9 x 69-71 mm.; each column
30-2 mm. wide, the intercolumnar space *c*.8 mm. wide.
SCRIPT: written in a 'fere humanistica' bookhand, apparently by Dionisius de
Castello throughout (see under Provenance), with 29 lines of text per page;
the written space 95-6 x 69-70 mm.

RUBRICATION: headings in red; capitals stroked in red ink; guide-letters for one-
and two-line initials usually visible within the initial area; oblique strokes next to
blue two-line initials were used to ensure a regular alternation of red and blue
initials when working on disbound sheets.
SEC. FOL.: (calendar, fol. 2r) 'Martius in prima'; (text, fol. 14r) 'V'. Iube deo.'

Binding

19th-cent. Parisian signed binding by (Alphonse?) Simier. Sewing-supports not
visible; bound in very dark green leather over pasteboards; the covers tooled in
gilt with an outer frame formed of lozenges and semi-circlets, enclosing another
frame of overlapping circle and foliate designs, the centre of each cover with a
four-pointed motif composed of heart-shaped leaves on curling leafy stems; the
spine with seven false raised bands; with repeated use of large and small heart-
shaped-leaf tools, in every compartment of the spine; lettered 'BREUIARIUM' in
the third compartment, and 'ANO [*sic*] | 1465' in the sixth; doublures of brown
leather framed by the turn-ins, both tooled in gilt around the edge with palmette
and quatrefoil roll patterns; the first and last flyleaves finely marbled on both
sides; the other flyleaves of unwatermarked wove paper; the edges of the leaves
and boards gilt; yellow, green and red endbands; one green silk bookmark;
stamped on the top edge of the lower board and on fols. ii verso and 482r
'SIMIER.R[ELIEUR].DU ROI.' (cf. MS. Buchanan g. 1). Boxed.

It seems that both René Simier, and his son, Alphonse (on whom see Charles
Ramsden, *French bookbinders 1789-1848* (London, 1950, repr. 1989), 190;
and Hellmuth Helwig, *Handbuch der Einbandkunde* (3 vols., Hamburg, 1953-5),
II, 179), each signed their work 'SIMIER.R[ELIEUR].DU ROI.' at different times
(for examples, see Etienne Ader and Léopold Carteret, *Bibliothèque Henri Béraldi,
cinquième partie: livres des XVIe, XVIIe et XVIII siècles romantiques et modernes dans
de belles relieures* (auction catalogue: Paris, 1935), pls. facing pp. 6, 38, 39, 105,
122, and 127); but the style of the present binding looks too late to have been
executed before the death, probably shortly after 1826, of René.

Provenance

1. Signed and dated by Dionisius de Castello, priest of S. Giovanni in Conca,
Milan, 1464-5; dated in red ink at the end of the Hymnal '.*1464*.'(fol. 291v),
and with a colophon in red ink at the end of the volume '.*1465. Deo. Gratias.
Amen. Finis*', and: '*Istud breuiarium est presbiteri dionisij de Castello. In sancto
Iohanne ad Concham mediolani porte romane intus beneficiato. manu sua propria
scriptum .M.CCCClxiiij°. et finitum die sabbati .xviiij°. mensis Ianuarij. 1465.
Ad honorem dei et gloriose eius matris uirginis marie.*' (fol. 480v). The entry at 1 Dec.
in the first calendar (fol. 6v) states that the relics of St. Castritianus are in the
church; the shield on fol. 13r appears to have been flanked by two letters in gold,
and perhaps topped by a third, all now erased.

2. Unidentified near-contemporary Italian owner(s): the additions (fol. 10r) of
Hermagoras and Fortunatus to the second calendar, and their commemoration
(fol. 481r) at the end of the volume, suggest an owner with a special veneration

of their cult—they were principal patrons at Udine, Gorizia, and Laibach (now Ljubljana); an omitted verse of a psalm is supplied in a humanistic semi-cursive script on fol. 254r; a smudged inscription is on fol. 200r: 'Breujarius Romanus [?] | uerbis johannis' (??).

3. Unidentified French collector, 19th cent.: a small gilt red leather bookplate (fol. i recto), shows a coat of arms with three fleurs-de-lis, a bordure with eight scallop shells, encircled by the chain of the Order of the Golden Fleece, with links composed of pairs of facing initial 'C's, surmounted by a closed crown, and flanked by two angel supporters holding banners with, and wearing, fleurs-de-lis, above the motto: 'DEUS ET DIES'; fol. 484v with a corresponding small red leather bookplate stamped in gilt with a tree of fleurs-de-lis, surmounted by a closed crown. The same arms and the same tree of fleurs-de-lis are on the covers of a binding sold at Sotheby's, 15 May, 1997, lot 61 (catalogue with colour pl.); this binding is signed by Lortic (cf. below), who is thought to have started business in 1840, which would make it impossible for the arms to be a variant of those of Charles X of France (1757-1836; *r*.1824-30), as had previously been proposed, presumably on the basis that the closed crown should only be used by royalty.

4. Baron François-Florentin-Achille Seillière (1813-73), French banker and book-collector (see Eugène Olivier, Georges Hermal, and R. de Roton, *Manuel de l'amateur de reliures armoriées françaises: onzième série (meubles)* (Paris, 1927), no. 1130): his sale at Sotheby's, 25 February 1887 and four following days, lot 180, bought by Ridler for £13; inscribed, presumably by Sotheby's, in pencil '985' within a triangle in the upper left corner of fol. ii verso (see Introduction, p. xxv). A cutting of the Sotheby's catalogue description is pasted to a sheet of plain paper and inserted loosely in [pr. bk.] Buchanan f.54, and inscribed by Buchanan: 'Belonged to same collector as Summa Angelica'. Since there is no copy of Angelus's *Summa Angelica* from Buchanan's collection in either the Bodleian or All Souls, this note presumably refers to the copy in the Seillière catalogue, lot 40, bound by Lortic (cf. above); Seillière presumably acquired the latter and the present manuscript from the same source. Buchanan attended the sale in person, and bought a number of printed books (see Introduction, p. xxv); he presumably bought the present manuscript from Ridler immediately afterwards, since it does not bear Ridler's price-code.

5. Rt. Hon. T. R. Buchanan (1846-1911); given to the Bodleian by his widow, Mrs. E. O. Buchanan, in 1941.

Bibliography
Sotheby, Wilkinson & Hodge, *La bibliothèque de Mello: catalogue of an important portion of the very choice library of the late Baron Seillière which will be sold by auction … 28th of February, 1887, and four following days* (London), lot 180.

van Dijk, *Handlist of Latin liturgical MSS.*, II pt. ii (1957), 308-9.

Pächt & Alexander, 2, no. 731, pl. LXX.

Watson, *Dated and datable, Oxford*, I, 25 no. 140, II, pl. 626.

MS. Buchanan g. 1

Book of Hours, Use of Rome, in Latin
Italy, Florence; late 15th century

Text
[Item 1 occupies quire I]

1. (fols. 1r-12v) Calendar, with an entry for most days of the year; each month headed by a note on the length of the calendar month in red; the left-hand columns consisting of only the golden number and dominical letter (i.e. omitting the Roman calendar, etc.); major feasts (in red) include Antony Abbot (17 Jan.), the Virgin *'ad niues'* (5 Aug.), and Francis (4 Oct.); feasts in ordinary ink include Gilbert of Sempringham (4 Feb.), Thomas Aquinas (8 [*recte* 7] Mar.), the Stigmatization of Francis (17 Sept.), the translation of Clare (2 Oct.), the octave of Francis (11 Oct.), and the dedication of S. Salvator (8 Nov.).

[Items 2-4 occupy quires II-VIII]

2. (fols. 13r-77r) Hours of the Virgin, Use of Rome: *'Incipit offitium* [sic] *beate marie uirginis secundum consuetudinem romane curie'*; with three lessons at Matins; followed by variant Matins psalms and antiphons for (fols. 60r-64v) Tuesdays and Thursdays, and (fols. 64v-68v) Wednesdays and Saturdays; and (fol. 68v-77r) seasonal variants.

3. (fols. 77r-80v) Hours of the Cross: *'Incipit officium sancte crucis'*.

4. (fol. 81r-v) Prayer attributed to St. Anselm: *'Oratio sancti anselmi* Domine deus meus si feci ut essem reus tuus ... et absterge quod est meum: Qui cum patre ...' (also found in MS. Lat. liturg. g. 5, pp. 242-244; see also Ker, *MMBL*, I, 105 art. 16, 170 art. 4, etc.); the prayer is based on a portion of Anselm's second Meditation, see Franciscus Salesius Schmitt, *S. Anselmi Cantuariensis archiepiscopi opera omnia* (6 vols., Edinburgh, etc., 1946-51), III (1946), pp. 82-3, ll. 86ff.)

[Items 5-11 occupy quires IX-XVIII]

5. (fols. 82r-94r) The Seven Penitential Psalms.

6. (fols. 94r-104v) Litany and collects; the litany including Jerome in red (all others in plain ink) sixth among nine bishops, confessors, and doctors; followed (fols. 101v-104v) by the ten usual collects (listed under MS. Buchanan e. 5), the fifth (fol. 102v) mentioning to '... famulo tuo .N. pontifici nostro ...'.

7. (fols. 105r-106v) Hours of the Holy Spirit, starting imperfect in Matins (in the prayer *Omnipotens sempiterne deus da nobis illam ...* at '[penteco]||stes transmisisti ...'), due to the loss of a leaf before fol. 105; and ending imperfect in Compline after the first versicle (at '... Deus in ad[iutorium]: *R'* ||'), due to the loss of a leaf after fol. 106.

8. (fols. 107r-153v) Office of the Dead, Use of Rome.

9. (fols. 154r-165v) The Gradual Psalms [Pss. 119-133]: '*Canticum graduum absolute incipitur: psalmi semper dicuntur sedendo: Orationes et uersiculi flexis genibus:*', each group of five psalms followed by responses, versicles, and a collect; the latter are: (i) (fols. 157v-158r) 'Absolue quesumus domine animas famulorum ...'; (ii) (fol. 161v) 'Deus cui proprium est misereri semper et parcere ...'; and (iii) (fol. 165v) 'Pretende domine famulis et famulabus tuis ...' (as in Randall, *Walters Art Gallery cat.*, vol. II, pt. 2, no. 169 fols. 19v-20v).

10. (fols. 166r-177v) Long Hours of the Holy Spirit: '*Incipit officium magnum sancti spiritus:*'.

11. (fols. 178r-179v) Psalm 90: '*Iste psalmus est deuotissimus et maxime uirtutis:*' (cf. MS. Lat. liturg. g. 4, fols. 128r-130r; also Ker, *MMBL*, I, 105 art. 15, 356 art. 3, etc.).

[Items 12-14 occupy quires XIX-XXI]

12. (fols. 180r-205r) Long Hours of the Cross: '*Incipit officium magnum sancte crucis:*', with three lessons at Matins.

13. (fols. 205v-207v) The Seven Prayers of St. Gregory, carrying an indulgence: '*Oratio piissima sancti gregorii pape qui concessit omnibus penitentibus et confessis dicentibus ... apud ymaginem pietatis: quatuordecim milia annorum indulgentie: ...*', with only six verses, in the following order: 'O Domine ihesu christe adoro te in cruce pendentem ... in cruce uulneratum ... in sepulcro positum ... resurgentem a mortuis ... pastor bone ... propter illam amaritudinem ...' (cf. versions pr. by Leroquais, *Livres d'heures*, II, 346; and Wordsworth, *Horae Eboracenses*, 81); the first ten lines of fol. 205v ruled, but otherwise blank, as if intended for a miniature (see the note under Decoration, concerning fol. 207v).

14. (fols. 207v-208v) Prayer to St. Sebastian: 'Omnipotens sempiterne deus: qui beati sebastiani martiris tui ... et inprouisa morte liberentur: Per christum ...'; preceded by a ten-line space (see the note under Decoration); fol. 209r-v ruled, otherwise blank.

[Items 15-28 occupy quires XXII-XXVI]

15. (fols. 210r-221r) Mass of the Virgin: '*Ad missam sancte marie maioris:*'; the postcommunion followed by five prayers (fols. 218v-221r):
>　(i) 'Aue sanctissimum pretiosissimum dulcissimum corpus christi ... in odorem suauitatis dominum nostrum ihesum christum.' (cf. the version pr. by Leroquais, *Livres d'heures*, II, 341);
>　(ii) 'Aue sanctissima christi caro summa uite mee dulcedo: ... et corpus meum in uitam eternam amen:';
>　(iii) 'Aue celestis potus ante omnia et super omnia ... ad remedium sempiternum in uitam eternam amen';

est i possibile tue potentie:
nec innocens tue iusticie: nec
in solitum tue clementie: ↳
Quid enim est ihesus nisi sal
uator: Ergo ihesu qui me cre
sti: no perimas: qui me redem
sti non condemnes: qui me cre
sti tua bonitate no pereat op
tuum mea iniquitate: cogno
sce ergo i me quod est tuum:
et absterge quod est meu: Q
cu pre et spiritu sancto uiuis
et regnas ds: P omia secula
seculo amen:

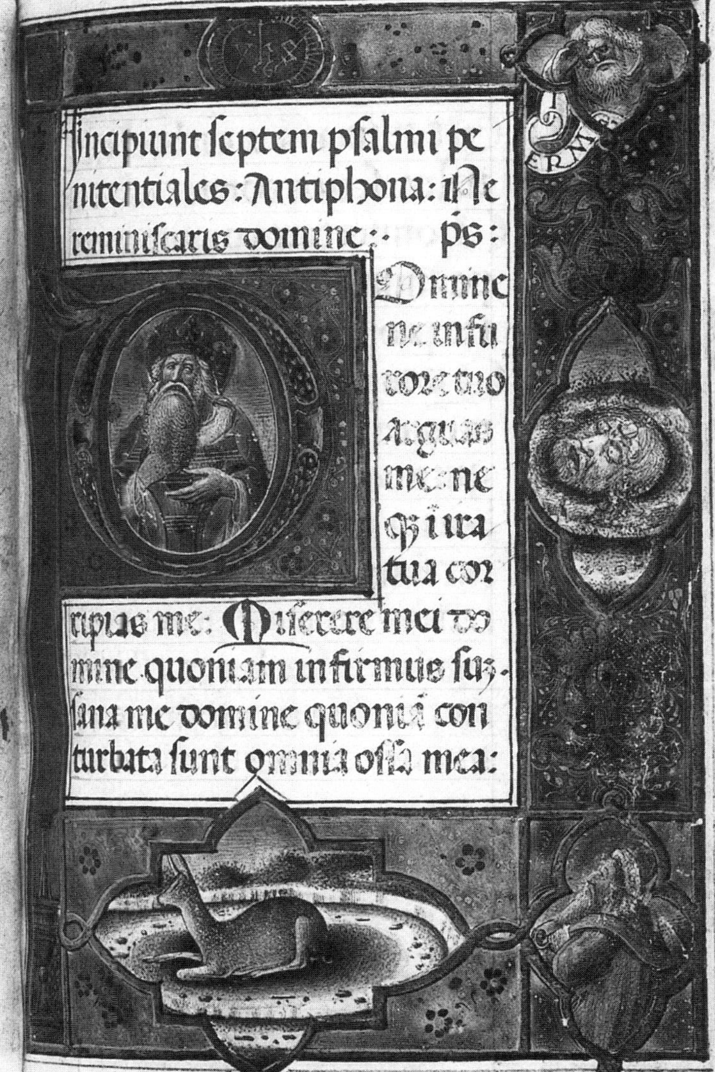

43. MS. Buchanan g. 1, fols. 81v-82r. [Enlarged]

(iv) 'Corpus tuum domine quod sumpsi et calicem quem potaui ... ubi tam
pura introierunt et sancta sacramenta:';
(v) 'Gratias tibi refero domine gratiarum actiones tue ... et gaudia sempiterna
sanctorum amen:'.

16. (fols. 221r-228v) Prayer to the Virgin: '*De domina nostra:*', in two sections,
the first (fols. 221r-226v): 'Domina mea sancta maria perpetua: uirgo uirginum
... suppliciter exoro et deuote', followed by a rubric: '*Hic lege septem aue maria et
nominarem pro qua petis et tu:*', and continuing, with a two-line initial (fols. 226v-
228v): 'Ut sicut ego certus sum quos dilectus filius tuus ... et in hoc seculo concede:'.

17. (fols. 228v-230r) Hymn to John the Evangelist: '*Sequitur oratio bona de sancto
iohanne apostolo et euangelista:* Contemplator trinitatis speculumque ueritatis
iohannes apostole ...' (*Repertorium hymnologicum*, no. 3846).

18. (fols. 230r-231r) Hymn on the Seven Joys of Mary Magdalen: '*De sancta
maria magdalena: oratio:* Gaude pia magdalena spes salutis uite uena lapsorum
fidutia: ...' (*ibid.*, no. 6895)

19. (fols. 231r-233v) Prayer attributed to St. Thomas Aquinas: '*Oratio sancti
Thome de aquino:* Concede michi misericors deus que tibi placita sunt ardenter
concupiscere ... tuis gaudiis in patria frui per gloriam: Qui uiuis et regnas.'
(pr. A. I. Doyle, 'A prayer attributed to St Thomas Aquinas', *Dominican Studies* 1
no. 3 (1948), 234-8, at 234, 236).

20. (fols. 233v-239v) Prayer for protection against one's enemies: '*Oratio contra
aduersarios.* O dulcissime et pijssime et clementissime domine ihesu christe uere
filius dei qui de sinu patris omnipotentis missus es in hunc mundum relaxare
peccata: ... et liberare me :N: de afflictione ... preparasti uere diligentibus te: tibi
gratias refero qui uiuis et regnas ...' (a version of this prayer is in MS. Lat. liturg.
g. 4, fols. 162v-169v, where it is attributed to Augustine).

21. (fols. 239v-240r) Prayer in the form of a series of petitions: '*Oratio:*',
'Benedicat me imperialis maiestas: ...' (pr. Wordsworth, *Horae Eboracenses*, 88).

22. (fols. 240r-246r) Hymn, in the form of an exposition of the *Salve regina*:
'*Deuotissima expositio super salue regina:*', with each word or phrase of the *Salve
regina* in red, followed by a quatrain: '*Salue:* Salue uirgo uirginum que genuisti
filium stella matutina: ...' (*Repertorium hymnologicum*, no. 18318); followed by
another quatrain (fols. 245v-246r): '*Qua finita dicuntur isti versus:* Has uideas
laudes qui sacra uirgine gaudes: ... Pretereundo caue ne taceatur aue:'
(*Repertorium hymnologicum*, no. 7687; James A. Corbett, 'A fifteenth-century
Book of Hours from Salisbury', *Ephemerides Liturgicae* 71 fasc. iv-v (1957), 293-
307, 302), this often occurs as a rubric before the exposition on the *Salve regina*.

23. (fols. 246r-247v) Passion narrative: '*Passio domini nostri ihesu c[h]risti
secundum Johannem:*' (the usual paraphrase of John 19:1-34, with additions from
John 18:4, and Matthew 27:30 & 27:34, cf. MS. Buchanan e. 9, fols. 116v-118r;
pr. Wordsworth, *Horae Eboracenses*, 123).

24. (fols. 247v-251v) The Athanasian Creed: '*Simbolum athanasii:* Quicumque uult ...'.

25. (fols. 252r-254v, rubric on fols. 251v-252r) Hymn in the form of an exposition of the *Ave Maria*, carrying an indulgence of Pope Honorius II: '*Incipit salutatio beate uirginis marie quam quicumque deuote dixerit habet indulgentiam ducentorum dierum ex parte domini honorii pape secundi:*', with each word or phrase of the *Ave Maria* in red, followed by a quatrain: 'Aue dei genitrix et immaculata uirgo celi gaudium toti mundo grata: ...' (*Repertorium hymnologicum*, no. 1761; pr. F. J. Mone, *Lateinische Hymnen des Mittelalters, aus Handschriften herausgegeben und erklärt, II: Marienlieder* (Freiburg im Breisgau, 1854), 100-3), here with an extra quatrain at the end: 'Ad haec uirgo celica: det nobis solamen: Et sanctis similiter pium confortamen: Omnes sancte uirgines pium quoque flamen: Qui regnat in secula seculorum Amen:'.

26. (fols. 255r-257v, rubric on fols. 254v-155r) Devotion to the Seven Last Words, attributed to Bede: '*Hanc orationem fecit uenerabilis beda presbiter de septem sacratis uerbis ... quicumque eam dixerit omni mane genuflexo ... mater domini apparebit in adiutorium sibi triginta diebus ante mortem suam: Oratio:* Domine ihesu c[h]riste pater meus qui septem uerba in ultima hora tue uite ... et iocunderis in regno meo per infinita secula seculorum: Amen' (very similar to the version pr. by Wordsworth, *Horae Eboracenses*, 141-2), each phrase introducing Christ's words written in red, e.g.: '... *Et sicut tu domine dixisti: +:* Pater ignosce crucifigentibus me: ....'.

27. (fols. 257v-259v) Sequence from the Mass for the Dead: '*Sequentia mortuorum:* Dies ire dies illa: ...' (*Repertorium hymnologicum*, no. 4626; pr. *Analecta hymnica*, LIV (1915), 269-70).

Decoration

Six (of an intended eight?—see below) historiated initials of varying size; each surrounded by full borders divided into panels by gold fillets (similar in arrangement to MS. Buchanan e. 7); some with a 'yhs' monogram of S. Bernardino in the upper border:

(fol. 13r) Hours of the Virgin. Nine-line initial D[omine] with the Virgin and Child; the outer border with three prophets, two of them holding scrolls, inscribed 'SACER'(?) (Zacharias?), and 'SACHIEL'(?) (Ezekiel?), the lower border with two angels supporting a wreath enclosing a blank shield (Pächt & Alexander, 2, pl. XXIX no. 324).

(fol. 82r) Penitential Psalms. Seven-line initial D[omine] with King David playing the psaltery; the outer border with the severed head of Goliath; two prophets, one holding a scroll inscribed 'IERM' (Jeremiah); the lower border with a deer resting in a landscape (pl. 43).

(fol. 107r) Office of the Dead. Eight-line initial D[ilexi] with a funeral scene: a priest and four other clerics standing over a shrouded corpse; the outer border with three further clerics and five skulls, the lower border with an elderly

white-bearded man holding and contemplating a skull; all are tonsured, and wear
grey habits, the priest has an orange and gold cope over his.
(fol. 154r) Gradual Psalms. Six-line initial A[d] with the Presentation of the
Virgin by Joachim and Anne, at the steps of the temple; the outer border with
three Old Testament figures, holding scrolls inscribed 'IXAIE'(?) (Isaiah?),
'ABRAAM' (Abraham), and 'MOIXE' (Moses), the lower margin with a horned
deer resting in a landscape.
(fol. 166r) Hours of the Holy Spirit. Seven-line initial D[omine] with Pentecost;
the outer border with four figures, one holding a scroll inscribed 'ABACVCO'
(Habacuc), the lowermost figure in a landscape which is continuous with the
scenes in the lower border: a saint pointing to rays of light, with a kneeling youth,
perhaps in a dry river-bed, the figure in the lower right corner also apparently
looking towards the source of light; the upper border with the cross-nimbed Dove.
(fol. 180r) Long Hours of the Cross. Eight-line initial D[omine] with the
Crucifixion, with the Virgin and John; the border with St. Peter, the Virgin, and
Mary Magdalen (or John the Evangelist?), the latter in a landscape continuous
from the lower border, which has the Man of Sorrows displaying his wounds.

On fol. 207v there is a ten-line space preceding the prayer to St. Sebastian, next
to which there is a note in the margin in Italian, in small cursive script in red ink,
presumably intended for an illuminator: '[q]*ui ua sancto | sebastiano*.'. The top ten
lines of fol. 205v have also been left blank, presumably also for a miniature (perhaps
representing the Mass of St. Gregory?), but no marginal note is evident there.

One six-line historiated initial, with a three-sided foliate and floral border:
(fol. 77r) Hours of the Cross. Crucifixion, with the Virgin and John; the lower
border with a gold cross amid the foliage and flowers.

Five-line foliate and floral initials on a square gold field at the start of the hours
of Lauds to Compline of the Hours of the Virgin (fols. 24v, 35r, 39r, 42v, 45v,
49r, 56r); similar (mostly) four-line initials at the hours of Lauds to Compline
of the Long Hours of the Cross (fols. 190r (six-line), 192r (five-line), 194r, 196r,
198r, 200r, 202v); a four-line initial in blue with red penwork to the exposition
on the *Salve regina* (fol. 240r); similar three-line initials to the Mass of the Virgin
and selected prayers (fols. 210r, 221r, 233v (red with purple penwork), 252r);
similar two-line initials to the KL monograms in the calendar; similar two-line
initials alternately in blue with red penwork, or red with purple penwork, to
psalms, lessons, canticles, hymns, etc.; plain one-line initials alternately in red
or blue, to verses and other minor textual divisions.

Pächt & Alexander attributed the illumination to 'the same hand as London, BL,
Add. MS. 19417. Closely related to the style of Giovanni di Giuliano Boccardi.'
(on whom see Levi d'Ancona, *Miniatura e miniatori a Firenze*, 149-54). Prof.
Alexander now suggests that the style of the present manuscript is perhaps
closer to that of Mariano del Buono di Jacopo (1433-1504?) (on whom see
Levi d'Ancona, *op. cit.*, 175-81; and Annarosa Garzelli, 'Le immagini, gli autori,
i destinatari', in *La miniatura fiorentina del Rinascimento, 1440-1525: un primo*

censimento ed. Annarosa Garzelli (Inventari e cataloghi toscani, 18-19: 2 vols.,
Florence, 1985), I, 5-391, and pls., at 189-215; and cf. MS. Buchanan e. 7,
attributed to the same artist). The comparison with BL, Add. MS. 19417
remains valid.

Physical Description
MATERIAL: parchment, generally of very fine quality.
DIMENSIONS: the leaves 117-8 x 89-90 mm., the decoration somewhat cropped.
NUMBER OF LEAVES: ii (modern paper, detached) + ii (modern parchment) + 259
+ ii (modern parchment) + ii (modern paper).
FOLIATION: modern, in pencil: i-iv, 1-263; a previous (17th-cent.?) foliation in
black ink in arabic numerals, in the lower right corner of rectos, is largely
cropped; it sometimes runs one or more in advance of the present foliation,
e.g. '42' (fol. 41r), '54' (fol. 53r), '18[?]' (fol. 178r), but sometimes runs behind,
e.g. '84'-'92' (fols. 83r-91r), so firm deductions cannot be made about whether
leaves were already missing when this foliation was supplied.
COLLATION: mostly in quires of 10 leaves: I^{12} (fols. 1-12) | II-VIII^{10} (fols. 13-81)
| IX-X^{10} (fols. 82-101), XI$^{10-2}$ (4th and 7th leaves, a bifolium, missing after fols. 104
and 106) (fols. 102-109), XII-XVIII^{10} (fols. 110-179) | XIX-XXI^{10} (fols. 180-209)
| XXII-XXVI^{10} (fols. 210-259); vertical CATCHWORDS in the script of the main text,
written sideways, downwards, on the right vertical bounding-line, slightly below
the bottom line of text, are present throughout except in quires which contain
the end of a major textual unit (i.e. quires I, VIII, XVIII, XXI, and XXVI), that on fol.
129v with a calligraphic flourish; early modern(?) QUIRE SIGNATURES 'f' and 'j'
at the lower right edge of the first rectos of quires VII and XI (fols. 62r, 102r)
(the series omits the calendar, but uses both 'i' and 'j'); modern pencil QUIRE
NUMBERS in the bottom gutter corner, largely cropped (e.g. fol. 82r, '9'), perhaps
by Simier (see under Binding, and cf. MS. Buchanan f. 4).
RULING: 15 lines ruled in pale brown ink, between single vertical bounding
lines extending the full height of the page, the horizontals possibly ruled with
a multi-nibbed implement (see e.g. fols. 2r, 116r, 139r, where the horizontals all
overshoot the vertical bounding line by about the same distance); the ruled space
65 x 45-6 mm.; single prickings in the fore-edge margin, about 4 mm. (i.e. one
line's height) below the bottom horizontal ruled line, and in the lower gutter
margin, perhaps for registering the ruling implement; the calendar with 16 ruled
lines, with single vertical bounding lines extending the full height of the page;
the ruled space 69-70 x 45-6 mm.
SCRIPT: written in a fine regular rounded Italian gothic bookhand, in two sizes
of script according to liturgical function, with 14 lines of text per page; the
written space 63-4 x 45-60 mm.; the calendar with 16 lines of text per page
(all but the start of February written above the top ruled line).
RUBRICATION: headings in red (not identical to the red of the pen-flourishing
of initials).
SEC. FOL.: (calendar) 'KL Februarius', (text, fol. 14r) [domi-]'nus tecum:'.

Binding
19th-cent Parisian signed binding by (Alphonse?) Simier (see the note under
MS. Buchanan f. 4). Sewing not clearly visible; red, white, and green endbands;
bound in dark blue leather over pasteboards; each cover with a gilt scrollwork
and foliate panel design; the spine with four false raised bands, dividing it into
five compartments, each with a simple panel in gilt, the second compartment
lettered: 'PRAECES PIAE'; 'SIMIER.R[ELIEUR].DU ROI' stamped at the bottom of the
spine, on fol. i verso, and on the bottom turn-in of the lower board; one red silk
bookmark; the edges of the leaves and boards gilt; two wove paper endleaves
and two modern parchment endleaves at each front and back of the volume.
The turn-ins of a previous binding have left slight impressions around the edges
of the first and last original leaves.

Provenance
1. Probably made without a specific patron in mind: the shield for a coat of arms
on fol. 13r has been left blank.

2. Unidentified 17th-cent.(?) owner prior to the present binding: responsible for
the ink foliation, which has been cropped.

3. Unidentified 18th/19th-cent. French bookseller (?), after the date of the
present binding: inscribed in pencil in the lower gutter corner of fol. ii recto:
'1345'.

4. Messrs. Boone, London booksellers (see Introduction, p. xxi): inscribed in
pencil in the top right corner of the upper pastedown and in the top left corner
of the lower pastedown with their price-code (cf. MSS. Buchanan e. 2 and e. 3;
see pls. 3-6).

5. John (or Thomas?) Buchanan, bought from Boone on 16 April 1862 for £30
(see Introduction, pp. xix, xxi): inscribed in pencil with the 'Descriptive list'
number, '1.', in the upper left corner of the upper pastedown, on a mark
apparently made by a small rectangular adhesive label.

6. Rt. Hon. T. R. Buchanan (1846-1911): given to the Bodleian by his widow,
Mrs E. O. Buchanan, in 1939, when it was accessioned as MS. Lat. liturg. e. 22;
re-referenced as MS. Buchanan g. 1 in 1941.

Bibliography
'Fifteen illuminated *Horae*', *BLR* 1 no. 7 (1939), 115-6, at 116 (as MS. Lat.
liturg. e. 22).

van Dijk, *Handlist of Latin liturgical MSS.*, IV, 318 (described as 'Roman use,
Palestine', but with no explicit reason given).

Pächt & Alexander, 2, no. 324, pl. XXIX.

L. M. J. Delaissé, James Marrow, and John de Wit, *The James A. de Rothschild
Collection at Waddesdon Manor: illuminated manuscripts* (Fribourg, 1977), 346.

MS. Buchanan g. 2

Psalter, in Latin
Flanders, Ghent(?); late 13th or early 14th century

Text
[Item 1 occupies quire I]

1. (fols. 1r-6v) Calendar, about one third full, most months headed by a note on
the length of the calendar month in red; major feasts (in red) include Remigius,
Germanus, Vedast, and Bavo (1 Oct.), Livin (12 Nov.); feasts in ordinary brown
ink include Vincent (22 Jan., crossed through in red, and with a red cross next to
the entry), Adelgundis (30 Jan.), Vedastus and Amandus (6 Feb.), Gertrude (17
Mar.), Guntram (partly erased) (28 Mar.), Ursmar (18 Apr.), Gudwal (6 June),
Lebuinus (25 June), Amalburga (10 July), Hilarianus (16 July), Bertin (5 Sept.),
Lambert (17 Sept.), Firminus (25 Sept.), Benedicta (8 Oct.), Severinus (23 Oct.);
Elizabeth of Thuringia (19 Nov.) is a contemporary addition; drypoint additions
include Dominic (5 Aug.); a group of 14th-cent. additions by a single hand,
relating to altars and indulgences, are: (i) 'Dominica secunda xl [i.e. quadragesime]
est dedicatio altaris sancti Eligii episcopi et confessoris tres anni indulgentiarum
et tres ca[...?]' written next to the first few days of March; (ii) 'Inuentio sancte
crucis est dedicatio ante crucem .xl. dies indulgentiarum', next to the feast of
the Invention of the Cross (3 May); (iii) 'Dominica proxima post festum beati
remigij episcopi dedicatio altaris sancti Judoci confessoris quadraginta dies
indulgentiarum et unam ca[...?]' written below the feast of Remigius, *et al.* (1 Oct.);
(iv) 'Dominica proxima ante festum omnium sanctorum dedicatio altaris sancte
marie magdalene unus annus indulgentiarum et .i. carn[...?]' written below the
feast of All Saints (1 Nov.); 15th-cent. additions in another hand are Louis
('Ludouici regis francie'; canonized 1297) (25 Aug.), and the rank 'chardenalis'
added to Jerome (30 Sept.).

[Items 2-5 occupy quires II-XXV, with a change of scribe at quire XIII, the start
of Ps. 80]

[fol. 7r is blank, fol. 7v has a full-page historiated initial incorporating the first
two words of the following text]

2. (fols. 7v-198v) Psalms 1-150; Psalm 80 starting imperfect in verse 13
(at [desi-]'||deria cordis eorum ...') due to the loss of a leaf before fol. 114;
14th-cent. corrections, omissions and antiphons supplied in the margins
(e.g. fols. 19v-20r, 104r).

3. (fols. 199r-217v) Canticles and Athanasian Creed: the six ferial canticles
followed (fols. 210v-217v) by the *Benedicite, Benedictus, Te Deum, Magnificat,
Nunc dimittis,* and *Quicumque.*

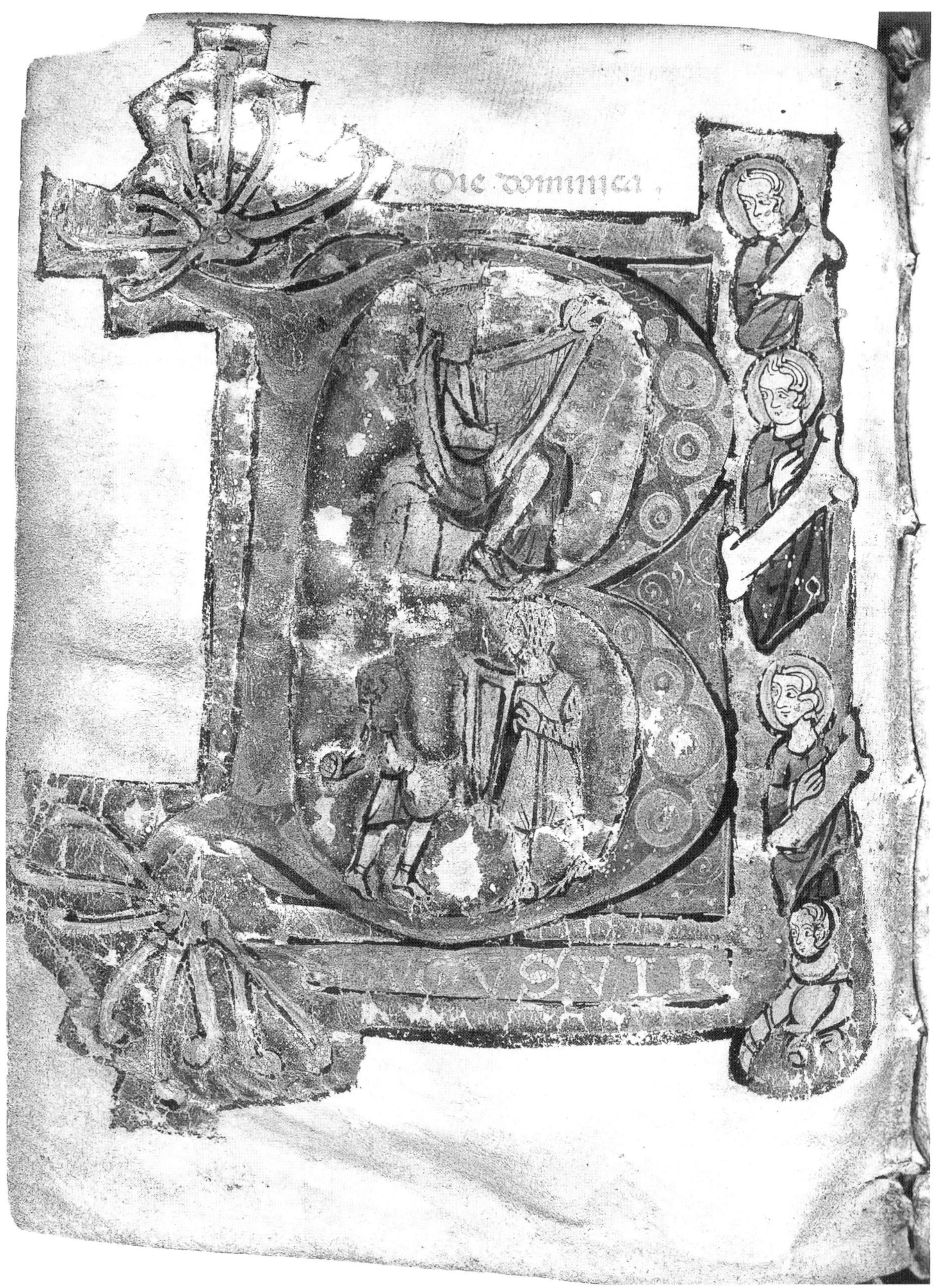

44. *MS. Buchanan g. 2, fol. 7v. [Considerably enlarged]*

4. (fols. 217v-222v) Litany and collects: the litany with Martial last among seventeen apostles and evangelists; Livin (2) and Lambert (17) among eighteen martyrs; Bavo, Landoald, Macarius, Amandus, 'Amauri' (Amor of Aquitaine, venerated in Liège ?) (1-5), and Servatius, Willibrord, Giles, Winnoc (16-19) among nineteen confessors; Vinciana (3), Amalberga, Gertrude (14-15), and Elizabeth (18) among eighteen virgins; followed by five collects (fols. 221v-222v): (i) 'Deus cui proprium est misereri ...' (pr. *Corpus orationum*, no. 1143); (ii) 'Omnipotens sempiterne deus qui facis mirabilia magna ...' (pr. *ibid.*, nos. 3938b-c); (iii) 'Pretende domine famulis et famulabus tuis ...' (pr. *ibid.*, no. 4587a); (iv) 'Ecclesie tue quesumus domine preces placatus admitte ...'; (v) 'Absolue domine animas famulorum famularumque tuarum ...' (pr. *ibid.*, no. 16).

5. (fols. 222v-230r) Office of the Dead, Cluniac(?) Use; the nine lessons are those of Ottosen's 'Group 1f' and the responses correspond to his numbers 14,72,24; 90,32,57; 68,28,38: Ottosen states that all the Offices he has studied with this series are of Benedictine houses connected with the monastic reform of either Cluny or William of Volpiano (see Ottosen, *Office of the Dead*, 53-64, 146-7); fol. 230v blank.

Decoration
One full-page historiated initial:
(fol. 7v) Initial 'B'[eatus]. King David harping in the upper compartment, David confronting Goliath in the lower compartment; the letter in pink on a blue and gold ground, the colours with white decoration; the right border with three three-quarter-length nimbed male figures each holding a scroll, and a human-headed hybrid; the lower border incorporating the letters 'EATVS VIR'; rubbed and worn, with some oxidisation of the white, and flaking of the gold (pl. 44).

Nine (of an original ten) eight-line initials, at the remaining ten-part divisions of the psalms (that to Psalm 80 missing, with an offset on fol. 113v), each in gold (with some flaking), edged in black, on a rose and blue 'quartered' field (some powdering), with white and silver (? now oxidised) tracery, with similar bar borders surrounding the text on all sides: Ps. 26 (fol. 36v); Ps. 38 (fol. 56r); Ps. 51 (fol. 73r); Ps. 52 (fol. 74r); Ps. 68 (fol. 91v); Ps. 97 (fol. 133v; pl. 45); Ps. 101 (fol. 136r); Ps. 109 (fol. 155v); a similar initial at the first Canticle, (fol. 199r) *Confitebor*, but without the bar borders; three-line initials in gold, edged in black, indented, with extensions running the height of the text area, on a field of rose and blue with white tracery (some powdering) to psalms and the 'KL' monograms in the calendar; one-line initials in burnished gold, edged in black, usually aligned between the left vertical bounding lines, to verses and other minor text divisions; line-fillers in gold edged in black, present only on the outer faces of the first bifolium of the text, i.e. fols. 8r and 17v.

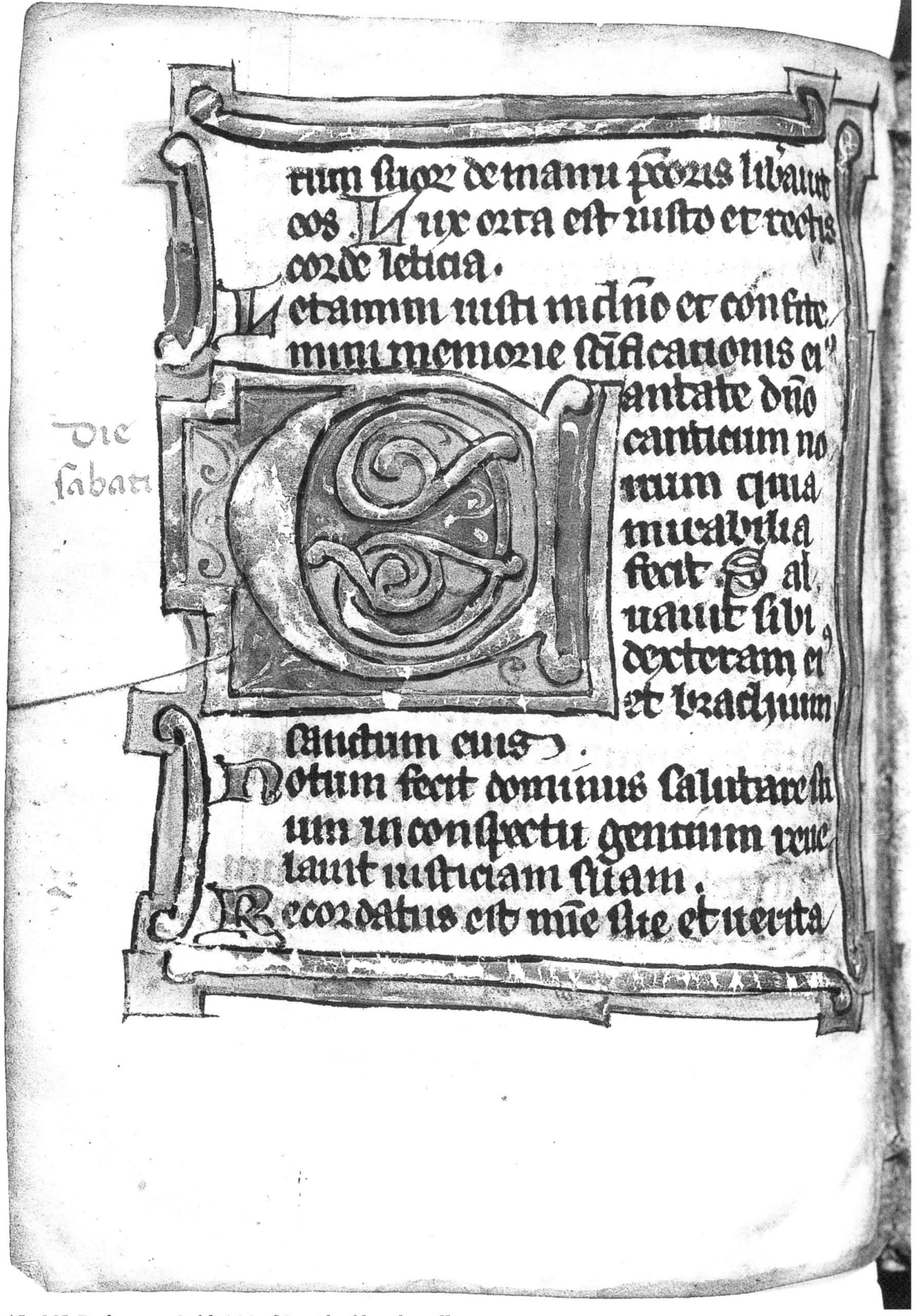

45. *MS. Buchanan g. 2, fol. 133v. [Considerably enlarged]*

Physical Description

MATERIAL: parchment; rather cockled.

DIMENSIONS: the leaves 110-5 x 80-5 mm. (rather cockled, so all measurements are approximate).

NUMBER OF LEAVES: 230.

FOLIATION: modern, in pencil: 1-230.

COLLATION: mostly in quires of 10 leaves: I^6 (fols. 1-6) | II$^{4-3?}$ (of two(?) bifolia, only the last leaf remains, see below) (fol. 7) | III-XII^{10} (fols. 8-107), XIII^6 (fols. 108-113) | XIV$^{10-1}$ (1st leaf missing, before fol. 114) (fols. 114-122), XV-XXIV^{10} (fols. 123-222), XXV^8 (fols. 223-230) | XXVI$^{8-8}$ (a whole quire cut out: unfoliated stubs remain); stubs between fols. 6 and 7 suggest that quire II may originally have been a quire of four (or more?) leaves, of which only the last survives; CATCHWORDS occasionally survive, in a smaller and somewhat more cursive script, in the bottom gutter corner (e.g. fols. 57v, 97v); LEAF SIGNATURES sporadically visible, lower right or left, perhaps more than one series, using various systems, including combinations of circlets and horizontal or vertical strokes (e.g. fols. 48r-52r, 98r-102r, 203r-206r), some in a green/blue ink (e.g. fols. 153r-157r).

RULING: 19 lines ruled in plummet, between a single vertical bounding line to the right, and double lines to the left to guide the placement of verse initials, the verticals extending the full height of the page, the first two and last two horizontals extending the full width of the page; there are up to 31 lines of writing in the calendar, but ruling lines are not visible; the ruled space *c.*70 x 50 mm.; prickings frequently survive at all three outer edges.

SCRIPT: written in a rounded gothic bookhand, with 18 lines of text per page; the written space 68-70 x 47-51 mm.; by two scribes, one writing the first 79 psalms (fols. 8r-113v), the other writing the remainder of the text (fols. 114r-230r), as is very common in 13th-cent. Flemish Psalters; it appears unlikely that either of these scribes wrote the calendar, but comparison is made difficult because it is written in a much smaller script; the Office of the Dead written in two sizes of script according to liturgical function.

RUBRICATION: headings in red, capitals touched in red on one bifolium of the last quire (fols. 225r-v and 228r-v), further rubrics added in the 15th? cent. (see under Provenance); many of the psalm initials have a drypoint symbol in the margin alongside, perhaps a letter 'g' (e.g. fols. 64r, 77r) perhaps a marker for the person executing the initials.

SEC. FOL.: (calendar) 'KL martius'; (text, fol. 9) [conturba- | |]'bit eos.'

Binding

Original sewing and remains of the binding (see pl. 2). Sewn on four split thongs; endbands sewn with green and red over plain thread; the upper board lacking; the thongs enter the lower board through its thickness, emerging in four horizontal channels on the outside, and fixed into holes with wood pegs; the endbands entering the board through smaller channels at the corners, at an angle of about 45 degrees, also pegged; the three outer edges of the oak board roughly bevelled on both the inner and outer face; two groups of three nail-holes in a triangular pattern are visible on the outer face at the fore-edge, for clasp-fittings (fol. 1 has rust-stained holes caused by the corresponding fittings of the upper board); two pairs of nail-holes visible on the inner face of the board near the outer corners, three still with traces of nails, perhaps for securing the turn-ins of a tanned leather covering, of which only tiny traces survive; the upper two thongs, half of the third thong, and the endbands all broken; the remaining bands weak. In a 20th-cent. box, lettered on the spine 'HORAE BEATAE | MARIAE | VIRGINIS' (*sic*) at the top, and 'MS. BUCHANAN | g. 2' at the bottom.

Provenance
1. The preponderance of saints in the calendar and litany whose relics were at Ghent (Livin, Bavo, Landoald, Macarius, Vinciana, Gertrude, etc.), point to that region, but the Office of the Dead, and the absence of some other Ghent feasts, such as the elevation and translation of the relics of Bavo, suggests that the book may have been intended for use in the diocese, rather than the town itself. The absence of St. Louis from the original calendar suggests that the book was made before, or not long after, 1297.

2. Unidentified 14th-cent owner: responsible for frequent corrections to the text (e.g. fols. 19r, 28v).

3. Unidentified 14th-cent. owner: additions to the calendar indicate the book's use by someone whose church had altars dedicated to Judoc, Eloi, and Mary Magdalen.

4. Unidentified 14th-cent. Netherlandish owner; inscribed (fol. 204r): 'in wil\s/e [??] nyet langherbeyde(n) sal'.

5. Unidentified 14th/15th-cent. Northern owner; responsible for the erasure and rewriting of earlier corrections (fols. 19v-20r).

6. Unidentified 15th(?)-cent. Italian owner; rubrics indicating the days and canonical hours added in a neat (14th/)15th-cent. Italian hand, e.g. (fol. 186r): '*Die veneris Ad vesperas*' (cf. pls. 44, 45).

7. Unidentified 15th/16th-cent. Italian owner; with erased, but partly legible, inscriptions in an untidy humanistic script: 'questo salmo se debe dire con deus laudem meam' (fol. 47v, next to Ps. 34); 'questo el quinto salmo che salmo[?] se debe dire per bono rispeto non domino(?) altro' (fol. 153v, next to Ps. 108, which begins 'Deus laudem meam'); similar, erased, inscriptions next to Ps. 21 (fol. 30r), and Ps. 54 (fol. 75r), and perhaps also Ps. 68 (fol. 91v); of approximately the same date is the marginal numbering of the psalms in lower-case Roman numerals, as far as Ps. 38 (numbered 'xxxvii', fol. 56r).

8. Female owner: a partly erased post-medieval(?) inscription at the end of the text, written in a 15th-cent. style of script, has been read by a previous Bodleian cataloguer as (fol. 230r): 'liber nobillissim[e] domine | eleza[bete] marie sho[...?]way', but the whole of the name is erased and very unclear.

9. Unidentified 19th-cent. English owner: the inner face of the lower board has a pasted-in slip of paper, inscribed: 'This is a complete Psalter of the 15th century.'

10. Rt. Hon. T. R. Buchanan (1846-1911); given to the Bodleian by his widow, Mrs. E. O. Buchanan, in 1941.

Bibliography
van Dijk, *Handlist of Latin liturgical MSS.*, II pt. i, no. 24.

Pächt & Alexander, 1, no. 290.

Richard Gameson, 'The Danson Psalter (Trinity College, MS 97)', in *Trinity College Oxford Report 1989-90* (Oxford, 1991), 71-83, at 74, 80.

MS. Buchanan g. 3

Ferial Psalter, in Latin

Italy, North-East, Venice(?), written for a Benedictine house of the Congregation of Sta. Giustina; 15th century, third quarter

Text

[Items 1-2 occupy quire I]

1. (fols. 1r-6v) Calendar, about half-full; graded with commemorations, feasts of twelve lessons, and *duplex maius* or *minus* feasts, but no feasts of three or nine lessons; January headed by a note on the number of months, weeks, and days in the year, in red; each month headed by a note on the length of the calendar and lunar month, in red; the Golden Numbers given in arabic numerals; major feasts (in red) include: Benedict ('*Sanctissimi patris nostri Benedicti ... duplex maius*') (21 Mar.), Placidus and his companions, '*duplex maius*' (5 Oct.), Justina, '*duplex maius*' (7 Oct.), Ambrose '*duplex minus*' (7 Dec.); feasts of twelve lessons in ordinary ink include Simeon (26 July), Dominic (5 Aug.), Cyprian & Justina (26 Sept.), Columban (21 Nov.); vigils are written as: 'Vigilia de precepto'; numerous erasures, regradings, and additions in January-June; contemporary additions include George, Felix, Fortunatus, and Achilleus (23 Apr., twelve lessons); regradings include some of three lessons, and others of twelve divided into eight and four lessons.

2. (fols. 7r-10v) Tables of the antiphons before Christmas (pr. S. J. P. van Dijk, ed., *Sources of the modern Roman liturgy: the ordinals of Haymo of Faversham and related documents (1243-1307)* (Studia et Documenta Franciscana: 2 vols., Leiden, 1963), II, 401-8).

[Items 3-6 occupy quires II-XII]

3. (fols. 11r-92r) Ferial Psalter, beginning imperfect in Ps. 6:9 (at '| | operamini iniquitatem ...'), due to the loss of a leaf before fol. 11; with Benedictine divisions (except Ps. 32; see under Decoration), and sub-divisions of psalms marked (e.g. Pss. 9:20, 17:26, 67:20, 103:25, fols. 13r, 16v, 46v, 68v, respectively).

4. (fols. 92r-97r) Canticles for Advent, Christmas, Quadragesima, and Easter; and (fols. 95v-97r) for the Common of Saints.

5. (fols. 97r-111r) Hymnal, including hymns for major feasts of the Temporale, the Dedication of a Church, Sts. Benedict and (fols. 107v-108v) Justina, and the Common of Saints.

6. (fols. 111r-113v) Litany and collects; the litany including Placidus and his companions, sixth among twelve martyrs; Benedict ('Sancte pater Benedicte') first among ten monks and hermits; and Justina second among fourteen virgins; followed (fol. 112r-v) by petitions including: 'Ut omnes nauigantes ad portum salutis perducere digneris'; and (fol. 113r-v) by the usual ten collects

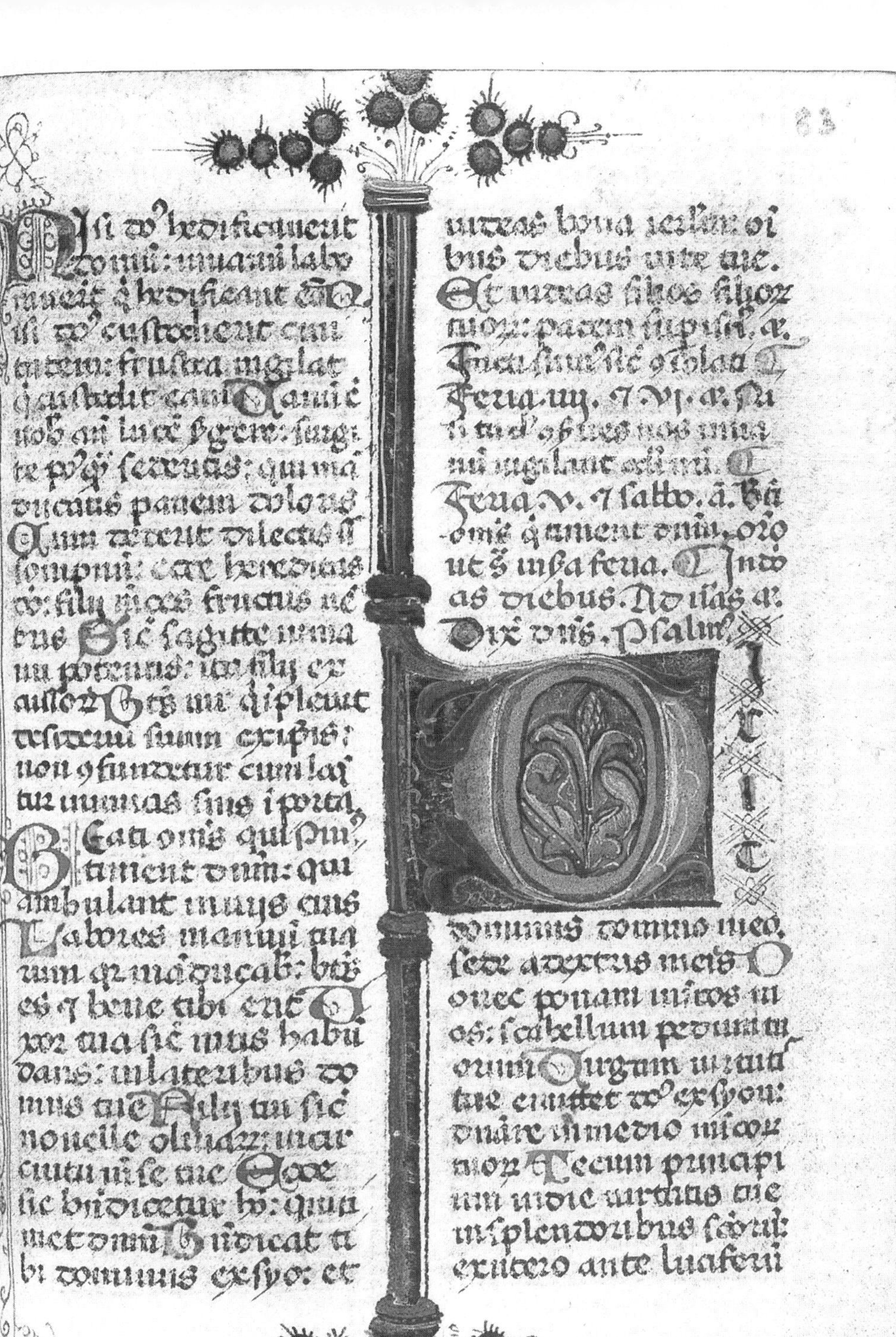

46. *MS. Buchanan g. 3, fol. 83r. [Considerably enlarged]*

(see MS. Buchanan e. 5, where they are listed); the fifth mentioning '... famulo tuo presidenti nostro ...'; the tenth ending imperfect (at '... omniumque misere | | [ris]'), due to the loss of a bifolium after fol. 113; fols. 114r-115v, ruled, otherwise blank.

Decoration

One eight-line initial in gold and colours, with a bar-extender running the whole height of the page, to Ps. 109 (fol. 83r; pl. 46); a similar six-line initial and extender to Ps. 101 (fol. 66v); a seven-line foliate initial on a gold ground, with foliate sprays and gold balls extending half the height of the page and into or towards the upper and lower margins, at the start of the hymnal (fol. 97r); similar four- to six-line initials, their extensions ranging from half to full height, to Pss. 20, 45, 59, 73, 85 (fols. 18v, 38r, 44v, 52r, 60r), the start of the canticles for Advent and Christmas (fols. 92r, 93r), the Common of Saints (fols. 95v, 96v), hymns for major feasts of the Sanctorale (fols. 97v, 98v, 101v, 103r, 104r, 108v), the Common of Saints (fols. 109r, 109v, 111r), and the litany (fol. 111r); four-line initial in red with purple penwork, the penwork extending almost the full height of the page, to Ps. 26 (fol. 21v); similar three-line initials alternately in red with purple penwork, or blue with red penwork, with similar penwork extenders, to psalms, canticles, etc. up to fol. 44r, thereafter two-line; one-line initials alternately in red or blue, to verses and other minor divisions; guide letters for coloured initials are visible throughout; paraphs in blue; simple red and blue line-fillers in the litany (fols. 111v-112v).

Physical Description

MATERIAL: parchment, rather water-stained at beginning and end; offsets indicate that the bifolium was already missing after fol. 113 when the water-damage occured.

DIMENSIONS: the leaves 73-5 x 104-5 mm.; the decoration cropped in all three outer margins.

NUMBER OF LEAVES: ii (paper, the first marbled and conjoint with the pastedown) + 115 + ii (paper, the second marbled and conjoint with the pastedown).

FOLIATION: modern, in pencil: i-ii, 1-117.

COLLATION: in quires of 10 leaves, with some losses: i^{10} (fols. 1-10) | II^{10-1} (1st leaf excised, leaving a stub before fol. 11) (fols. 11-19), $III-XI^{10}$ (fols. 20-109), XII^{10-4} (5rd and 6th leaves, a bifolium, missing, 9th and 10th leaves excised) (fols. 110-115); CATCHWORDS survive at the end of every quire except the first and last, written in the same script as the main text, horizontally in the lower margin, between the ruled vertical intercolumnar bounding lines, about two lines' height below the bottom line of text, surrounded in a saltire pattern by four designs in paler ink, each like a cross of St. Andrew on a quatrefoil.

RULING: 33 lines ruled in very pale brown ink, in two columns, each column between single vertical bounding lines extending the full height of the page; the ruled space 76-7 x 54-5 mm.; the inter-columnar space *c*.6 mm.; single prickings survive in the upper fore-edge margin, 4-5 mm. above the top ruled line.

SCRIPT: written in a neat rounded gothic bookhand, with 32 lines of text per page, in two columns; the written space of each column 74-6 x 23-4 mm.
RUBRICATION: headings in red.
SEC. FOL.: (calendar, fol. 2r) 'KL Martius'; (tables, fol. 8r) 'Ad laudes'; (text, fol. 11r) 'operamini iniquitatem:'; (text, fol. 12r) 'deducat Exurge'.

Binding

Sewn on three(?) cords (not clearly visible); bound in Italian 18th(?)-cent. mottled brown leather over pasteboards; rebacked, the old spine laid on, with gilt foliate ornament and a pale brown leather title-piece lettered: 'OFFIC | DELLA | B.V.M', slightly damaged along the side of the upper joint; marbled pastedowns and conjoint flyleaves; the edges of the leaves coloured red, later than the date of the binding, since the red also affects underlying corners of the pasteboards which are exposed by damage.

Provenance

1. Made for a Benedictine House (as evidenced by the grading of feasts with twelve lessons in the calendar, the Benedictine divisions and sub-divisions of the psalms, and the wording of the 21 March feast of Benedict) of the Congregation of Sta. Giustina (as evidenced by the emphasis on St. Justina in the calendar, litany, and hymnal; the emphasis on St. Placidus in the calendar and litany; the wording of vigils 'de precepto'; and the collect mentioning 'presidenti nostro'); the petition for sailors might hint at a coastal origin, since it occurs also in manuscripts of the Congregation written for S. Giorgio Maggiore, Venice (e.g. MSS. Canon. Liturg. 204 and 210), but not in the Breviary of the Congregation printed in 1484; yet it also occurs in a breviary written for nuns of the Congregation in the diocese of Brescia (MS. Canon. Liturg. 164).

2. ? Monastery of SS. Felice e Fortunata, Vicenza (on which see Cottineau, *Répertoire topo-bibliographique*, II, col. 3360): according to van Dijk, and accepted by Pächt & Alexander, the added feast of these two saints in the calendar may point to the monastery dedicated to them; it was incorporated into the Congregation of S. Giustina in 1462. The fact that the feast is graded with twelve lessons, however, rather than as a *duplex*, casts some doubt on this.

3. Unidentified 18th/19th-cent owner; inscribed (fol. ii recto): 'Horae diurne'.

4. Unidentified 19th-cent owner: inscribed in pencil: 'LB13[?] V15±[?]' at the top left of fol. i verso.

5. Raguin, Paris bookseller, by 1875 (see Introduction, p. xxiv, and below); inscribed in pencil: 'Bu.or'(?) in the top left corner of fol. 117r.

6. Rt. Hon. T. R. Buchanan (1846-1911), 1875: fol. ii recto with a slip of paper glued in vertically, inscribed in ink by Buchanan '[Ho]ræ B.V.M. MS. of 15th century. | Bought from Raguin Nov. 1875 -' (cf. especially MS. Buchanan d. 2, and the printed books, Buchanan e.65 and e.136); given to the Bodleian by his

widow, Mrs E. O. Buchanan, in 1941; traces of a rectangular paper label with at least one perforated edge in the lower left corner of the upper board are probably the remains of a Bodleian shelfmark label.

Bibliography
van Dijk, *Handlist of Latin liturgical MSS.*, II, 97.

Pächt & Alexander, 2, no. 885.

MS. Buchanan g. 4

Prayers and Devotions (perhaps an imperfect Book of Hours), in Latin and Italian
Italy; 15th century, second half

Text
[Items 1-2 originally occupied quires II-III; the start of item 1 was later copied
onto the added quire I]

1. (fols. 2r-15r) The Seven Penitential Psalms; fol. 1r-v ruled, otherwise originally
blank; fol. 2 is a supply leaf containing Ps. 6:1-6 (to '... inferno autem | |'; see
also under Decoration).

2. (fols. 15r-24v) Litany and collects; the litany with 'Sancte pater' Benedict (1),
Placidus (6), and Romuald ('Romuade') (8) among eight monks, hermits, priests,
and deacons; followed (fols. 22r-24v) by the usual ten collects (listed under MS.
Buchanan e. 5), the fifth mentioning '... famulo tuo .N. ...'; fols. 25r-26v ruled,
otherwise blank.

[Items 3-13 originally occupied the present quires IV-VIII; the start of item 3 was
later copied onto the last leaf of quire III]

3. (fols. 27r-51v) Office of the Dead, omitting Vespers, and thus beginning at
Matins, with only three lessons, corresponding to those of the Use of Rome; the
first leaf is a supply leaf containing Ps. 94:1-59 (to '... adoremus. Quoniam | |';
see also under Decoration).

4. (fols. 52r-53r, rubric on fol. 51v) The Verses of St. Bernard: '*Isti sunt uersibus*
[sic] *sancti bernardi abbatis. O bone ihesu:-* Illumina oculos meos ...', the verses
in the same order as in MS. Buchanan e. 9, fols. 118v-119r (*q.v.*) followed by a
versicle, response, and (fol. 53r) the usual prayer, here incorporating the name
of the original owner: 'Omnipotens sempiterne deus qui ezechie regi iude ...
concede mihi indignum famulum tuum. iohannem. ... misericordiam consequi
merear. Per ...'.

5. (fols. 53v-54r) Indulgenced prayer, here attributed to Pope Innocent [III
(1198-1216)?]: '*Innocentius papa concessit omni dicenti semel in die istam orationem.
indulgentiam omnium peccatorum suorum.* Deus qui uoluisti pro salute mundi ...
[masculine forms] ... perduxisti latronem crucifixum. Qui uiuis' (cf. Leroquais,
Livres d'heures, II, 344; Wordsworth, *Horae Eboracenses*, 83; de la Mare, *Lyell cat.*,
64 item e, where it is attributed to Boniface IV).

6. (fols. 54v-56r) Prayer to be said before Communion: '*Oratio deuota dicenda ante
comunionem.* Domine yhesu christe qui dixisti. qui manducat meam carnem et
bibit meum sanguinem. ... [masculine forms] ... Ubi te semper uideam. cum deo
patre et spiritu sancto in secula seculorum. Amen.'

7. (fols. 56r-57r) Prayer to be said after Communion, carrying an indulgence of Pope Boniface: '*papa bonifatius concessit omni dicenti post perceptionem corporis christi indulgentiam .xl.ᵃ dierum.* Gratias tibi ago domine sancte pater qui me famulum tuum nullis mentis ... et sempiternum gaudium. Per eundem christum ...'.

8. (fol. 57r-v) Hymn, here attributed to St. Bernard: '*Beatus bernardus conposuit infrascriptam orationem. affirmans quicumque eam flexis genibus dixerit omnibus diebus uite sue numquam in peccatis morietur. oratio.* Ave caro christi cara. inmolata crucis ara. pro redemptis hostia. Morte tua nos amata. ... pater misericordiarum. Amen.' (*Repertorium hymnologicum*, no. 1710).

9. (fols. 58r-60r, rubric on fols. 57v-58r) Prayer, here attributed to St. Augustine: '*Oratio sancti augustini ualde utilis et deuota. Quicumque eam dixerit semel in die non peribit in igne. ... Et si quid iustum petierit a deo i[m]petrabit. oratio.* Deus propitius esto mihi peccatori et custos omnibus diebus uite mee. ... ad tuam sanctam gratiam facias peruenire. Amen.' (a shorter version is pr. in Wordsworth, *op. cit.*, 125).

10. (fols. 60v-61r, rubric on fol. 60r-v) Prayer in Italian, here attributed to St. Augustine: '*Questa oratione fece sancto augustino laquale e molto utile et deuota. Incipit.* Signor rodio [sic] mio misericordia mia refugio mio et desiderio mio atte rifuggo ... raccomando lo spirito mio. Amen.'

11. (fols. 61v-62r, rubric on fol. 61r) Prayer to one's guardian angel: '*Oratio ad proprium angelum.* Superne curie ciuis angele sancte. qui fragilis uite mee deputatus es custos ... et presenta eam in uitam eternam. Amen.'

12. (fol. 62r-v) Commemoration of the archangel Raphael: '*Conmemoratio beati raphaelis archangeli. antiphona.* Angelum nobis medicum salutis ...', with versicle, response, and the prayer 'Deus qui raphaelem archangelum thobie famulo tuo properanti preuium direxisti. ... .*LAUS DEO.*' (the latter pr. J. Lemarié, 'Textes relatifs au culte de l'archange et des anges dans les bréviaires manuscrits du Mont-Saint-Michel', *Sacris Erudiri* 13 (1962), 113-52, at 141); fol. 63r ruled, otherwise originally blank; fol. 63v originally blank.

13. (fol. 63r-v) (?) Pen trials, of uncertain date; inscribed: 'mapilon' or 'mopilon' at the start of the top line of fol. 63r, and '[T]ota die' at the top of the verso.

Decoration
Two historiated initials (9- and 7-line) on inserted leaves, perhaps late 15th cent., or later, each on a square gold field with foliate tendrils extending into the margins: (fol. 2r) Penitential Psalms. Initial D[omine]: a group of buildings (perhaps a monastery?), including a circular tower with three storeys, on top of which is a cross and pennant (pl. 47).
(fol. 27r) Office of the Dead. Initial U[enite] (but shaped more like an 'O' or 'D'): group of buildings, similar in some details to those on fol. 2r.

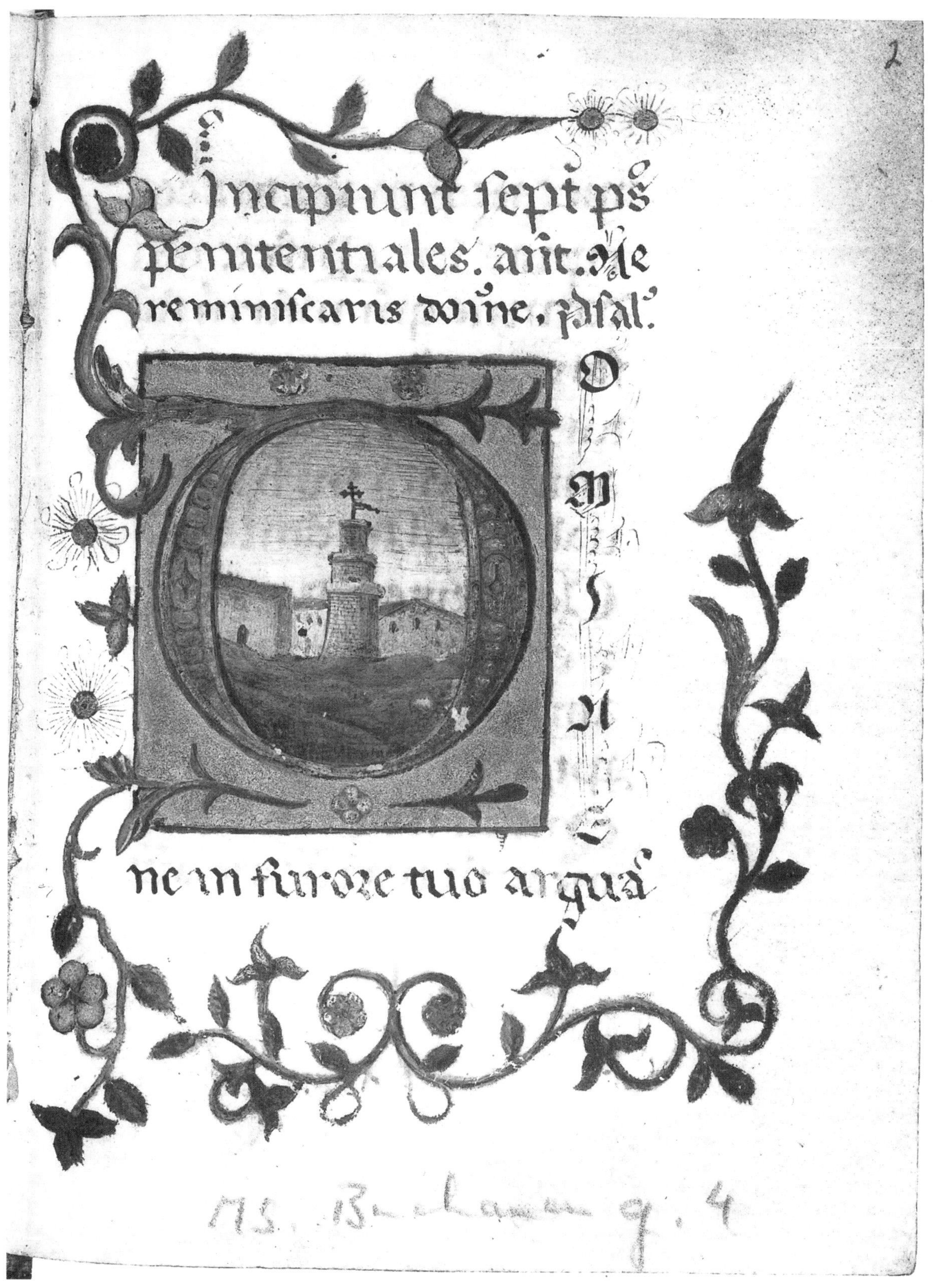

47. *MS. Buchanan g. 4, fol. 2r. [Considerably enlarged]*

Two-line initials, alternately in blue with red penwork or red with purple penwork, the penwork extending almost the full height of the page, at the start of psalms, collects, lessons, etc.; one-line initials alternately in red or blue, at the start of verses and other minor textual divisions.

Physical Description

MATERIAL: parchment.

DIMENSIONS: the leaves 93-4 x 67-8 mm.

NUMBER OF LEAVES: i (modern paper, conjoint with the pastedown) + 63 + i (modern paper, conjoint with the pastedown).

FOLIATION: modern, in pencil: i, 1-64.

COLLATION: mostly in quires of 10 leaves: I^2 (fols. 1-2) | II^{10-1} (1st leaf excised, leaving a stub before fol. 3) (fols. 3-11), III^{10} (fols. 12-21), IV^6 (fols. 22-27) | V^{10-1} (1st leaf excised, leaving a stub before fol. 28) (fols. 28-36), VI-VII^{10} (fols. 37-56), VIII^{8-1} (with the stub of an excised leaf after fol. 58) (fols. 57-63)—the structure of the final quire is rather complicated, see the *Note* below; each of the two main original scribes (see under script) used a different system of CATCHWORDS: (i) written sideways vertically downwards, on the inner vertical bounding line, between a pair of dots (fols. 11v and 21v); (ii) written horizontally in the centre of the lower margin, surrounded by four short wavy lines (fols. 36v, 46v, and 56v).

RULING: 14 lines ruled in very pale brown ink, sometimes almost invisible, between single vertical bounding lines extending the full height of the page; the ruled space 54-5 x 35-6 mm.; single PRICKINGS visible, often a Y-shaped puncture, in the fore-edge margin *c*.4 mm. below the bottom ruled line.

SCRIPT: written in gothic bookhands, with for 13 lines of text per page; the written space 52-3 x 34-7 mm.; by three scribes: (i) fols. 3r-24v; (ii) fols. 28r-62v (using a distinctive *signe-de-renvoie* to supply an omission, fol. 43v); and (iii) fols. 2r-v, and 27r-v (i.e. the supply leaves; somewhat clumsy, and perhaps artificial—see e.g. the unusual abbreviation 'do(m)ine' in pl. 47).

RUBRICATION: each scribe responsible for his own headings, in red.

SEC. FOL.: 'quis confitebitur'.

Note

The rather tight and fragile binding makes for some uncertainty. The stub before fol. 59 has traces of pen-flourishing on its recto which correspond to the pen-flourishing of the initial on fol. 58; it therefore seems likely that what is now the stub was originally the second leaf of the quire, and that this was cancelled after it had been written and decorated; the text was then re-written on the conjugate half of the same bifolium (which would have been the ruled but otherwise blank penultimate leaf of the quire), and bound in its present position, as fol. 58.

Another anomaly is the offset of purple penwork decoration in the gutter [!] margin of fol. 47r, with no such decoration on the facing page, and no loss of a leaf: to produce an offset here, another leaf/quire must presumably have been

laid head-to-tail on top of this one by the pen-flourisher before binding, and
while the ink was still wet.

Binding
Sewn on two cords; bound in 17th/18th?-cent. brown leather over pasteboards;
with a double gilt fillet framing the covers (largely obscured), five (or six?) similar
horizontal double fillets dividing the spine (largely obscured); each cover with an
applied panel of 19th-cent. enamelled glass (the upper panel badly cracked) with
a semée of gold stars on a deep blue ground, and with gold and silver oak-leaf
motifs around the edges; these panels each with an openwork gilt metal framing
(originally attached with a nail in each corner; three of the nails on the upper
cover are now detached) in the form of branches, foliage, flowers, and fruit(?);
with a silver(?) clasp (fastening from bottom to top); the spine with a convex
gilt metal panel (damaged and repaired) with fleurs-de-lis and scrolls in relief,
attached with a nail at each corner; yellow wove paper flyleaves conjoint with the
pastedowns; fol. 63 apparently the pastedown of a previous binding; the edges
of the leaves gilt; boxed (pl. 2).

Provenance
1. Made for an Italian-speaker named Giovanni/Iohannes (see text items 4
and 10); it is probable that the manuscript is the second half of a Book of Hours.

2. Unidentified owner: there is an erased ownership(?) inscription at the upper
edge of fol. 1r, not legible even under UV light, probably added after the binding,
since it appears to be offset onto the flyleaf, fol. i verso.

3. Thomas Arthur / William Ridler, London booksellers (see Introduction, pp. xxii-
xxiv); inscribed in pencil on the upper pastedown with their characteristic price
and pricecode: '£10-18-0' (the '10' altered from '11'), upper centre, with their
price-code 'm/sd/-' (i.e. £8 15s), at the centre fore-edge, sloping upwards
(cf. MSS. Buchanan b. 1 and d. 1).

4. Rt. Hon. T. R. Buchanan (1846-1911), probably bought from Arthur or
Ridler after 1874 (see Introduction); given to the Bodleian in 1941 by his widow,
Mrs. E. O. Buchanan.

Bibliography
van Dijk, *Handlist of Latin liturgical MSS.*, IV, no. 332.

Pächt & Alexander, 2, no. 984.

General index

Unidentified German prince-archbishop,
18th cent.
MS. Buchanan e. 2
see also Owners and donors
Booksellers and auctioneers
Unidentified
MS. Buchanan d. 4
MS. Buchanan e. 3
see also Arthur (Thomas); Boone
(Thomas and William); Ellis (F. S.);
Leighton (J. & J.); Muller (Frederik);
Ridler (William); Sotheby's; Trigt
(G.-A. van)
Boone (Thomas and William), *19th cent.,*
booksellers, of London
sold (1863)
MS. Buchanan e. 2
MS. Buchanan e. 3
MS. Buchanan e. 4
MS. Buchanan g. 1
Bourdichon (Jean), *illuminator*
style of
MS. Buchanan e. 4
Bracciolini (Poggio) *see* Poggio Bracciolini
Brendan, *c. 468-c 575, St., 'the Navigator'/*
'the Voyager'
in calendar [16 May]
MS. Buchanan e. 18 (17 May)
Breviary
in Latin
Use of Rome
MS. Buchanan f. 4
Use unidentified
MS. Buchanan f. 3 (bifolium)
Bridget, *c. 451-525, St., of Kildare, Ireland*
in litany
MS. Buchanan f. 2
Bridget, *c. 1303-1373, St., of Sweden*
in calendar [28 May, 23 July, 7 Oct.]
MS. Buchanan f. 2
in litany
MS. Buchanan f. 2
Bridgettine Order
breviary of
MS. Buchanan f. 2
Bruges *Flanders*
MS. produced in
MS. Buchanan e. 18
Bruni (Leonardo) *see* Aretinus (Leonardus)
Buchanan (John), father of T. R. Bucha-
nan
probably owned
MSS. Buchanan e. 2-e. 5, e. 7-e. 14,
f. 1, g. 1
Buchanan (Thomas) d. 1864, uncle of T.
R. Buchanan
owned
MS. Buchanan e. 5

Buchanan (Thomas Ryburn), *1846-*
1911, Rt. Hon.; and Buchanan (Emily
Octavia), *his wife*
owned
all MSS. with shelfmarks beginning
'MS. Buchanan'
Calendar
in Dutch
MS. Buchanan f. 3
in French
MS. Buchanan e. 2
MS. Buchanan e. 3
MS. Buchanan e. 4
MS. Buchanan e. 8
MS. Buchanan e. 9
MS. Buchanan e. 10
MS. Buchanan e. 13
MS. Buchanan e. 14
in Latin
MS. Buchanan e. 5
MS. Buchanan e. 7
MS. Buchanan e. 12
MS. Buchanan e. 18
MS. Buchanan f. 2
MS. Buchanan f. 4 (Ambrosian
and Roman)
MS. Buchanan g. 1
MS. Buchanan g. 2
MS. Buchanan g. 3
rubrics relating to
MS. Buchanan f. 4
Illustrations *see* Iconography,
Occupations of the Months; and
Iconography, Zodiac Signs
Calixtus III, *d. 1458, Pope*
Office instituted by
MS. Buchanan f. 4
Candidus, *St., see* Maurice
Canonici (Matteo Luigi) *1727-1806, of*
Venice
possibly owned
? MS. Buchanan d. 4
Canticles
in Latin
MS. Buchanan f. 2
MS. Buchanan g. 2
MS. Buchanan g. 3
Carmelite
Office of the Dead, Use of
MS. Buchanan e. 7
Cassinese Congregation
MS. made for a house of
MS. Buchanan g. 3
Castritianus, *d. 137, St., Archbishop of*
Milan
in calendar [1 Dec.]
MS. Buchanan f. 4

Ritus?, *unidentified, St., Bishop*
in calendar [14 Apr.]
? MS. Buchanan e. 5 ('Riti episcopi')
Roche, *14th cent., St.*
in calendar [16 Aug.]
MS. Buchanan e. 11
suffrage to
MS. Buchanan e. 4
Rohan Master *see* Master of the Rohan
Hours
Romanus, *d. 258, St.*
in calendar [usually 9 Aug.]
MS. Buchanan e. 7 (31 March)
Romanus, *d. 463, St., Abbot of Condat*
in calendar [28 Feb.]
MS. Buchanan f. 1 (see Provenance)
Romanus, *c. 561-639, St., Bishop of Rouen*
in calendar [23 Oct.; transl. 17 June]
MS. Buchanan e. 3 (23 Oct. only)
MS. Buchanan e. 13
in litany
MS. Buchanan e. 3
MS. Buchanan e. 14
suffrage to
MS. Buchanan e. 3
Rome *Italy*
SS. Pietro e Paolo, dedication of church
of
in calendar [18 Nov.]
MS. Buchanan f. 4
SS. Salvatore e Teodoro, dedication of
church of
in calendar [9 Nov.]
MS. Buchanan g. 1 (8 Nov.)
Romuald, *c. 952-1027, St., Abbot, founder
of the Camaldolese hermits*
in litany
MS. Buchanan g. 4
Rose, *St., of Viterbo*
in litany
? MS. Buchanan e. 4
Rouen *France*
MSS. produced in
MS. Buchanan e. 3
MS. Buchanan e. 13
Roussel (Symeon de), *17th cent.*
owned (1694)
MS. Buchanan e. 9
Rufinus, *unidentified St.*
in calendar [19 April, 27 Aug.]
? MS. Buchanan e. 11 ('Rufin'),
Sabinianus, *d. c. 300, St., Bishop of Sens*
suffrage to
MS. Buchanan e. 9

Sacrament, the Holy
Office of, in Dutch
MS. Buchanan f. 3
ritual of the Last, in Latin
MS. Buchanan f. 4
Saint-Omer, *France*
MS. perhaps made for
MS. Buchanan e. 9
San Marco, Dominican Convent,
see Florence
Saints
see Achilleus; Adalbert; Adrian; Agnes;
Albinus; Aldegund; Aldhelm; Alexander;
Alexis; All saints; Alphege; Amalberga;
Amand; Ambrose; Amor; Anastasia;
Andrew; Anne; Ansbert; Anselm;
Antoninus; Antony, *abbot*; Antony, *of
Padua*; Apollonia; Aquilinus; Arnulf;
Augustine; Aurea; Austreberta; Avia;
Barbara; Barnabas; Bartholomew; Basil;
Bavo; Becket, Thomas; Bede; Benedict;
Benedicta; Bernard; Bernardino; Bertin;
Blaise; Boniface; Bonus; Brendan;
Bridget, *of Ireland*; Bridget, *of Sweden*;
Castritianus; Catherine, *of Alexandria*;
Catherine, *of Siena*; Christopher; Clare;
Clarus; Claudius; Clement I; Cloud;
Columba; Columban; Cunibert;
Cuthbert; Cyprian; Denis; Desiderius;
Dominic; Donatian; Donatus; Dunstan;
Dympna; Edmund; Eleven Thousand
Virgins; Elisabeth; Eloi; Erasmus; Eulalia;
Eustace; Eustaise; Eustorgius; Eutropius;
Evodius; Fabian; Felix; Ferrer, Vincent;
Fiacre; Firmin; Fortunatus; Francis;
Gabinius; Gallus; Gatianus; Gaudus;
'Gelliis'; Geneviève; George; Gerald;
Gereon; Germain; Germanus; Gertrude;
Gervase; Ghislain; Gilbert; Giles;
Gorgonius; Gregory I; Gudwal; Gummar;
Guntram; Helory, Ivo; Herculanus;
Hermagoras; Hilarianus; Hildebert;
Hippolytus; Honorina; Hubert; Hugh, *of
Rouen*; Hugh, *of St.-Victor*; Humbert; Ivo;
James; Jerome; John *the Baptist*; John *the
Evangelist*; Judoc; Julian; Juliana; Justina,
of Piazenza; Justina, *of Padua*; Lambert;
Landericus; Landoald; Laurence;
Lazarus; Lebuin; Leger; Leo; Leufred;
Livin; Louis IX; Louis, *of Toulouse*; Lubin;
Luke; Lupus; Macarius; Madelberta;
Magloire; Magnus; Malo; Mamertus;
Manvoeus; Marcellus; Margaret; Mark;
Martha; Martial; Martin; Mary
Magdalen; Mastidia; Maternus;
Matthew; Matthias; Maurice; Maurus;

'uerbum caro'
   MS. Buchanan e. 13
'vestri; probauerunt'
   MS. Buchanan e. 14
'V'. Iube deo'
   MS. Buchanan f. 4
Seillière (*François-Florentin-Achille*), *1813-1873, Baron*
  owned
   MS. Buchanan f. 4
Sens *France*
  MS. perhaps owned in diocese of
   MS. Buchanan e. 9
Sept requêtes *see* Requests of Our Lord
Servatius, *c. 338-384, St., Bishop of Tongern*
  in calendar [13 May]
   MS. Buchanan e. 18
   MS. Buchanan f. 1
   MS. Buchanan f. 2
  in litany
   MS. Buchanan g. 2
Seven Penitential Psalms *see* Psalms
Seven Prayers of St. Gregory
see Gregory I
Seven Requests of Our Lord
see Requests of Our Lord
Seven Verses of St. Bernard *see* Bernard
Severinus, *St., Bishop of Tongeren*
  in litany
   MS. Buchanan f. 2
Severinus, *d. c. 403, St., Bishop of Cologne*
  in calendar [23 Oct.]
   MS. Buchanan f. 3
   MS. Buchanan g. 2
Severus, *St., Bishop of Avranches*
  in calendar [1 Feb. at Rouen]
   MS. Buchanan e. 13
  in litany
   MS. Buchanan e. 3
Severus, *St., one of the 72 Disciples of Christ*
  in litany
   ? MS. Buchanan e. 9
Silvester, *d. 335, St., Pope 314-35*
  in litany
   MS. Buchanan e. 12
Silvinus, *d. c. 718, St., regionary Bishop*
  in litany
   MS. Buchanan e. 9
Simeon, *d. 1016, St., of Padalirone, diocese of Padua*
  in calendar [26 July]
   MS. Buchanan g. 3
Simier (Alphonse and René), *early 19th-cent., bookbinders, of Paris*
  bound
   MS. Buchanan f. 4
   MS. Buchanan g. 1

Simon & Jude, *Sts., Apostles*
  suffrage to
   MS. Buchanan e. 9
Sixtus IV, *d. 1484, Pope*
  indulgence attributed to
   MS. Buchanan f. 1
Soranzo (Jacopo) *1686-1761*
  possibly owned
   MS. Buchanan d. 4
Sotheby, Wilkinson & Hodge, *auctioneers, see* Sotheby's
Sotheby's, *auctioneers, of London, formerly styled 'Baker, Leigh & Sotheby' (-1861); 'Sotheby, Wilkinson & Hodge' (1861-1924); 'Sotheby & Co.' (1924-1975); and 'Sotheby Parke Bernet & Co.' (1975-1984)*
  17 June 1875
   MS. Buchanan e. 18
  25 Feb. 1887
   MS. Buchanan f. 4
  25 Feb. 1889
   MS. Buchanan c. 1
  5 Dec. 1898
   MS. Buchanan c. 1
   MS. Buchanan d. 4
   MS. Buchanan e. 15
Spes, *St.*
  in litany
   MS. Buchanan f. 1
Stephen, *St., Deacon, 'the first martyr'*
  suffrage to
   MS. Buchanan e. 8
   MS. Buchanan e. 9
Stia, Giovanni di Piero da *see* Giovanni di Piero da Stia
Stuart (William), *1798-1894, of Aldenham Abbey and Tempsford Hall*
  owned
   MS. Buchanan e. 18
Suffrages to saints *see under individual saints' names*
Sulpice, *d. c. 647, St., Archbishop of Bourges*
  in litany
   ? MS. Buchanan e. 10
Sulpitius, *d. 844, St., Bishop of Bayeux*
  in litany
   ? MS. Buchanan e. 14
Susanna, *St.*
  in litany
   MS. Buchanan e. 4
Swithun, *d. 863, St., Bishop of Winchester*
  in calendar [2 Jul.]
   MS. Buchanan e. 14
Taurinus, *d. 412, St., Bishop of Evreux*
  in calendar [invention 5 Sept.]
   MS. Buchanan e. 14
  in litany
   MS. Buchanan e. 14

Index of incipits

Incipits of French, Italian, and Netherlandish texts follow those in Latin.

Abbreviations used in this index:

CO *Corpus orationum*

HE *Horae Eboracenses*

RH *Repertorium hymnologicum*

Latin

Absolue quesumus domine animas
famulorum ... (CO, no. 16)
    MS. Buchanan g. 1, fol. 157v
    MS. Buchanan g. 2 (see text 4)

Actiones tuas quesumus domine ...
(CO, no. 74)
    MS. Buchanan e. 5 (see text 9)
    MS. Buchanan e. 7 (see text 4)
    MS. Buchanan f. 4 (see text 12)
    MS. Buchanan g. 1 (see text 6)
    MS. Buchanan g. 3 (see text 6)
    MS. Buchanan g. 4 (see text 2)

Ad haec uirgo celica, det nobis solamen,
Et sanctis similiter pium confortamen: ...
    MS. Buchanan g. 1 (see text 25)

Angele qui meus es custos pietate ...
(HE, 35)
    MS. Buchanan e. 3, fol. 78r
    MS. Buchanan e. 8 (see text 13)

Angelum nobis medicum salutis ...
    MS. Buchanan g. 4, fol. 62r

Animabus quesumus domine ...
(CO, no. 260)
    MS. Buchanan e. 3 (see text 7)

Apprehendit pylatus Ihesum *see* In illo
tempore. Apprehendit ...

Aue caro Christi cara, inmolata crucis ara ...
(RH, no. 1710)
    MS. Buchanan g. 4, fol. 57r

Aue celestis potus ante omnia et super
omnia ...
    MS. Buchanan g. 1 (see text 15)

Aue cuius conceptio ... (RH, no. 1744)
    MS. Buchanan e. 3, fol. 14v
    MS. Buchanan e. 4, fol. 19v
    MS. Buchanan e. 5, fol. 99r

Aue dei genitrix et immaculata uirgo celi
gaudium toti mundo grata ... (RH, no. 1761)
    MS. Buchanan g. 1, fol. 252r

Aue dextera manus cristi ...
    MS. Buchanan e. 4, fol. 187v

Aue Maria ... Indulgetc nobis propter deum
et piissimam matrem eius mariam ...
    MS. Buchanan f. 2, fol. 317v

Aue Maria ... Martir cum martiribus
transgladiata ...
    MS. Buchanan e. 2, fol. 165r

Aue regina celorum. Aue domina
angelorum. ... (RH, no. 2070)
    MS. Buchanan f. 4, fol. 292r

Aue sanctissima Christi caro summa uite
mee dulcedo ...
    MS. Buchanan g. 1 (see text 15)

Aue sanctissimum pretiosissimum
dulcissimum corpus Christi ...
    MS. Buchanan g. 1, fol. 210r

Auete omnes anime fideles ...
    MS. Buchanan e. 4, fol. 161v
    MS. Buchanan e. 8, fol. 136v
    MS. Buchanan e. 14, fol. 61r

Benedicat me imperialis maiestas ...
    MS. Buchanan g. 1, fol. 239v

Bis duo dat maratrum. febres fugat. atque
uenenum. ...
    MS. Buchanan f. 4, fol. 292r

Christe qui lux es et dies ... (RH, no. 2934)
    MS. Buchanan e. 8 (see text 14)

Christe redemptor omnium, conserua tuos
famulos ... (RH, no. 2959)
    MS. Buchanan e. 8 (see text 14)

Christe redemptor omnium ex patre patris ...
(RH, no. 2960)
    MS. Buchanan e. 8, fol. 151r

Concede michi misericors deus que tibi
placita sunt ardenter concupiscere ...
    MS. Buchanan g. 1, fol. 231r

Concede quesumus omnipotens et
misericors deus ut qui beati potenciam
martiris tui atque pontificis ...
(cf. CO, no. 783)
    MS. Buchanan e. 9 (see text 5)

Confiteor deo omnipotenti et beatissime
semper virgini Marie beate Birgitte beato
Augustino et omnibus sanctis dei ...
    MS. Buchanan f. 2, fol. 317v

Consciencias nostras quesumus domine
visitando purifica ... (CO, no. 800d)
    MS. Buchanan e. 14 (see text 4)

Contemplator trinitatis speculumque
ueritatis Iohannes apostole ...
(RH, no. 3846)
    MS. Buchanan g. 1, fol. 228v

Corpus tuum domine quod sumpsi et
calicem quem potaui ...
    MS. Buchanan g. 1 (see text 15)

Da nobis quesumus omnipotens deus, velle,
cogitare, facere ...
    MS. Buchanan e. 18, fol. 144r

Deus a quo sancta desideria ...
(CO, no. 1088a)
    MS. Buchanan e. 5 (see text 9)
    MS. Buchanan e. 7 (see text 4)
    MS. Buchanan e. 18 (see text 8)
    MS. Buchanan f. 4 (see text 12)
    MS. Buchanan g. 1 (see text 6)
    MS. Buchanan g. 3 (see text 6)
    MS. Buchanan g. 4 (see text 2)

Deus cui proprium est misereri semper
et parcere suscipe ... (CO, no. 1143)
    MS. Buchanan e. 2 (see text 7)
    MS. Buchanan e. 3 (see text 7)
    MS. Buchanan e. 4 (see text 7)
    MS. Buchanan e. 5 (see text 9)
    MS. Buchanan e. 7 (see text 4)
    MS. Buchanan e. 8, fol. 95v
    MS. Buchanan e. 9 (see text 7)
    MS. Buchanan e. 10 (see text 6)
    MS. Buchanan e. 11, fol. 59r ('Deus
    qui [sic] proprium ...')
    MS. Buchanan e. 12, fol. 29r
    MS. Buchanan e. 13, fol. 89r
    MS. Buchanan e. 14, fol. 42r
    MS. Buchanan e. 18, fol. 93r
    MS. Buchanan f. 4 (see text 12)
    MS. Buchanan g. 1 (see text 6,
    and fol. 161v)
    MS. Buchanan g. 2, fol. 221v
    MS. Buchanan g. 3 (see text 6)
    MS. Buchanan g. 4 (see text 2)

Deus cuius misericordie non est numerus,
suscipe propicius preces humilitatis nostre.
... (CO, no. 1178)
    MS. Buchanan f. 2 (see text 8)

Deus cuius unigenitus assumpte
humanitatis ...
    MS. Buchanan e. 4 (see text 14)

Deus propitius esto mihi peccatori et custos
omnibus diebus uite mee. ...
    MS. Buchanan g. 4, fol. 58r

Deus qui culpa offenderis ... (CO, no. 1511)
    MS. Buchanan e. 5 (see text 9)
    MS. Buchanan e. 7 (see text 4)
    MS. Buchanan f. 4 (see text 12)
    MS. Buchanan g. 1 (see text 6)
    MS. Buchanan g. 3 (see text 6)
    MS. Buchanan g. 4 (see text 2)

[D]eus qui ecclesiam tuam beati Thome
confessoris tui eruditione clarificas ...
(CO, no. 1562)
    MS. Buchanan f. 4, fol. 480v

Deus qui in sancta cruce pro salute nostra
pendens ...
    MS. Buchanan e. 11, fol. 81r

Deus qui manus tuas et pedes tuos ...
    MS. Buchanan e. 4 (see text 4)
    MS. Buchanan e. 9, fol. 118r

Deus qui nobis sub sacramento mirabili ...
(Bruylants, 393)
    MS. Buchanan e. 18 (see text 11)

Deus qui nos conceptionis natiuitatis ...
    MS. Buchanan e. 4 (see text 3)

Deus qui nos patrem et matrem ...
(CO, no. 1903)
    MS. Buchanan e. 10 (see text 6)
    MS. Buchanan e. 13 (see text 6)
    MS. Buchanan f. 2 (see text 8)

Deus qui Raphaelem archangelum Thobie
famulo tuo properanti preuium direxisti. ...
    MS. Buchanan g. 4 (see text 12)

Deus qui uoluisti pro salute mundi ...
    MS. Buchanan g. 4, fol. 53v

Deus venie largitor ... (cf. CO, no. 2205)
    MS. Buchanan e. 10 (see text 6)
    MS. Buchanan f. 2 (see text 8)

Dies ire dies illa ... (RH, no. 4626)
    MS. Buchanan g. 1, fol. 257v

Domina mea sancta Maria perpetua, uirgo
uirginum ...
    MS. Buchanan g. 1, fol. 221r

Domine deus meus si feci ut essem reus
tuus ...
    MS. Buchanan g. 1, fol. 81r

Miserere obsecro domine misereris
animabus seruorum tuorum et ancillarum
tuarum ...
    MS. Buchanan f. 2 (see text 8)

Miserere quesumus domine clementer
animabus omnium benefactorum nostrorum
defunctorum ... (CO, no. 3366)
    MS. Buchanan f. 2 (see text 8)

Missus est Gabriel angelus ad mariam ...
    MS. Buchanan e. 4, fol. 177r

Nos autem gloriari oportet in cruce domini
nostri Ihesu Christi ...
    MS. Buchanan f. 4, fol. 481r

O deus pontificum et honor certantium ...
    MS. Buchanan e. 9 (see text 5)

O Domine Ihesu Christe adoro te in cruce
pendentem ...
    MS. Buchanan g. 1, fol. 205v

O dulcissime et pijssime et clementissime
domine Ihesu Christe uere filius dei qui de
sinu patris omnipotentis missus es in hunc
mundum relaxare peccata ...
    MS. Buchanan g. 1, fol. 233v

O gloriosa domina que filium dei portasti ...
    MS. Buchanan e. 4, fol. 186v

O intemerata ...
    ... orbis terrarum. De te enim ...
        MS. Buchanan e. 2, fol. 156r
        ('... terrarum ex [*sic*] te ...')
        MS. Buchanan e. 4, fol. 14v
        ('... de te. De te [*sic*] enim ...')
        MS. Buchanan e. 5, fol. 96v
        MS. Buchanan e. 9, fol. 20r
        MS. Buchanan e. 12, fol. 6v
        MS. Buchanan e. 13, fol. 22v
    ... orbis terrarum. Inclina aures tue
        pietatis ...
        MS. Buchanan e. 10, fol. 23r
        MS. Buchanan e. 11, fol. 79r
    ... orbis terrarum. Inclina mater
        misericordie aures tue pietatis ...
        MS. Buchanan e. 3, fol. 13r
        MS. Buchanan e. 18, fol. 134r

O mirum Syroneum Senonensis ecclesie.
sit presulum. ...
    MS. Buchanan e. 9, fol. 75r

O salutaris hostia, que celis pandis
hostium ... (RH, no. 13680)
    MS. Buchanan e. 18, fol. 137v

O sancta trinitas atque indiuisa unitas
uera ...
    MS. Buchanan e. 2, fol. 169r

O uirgo et martyr Barbara, quasi pulchra
luna plena ...
    MS. Buchanan e. 3, fol. 77v

Obsecro te ...
    MS. Buchanan e. 2, fol. 160v
    MS. Buchanan e. 3, fol. 11r
    MS. Buchanan e. 4, fol. 12r
    MS. Buchanan e. 5, fol. 93r
    MS. Buchanan e. 8, fol. 21v
    MS. Buchanan e. 9, fol. 17r
    MS. Buchanan e. 10, fol. 19v
    MS. Buchanan e. 11, fol. 81v
    MS. Buchanan e. 12, fol. 5v
    MS. Buchanan e. 13, fol. 18r
    MS. Buchanan e. 18, fol. 131r

Omnipotens eterne deus edificator et
custos ... (CO, no. 3787)
    MS. Buchanan f. 2 (see text 4)

Omnipotens sempiterne deus cui nunquam
sine spe misericordie ... (CO, no. 3809)
    MS. Buchanan f. 2 (see text 8)

Omnipotens sempiterne deus, miserere
famulo tuo ministro ...
    MS. Buchanan e. 5 (see text 9)
    MS. Buchanan e. 7 (see text 4)
    MS. Buchanan f. 4 (see text 12)
    MS. Buchanan g. 1 (see text 6)
    MS. Buchanan g. 3 (see text 6)
    MS. Buchanan g. 4 (see text 2)

Omnipotens sempiterne deus, qui beati
sebastiani martiris tui ...
    MS. Buchanan g. 1, fol. 207v

Omnipotens sempiterne deus qui Ezechie
regi Iude ...
    [ends:] ... misericordiam consequi
      merear. Per ...
        MS. Buchanan e. 18, fol. 143v
        MS. Buchanan g. 4, fol. 53r
    [ends:] ... misericordiam tuam impetrare.
    Per...
        MS. Buchanan e. 11, fol. 59v
    [ends:] ... misericordiam tuam inuenire.
    Per ...
        MS. Buchanan e. 9, fol. 119r

Omnipotens sempiterne deus qui facis
mirabilia magna ... (CO, no. 3983b-c)
    MS. Buchanan g. 2 (see text 4)

Omnipotens sempiterne deus, qui gloriose
uirginis matris Marie ... (CO, no. 3859)
    MS. Buchanan e. 5 (see text 7)
    MS. Buchanan e. 8 (see text 6)
    MS. Buchanan e. 18 (see text 6)
    MS. Buchanan f. 4, fol. 292r

French

Aduocate pour les pecheurs (Sinclair, no. 3927)
    MS. Buchanan e. 3, fol. 77r

Argent faict raige | Amour faict mariaige | ...
    MS. Buchanan e. 11, fol. 85v

Bien te doy hain[?] et blasmer ...
    MS. Buchanan e. 11, fol. 84v

Doulce dame de misericorde ...
    MS. Buchanan e. 9, fol. 108r
    MS. Buchanan e. 10, fol. 166v

Doulx dieu doulx pere sainte trinite ...
    MS. Buchanan e. 9, fol. 113v
    MS. Buchanan e. 10, fol. 171v

E tres certaine esperance ...
    MS. Buchanan e. 2, fol. 166r

Ma joie nest que de pleurer ...
    MS. Buchanan e. 11, fol. 84v

Mere de dieu qui fustes mise ... (Sonet, no. 1121)
    MS. Buchanan e. 3, fol. 74r

Mon vieng amor[?] fin[?] ...
    MS. Buchanan e. 11, fol. 84v

Noble mere du redempteur ... (Sonet, no. 1241)
    MS. Buchanan e. 3, fol. 77v

[O?] bien doret [...] le coeur mary femme ...
    MS. Buchanan e. 11, fol. 84r

O tres certain esperance ... *see* E tres certaine esperance ...

Qui veult en paradis aler ... (Sonet, no. 1748)
    MS. Buchanan e. 3, fol. 78r

Saincte barbe comme ie croy ... (Sinclair, no. 5067)
    MS. Buchanan e. 3, fol. 77v

Saincte larme glorieuse ... (Sonet, no. 1859)
    MS. Buchanan e. 4, fol. 192v

Saincte vraie croix aouree. Qui du corps dieu fus aournee. ...
    MS. Buchanan e. 9, fol. 116r
    MS. Buchanan e. 10, fol. 174r

Vecy l'homme saint innocent et iuste ...
    MS. Buchanan e. 12, fol. 41r

Italian

Signor rodio mio misericordia mia refugio mio e desiderio mio ...
    MS. Buchanan g. 4, fol. 60v

Netherlandish

Alre heilichste siele christi heilige mi O ghebene dide ende gloriose licaem christi ...
    MS. Buchanan f. 3, fol. 193v

Danc segghe ic di o almachtighe god dattu mi onwaerde ...
    MS. Buchanan f. 1, fol. 162v

Die soete naem ons heren ihesu christi ...
    MS. Buchanan f. 1, fol. 90r

Doe sinte andries quam totter stede daer dat cruce bereit was ...
    MS. Buchanan f. 1, fol. 127v

God die ons daer bewijst menichuoldicheit ...
    MS. Buchanan f. 3 (see text 10)

God dient properlike toe behoert ...
    MS. Buchanan f. 3, fol. 103r

God gheue den leuendighen gracie ende ontfarmherticheit ...
    MS. Buchanan f. 1, fol. 56v

Gods ziel heilighe mi. Gods lichaem behoede mi. Gods bloet drinke mi ...
    MS. Buchanan f. 1, fol. 164v

Heer ic en bins niet waerdich dattu comest onder mijn dac ...
    MS. Buchanan f. 1, fol. 162r

Heilighe enghel godes den ic beuolen bin ...
    MS. Buchanan f. 1, fol. 38r

Ic aenbede di verborghen waerheit ...
    MS. Buchanan f. 3, fol. 195r

Ic bidde di alre mildeste heer ihesu christi omme die sonderlinghe hoge ...
    MS. Buchanan f. 3, fol. 191r

Ic bidde dij lieue ghenadighe here dat dese ontfanghenisse ...
    MS. Buchanan f. 1, fol. 163v

Ic hebbe gheseit here ontferme mijns ...
    MS. Buchanan f. 3, fol. 101v

O almachtighe ende ghenadighe god ic onwaerde sondighe mensche ...
    MS. Buchanan f. 1, fol. 161v

O almechtige god ic bidde di omme dine heilige vijk wonden ...
    MS. Buchanan f. 3 (see text 9)

O almechtige god wi bidden verleen ...
    MS. Buchanan f. 3 (see text 14)

O alre guedertierenste here ihesu christi sich op mi mitten oghen dijnre barmherticheit ...
    MS. Buchanan f. 3, fol. 205v

O du vlietende borne der ewicheit woe bistu wi aldus verseghen ...
    MS. Buchanan f. 3 (see text 13)